ENGLISH MASTER PAINTERS
Edited by SIR HERBERT READ

WILLIAM ETTY

RECLINING FEMALE NUDE

19 × 25 (241)

DENNIS FARR

WILLIAM

ETTY

ROUTLEDGE & KEGAN PAUL

First published in 1958
by Routledge & Kegan Paul Limited
Broadway House, 68–74 Carter Lane
London E.C.4
Printed in Great Britain by
Butler & Tanner Limited
Frome and London

CONTENTS

LIST OF PLATES

Catalogue numbers appear in brackets following the measurements which are given whenever appropriate in the caption accompanying each plate.

PREFACE

THE material for much of this book first appeared as a thesis and I would like to thank the Committee of the Central Research Fund, University of London, for their generous financial help during the earlier stages of my work. I also owe a particular debt of gratitude to the Director and members of the staff of the Courtauld Institute of Art for their advice and encouragement. I received much valuable criticism from Mr. David Thomas, and later, from Mr. T. S. R. Boase and Dr. Margaret Whinney, to all of whom I am most grateful. I wish to thank also Mr. Stephen Rees-Jones who has given me expert guidance in connection with Etty's painting techniques, and Dr. L. D. Ettlinger of the Warburg Institute, who advised me over some iconographical problems. My research has been considerably helped by the keen interest and efforts of Ir. Thomas H. Etty, whose kind hospitality towards me during my visits to Holland gave added pleasure to my task. Both he, and other members of the Etty family, including Mr. and Mevr. Jacobus J. T. Bosch, Mr. Thomas Verloop, the late Mr. Edward Etty and Wed. Etty-Hoeyenbos, have allowed me to see paintings, drawings, MS. diaries and letters in their possession. I am greatly indebted to Mr. George H. Scott, who gave me his typescripts of the original Etty–Bodley MS. letters, until recently in his possession and which are now in the City Reference Library, York; to Mr. Nicholas Gillott, who allowed me to see the Etty–Gillott MS. letters as well as the account books once belonging to Joseph Gillott, and to Mr. Richard James of the Barber Institute of Fine Arts, Birmingham, who permitted me to use his own notes on these; also to Mr. James M. Biggins, of the City Reference Library, York, who lent me his transcriptions of all the Etty papers (ex-Richard E. Smithson collection) under his care.

I would like to thank the many private collectors who have responded so readily to my requests for information about their paintings, some of whom allowed their works to be specially photographed. I must single out for especial mention Mr. Anthony Bacon, Mr. Peter Claas, Emeritus Professor E. G. R. Taylor, D.Sc., F.R.G.S. and her son, Commander Dunhill, R.N., Lord Fairhaven, Mrs. E. M. Gabriel, Mr. W. A. Martin, Lord Methuen, the Earl of Normanton, Mr. Gerald Reitlinger, the Earl of Sandwich, and Mr. Alfred Wolmark, all of whom have borne my questions with unfailing patience. My cordial thanks are due to the Rev. Canon Tissington Tatlow,

PREFACE

D.D., who transcribed extracts from the parish records of St. Edmund the King and
Martyr, London; to Mr. W. W. Boulton, Secretary of the General Council of the Bar;
to Miss Helen McCormack, Carolina Art Association, U.S.A.; to Mr. G. N. Paul
Crombie, Secretary to the Company of Merchant Adventurers of the City of York;
to Mr. E. L. Gifford, of Messrs. Truefitt and Hill, London; to Mr. Sidney C. Hutchin-
son, F.S.A., Librarian of the Royal Academy; to Mr. Oliver Millar, M.V.O., Deputy
Surveyor of the Queen's Pictures; to Dr. Phoebe Stanton, formerly of the United States
Information Service in London; to Mr. H. A. C. Sturgess, M.V.O., Librarian and
Keeper of the Records of the Honourable Society of the Middle Temple; to the Reference Librarian of the City of Colchester; to the staff of the Guildhall Library, London;
and to the Archivist, Liverpool Record Office.

My colleagues of the museums and art galleries, both here and abroad, deserve my
special gratitude for their co-operation during the compilation of the catalogue to this
book, and I must ask them to accept this general acknowledgment. However, I would
like particularly to thank Mr. Hans Hess of the City of York Art Gallery, who with
Mr. John Jacob, have given me every possible help over a long period. I would also like
to thank Mr. Kenneth Garlick, Barber Institute; Mr. Douglas Hall, Manchester;
Mrs. Hannah W. Howells, Frick Art Reference Library, New York; Mr. David Loshak,
University of Michigan, U.S.A.; and Mr. John Steer, University of Glasgow, all of
whom have given me considerable help in tracing pictures and information. I am
indebted to Messrs. Christie, Manson and Woods, Ltd., for their unfailing help and
courtesy in answering my questions concerning picture auctions; to Messrs. Sotheby
for similar assistance; and to all those British and foreign dealers who have supplied
information for my catalogue.

I wish to thank and acknowledge all private collectors who have allowed me to
reproduce paintings and drawings in their possession; and I wish to thank the following
public institutions for similar facilities: The Williamson Art Gallery and Museum,
Birkenhead; The Museum and Art Gallery, Birmingham; The Russell-Cotes Art
Gallery and Museum, Bournemouth; The Trustees of the National Gallery of Ireland,
Dublin; The Dunedin Public Art Gallery Society Inc., New Zealand; The Trustees of
the National Gallery of Scotland, Edinburgh; The President and Council of the Royal
Scottish Academy, Edinburgh; The City Art Gallery, Leeds; The Trustees of the
British Museum, London; The Trustees of the National Gallery, London; The President
and Council of the Royal Academy of Arts, London; The Trustees of the Tate Gallery,
London; The Courtauld Institute of Art, University of London; The Victoria and
Albert Museum, London; The City Art Gallery, Manchester; The Museum of Fine
Arts, Montreal; The Metropolitan Museum of Art, New York; The New-York Histori-
cal Society, New York; The Art Gallery of Western Australia, Perth; The John G.
Johnson Collection, Philadelphia; The Trustees of the Lady Lever Collection, Port
Sunlight; The Harris Museum and Art Gallery, Preston; The Rhode Island School of
Design, Providence, U.S.A.; The Ashmolean Museum, Oxford; The Southampton
Art Gallery; The Company of Merchant Adventurers of the City of New York; The
City Art Gallery, York; and The Yorkshire Philosophical Society, York.

Finally, I wish to thank Dr. George Zarnecki and the Photographic Department of
the Courtauld Institute for their invaluable help in photographing the collection of

PREFACE

drawings at York and works in private collections. My warmest thanks are due to Mr. John Pryor, who undertook the onerous task of editing the first draft of my MS.; to Miss Joanna Drew, who read the final text; and to Mrs. R. Stoltenhoff, who typed notes and indexes.

DENNIS FARR

December, 1957

CHAPTER ONE

CHILDHOOD : 1787–1805

WILLIAM ETTY'S reputation as an artist has survived several fluctuations in fortune, and today he occupies a secure and enviable niche in the history of British art as an extremely gifted minor master. He has been acclaimed an accomplished painter of the nude human form and modern taste prefers his smaller, individual studies rather than the grand history pieces. Yet in his own day he was not unique as a painter of the nude; indeed, from the late eighteenth century onwards, British artists striving after the grand manner had perforce to study the nude since their subject-matter demanded a thorough knowledge of it. Where Etty differs from his contemporaries is in his intensive study of its problems and unwearied devotion to the Life School. This single-mindedness springs from a combination of two elements: firstly, Etty's own driving energy, sense of dedication and ambition to become one of the leading British history painters of his day; secondly, the informed artistic opinion in England at the turn of the century which had finally acknowledged history painting as the most noble (if the most unremunerative) calling for an artist. A third, and by no means unimportant factor was the financial support which Etty enjoyed from his brother Walter during the early part of his career.

If Etty's life and work are studied against the more general pattern of artistic life in England and Europe at the beginning of the nineteenth century, it will be realized that he arrived on the scene at a moment when a series of conflicting ideas were struggling for supremacy, and at a time, too, when contact between France and England yielded a rich harvest for both countries. Curiously, however, Etty was attracted by elements in French academic painting which would seem to be at odds with his sensuous use of paint and rich colour, and this duality or compromise is found again and again in his work. This struggle to reconcile opposites never assumed the heroic proportions that mark the career of Delacroix; the tension is less and Etty appears to give up the contest ten years before his death. There are signs, too, that he never understood the implications of French romantic painting, nor did he ever fully realize his own gift for direct, naturalistic painting. To some extent the fault was innate, since imaginative power can never be taught or picked up at random; and partly was it the result of national taste and patronage. For it must be remembered that like so many British painters, Etty began life under conditions least favourable to an artistic career, and was certainly ill-equipped to become a history painter. Not only did he lack education, for which, as will be seen,

I

he could hardly be blamed, but the whole system of artistic training, tradition and patronage in this country had never encouraged the growth of a school of painters capable of designing on a grand scale and able to achieve that monumental feeling for painting as part of an architectural scheme of decoration.

Much of the early biographical detail may be found in Alexander Gilchrist's two-volume *Life of William Etty, R.A.*, published in 1855. This zealous amateur biographer had been commissioned by the publisher David Bogue on the strength of his critical essay printed anonymously in the *Eclectic Review* at the time of Etty's retrospective exhibition at the Society of Arts in 1849. I have been fortunate enough to be able to examine almost all the original MS. diaries, letters and notebooks which were used by Gilchrist, besides having access to additional material which was either unknown to Gilchrist or at all events not published by him.

William Etty, the seventh child of Matthew and Esther Etty, was born on 10th March, 1787, at a house in Feasgate, York, and was baptized the same day. Thirty-two years earlier another artist, John Flaxman, had been born in York, and he was to exert a considerable influence upon the work of his younger fellow-citizen. Etty's father was a miller, baker and confectioner, being especially known among York folk for his gingerbread. Unlike Constable's father, however, Matthew Etty was not a wealthy man, and although his small business was flourishing, a large family made heavy demands upon his purse. His wife was the youngest daughter of William Calverley, and she was only seventeen when in July, 1771, she married Matthew, a man eleven years her senior and tenant of a small flour mill on her father's estate at Hayton. She appears to have sacrificed herself somewhat by this marriage, at least materially, for her social position as a squire's daughter was exchanged for that of a tradesman's wife.

However, this is not quite all the story. Esther's father had begun life as a rope-maker and had unexpectedly inherited the Hayton estate, or more accurately, watched over the interests of his eldest son (to whom the estate was actually bequeathed) until he should become of age. The Calverleys had married into the Rudston family,[1] but the Calverley branch had since degenerated to the status of poor relations. Their fortunes only revived as a result of a quarrel in the Rudston family, during which Elizabeth Cutler (daughter and heiress of Sir Thomas Rudston, the third and last baronet of Hayton) disinherited her nephew and, being childless, adopted Rudston Calverley, William's eldest son, stipulating that the surname Rudston should be written both before and after that of Calverley. Mrs. Cutler died in 1745. Esther, the youngest child, was born in 1754 and was thus able to benefit from her family's changed circumstances. It is of some importance that the artist's mother was a person of some refinement, and of strong character. The business side of the Etty household came under her management

---

[1] For further details concerning the history of these families, consult: William Gaunt, M.A., and F. Gordon Roe, *Etty and the Nude*, Leigh-on-Sea, 1943, pp. 27–8, and the family tree printed at the beginning of that book.

The tracing of the Rudston and Calverley families back to Walter Rudston and his wife Frances Constable, with its two branches—Sir Walter Rudston, 1st Baronet of Hayton (created 1642), on the Rudston side; and his brother, William Rudston, whose daughter, Hester, married the first William Calverley—seems quite convincing.

Rudston Calverley-Rudston assumed full title by Royal Licence in 1802, after the death of his mother, Jane, in 1801. Gilchrist misquoted the family name Rudston as 'Rudstone'.

as did the purely domestic, and Gilchrist describes her as 'a really remarkable woman, of superior intellect and much practical *force*; who could cope with the varying exigencies of a humble and arduous fortune, and who won the respect of those who knew her'.

Her appearance was no less distinguished, combining strong aquiline features with an intense penetrating expression, softened over the years by age and sadness. Etty painted a portrait of his mother in her declining years, and Sir Thomas Lawrence remarked of her that she had the 'face for a Madonna'. A descendant of the family still possesses a small copy of the head from this early portrait of his mother, which Etty painted for his brother Charles to take with him on his voyages abroad.

Matthew Etty was also reputed to have been of a studious disposition and not without some rudimentary education, probably self-acquired. He was hard-working but of easy temperament, and a rather less dominant personality. Shrewdness, plus a characteristic Yorkshire stolidity and sense of humour were qualities in the husband complementary to those of his wife. As his son William's portrait of him would suggest, he was of small stature, but powerfully built, and a man of humble origin. John Etty (1705–79), his father, was a wheelwright at Holme-on-Spalding-Moor, five miles south of Hayton. The surname was a common one in Yorkshire, and Gilchrist found five distinct families of that name living within the North Riding at the end of the eighteenth century. John Etty married Martha (whose maiden name is unknown), and they had three children, a son who died when still a baby in 1738, followed by the birth of two more sons: William in 1740 and Matthew in 1743. William was to be the artist's 'noble and beloved uncle' referred to in *The Art Journal*, 'Autobiography' (1849), who financed him during his early years in London, for unlike Matthew, William became quite wealthy as a partner in the then prosperous gold-lace business of Bodley, Etty, and Bodley. There was some inter-marrying, and William married an Elizabeth Bodley (1745–1829), and it was her daughter Martha who became the wife of a cousin, Thomas Bodley.[1] It was with this last couple that William (the artist) maintained a life-long friendship, evidence of which survives in the form of many letters between William Etty and his cousin Thomas Bodley. These are now in the City Reference Library, York, and are of the greatest interest for the considerable amount of information that they contain about every aspect of Etty's career.

To return to Matthew and Esther, we find that the newly-created Squire of Hayton (who by now had come of age), appalled by his sister's marriage beneath her station, repudiated her and dismissed her husband from the mill. Matthew's elder brother William, in an unsuccessful attempt to heal the breach, is said to have offered to double whatever the amount of the dowry might be that Rudston Calverley-Rudston would have allowed his sister in the normal course of events. The whole of this episode sounds like the plot of a bad melodrama, but it was real enough and not without some unfortunate repercussions, for it meant that a gifted painter had to overcome formidable difficulties before fulfilling his vocation. Nevertheless, such a relationship, if acknowledged, might have been a hindrance, for a newly-admitted member to the landed classes would have fully shared their intense prejudice against the fine arts as a career

---

[1] *See* pp. 31 and 75, *The Parish Registers of St. Edmund the King and Martyr, Lombard Street, London, 1670–1812.* Transcribed by William Brigg, B.A., privately printed for the transcriber, London, 1892.

for a young gentleman and it is not inconceivable that Etty would have been dissuaded from pursuing his vocation.[1]

After two attempts to establish themselves, first at Pocklington, then at Eastrington, the Etty ménage finally moved to York in 1777. Five years previously their first son, William, had been born, but died at the age of only twelve. This child had also shown some artistic ability, never allowed to develop, and it was not until the birth of another William in 1787 that this latent talent again displayed itself and fortunately matured. Of ten children, only five survived: Walter (1774–1850), John (1775–1865), Thomas (Matthew's fourth son, and perhaps the fourth child, born in 1779), William (1787–1849) and Charles (1793–1856).

As a child, Etty soon demonstrated his gifts as a draughtsman: any blank space on floor or wall was a tacit invitation which he was quick to accept. There is also an engaging anecdote, handed down in the family, that William was always late when delivering the gingerbread and cakes for his mother, since he was always stopping to draw on any large paving-stone *en route*! At the end of his life Etty recalls some of these early efforts in the Autobiography: 'My first panels on which I drew were the boards of my father's shop floor; my first crayon, a farthing's worth of white chalk; . . .' later on, Thomas, his sailor brother, brought home for him a box of water-colours, a memorable occasion. These, and many other trivial instances of modest effort and encouragement have been recorded, and they are no more than the first hints of what was to follow; besides, many other children have shown similar aptitude which fades as manhood is reached. But not so Etty, although he had to pass through a testing period of hopes frustrated and ambition thwarted. When the time came for him to go to school, the family budget was fully extended by the addition of at least two more children, and Etty's education suffered from this abundance of brothers and sisters. Mistress Mason, of Feasegate, had charge of him at the age of four or thereabouts, to be followed by Mr. Shepherd of Bedern, whose school was situated on the outskirts of York. Here he spent two years, absorbing a somewhat unambitious curriculum, and at the age of ten he became a boarder at Mr. Hall's 'Academy' in Pocklington, only to leave after about two years' attendance. This can hardly be called a distinguished schooling, and was not the best start in life. His schoolfellows spoke of Etty as a 'very still boy', shy and retiring, but filling his schoolbooks with sketches, often teased and always eager to escape from an uncongenial schoolboy world. Nor was Etty's appearance prepossessing: a large head with unruly sandy hair, a face strongly marked by small-pox scars, and a stocky figure with rather large hands and feet, could give little idea of the qualities of the man. Indeed, his physical appearance, linked with a precarious livelihood, made him a somewhat shy lover, and doomed to failure all his many matrimonial projects in later years. Though fluent with a brush, he never possessed a ready tongue, and even when writing he often had difficulty in expressing with precision his strongest emotions and ideas, although on occasion he could turn a felicitous phrase. Despite these apparent handicaps, a gentle and affectionate nature was to win many friends for him.

One particular home influence may be noted here, which was later to undergo an

[1] P. G. Hamerton, *The Portfolio*, London, 1875, VI, p. 89, in an article about William Etty, was the first to express this view. *See also* A. P. Oppé, *Early Victorian England*, London, 1934, chap. X, pp. 123–4, for further details about the social status of an artist at this period in England.

interesting change of direction. This was Etty's strict Wesleyan Methodist upbringing. As he says in his Autobiography, '. . . a love and fear of Almighty God . . . was impressed on my mind by my dear parents, and echoed feelingly in my heart . . .: and I may safely say, I never for one moment forgot the path of virtue without the bitterest feeling of remorse and ardent desire to return to it. . . .' Even so, he was soon to be deterred by the austereness of his parents' form of worship, and preferred to visit the parish church, or better still, the Minster, where colour and tradition made an immediate appeal to his instinctive love of these things. Etty's devotion was sincere and unruffled by doubt, optimistic and child-like in its simplicity, always an emotional process which never became, even in old age, either rigidly dogmatic or illumined by profound contemplative experience.

Preoccupied with the need to provide her son with a trade by which he could become self-supporting, Esther Etty decided to apprentice William to a printer. What could be more respectable or, as it happened, more opportune? For at that moment, a neighbour's daughter had just married a printer about to set up on a newer and larger scale in nearby Hull. Thus on 8th October, 1798, Etty became an apprenticed compositor to Robert Peck, publisher of the *Hull Packet*, the appearance of which every Monday morning meant that Sunday was no day of rest for its staff. It was a harsh, stultifying existence, leisure hours were few, and the work mentally and physically exhausting. But the urge to draw and to paint could never be extinguished, and although such unusual activities were frowned upon by the master, Etty continued to indulge his secret ambition despite the limited opportunities. The situation was not without some relief, and Etty began to lay the foundations of a wider knowledge by reading such books as he could obtain in his spare evenings, and his brother Walter extracted a promise from Peck that the apprentice should not be hindered in his studies during his free time. Added to this, Etty had earned a favourable reputation for his industry and good character.

The subjects of his sketches were more often than not taken from the everyday incidents of his life, observed and recorded with varying degrees of success. Drawings, carefully executed, of 'a pistol, a drum, a palette, a pewter-pot, an open knife or book, a printer's shears; nay, parts even, of the human figure'[1] are numerous, while at the same time prints are also copied, probably in most cases from memory, as they would be beyond the reach of an apprentice's purse. The medium varies also; experiments are made with water colours and with a crude concoction of water colour ground in oil. Although Gilchrist had seen examples of these early sketches, none appears to have survived, and now they would perhaps be difficult to recognize as from Etty's hand.

The years dragged on, and Etty's patience must have been sorely tried, although it is characteristic of him that he should feel bound to fulfil conscientiously his term of apprenticeship, and his exemplary conduct under these conditions contrasts strongly with that of two of his contemporaries, John Martin and B. R. Haydon, the latter admitting himself to be 'an excessively self-willed, passionate child'.[2] Not that Etty was any less determined upon his choice of a career, but his ardour glowed with a

[1] Alexander Gilchrist, *Life of William Etty, R.A.*, 2 vols., London, 1855, I, p. 27.
[2] *The Autobiography and Memoirs of B. R. Haydon*, ed. Tom Taylor, London, 1926, I, p. 7, and Thomas Balston, *John Martin. His Life and Works*, London, 1947, pp. 20–1.

steadier flame, quite unlike Haydon's flickering light, at one moment at white heat, at the next almost extinguished by despair. As a painter Haydon was a failure, but one might regret that Etty did not possess a little of Haydon's intellectual brilliance and range, which allied with his own consummate painterly skill, would have enabled him perhaps to achieve the goal that was for Haydon nothing more than a chimaera, a pathetic self-delusion, namely, to be the founder of a new and vital school of history painting.

This may seem to be anticipating future events, but the force of this analogy may be illustrated by this passage from Etty's Autobiography, in which he speaks of the termination of his indenture, on the 23rd October, 1805: 'I was now *entirely* emancipated from servitude and slavery; I was flapping my young wings in the triumphant feeling of *liberty*! Not the liberty of licentiousness and jacobinism, but natural rational freedom of *body, mind and will*, to which for seven long years I had been an entire stranger!'

Etty is no revolutionary, and takes pains to define the brand of liberty he means, but perhaps it is not an unfamiliar paradox that, with some obvious exceptions, an artist should value personal freedom in so far as it is necessary for him to preserve his artistic integrity, and yet be either unconscious of, or unconcerned by, the need for political liberty. The July Revolution of 1830, into which Etty was to wander quite by accident, left him (an Englishman, it is true) unmoved, except to be mildly irritated that it should interfere with his painting at the Louvre. Yet Delacroix found it an inspiration, although in 1848 even he was to react against the trends of his day. To this extent Etty is at least consistent, both in his toryism and insular outlook; his views on political reform remain as unchanged in 1848 as in 1832. Indeed, his character hardly changes throughout his life, there are no quirks or unexpected late developments, and he seems impervious to the influence of foreign ideas on his own way of life, although his attitude towards them does mellow with continually renewed acquaintance.

At last, Etty was set free, and was rewarded for his diligence by an appreciative testimonial from Peck when his indentures were endorsed as having been '. . . faithfully fulfilled to the satisfaction of the Master and the credit of the Apprentice'.[1] He had, however, to spend three more weeks in gloomy Hull, working as a journeyman printer, until his uncle William gave way to his nephew's repeated entreaties, and allowed him to come to London for a few months to try his mettle. Walter, his eldest brother, was working in the gold-lace business, and took him under his care. This was to be the start of a wonderful relationship between the two men; the elder sustaining and protecting his more gifted, but more vulnerable, younger brother. The artist's financial needs were supplied by Walter, and it was he who attended to the mundane task of keeping accounts, a very necessary thing when managing the affairs of an almost helplessly impractical person like Etty. It was just this sympathy and encouragement given by Walter and by his cousin Thomas Bodley that provided him with the vital stimulus so necessary to the artist in his prolonged struggle for recognition in one of the most hazardous of professions.

What benefit did Etty derive from his enforced period of marking time? Very little, it must be confessed, but he did acquire a habit of unsparing application to a given task, and it brought out in him the best of his qualities of will-power and determination

[1] Autobiography, *The Art Journal*, XI, London, 1849, p. 13.

to succeed. He learnt the painful art of hardening, if not fully adapting himself to uncongenial circumstances, a useful asset when later travelling abroad. Nevertheless, it might be argued that the foundations of his greatest strength were also those of his greatest weakness. A restricted early environment can have a subtle, cramping effect on the mind, probably imperceptible to the victim of such a state of affairs, and active long afterwards. When Etty should have been enriching his knowledge and experience at his most impressionable age, he was wasting his mental and physical energies at a printer's bench, and this fact cannot be entirely dismissed when discussing his life and work. Enthusiasm, and a particular natural ability, cannot always counteract damage of this kind, and this may in part account for the 'perpetual student' frame of mind which led Etty to make such regular visits to the Life School of the Academy long after his days of studenthood were past. He set an example of conduct meritorious in itself, and from which the Academy students were to profit; but it was a mixed blessing for Etty, and it inevitably made for a certain narrowness of outlook to the extent that his sources of experience were necessarily confined, and it was perhaps for just this reason that he was betrayed into occasional lapses of aesthetic taste. But it should at once be made clear that the so-often shallow, Victorian standards of prim morality cannot be the basis for a judgment of this kind. For it is a commonplace that the elements in Etty's art once considered as outrageously indecent (even as early as the 1820's), now appear either as innocuous or as positive merits in his work. One might go further and say that it is only when Etty shows himself as a child of his times, and only when he bows to the superficial conventions of his own day, that he loses force and his work fails to carry conviction. There can be no doubt that he often found himself in a dilemma. When he allows his true artistic instincts to prevail, he triumphs; when his primness is strongest, then he falters. This is a simplification, of course, but it seems to be the fundamental contradiction in Etty's personality which will often make itself manifest both in his work and in his thoughts.

Enough has been said by way of preparation for a study of Etty's artistic career, which began in earnest on his arrival at his uncle's house in London on 23rd November, 1805.[1]

[1] From an entry in a Notebook of 1839–49, in the collection of Mr. Jacobus J. Thomas Bosch.

CHAPTER TWO

STUDENT YEARS: 1806–1815

A T 3 Lombard Street, William's uncle greeted him with friendly sympathy, not unnaturally a little tempered by doubts about the true extent of his nephew's powers. Obviously, the young man should receive some training at once, and this meant gaining admittance to the Royal Academy Schools. However, it was imperative that the candidate seeking admission should be able to produce drawings done from casts of the Antique statues, of sufficient quality to merit acceptance. Fully aware of the leeway to be made up, Etty set to work with a will to reach the required standard of proficiency, and for just over a year he spent much of his time drawing from prints or from nature, which probably meant that he continued his recording of incidental events around him, as at Hull. He speaks of Gianelli's plaster-cast shop near Smithfield as his first 'Academy', where he drew '. . . in heat and cold; sometimes, the snow blowing into my studio, under the door, white as the casts.'[1] Such a shop would have been one of the few places in London where facilities for drawing from the Antique were available. No doubt there were other students working with Etty at Gianelli's, although there is no mention of them in Gilchrist, nor do any other painters of this period mention Gianelli. The British Museum was, of course, another important centre for studies of this kind, but its collections had not yet been enriched by Lord Elgin's acquisitions from Greece. Sass's school was not opened until 1818.

The Missionary Boy [pl. 2a] is perhaps the first large oil painting surviving from Etty's early student days. This picture, now at York, raises several problems for it appears to be quite unrelated to subsequent work, and we have no well-authenticated paintings of the same period which could prepare us for it. Its title cannot adequately be explained, although it would suggest that the picture is intended to be a portrait, perhaps of a child preacher known to Etty in London, or maybe at York. On the other hand

---

[1] Autobiography, *The Art Journal*, XI, London, 1849, p. 13. Etty's Gianelli was almost certainly J. B. (i.e. John Baptist or Giovanni Battista) Gianelli, who is mentioned as a tradesman with premises at 33 Cock Lane in Holden's *Triennial Directory*, 1805 and 1809; the *Consolidated Rate Book*, 1810; and *Johnson's Directory*, 1817—in the last specifically as a Plaster of Paris manufacturer. Giovanni Battista's more notable brother, Giovanni Domenico Gianelli, did not settle in London till 1809 (Thieme-Becker, *Künstlerlexikon*, XIII, pp. 581–2).

there appear to be no contemporary records of such a seven-day wonder, and it may only represent a Christian convert rather than a preacher, in which case the title of *The Mission Boy* might seem more apt. The signature 'W. Etty' is no proof of authenticity, since this same form of signature appears on several other paintings manifestly not by him, but which seem to be imitations of his more mature works. Furthermore, Etty never signed any of his pictures on the front in this way so far as is known, not even as a student. However, there are the fragments of two inscriptions, one on the actual millboard, and the other an old label stuck to the frame, and these when pieced together give the following reading: 'I well remember . . . missionary boy at Hull painted [at?] York by W. Etty R.A.' The artist has obtained a certain coarse plasticity in his forms, but the modelling of both head and body is extremely hard; somewhat naïvely he has avoided the test of painting in the hands, and this detracts from the vigour of the general conception. Much of the character of the work derives from the colours used, and these give a freshness and conviction to what would otherwise be a feeble attempt. The boy's swarthy skin, black hair and scarlet cap are enhanced by a deep ultramarine background, which also sets off to great advantage his pale lilac tunic and mustard-coloured waistcoat. A dark blue sash with orange and grey embroidery, a pale greyish brown neckerchief, and the red tablecloth complete a surprisingly harmonious colour scheme. The painting is nearly life-size, and it is most unlikely that he would have been allowed to paint such a thing in the Academy Schools, but it is not impossible for him to have done it in his spare moments, in order to earn a little towards meeting his expenses—quite a usual practice among art students of the time.[1] The possibility that this picture is by George Franklin, Etty's assistant, cannot entirely be overlooked. If this were so, then the painting would have to be dated very much later to about 1820.

The moment came when Etty felt that he could put himself up for admission to the Academy Schools. He made the attack in careful stages, first obtaining a letter of introduction to John Opie, R.A., from Mr. Sharp, Member of Parliament for Hull. Armed with this, he went to Opie and showed him a drawing of a *Cupid and Psyche* done from the Antique. This evidently met with Opie's approval, for he sent the young man on to Henry Fuseli, who was then Keeper of the Royal Academy. A vivid account is given in the Autobiography of this early meeting with Fuseli, who, formidable yet carelessly attired, received the newcomer, awed by the old artist's reputation and fascinated by the unfamiliar world of fantasy surrounding him. By a strange coincidence, Etty's choice of *Cupid and Psyche*, although a common enough academic theme, anticipates a long sequence of paintings with this as their *leitmotiv*. Etty was accepted on probation, and it was only after he had executed satisfactorily the necessary studies from the *Laocoon* and from the *Torso* of Michelangelo[2] that he was made a full student,

---

[1] Oppé, *op. et loc. cit.*, p. 126.

[2] No inventory exists of casts belonging to the Academy Schools of the period, and it is difficult to know what Etty intended by 'the *Torso* of Michael Angelo'. Possibly he refers to a cast of the *Belvedere Torso* (Vatican), so admired by Michelangelo as almost to become known as 'Michelangelo's Torso'. Another possibility is the *River God* model (described by Vasari in great detail), but Professor J. Wilde doubts that casts were made from this work (now in the Bargello Museum, Florence), since there are no obvious traces on it of the application at any time of such a process. There are virtually no Michelangelo statues that would provide a cast from the torso, except perhaps the *David*.

on 15th January, 1807.[1] Thus began a long and for the most part happy association with the Royal Academy, one of whose most loyal and devoted members he was to become. The Academy represented for him, as for Constable and Turner, an institution which would set up and maintain in England a standard of artistic achievement comparable with that of its older Continental rivals.

Among his more immediate contemporaries at the Academy were Collins, Wilkie, Haydon and Hilton; Constable had been admitted in 1799, and Eastlake did not arrive until 1809. The men who most attracted Etty were Haydon and Hilton. Their ambition to paint history pieces stimulated Etty's own ideas, and he acknowledges this towards the end of his life, saying, 'Poor Haydon, ardent, mistaken in some respects, but still glorious in his enthusiasm, drew at the same time; his zeal and that of Hilton in the cause of historic Art urged me to persevere, and, by their example and precept, I certainly benefited and was encouraged.' [2] Despite these words, Haydon and Etty never seem to have been intimate, and since they were of entirely different temperament, this is not altogether surprising. Haydon, when speaking of this period, reveals this fact almost as an aside: 'I do not remember to have seen during this quarter of 1805 either Mulready, Collins or Hilton . . . Etty I never saw, and Wilkie had not yet come up.' [3] In any case Etty's natural shyness would have prevented him from making himself very noticeable among a group of high-spirited students.

The year Etty arrived at the Academy, 1807, was notable for the series of four lectures on painting delivered by John Opie during February and March. In them Opie expresses certain ideas which may well have set off Etty's own thoughts along the path he subsequently chose. They contain some very sound and straightforward advice, but are more partisan and more limited in scope than those of Reynolds, and cannot fairly be compared with them: Reynolds often dealt with questions of far greater general significance, while Opie chooses to talk about the more immediate problems facing an artist. His four lectures treat of 'Design', 'Invention', 'Chiaroscuro' and 'Colouring' respectively, and they were given in that order. The language used has not quite the same sustained literary quality which gives Reynolds's *Discourses* their peculiar charm, but Opie can at times evoke a powerful imagery and subtlety of expression. Independent in mind and outlook, he strongly disagrees with Reynolds's views on the part colour should play in the formation of a grand style of painting. Opie seems to have had great sensitivity to colour, at least when talking about it. But his ability to handle colour effectively in practice is less easy to assess despite the experiments he made in this direction when painting his self-portraits. At the very beginning of his first lecture, Opie said: 'The empire of the art [of painting] extends over all space and time: it brings into view the heroes, sages, and beauties of the earliest periods, the inhabitants of the most distant regions, and fixes and perpetuates the forms of those of the present day; it presents to us the heroic deeds, the remarkable events, and the interesting examples of piety, patriotism, and humanity of all ages; and according to the nature of the action depicted, fills us with innocent pleasure, excites our abhorrence of crimes, moves us to pity, or inspires us with elevated sentiments.' [4] This, of course, is nothing more than a

[1] *Royal Academy Council Minutes*, III, 15th January, 1807.
[2] Autobiography, *loc. cit.*, p. 37.   [3] B. R. Haydon, *Autobiography and Memoirs*, I, p. 24.
[4] John Opie, R.A., *Lectures on Painting*, London, 1809, Lecture I, pp. 7–8.

definition of history painting, but, over forty years later, Etty echoes Opie's words in this way: 'My aim in all my great pictures has been to paint some great moral on the heart: "The Combat", *the beauty of Mercy*; the three "Judith" pictures, *Patriotism*, and self-devotion to her people and her God; "Benaiah, David's chief captain", *Valour*; "Ulysses and the Syrens", the importance of resisting *Sensual Delights*, or an Homeric paraphrase on the "Wages of Sin is Death"; the three pictures of "Joan of Arc", *Religion, Valour, Loyalty*, and *Patriotism*, like the modern Judith; these in all, make *nine* colossal pictures, as it was my desire to paint three times three.' [1]

The aim is thus virtually the same, for one should not be misled by the slightly Victorian flavour of Etty's language. Fuseli, lecturing as Professor of Painting four years earlier than Opie, had spoken thus: 'Invention in its more specific sense receives its subjects from poetry or authenticated tradition; they are *epic* or sublime, *dramatic* or impassioned, *historic* or circumscribed by truth. The first *astonishes*; the second *moves*; the third *informs*. The aim of the epic painter is to impress one general idea, one great quality of nature or mode of society, some great maxim, without descending to those subdivisions, which the detail of character prescribes: . . .' and if 'the necessity of a moral tendency or of some doctrine useful to mankind in the whole of an epic performance' is admitted, 'are the agents sometimes to be real beings, and sometimes abstract ideas?' Answering this question, Fuseli considered 'it is that magic which places on the same basis of existence, and amalgamates the mythic or super-human, and the human parts of the Ilias, of Paradise Lost, and of the Sistine chapel, that enraptures, agitates, and whirls us along as readers or spectators'. [2] Yet it should be recalled that history painting, still accorded the place of honour as the highest form of art, had moved some way from Reynolds's Augustan ideals as propounded in his *Fourth Discourse*. By the time of Opie's lecture, three distinct interpretations of history painting may be seen active in British art, and Opie belonged to the newest group, that of Shakespearean illustrators. His definition of the art allows much greater freedom of subject-matter and treatment, a freedom inspired by the examples of West, Copley and Fuseli. Nor should it be forgotten that an entirely new conception of history painting had been evolved. This was the documentary method of painting, best represented by the works of John Singleton Copley, whose *Death of Major Pierson* of 1783 is one of the finest of his series of modern history paintings produced during the last twenty years of the eighteenth century. Not only does this painting foreshadow the great French romantic histories such as *Les Pestiférés de Jaffa*, but it also prepares the way for those vast, meticulous pictorial reconstructions of events of national history to be found in the Houses of Parliament and other public buildings of the last century. Opie's distaste for the over-idealized undoubtedly finds support in this fresh approach to history painting.

[1] Autobiography, *loc. cit.*, p. 40. The italics are Etty's.

[2] Henry Fuseli, R.A., *Lectures on Painting*, London, 1820; Third Lecture, pp. 123–4; Fourth Lecture, pp. 161–2. Both lectures discussed 'Invention', but the first three of this series of six lectures were given in 1801, and were either continued after Fuseli's re-appointment as Professor of Painting in 1810, or in 1806, when he had been asked to lecture again, because Opie, Fuseli's successor, had not then prepared his own series.

Etty himself once attempted to divide his ideas for paintings under various headings such as: 'Subjects of Grandeur'; of 'Terror or Emotion'; of 'Poetry'; of 'Feeling'; and of 'Sunshine' (Gilchrist, *op. cit.*, I, pp. 86–7). But the system does not seem to have been a very rigid or logical one.

Hence, in his first lecture, he also makes some sarcastic attacks upon the French school, and especially upon the French artists' use of colour. David is castigated for using colour that is barren and cold, and that of the 'learned Poussin' provokes the epithet 'brick-dust'; Opie is convinced that there should be no incompatibility between the 'ideal' and nature; he cannot believe 'that the flesh of heroes is less like flesh than that of other men; or that the surest way to strike the imagination, and interest the feelings, is to fatigue, perplex, and disgust, the organ through which the impression is made on the mind'.[1] The whole school is then scornfully dismissed: 'It seems, indeed, to be the fate of this school to be ever in extremes.'[2] As a student, then, Etty was exposed to a certain amount of anti-French feeling which might have strengthened his own prejudice against contemporary foreign painting generally, but which in fact did nothing to prevent his expressing later great admiration for Poussin and for some of the French academic painters of his own generation. In the following lecture Opie, discussing 'Invention', quotes Raphael and Michelangelo as examples worthy of the most careful study—the first for his ability to express subtlety of emotion, the second for his unrivalled richness of invention and epic grandeur of conception.[3] This second lecture also contains a blunt statement about the chief defect of English painting—its lack of inventiveness in figure design—for which Opie considered that an unenlightened public, with a correspondingly limited patronage, was to blame. 'So habituated', he says, 'are the people of this country to the sight of portraiture only, that they can scarcely as yet consider painting in any other light; they will hardly admire a landscape that is not a view of a particular place, nor a history unless composed of likenesses of the persons represented; and are apt to be staggered, confounded, and wholly unprepared to follow such vigorous flights of imagination, as would . . . as *will* be felt and applauded with enthusiasm, in a more advanced and liberal stage of criticism.'[4] This was a cry from the heart later echoed with equal feeling by Constable, Haydon and Etty, who were among the more obvious sufferers from this dearth of patronage. Naturally enough, these artists felt that their ideals were doomed to oblivion for want of an opportunity to embody them in some tangible form of expression: but the patronage of the day did impart some positive characteristics to the English school, as the successes of Wilkie and Mulready amply show. However, in his next lecture, after again deploring the lack of prestige accorded the arts in England, Opie refers to the foundation of the British Institution as a ray of hope which might lead to a rebirth of an age of taste in this land.

Perhaps it is in the final lecture that Opie appears at his best, and certainly his remarks on the use of colour must have impressed the young Etty. Opie devotes five pages of his lecture to a discussion of Titian, whom he regarded as the greatest colourist the world had known, and one whose work would amply repay intelligent study by every young artist. He also notes Titian's own continual study and effort towards improvement in his art, lasting even into old age, a hint which Etty may well have taken to inspire his own assiduousness. After discussing Giorgione, Tintoretto and Veronese, Opie turns his attention to Rubens, and demonstrates the differences in technique which distinguish the works of Titian and Rubens: the former mingling his colours imperceptibly; the

---

[1] *Op. cit.*, Lecture I, p. 18.   [2] *Ibid.*, p. 31.
[3] *Op. cit.*, Lecture II, pp. 78–9; *cf.* Reynolds's *Fifth Discourse*.   [4] *Ibid.*, p. 76.

latter laying his tints side by side and only slightly mixing them. Etty mastered these techniques and sometimes used both, slightly modified, in the same picture. When describing the function of colour, Opie hits upon a delightful phrase, telling his audience that 'Colouring is the sunshine of the art [of painting], that clothes poverty in smiles, and renders the prospect of barrenness itself agreeable, while it heightens the interest, and doubles the charms of beauty . . . like sound in poetry, colouring in painting should always be an echo to the sense. The true colourist, therefore, will always . . . consider the nature of his subject, whether grave or gay, magnificent or melancholy, heroic or common; and, according to the time and place, . . . such will be the predominant hues of his piece.'[1] Opie probably did not realize the logical conclusion of his remarks about colour and poverty, and he can be acquitted of any charge of hypocrisy. (Not so Wilkie, whose attitude towards representations of poverty in painting comes out most clearly in the sentiments about peasant life expressed in letters to friends during his stay in Ireland nearly thirty years later.[2] He was interested only in the picturesque, and it was left to Daumier to reveal the sordidness of poverty in nineteenth-century art.)

It has been necessary to discuss these lectures in some detail, especially as very little attention seems to have been paid to them by historians. Although Opie's first lectures before the Royal Institution were unsuccessful, the defects which marred them—they were ill-ordered and too technical—were soon remedied, and in addition, Opie found Royal Academy students more congenial to him than the fashionable society audience of previous occasions. There is no proof whatsoever that Mrs. Opie helped her husband write these Academy lectures, and if she read the Royal Institution lectures before their delivery one can only say that whatever advice she gave did nothing to improve them. The Academy lectures are well written and reveal Opie as a man of strong intellect. Lucid, and for the most part carefully reasoned, they must have been an admirable guide to students. They certainly impressed Haydon as such, and he praised Opie for his 'natural sagacity and shrewdness' and as a man 'of strong natural understanding— honest, manly and straightforward'.[3] Published in 1809, two years after Opie's death, they must have acquired some importance as a textbook, being shorter and more concise than Reynolds's *Discourses*.

There is a glimpse of Etty as a student, in an incomplete letter to his parents of 10th April, 1807, and of which this is only the lower half of the page :[4]

I am very well (thank God) as I hope this will meet you all; as great an enthusiast in

---

[1] *Op. cit.*, Lecture IV, pp. 138–9.

[2] Allan Cunningham, *Life of Sir David Wilkie*, London, 1843, III, pp. 100–8.

[3] B. R. Haydon, *Autobiography and Memoirs*, I, p. 53.

[4] This letter, hitherto unpublished, is an odd one out of a collection of 80 written by Etty to Joseph Gillott, of Birmingham, covering the period 1844–9. On the envelope containing this fragment are the following words, which are self-explanatory:

'*An autograph*—a curiosity
'Tis Forty years ago!
Dear Joseph Gillott, Esqe
"So You will excuse it!"
        and its *Tone* of *Color*
Betsy found it last week
        April 19, 1847.'

my Art as ever. I like London extremely well, and hope in the end, ['to show' deleted] however vain the idea, that my name will not perish with ['the' deleted] my breath ['of my nostrils' deleted] but I have not time to launch into eloquent harangues on Painting, for tis just post time, so you will excuse it.

Give my best love to Thomas and his family, who I hope are well; respects to Mr. and Mrs. Peck, etc.

And believe me,
Dear Parents,
Yr. Aff.ᵉ Son
Wm Etty

London, Friday, April 10. 1807.
Addressed [on verso] to: Mr. M. Etty
At Mr. T. Etty's
Church Lane
Hull.

The character of this earnest and serious-minded young man is thus revealed in a particularly intimate way. He still has to grope for words sufficiently expressive of his ambitions and feelings, but the simplicity of his sentiments makes an immediate appeal. The letter is carefully written in a large scrawling hand, with a legibility soon to deteriorate. Etty wrote a large number of letters during his lifetime, some of which are long, florid and often repetitive, but always in a difficult style of handwriting which occasionally defies accurate transcription.

Three months after this letter was written, Etty embarked upon a new venture. He had expressed an admiration for the work of Thomas Lawrence, Esq., R.A. (as he then was), and felt that a period of study under the eye of that already famous artist would be of considerable help. Thus, after first obtaining a letter of introduction from Fuseli, the obliging Uncle William had an interview with Lawrence, and it was agreed that upon the payment of a premium of one hundred guineas Lawrence would accept Etty as a private pupil for a year. On 2nd July, 1807, the uncle paid the fee, an act of unstinted generosity never to be forgotten by his nephew.[1] That this uncle had every sympathy with the aspirations of his protégé may in part be explained by the fact that he himself was also talented as a draughtsman and engraver. Lawrence, for his part of the bargain, promised to set aside a room in the attic of his house in Greek Street, Soho, where the pupil would be at liberty to copy from pictures, and to seek advice from him whenever he should happen to be disengaged. At this point it may be remarked that Etty's career closely resembles that of Northcote, for both men had been forced to spend their early years in uncongenial occupations, with a correspondingly late start in their true vocation.

Like Northcote, Etty received no specific instruction in painting from his master, and he experienced some agonizing difficulties when trying to imitate Lawrence's highly

[1] Joseph Farington, R.A., wrote in his *Diary* on 2nd July, 1807, as follows:
'. . . Lawrence called. His new pupil, the nephew of Mr. Etty, Banker, is come to Him this morning, & is to pay 100 guineas for instruction for one year . . .' This extract is from p. 3765 of the British Museum typescript copy of the original MS. *Diary* now in the Royal Library, Windsor.

sophisticated style, without being himself fully grounded in the essentials of his art. 'Lawrence's execution was *perfect—playful*, yet *precise*—elegant, yet *free*; it united in itself the extreme of possibilities. I tried, vainly enough, for a length of time, till *despair* almost overwhelmed me; I was ready to run away; my despondency increased.' [1] Throughout this time, Lawrence was far too busy to give very much advice or assistance, and when, at last, his pupil did succeed in imitating Lawrence's work, it was largely as the result of his own persistence and experiment. The time spent at Lawrence's house was not entirely wasted, since Etty claimed that he found copying the old masters comparatively easy once he had discovered the correct method of approach and solution to the problems involved by such work. Gilchrist shared C. R. Leslie's prejudice against Lawrence's influence on English portraiture, considering it evil and stultifying; he makes it quite clear that he feels Etty's survival unscathed by this experience to be fortunate.

When the year with Lawrence had expired, Etty was once again free to study according to his own inclinations, and there can be no doubt that he had sometimes found copying an irksome business. Despite this, he continued to work for Lawrence when required, and at Somerset House he copied Reynolds's *Queen Charlotte* (of 1780), besides executing other commissions at his own home, to the satisfaction of his master. Hack work of this kind was a very necessary, if uninspiring, method of earning money. [2] Otherwise, he continued to follow the usual Academy course of drawing from the life during the evenings, and copying old masters at the British Institution exhibitions. Tangible success still eluded him, and his efforts in the annual Academy competitions were repeatedly unsuccessful. Wilkie, although only two years Etty's senior, was made an Associate in 1809, but Etty had to wait until 1811 before he even got a picture accepted at the Academy, and in that year Wilkie became a full Academician.

The year 1809 was saddened for Etty by the death of his uncle on 25th May. In addition to the sharp grief of this personal loss, there was the need to find lodgings for himself, and for some time to come he led an unsettled existence, moving from one place to another, and some of these changes he has noted down, as, for example, 'Came to Mr. Underdown's Apartments on Friday, August the 24th. 1809.' Or again, 'took possession of Mr. James's apartments, December 11th, 1809'. [3] On the other hand, his kind

---

[1] Autobiography, *loc. cit.*, p. 37.

[2] It is known that Lawrence acquired some unfinished copies of both the *George III* and the *Queen Charlotte*, and had them completed in his studio. (*See also* the entry for Sunday, 26 January, 1794, in Joseph Farington's *Diary*; p. 113 of the British Museum typescript copy.) In *Sketchbook V* (York Art Gallery) of about 1809, this note is written on the back inside cover: 'June 27 received of T. Lawrence 30 Guineas.' Presumably a payment for a copy (or copies) executed by Etty, perhaps even referring to the *Queen Charlotte*. Across two other pages in the same sketchbook is written:

'Dr. / June 27 / Borrowed of Mr. T. Bodley £8. 0. 0.
Received of Mr. Lawrence £31. 10. 0.
Cr. / ,, ,, / Paid in the hands of. Bodley 30. 0. 0.
Paid Ditto Ditto 30. 0. 0.'

A reference to '2 Queens' occurs in a letter to Walter Etty, 19th June, 1811 (Appendix I, *Letter 1*).

[3] The first quotation is from *Sketchbook V*, front inside cover; the second is from Gilchrist, *op. cit.*, I, p. 43, and refers to another sketchbook, now lost.

Etty did not remain anywhere for very long until 1814. The Royal Academy Exhibition catalogues give his addresses as: 1811, 15 Bridge Street, Blackfriars; 1812–13, 23 Pavement, Moorfields; 1814–19,

uncle had left him a handsome legacy, and his brother Walter now became a partner in the gold-lace concern, thus enabling him to give more substantial help to William.

Sketchbooks of this period survive, containing many drawings done from a wide variety of subjects.[1] Most of these are in pencil, but there are also a few in pen-and-ink. Apart from studies of drapery, architectural fragments, and from the Antique, there are many drawings of women with young children, their mothers either leading them or carrying them in their arms. These lively records done from nature most closely resemble the work of Flaxman, differing only in that they are often softer in outline and less angular. Arms and legs are fluently drawn, although at this stage Etty does not show a complete mastery of anatomical problems. These drawings often possess a firmness and a monumental quality close to Flaxman in style, yet there is a tendency to elongate the figure and to draw the hands and feet in a mannered way more reminiscent of Fuseli, or perhaps even Lawrence [pls. 4a, 4b, 8a, 8b]. A few years later, this element disappears, and although Etty achieves a delightful crispness of outline (especially when making small studies of hands or feet), he no longer uses these rather affected distortions of form. Above all it is noticeable that Etty draws freely and can use his pencil sensitively, usually indicating the mass of an object by subtleties of line rather than by contrasts of light and shade. He rarely composes his figure sketches into any large groups or compositions, and prefers to view each figure as an isolated unit. This is not insignificant, for so many of his large paintings are composed either of a few figures which fill most of the picture-space, or of a lot of figures which do not always blend to form a strong composition. Undoubtedly these early sketchbooks contain only the first few words of Etty's artistic vocabulary, but his method of using them seems almost to be formed from the beginning—a method which contained within itself serious weaknesses. The slightly sweet domestic sentiment of the drawings of groups of children is in feeling not unlike the work of Stothard or Westall, but Etty's vigorous draughtsmanship usually prevents any lapse into insipidity.

Apart from the stylistic affinities of these drawings with those by Flaxman already noted, there is some evidence that the studies of draped figures in movement may be the direct outcome of Flaxman's own teaching [pl. 9a].

In 1810 Flaxman was appointed Professor of Sculpture at the Royal Academy, and in Lecture VIII entitled *Drapery*, he gives detailed, painstaking descriptions of the transitions from the simple to the more complex drapery forms. A glance at the Jasper ware plaques of *The Dancing Hours*, for example, shows that Flaxman had put his theories into practice. The original nine lectures (the tenth, *Modern Sculpture*, was written only in 1826) although now rather dull reading, would have formed for the student an introduction to antique sculpture, since Flaxman draws the greater part of his examples from Greek art of the fifth and fourth centuries B.C. Lecture IX, *Ancient Art*, is virtually a catalogue of the famous works by Praxiteles, Alcamenes, Myron, Phidias and so on. It need hardly be remarked that as soon as the Elgin Marbles were available he exhorted students to study these, in addition to the existing collections of vases, bronzes and sculptures in the British Museum. Flaxman also discusses the attri-

20 Surrey Street, Strand; 1820, 92 Piccadilly; 1821-4, 16 Bishop's Walk, Westminster Bridge, Lambeth (renamed Stangate Walk in 1822); 1825-49, 14 Buckingham Street, Strand.

[1] *Sketchbooks III* and *V* (City Art Gallery, York).

butes of the various gods and goddesses of antiquity, and recommends his audience to examine albums of engravings of, for example, the *Museum Pium Clementinum*, the *Museum Romanum*, and *Museum Florentinum*, copies of some of which were in the library of the Royal Academy.

As a draughtsman Etty has frequently been criticized, usually on the basis of his later and more numerous nude studies, in which the extremities are very often left unfinished. Against this must be set the failing eyesight and rheumatic infirmities of the last ten years of his life, which resulted in a decline in precision and dexterity; but the many drawings which survive from an earlier period contradict the charge that it was a fundamental weakness of his. Those at York are particularly useful in that they span almost the whole of his career, giving a very good idea of his development, of the variety of his interests, and of the things which most attracted him during his Italian stay of 1822–3. No work exhibited at the Academy between 1811 and 1818 seems to have survived; and except from a few family portraits, very little idea of Etty's early style can be gained from a study of his pictures. At the end of his life, a writer in the *Eclectic Review*,[1] discussing the Society of Arts exhibition of 1849 devoted to Etty, commented upon this lack of early works, and it seems that they had sunk into oblivion even at that date. The drawings of this period have thus an additional importance.

Nevertheless, Etty did not gain fluency as a draughtsman without some preliminary struggles, and the drawings of 1809 to 1818 show him striving to improve his knowledge of anatomy and proportion. Repeated rejection of his work by the Academy during the first four years of his career in London made him realize that he had much to learn. 'I began to think', he confesses, 'I was not *half* the clever fellow I had imagined, and indeed I even began to suspect that I was no clever fellow at all. I thought there must be some radical defect; my master told me the truth in no flattering terms; he said I had a very good eye for colour, but that I was lamentably deficient in all other respects almost. I believed him.'[2] The shock was a salutary one, and with characteristic energy he set about repairing his deficiencies. He went back to school and, among other things, he studied anatomy more carefully and in greater detail, sketching from the anatomical 'atlases' of Albinus[3] and painting from the life. He also made finished pencil studies from prints of the various Italian collections of antique statues, albums of which he referred to at the Royal Academy and at the excellent library of the London Institution.

This intensive application was rewarded in 1811, when two of his pictures were publicly exhibited for the first time. One was a *Sappho*, shown at the British Institution; this picture Etty had the good fortune to sell for twenty-five guineas. The other was *Telemachus rescues Antiope from the Fury of the Wild Boar*, accepted by the Academy later that year. Thus from the very beginning he chose the kind of subjects that were to occupy his attention throughout his life, and the titles of these early pictures show where his interests lay. The next year, for example, he exhibited three works, *Cupid Stealing the*

[1] *Eclectic Review*, London, September, 1849. The writer was in fact Alexander Gilchrist and the article was later published as a pamphlet by Rickerby, London. Of the paintings exhibited at the Society of Arts the earliest was *Hercules killing the Man of Calydon with a Blow of his Fist* of 1820.

[2] Autobiography, *loc. cit.*, p. 37.

[3] Bernhard Siegfried Albinus (1697–1770) was a famous German professor of anatomy who published several illustrated treatises on the subject which became the standard works of their time.

Ring (British Institution), *A Domestic Scene* and *A Portrait* (both at the Academy); in 1813, four were hung, including one entitled *The Whisper of Love* (presumably a Cupid and Psyche group); and in 1814 he showed one painting at the Academy, *Priam supplicating Achilles for the Dead Body of his Son Hector*.[1] It would be interesting to see these paintings, if only to discover what classical models he had used as his starting point in the history pieces; for one would not expect to find work of very great originality at this stage. Judging by some family portraits of these years, it may be supposed that the handling of the paint would be dry, without very much impasto, and generally thinly applied. The colours would probably be fairly restrained, and cool in tone.

Other paintings of these years are an important reminder that Etty also had to rely on homelier subjects that were more acceptable to public taste and which sold more easily. Most of the pictures were small and included such themes as *Courtship* (British Institution 1815), *The Fireside* (R.A., 1813) or *Portraits of a Family* (R.A., 1815). According to Gilchrist[2] *The Fireside* was of a group seated around a tea-table, with details of still-life—muffins, poker and tongs, etc.—quite cleverly but painstakingly done, and not in a style readily associable with Etty's mature years. He painted his first portraits early in his career, and some of his finest work is of this type. Much of it is relatively unknown, and after 1820 he rarely exhibited portraits, preferring to gain repute as a history painter —although a small but steady flow of portraits continues to the end of his activity. The sitters are usually from his immediate circle of friends and relations; and the works perhaps gain in quality because they were never intended as mere commercial propositions. This also explains why there are so few mediocre portraits by him, although a lack of sympathy with his subject is always marked by a correspondingly sharp drop in vitality: his bad portraits are very bad indeed simply because he never needed to cultivate the professional portraitist's skill in making the dullest or the most uncongenial of sitters look moderately presentable. Etty seemed incapable of viewing the world with a certain detachment of feeling as Reynolds could, and this implies a lack of critical perception, certainly in worldly matters and sometimes in artistic evaluations as well, which is fully borne out by a study of his life.

There is an interesting letter of 19th June, 1811, from William, who was at York on holiday, to his brother Walter in London,[3] which gives a very good idea of Etty's increasing self-confidence. It is in marked contrast with that of 1807 quoted earlier. It fairly bristles with information of every kind—not least important that he had visited Burghley House and Castle Howard, and had seen their fine collections of pictures. At Burghley he would also have been able to examine Stothard's decorations on the staircase painted between 1799 and 1802, one of the few examples of large-scale wall decoration done for a private patron of that time. In these, he could have observed an English artist turning to Rubens for inspiration, just as he himself was to do later. The

[1] Gilchrist, *op. cit.*, I, p. 48, says of the *Priam* that it was a subject rarely attempted by the students at the Academy. There is, however, a Fuseli drawing (exhibited at Zürich, 1926, No. 138) of *Priam supplicating Achilles*, which might have inspired Etty's own work. Flaxman's *Iliad* (1793) may be regarded as another possible source.

[2] *Op. cit.*, I, pp. 48–9. Gilchrist, however, had to rely on others who had seen these pictures for his information about them. This picture may be the one in the possession of Ir. Thomas H. Etty (Catalogue No. 112).

[3] *See* Appendix I, *Letter 1*.

letter also refers to his parents, and he notes that although his mother is in very good health, his father is much changed and aged considerably. His father's infirmities make the task of painting his portrait a difficult one; the strain and fatigue of the sitting sorely try his weakened powers of endurance. But complications of this kind did not bedevil the progress of three other portraits begun at this time—those of his mother, of his brother John's eldest daughter Kitty and of her sister Betsy. As he says, he is kept busy, but has found time to cast an approving eye upon John's building activities in Walmgate—evidence, incidentally, of improved family fortunes. Finally, it would appear that he is continuing to make copies for Lawrence, and 'the 2 Queens marked E on the back', which he asks Walter to tell either Strowger or Levell to take to Lawrence, are perhaps further copies of Reynolds's *Queen Charlotte*.[1] The letter ends on a happy note of congratulation to his brother upon the addition of a daughter to his family.

Three of the portraits mentioned in the letter still exist, and may be related with some certainty to paintings remaining in the possession of descendants of the Etty family. The portrait of *Miss Catharine Etty* (later to become the wife of Robert Purdon, and the 'Kitty' mentioned in the letter) [pl. 2*b*] possesses a naïve delicacy and charm which reconcile one to the rather stiff pose and flat surface modelling characteristic of the artist's early style. The young woman is set against a plain background of dark brown merging into a deep red at the bottom of the picture. A black velvet shawl makes a strong contrast with the white, thick-spotted muslin dress she is wearing, while further points of colour are provided by the gold filigree buckle, necklace and earrings, a pink rose pinned to her dress, and a dark red comb set in her auburn hair. The flesh tints are predominantly creamy-white, with touches of pink on the cheeks. The lips are firmly modelled, and the whole head has a plasticity that is much less evident in the treatment of the rest of the figure, particularly in the part below the waist. Although the hair has been fluently brushed in, Etty has rather laboured the rendering of the ear. It is noticeable that he is already beginning to paint fairly thinly in the shadows, especially in the areas around the chin and in the shadows cast by the falling locks of hair. There is sensitivity in parts, yet the whole still gives evidence of Etty's painstaking care, notably in the slightly mechanical painting of the highlights on the necklace and the almost flat treatment of the nosegay, where a minor problem of perspective has not quite been solved. It is a sincere, honest piece of craftsmanship and makes its appeal more by the winsomeness of the subject than by purely painterly qualities.

The portrait of *Matthew Etty* [pl. 3*a*] has much more sparkle about it, and there is a surer, richer use of paint, imparting both a greater plastic effect and increased variety of texture. His father's disabilities have made it difficult for Etty to obtain an easy coherent pose, and he has tried to overcome this problem by showing him seated at a table reading a Bible. Skilfully, the artist has exploited this slight awkwardness in the relation of figure to book, and the very bulk and solidity of the Bible gives, in a surprisingly effective way, great monumentality to the whole composition. Furthermore, the painting of the head is much more interesting than that of the *Miss Catharine Etty*; the thick pigment used on the white shirt ruff and the grey and black silk waistcoat displays a more complete mastery of handling; and there is a similar increased subtlety

---

[1] *See* note 2, p. 15 above.

in recording the sitter's features. The roughness of the old man's weather-beaten cheeks and jowl has been suggested by cross-hatching with a dry, thin solution of paint over the canvas, and the close-cropped hair, sandy but greying a little, is equally thinly painted but of smoother finish. Perhaps the outstanding feature of this portrait is the literal, unidealized treatment of the sitter, and it is just this unsophisticated quality which gives the picture so much of its power. A parallel for this in the work of an old master must surely be Rembrandt's *Old Woman Reading* at Wilton House, and perhaps Etty knew this painting. There is, of course, more incident in an old man's head than in a young woman's, allowing greater opportunities to a painter, and it may be that this portrait was finished later than the *Miss Catharine Etty*; six months would make a considerable difference at this stage of Etty's career. The striking portrait of *John Etty* [pl. 3*b*] must also date from about this time, and is an interesting adaptation of the *Matthew Etty* composition. Accurate dating of early works is not made easier by the fact that there are few surviving, or at least located, works of certain date before 1818 to serve as a yardstick.

Conveniently, 1815 acts as a bridge between Etty the student and Etty the distinct artistic personality; although five years have still to pass before he makes his mark publicly with works of outstanding originality. It was in 1815 that he made his first journey abroad. Very little is known about this journey, and evidence for it rests entirely upon a letter to his brother Walter, in which he describes his experience of a stormy crossing to France.[1] It makes interesting reading, and recounts in great detail the hazards of winter travel, miseries aggravated by the insolence and rapacity of the boatmen and, of course, the sufferings of the sea-sick. Divided into two parts, the letter was begun at Dover and finished at Calais, and covers the period Monday–Tuesday, 2nd–3rd January, 1815: Etty has dashed down his impressions in a racy narrative, adding snatches of dialogue to give local colour. Beyond the facts that he is alone, is making for Paris and has letters of credit for £100, nothing is known about the length of his stay, or of his later movements and acquaintances.

Paris, crowded with the troops of many nations, was at this time a fascinating place to visit. On 1st May, 1814, the first Treaty of Paris had been signed, and France was slowly regaining breath after having secured a generous peace settlement. The Louvre was still full of the accumulated loot from the foremost European collections, and there was every inducement for an artist to travel to France. Indeed, at the end of that same month, Wilkie and Haydon had set off together for six weeks' holiday there. Others were not slow to follow their example: Eastlake had arrived in Paris on 1st January, 1815, a few days ahead of Etty (always assuming the latter to have reached Paris). Within three weeks of his escape from Elba on 1st March, Napoleon was in Paris, and this at least provides a *terminus postquem* for the duration of Etty's stay in France, as it did for Eastlake's, who left Paris on 19th March, and after some delays returned safely to England that same month.

This first visit abroad must have been a great experience for Etty and should have been a useful preparation for his longer travels to Italy the following year. He came to France with a mind ready to receive new ideas and sights: 'I like', he writes, 'what little I have seen of France already the scene is novel and interesting,—I will tell you more

[1] *See* Appendix I, *Letter 2.*

bye and bye.' Nothing else seems to have survived, and even Gilchrist makes no mention whatsoever of this expedition. A further puzzle is provided by the fact that Etty himself omits any reference to it in his Autobiography. Both Haydon and Eastlake, however, have left inimitable personal records of the France of this period, and Etty, although lacking quite their acute perception and social aplomb, was never an insensitive traveller and would have shared much in common with them. His artistic education, in the wider sense, had begun.

CHAPTER THREE

RECOGNITION AND SUCCESS : 1816–1821

THE year 1816 had little sweetness for Etty. True, he had exhibited five pictures, three at the British Institution and two at the Academy; but they were small works, and there is no clear indication of whether they were sold.[1] His contemporaries Hilton, Collins and Mulready had already been elected Associates of the Royal Academy, yet he, with Constable his senior, still awaited recognition. However, to improve himself, Etty decided upon a journey to Italy, an idea he had long cherished. He intended to stay a year, and by the middle of 1816 plans were already being made; but there were complications, for he writes to his brother on 24th July, posing a somewhat ingenuous question.[2] Briefly, he was in love: should he marry and take his wife with him to a foreign country?—or should he pursue his career alone? Strange as it may seem that a man of twenty-eight should seek a brother's advice on such a personal matter, the letter clearly demonstrates William's dependence upon his brother and his faith in his wisdom. But perhaps more than anything else it betrays the first signs of the loneliness which was to haunt him for the rest of his life. Although it would be misleading to overemphasize this fact, it cannot be entirely ignored, for one can detect a feeling of disappointment implicit in the personal memoranda and diaries of his later years. By 1830, for example, he is apparently resigned to live a bachelor and comforts himself with the observation 'that it is best I have not married because I have not noisy Children and can have nice Books, and Pictures etc.'. Ten years later he writes in his notebook 'Never to Marry—Virago of Wife'! Whilst on the 6th July, 1843, he solemnly resolves that 'this day [Thursday] being in sound Mind and Body I declare it to be my *Firm Intention* NEVER TO MARRY. In which resolution I pray GOD to help me that I may devote myself more purely to my Art, my Country, and my GOD!'[3] It must have been surely very much harder for him to act quite so resolutely in 1816, but there can be little doubt about Walter's views at this juncture, nor about the lady's, and Etty set off on his travels alone.

Rejected and dejected, he did not enjoy the foreign tour which he began in early September, landing at Dieppe and journeying through Rouen to Paris. The French capital did not appeal to him greatly on this visit, and while he grudgingly admitted

---

[1] Little idea can be gained of the pictures from their titles: *Contemplation, Portrait of a Lady, A Study,* the rather enigmatic *Discovery of an Unpleasant Secret* and *The Offering of the Magi*, which last suggests an attempt at a more ambitious subject.   [2] *See* Appendix I, *Letter 3.*

[3] From notebooks in the possession of Mr. Jacobus J. T. Bosch and Ir. Thomas H. Etty.

the French to be a lively and cultured race living in a beautiful country, yet he much preferred England. The vexations of customs and passport examinations were further burdens, and on 8th September he wrote to his cousin Martha, Thomas Bodley's wife, 'I hope I shall like Italy better than Paris, or I think I shall not feel resolution to stop a year. If I don't, I shall content myself with seeing what I think worth while; and then return . . . I am better in health, much, than when I left; shall feel still better when I am getting on. I know not how it is:—I feel much better when I am advancing, worse when I am set down. I am a strange mortal; must have either a weaker head or stronger feelings than most. Or else, the circumstances, under which I left operate on me.'[1] With spirits momentarily revived he began to warm towards Paris, and by the time he arrived at the foot of the Juras he could delight in the golden beauty of a late summer's evening amid magnificent scenery. Climbing for the first time the mountain road into Switzerland he was awed by the grandeur of the Alps; and again, beyond Geneva and through the Simplon his sensitive nature, like Turner's, responded to the brilliant colours and immensities of his surroundings. On the other side, the vineyards of Piedmont, now harvested, fascinated the artist by their rich variety of autumnal colours. These enjoyments were marred to some extent by his own awkwardness as a traveller, by bad inns and by an injury to his knee. Always the English-man, he demanded tea even in the remotest Swiss mountain villages, and though equipped with his own tea-making apparatus, getting the necessary milk was often a problem.

Having arrived at Florence without serious mishap, he yet longed to be back in England, and on 5th October he wrote to his brother of his intention to return home. Shamefacedly, he confessed his failure, but strongly defended his decision: his illness, the bad roads and the expense of a visit to Rome and Naples which could not be justified by any immediate advantage—all were heaped together to bolster his argument. His morale was shaken: 'I feel so lonely, it is impossible for me to be happy. And if not happy, I cannot apply vigorously to my studies . . . I am sick to death of travelling in a country where the accommodations are such as no Englishman can have any idea of,—who has not witnessed it: the vermin in the bed, the dirt and filth. But I can't enter into particulars.'[2] He had learnt his lesson: he was cured, so he thought, of his wander-lust, and confirmed in his opinion of the natural superiorities of his own land. His real error perhaps lay in visiting a foreign land when emotionally upset, without some congenial travelling-companion able to attend to practical details; a mistake never repeated. That he felt the need for some such person from the start is made clear in his letter to Martha Bodley, where he expressed the wish that his friend Jay could have been with him to make the tour more enjoyable. This friend was probably the Reverend William Jay, of Bath, whose portrait he was to paint just over a year later. Altogether, he spent about a month in Italy, and besides seeing Florence and Milan, he stopped briefly at Lodi, Piacenza, Parma, Reggio, Modena and Bologna. All these he must have passed *en route* for Florence, since his return journey was made by way of Pisa, Leghorn, Genoa and Turin, crossing at Mont Cenis and travelling up through Lyons to Paris, where he paused on 26th October.

[1] Gilchrist, *op. cit.*, I, pp. 59–64.
[2] *Ibid.*, pp. 72–5, both for this quotation, and for other information about the first Italian journey.

In Paris, a city now more familiar to him, Etty attempted to study more diligently than in Italy, and he attended the Académie. He further varied his activities by entering the studio of Jean-Baptiste Regnault, one of the most fashionable academic painters of the day, and one of the greatest rivals to David and his school. As a pupil of Vien at the French Academy in Rome, Regnault would have inherited much of the teaching of Mengs and Winckelmann, with its emphasis upon Greek and Roman antiquity as the only true model for subsequent generations of history painters. Unlike David, however, Regnault lacked the originality and imagination which distinguished his contemporary, and his chief virtue was as a teacher.[1] The same might also be said for his pupil, Pierre-Narcisse Guérin, whom Etty was later to admire. Accustomed to the more sedate Royal Academy schools, Etty found Regnault's *atelier*, crammed with volatile and noisy young Frenchmen, not much to his taste, and he left after only about a week. He quotes Regnault as saying that the English method of painting from the life model was a bad one, and that one's studies should be finished part by part, 'putting as you go on, the bones and muscles in their proper places'. This is an interesting point, for it implies a greater thoroughness in French academic teaching and provides a little more evidence for the far higher general standard of technical proficiency which is so noticeable a feature of the school as a whole. Nevertheless, Etty found Regnault's methods unpalatable, and continued in his own style. At the Académie he persevered, and his work, mainly sketches from the Antique and life studies, found admirers among his fellow-students.

This part of the journey seems to have been far more profitable than the Italian episode, an impression further strengthened by the fact that he spent a considerable time in print shops gathering a large stock, later to be of great value to him. Besides amassing this type of iconographic treasure-trove, he made his own sketches from Le Brun's *Battles*, and a few of these drawings may still be seen in the sketchbooks at York. He also patronized the famous Parisian colourman and brushmaker Derveaux—whom he miscalled 'Dagneaux'[2]—buying some of his superlative brushes. But by 23rd November he was back in London, to his great joy and relief. One cannot help but compare and contrast this miserable adventure with Géricault's precipitate flight from Paris the same year. Both men were trying to escape from personal unhappiness; yet Géricault, by nature so highly-strung, demanded a much more extreme antidote, and in an effort to assuage his anguish he 'lost' himself for a year in the fashionable society of Rome and Florence.

After six years' obscurity Etty received a favourable criticism of his two paintings at the Academy of 1817—criticism that was more valuable for the attention it drew to the painter than for any display of the critic's sensibility. At this time, most art criticism in England ranged from the harshly vituperative, through the non-committal, to the wildly adulatory. Not until the time of Ruskin, Samuel Phillips and Tom Taylor was it much esteemed or considered an art in itself. But it would be unfair to the newer school of more intelligent criticism if one were to leave out the names of William Hazlitt

---

[1] *See* M. E. J. Delécluze, *Louis David, son école et son temps*, Paris, 1855, pp. 301–2; *also* J. Locquin, *La Peinture d'histoire en France de 1747 à 1785*, Paris, 1912.

[2] W. T. Whitley, *Art in England 1800–1820*, p. 194, has drawn attention to the strong probability that 'Dagneaux' and 'Derveaux' are, in fact, identical.

and John Landseer—honourable exceptions from the general mediocrity. Other critics writing for the Radical papers *Champion*, *Morning Chronicle* and *Examiner*, may also be mentioned as a welcome change from the declining Beaumont and Carr tradition of criticism. This tradition died hard, however, for as late as 1845 the artist George Foggo published his *Critical Notes on Paintings in the National Gallery*, a work consisting of little more than a crude statement of the author's whims and fancies; whereas John Landseer's critical catalogue *Fifty of the Earliest Pictures contained in the National Gallery of Great Britain*, which had appeared over ten years previously, is very different in quality. Nevertheless, it is pleasant to recall that William Carey, in the *Literary Gazette*,[1] wrote the following: 'Mr. W. Etty's sketch of Bacchanalians, No. 376, is a fine classical invention. The upper part of the female is designed with a noble flow of outline. The Cupid is incorrect, but full of spirit. The brilliant harmony of the colouring is produced by delicious oppositions. There is a certain graceful negligence in the whole, and a true poetical feeling, which affords a splendid promise, if this artist studies to combine *purity of form* with his fine vein of imagination.' In fine, he picks upon a merit and a defect; good colour is offset by a weakness in drawing. Carey was a prolific writer upon several subjects, and although often tedious, he was the first to recognize Etty's abilities (a fact which he never let be forgotten).

There can be no doubt whatsoever that Etty's artistic powers were now increasing steadily, certainly in portraiture, of which there were several examples at the Academy exhibitions. In 1818 he showed two, one of which was a *Portrait of the Rev. W. Jay, of Bath*, and the following year three were exhibited, *Portraits of a child, and favourite dog*, *Portrait of Miss Jay* and a *Portrait of a gentleman* (probably the *John Thornton* in the Merchant Adventurers' Hall, York).[2] The portrait of the Reverend William Jay is known to us only from a stipple-engraving published in the *European Magazine* for January 1819 [pl. 11*a*], where it served as a frontispiece to a biographical account of this gifted dissenting minister, whose abilities as a preacher had been praised by no less a person than Sheridan. The engraving is of a half-length portrait showing Jay seated, half turned to the left, and comfortably posed with his left arm resting upon the chair arm and making the base of a solid, triangular composition. Even from the engraving it is apparent that Etty has succeeded in obtaining a powerful characterization of his sitter, and for likeness it compares very favourably with a portrait of Jay by his son-in-law, William Jay Bolton, painted over twenty-five years later.[3] As if to compensate for the absence of the original Etty portrait, a portrait of William Jay's eldest child Anne and another of his son-in-law, the Reverend Robert Bolton, have since come to light. The portrait of *Miss Mary Arabella Jay* [pl. 33] has also re-appeared, but whereas this

[1] *Literary Gazette*, No. XVII, Saturday, 17th May, 1817, p. 264. The article is signed 'W.C.' and it is part of a series of reviews of current exhibitions. *See also: The History of 'The Times'*, II, London, 1938, pp. 437–9, for further details about art criticism in England, with special reference to *The Times*.

[2] The *Portrait of Miss Jay* must depict Mary Arabella, William Jay's second daughter and the third child of a family of six. The Rev. William Jay (1769–1853) married Miss Anne Davies in January 1791, and after Mary Arabella came two sons and a daughter. This painting is now in the National Gallery (No. 6268).

[3] This picture by W. J. Bolton is now in the collection of The New-York Historical Society, New York, which also possesses the two Etty portraits of *The Rev. Robert Bolton* and of his wife (*Mrs. Robert Bolton and her Children*).

is more or less in the Lawrence tradition, nothing could come as a greater surprise at this date than the two pictures of husband and wife; and they alone would qualify the artist for considerable respect. Their history is well known, but Gilchrist's apparent ignorance of their existence is excused by the fact that the Bolton family emigrated to America in 1822. All four portraits were painted at the same time: 'Etty, the artist, then rising into reputation was the guest for some weeks in Mr. Bolton's house in Liverpool painting family portraits. His likeness of Mr. Jay placed in the Royal Academy Exhibition of the year [1818] and engraved twice was painted at this time.'[1]

Almost life size, the portrait of *The Reverend Robert Bolton* [pl. 6] is distinguished by an austere grandeur untainted by any hint of pompousness. Boldly conceived, it is executed with a competence fully equal to the task, and the quiet dignity of the subject is enhanced by the slightly quizzical expression suggested in the eyes and mouth. The general tone of the painting is cool, the black coat, white cravat, and restrained flesh tints are harmonized with the warmer stone colours in the pillar and balustrade, whilst in the background ultramarine is the dominant colour.[2] Firmly and sensitively modelled, the figure stands free in a clearly defined, though limited, space. Depth and atmosphere are implied by the 'backdrop' of sea and ship, rather than deliberately created by means of linear perspective; although by a fortuitous optical illusion, the balustrade against which the figure stands appears to break back in space on the right-hand side. The paint is still fairly dry in handling, although the cravat (which neatly breaks the hard edge of the coat lapel) and head are broadly painted and the whole body is strongly lighted from one side giving a controlled decisiveness to the portrait. As a painting, it follows the long tradition of Reynolds and Lawrence, yet it is marked by a sincerity and simplicity characteristic of Etty.

Equally fine, and of the same size as *The Reverend Robert Bolton*, is the portrait of his wife, *Mrs. Robert Bolton and her Children* [pl. 7]. Anne Bolton is shown with two of her children, Robert and Anne, an arrangement which at once evokes a more tender mood. This picture is also much warmer in colour; the figures are set against a very dark background, with a deep maroon curtain on the right, and this red is echoed by embroidery of the same colour on the wrap across Mrs. Bolton's knees. The children's fair hair and the rosy complexion of all three sitters adds to this warmer tone, which is, however, balanced by the white satin bodice and white dress of the mother. The posing of the figures compares quite closely with that adopted by Lawrence in his portrait of *Lady Acland and her Children* exhibited at the Academy of 1818, but Etty's figures are far more

---

[1] Robert Bolton, *The Genealogical and Biographical Account of the Family of Bolton in England and America*, New York, 1862, p. 155. The Boltons were obviously quite wealthy, and Farington's *Diary* reveals an interesting snippet of information about Robert Bolton's father: '... Mr. Bolton, a merchant of Liverpool, has given in his income, on an average of 3 years £40,000 ...' (Monday, 1st April, 1799; p. 1511, British Museum typescript copy of the original MS.). Despite this wealth, however, Bolton *père* still owed Etty £30, and Jay owed £15, even as late as 1827 (letter in the British Museum, Add. MS. 38794 E, fols. 115–16). The portrait of the *Rev. William Jay* was first engraved by J. Thomson (1819), and again in 1854 by W. Holl when it formed the frontispiece to *The Autobiography of the Rev. William Jay*, ed. George Redford, D.D., LL.D. and John Angell James. The painting is there described as being of Jay 'in his 48th year', and as in the possession of the Rev. Robert Bolton.

[2] I am indebted to Miss Carolyn Scoon, Assistant Curator of the New York Historical Society, for details about the colours used in both the Bolton portraits.

static than those of the Lawrence portrait, and he replaced a restless internal movement by a statuesque, compact grouping reminiscent of Reynolds's *Jane, Countess of Harting-ton, with Charles, Viscount Petersham and the Hon. Lincoln Stanhope*, of 1786–7. Especially remarkable is the neo-classical pose of the wide-eyed little girl as she stands on her mother's knee. Despite the weight and solidity of these figures, the whole composition appears relatively flat, an impression heightened by the dark, unbroken background which effectively cuts off all suggestion of further recession beyond the plane formed by the curtain and table. Incidentally, the bowl of flowers must be among the earliest of Etty's attempts to paint this type of subject. Perhaps the artist who comes nearest in spirit to this portrait would be Opie, for there is a rugged domesticity here which is alien to Lawrence, and nowhere is the effect spoilt by a discordant note of false sentimentality.

Towards the end of 1818 Etty was involved in an unfortunate controversy over the result of the competition for a medal in the School of Painting, a new department of the Academy established in 1816. John Julius Angerstein had lent his *Ganymede* (then believed to be by Titian) and Etty had entered a copy of this picture for the competition, which he would have won easily but for the protests of two of his fellow candidates. Their objections were first that Etty, as a professional artist and a student of almost twelve years' standing, was no longer eligible to compete under the rules of the Academy; and second that during the work he had removed his canvas from the Academy premises for a short time, thus breaking a strict Academy rule. The Council had little choice but to disqualify Etty and award the premium to John Stevens, one of the objectors. The essence of the dispute is contained in the Academy Minutes for 5th November and 17th November, 1818, and Gilchrist quotes from a rough draft of Etty's letter to the Council defending his actions.[1] The obvious merits of his work did not go unremarked, however, and on 10th December Shee, acting as President in Benjamin West's absence, passed on the Council's 'high approbation' of his painting. Before the distribution of the premiums he had been asked to leave his copy at the Academy for the inspection of the General Assembly; after seeing it West was so pleased that he asked Etty to call upon him.

Success of this kind did not, of course, advance Etty much towards public recognition. An interesting picture exhibited at the British Institution in 1819 appears to have escaped attention. This was the *Manlius Hurled from the Rock*, [pl. 10a] depicting the fateful moment of Manlius Capitolinus's punishment. Although only of medium size, the painting is noteworthy for its grandeur of scale and for the manner in which the subject has been treated. Yet a public accustomed to the elaborate compositions of West and Wilkie could scarcely be expected to consider Etty's picture as anything but austere and perhaps meaningless. He had still to learn the art of titillating the spectator's eye; certainly the painting hardly rises much beyond a clever, carefully finished Academy nude, and it is possible to trace with some accuracy the way in which the model was posed. One has only to imagine the figure placed at the edge of a dais, head and chest projecting over, with the weight taken on the left hand and arm. In fact, Manlius is slithering off the Tarpeian Rock, rather than actually falling through space. Nevertheless,

---

[1] *Royal Academy Council Minutes*, VI, pp. 14–18; and the *General Assembly Minutes*, III, p. 276. Whitley, *Art in England, 1800–1820*, pp. 292–3, gives slightly abbreviated extracts from the *Council Minutes*. For Etty's defence *see* Gilchrist, *op. cit.*, I, pp. 79–83.

problems of foreshortening and flesh modelling are skilfully solved; the careful drawing and dry impasto are qualities found in the smaller life studies of this date. Probably somewhat earlier than the *Manlius*, because much less fluently finished, is the *Male Nude with a Staff* [pl. 5*b*], now at York Art Gallery. A very accomplished drawing [pl. 5*a*], also at York and done from the same model, leaves one in no doubt about Etty's powers as a draughtsman when he set his mind to a task. Before leaving the *Manlius*, it is tempting to recall Thomas Banks's diploma work *The Falling Titan* as a possible stimulus to Etty's imagination, for it is noticeable that Etty, by concentrating on one monumental figure, has treated his picture in a manner more readily associated with the sculptor than the painter. The most fertile source of inspiration, however, would have been the engravings of Michelangelo's Sistine ceiling, especially the *Creation* scenes at the end of the vault; and the almost superhuman male type developed by that artist is discernible in the heroic proportions of Manlius.

During the following year, 1820, Etty exhibited a very mixed bag of pictures, and the subjects range from Italianate grand manner to Dutch genre: at the Academy he showed *The Coral Finder: Venus and her Youthful Satellites arriving at the Isle of Paphos* along with *Drunken Barnaby*. Of the two *Drunken Barnaby* [pl. 10*b*] is perhaps the more interesting, for it reveals Etty attempting a popular type of subject more familiar to Mulready or even Wilkie. The incident chosen is described by Barnaby Harrington:

> Thence to Cock at Budworth, where I
> Drank strong ale as browne as berry;
> Till at last with deep-healths felled,
> To my bed I was compelled:
> I for state was bravely sorted,
> By two poulterers well supported.

The artist has painted a spirited picture, keeping close to the details of the narrative. Helpless, Barnaby is being carried by a farmer and a shepherd, while the buxom inn-keeper's daughter, or barmaid, looks on in amusement from the inn doorway. The general tone of the picture is warm and gay as befits the subject, and the bright reds and blues used for the clothes mingle with the softer browns and greens of the landscape and building. Particularly delightful, because so unexpected, are the lively groups of hens and cockerels in the foreground, and the landscape vista across a valley seen through some trees lining the lane, along which rides a woman on a donkey, accompanied by two boys. Of all the figures, that of the young woman provides a clue as to the artist. Robust and plump, rosy-cheeked, she is the precursor of a female type which occurs often enough in Etty's work of the next decade; a type sometimes more idealized, but recognizably of the same family.

Yet this excursion into domestic genre was but a passing phase, and his predilection for nobler themes had been emphasized earlier that year, when he sent to the British Institution a highly finished sketch for *Pandora, formed by Vulcan and crowned by the Seasons*; *Hercules killing the Man of Calydon with a Blow of his Fist*; and a *Magdalen*, a small study. The *Pandora* attracted both praise and blame; William Carey, writing in the *New Monthly Magazine*,[1] was as extravagant in his plaudits as were his opponents in their

---

[1] *New Monthly Magazine*, 1st March, 1820, p. 336.

abuse. Carey thought Etty was 'advancing with the steps of a giant. His sketch of *Pandora* . . . is a piece of poetry in colours, conceived with much richness and grandeur of fancy, and executed with a daring fury of pencil and foreshortenings of great beauty.' And much more in the same strain, which provoked rival critics to complain of Carey's 'tasteless ignorance' in praising 'this Pandora and two other paltry productions by the same lame workman, Etty'.[1]

Journalistic scuffles such as these attracted attention to Etty's name, and *The Coral Finder* found a purchaser, and brought the artist a commission from another admirer, Sir Francis Freeling, Secretary to the Post Office. *The Coral Finder* [pl. 12] was the first of those serene mythological compositions which Etty made so peculiarly his own, and which surprised both the public and his fellow artists by their freshness and apparent originality. Elements show themselves in this painting that recur time after time in later years: not only the protagonists, but even their trappings and draperies, reappear with only minor alterations of pose, situation and number. Venus, lying in the pose of a *Venus Victrix*, is gently propelled in a golden barge towards the shores of the Island of Paphos. The yellow roofs of the island's gleaming white temples are just visible through the dark green trees on the foothills of the slate-blue mountains, which rise up in the background beyond. The figures are colourfully attired: the oarsman has around his waist a vermilion cloth shot with white and blue that echoes the red cloak of the flying *putto*. Venus and Cupid are clad in white, and Venus lics on a crimson couch over which has been draped a dark blue cloth patterned with golden stars. The flesh is carefully modelled and almost enamel-like in finish, but it never becomes lifeless, for the shadows on the faces of the oarsman and the *putto* scattering pink and white roses are painted with a strong Indian red, and the lighter flesh of Venus contains subtle pinkish-mauve tints in its shadows. But the Etty palette is at this stage somewhat lush and a trifle gaudy, for he has still much to learn in harmonizing these strong colours well enough to avoid a certain brittleness of effect. The landscape is not unlike the imaginary scenes painted by Niccolò dell'Abbate, and it is possible that Turner may have borrowed from Etty when painting his *Ulysses Deriding Polyphemus*. But Etty had himself borrowed freely from a Titian prototype. The flying *putto* and relationship of landscape to the main figures follow Titian's *The Rape of Europa* composition far too closely for the resemblance to be merely accidental. Etty also had before him the example of William Hilton, who in 1818 had painted an *Europa* (now at Petworth) based quite unashamedly upon the Titian composition which, by then, was well known in England. Not only had the original passed from the Orléans Collection to the Earl of Darnley, but a copy, now in the Wallace Collection, had been sold at Christie's in 1811 by W. Y. Ottley.

The Coral Finder does not entirely prepare one for the ambitious work exhibited at the Academy of 1821. Sir Francis Freeling, unable to acquire *The Coral Finder*, commissioned Etty to paint a subject which for some time past had been in the artist's mind awaiting such an opportunity. This was *Cleopatra's Arrival in Cilicia* [pl. 13], based upon a description of this event in Plutarch's *Life of Antony*, and Shakespeare's *Antony and Cleopatra*. It is an extraordinary painting and must have burst like a bombshell upon

---

[1] *Ridolfi's Critical Letters on the Style of Wm. Etty, Esq., R.A. and on his Destroying Angel, inflicting Divine Vengeance on the Wicked: reprinted from the Yorkshire Gazette of October and November, 1832: with Additional Notices etc.* . . ., publ. 1833 for Wm. Carey ('Ridolfi'), p. 73.

the Academy and public alike. Although the central figures of Cleopatra and her attendants are strongly reminiscent of the Venus in *The Coral Finder*, it would be a mistake to think of *Cleopatra's Arrival* merely as an elaboration of the earlier theme. In conception, it owes most to French academic painting of the period, and if we compare this picture with, for example, Regnault's *Allégorie à la gloire de Napoléon*,[1] [pl. 15*b*] one sees a similar complex, over-crowded composition, but without quite such marked discrepancies of scale as are to be found in the Etty. There is a limited depth in both, and both give a curious effect of arrested motion. The poses of the figures, certainly in the *Cleopatra*, are fluently and cleverly contrived as individual groups, but fail to cohere within the general framework of the composition, and a confused *mêlée* of bodies is crammed into a very inadequate and ill-defined space. The boat is absurdly out of proportion, and it is hard to believe that men, not mice, work the oars. But although it is easy to scoff at such defects, the fact remains that it is a vividly imagined work, and contains many masterly pieces of draughtsmanship as well as of colour. Not least among these are the figures thronging the roof of the temple, the flying *putti*, the kneeling Egyptian slaves, the harpist and the mother holding up her baby, all finely conceived —particularly the mother and child, for which Etty used some of his many drawings of children quickly sketched from life in previous years. As so often happens, a young artist's first grandly conceived work contains elements enough for three or four paintings no less ambitious but more maturely planned, and Etty never again makes the mistake of over-burdening his picture to the detriment of the main theme.

Cleopatra's Arrival does, however, demonstrate Etty's eclecticism, a feature common to all academic painters and indeed encouraged by their early training. It is no accident that Etty should look to Regnault for inspiration, because Regnault himself borrows freely from the Carracci, Poussin and Mengs, as well as from the sculpture of Greek and Roman antiquity. But there are other echoes, and in addition to the Venetian elements seen already in *The Coral Finder* may be noted a revived interest in Rubens; the figures of the Triton and sea-nymphs are similar to those in *The Landing of Marie de Médicis*, from Rubens's great cycle in the Louvre. Stothard's Burghley House decorations may also have been one of the earliest examples which prompted Etty to seek Rubens as a guide in his own work.

Etty's painting was hailed by the public in no uncertain manner, and Sir Thomas Lawrence jokingly remarked to his former pupil that they 'leave Mark Antony [*i.e.* Lawrence] whistling in the market-place, and go to gaze on your *Cleopatra*'.[2] C. R. Leslie wrote to his friend Washington Irving, then in Paris, '. . . Etty's *Cleopatra* is a splendid triumph of colour. It has some defects of composition, but is full of passages of that exquisite kind of beauty, which he alone can give . . .' The *Gentleman's Magazine*[3] noticed Etty for the first time, acknowledging his picture to be outstandingly the best of

[1] *Allégorie à la gloire de Napoléon* (now at Versailles): commissioned by the French Senate in 1804, and finished in 1805, this painting was in the Palais du Sénat, Paris, until 1812. C. Normand engraved this picture in 1809, and it is possible for Etty to have known the engraving even if he had not seen the original picture.

[2] Autobiography, *loc. cit.*, p. 37.

[3] *Autobiographical Recollections of C. R. Leslie*, ed. Tom Taylor, London, 1860, II, pp. 112–14. The letter is dated 'London, May 25, 1821'. *Gentleman's Magazine*, XCI, May 1821, p. 446.

its kind. Yet *The Times* contains no review of this year's Academy Exhibition and it is not until January 1822, when discussing the exhibition at the British Gallery (*i.e.* British Institution), that it allows itself to admonish Etty in the following terms: '. . . we take this opportunity of advising Mr. Etty, who got some reputation for painting *Cleopatra's Galley*, not to be seduced into a style which can gratify only the most vicious taste. Naked figures, when painted with the purity of Raphael, may be endured: but nakedness without purity is offensive and indecent, and in Mr. Etty's canvass is mere dirty flesh. Mr. Howard, whose poetical subjects sometimes require naked figures, never disgusts the eye or mind. Let Mr. Etty strive to acquire a taste equally pure: he should know, that just delicate taste and pure moral sense are synonymous terms.' [1] The 'canvass' referred to was a preliminary study for another painting destined to become famous, Etty's *Youth on the Prow and Pleasure at the Helm*. After making allowance for the pompous virulence of this review, it is obvious that Etty must have struck a new note to provoke such a reaction, as this is probably the earliest of many subsequent chidings for alleged impropriety—and not only from *The Times* reviewer. On the other hand, this rebuke should not be thought too surprising for its period, since even at the height of the raffishness which characterized the behaviour of the Prince Regent (now George IV) and the old Whig aristocracy, a new movement was gaining ground, that of the cult of respectability. In 1809 Miss Hannah More won fresh triumphs for her campaign against the lax morals and irreligion of the aristocracy with her book *Coelebs in Search of a Wife*, which quickly ran to several editions and had an unbelievably virtuous, pompous and almost sexless character for its hero. Bowdler's *Family Shakespeare* appeared in 1818, only to be outshone by the Rev. James Plumptre's heavily censored version of *Robinson Crusoe* ten years later. It was now also that the 'Clapham Sect' of Evangelical sabbatarians began to group itself around the Rev. John Venn, rector of Clapham.

What seems to have annoyed and even startled his critics is the literalness with which Etty recorded the female nude. His women are sensuous and full-blooded, and although they are often in classical poses, there is little attempt to idealize or to 'etherealize' the female form as Howard did or as G. F. Watts was later to do. The flesh of the women in the *Cleopatra* is of a warm pinky tone, quite unlike the colouring used by David or Regnault, or indeed, by Etty's contemporary, Ingres. Ingres's female nudes are often more subtle in their appeal, but Etty has more directness, a quality admired by Delacroix. Whether Sir Francis Freeling was alarmed by *The Times* attack is uncertain, but it seems that he later persuaded Etty to drape some of the figures in the foreground of the *Cleopatra*, although in 1829 he relented and allowed the artist to restore the figures to their original state. In addition to the *Cleopatra*, Sir Francis commissioned him to paint the *Cupid and Psyche Descending* exhibited at the British Institution, 1822, and in the same exhibition Etty showed the companion picture *Venus and Cupid Descending* [pl. 18].

Etty's emergence from obscurity was accompanied by an improvement in his domestic affairs. Always temperate by nature and habit, he demanded little enough of life's luxuries, but a letter to Walter shows that by about 1818 he had acquired an assistant, George Franklin, though he was still relying on his brother for gifts in money and in kind.[2] Of George Henry Franklin very little can be gleaned except from

[1] *The Times*, 29th January, 1822. 'Mr. Howard' is Henry Howard, R.A. (1769–1847), portraitist and history painter, and Secretary to the Academy.   [2] *See* Appendix I, *Letter 4*.

incidental remarks scattered through the Etty MSS.; but it is clear that Franklin assisted his master by preparing canvases, grinding colours and acting as Etty's general factotum, even to the extent of packing his trunks and reserving seats on the York coach. As an artist he was poorly equipped. He tried nearly every kind of subject, but with the exception of 'those from humble landscape and still-life' which 'showed fidelity and cleverness; the rest were generally vague and tame'.[1] On one occasion when he exhibited a painting at the Academy (*The Bather*, 1828) Anderdon wrote in his catalogue 'George Franklin, imitator of Etty'[2]—and an unsuccessful one as well. The writer in the *Literary Gazette* also sounded a warning note which should not go unheeded when one judges one of the many undistinguished 'Etty' studies which still appear from time to time: 'One or two Academy studies of Etty's there were [*i.e.* in Franklin's possession], but in the last degree insignificant, and even dubious.' Franklin died in poverty, after serving Etty devotedly for nearly thirty years—a circumstance which might have been avoided but for the estrangement which took place between the two men towards the end of Etty's life, and which resulted in Franklin being ignored in Etty's will. The cause of this quarrel is probably now beyond hope of discovery.

Despite the first flush of triumph, Etty continued upon a strict course of study, and Fuseli, in his report to the Academy Council for 1821, took the opportunity of mentioning this exemplary conduct. Speaking of the Life School, he notes a general improvement, and justifies the practice of painting from the Life by artificial light, because it allowed the students to grasp more clearly the physical structure of the human form, as well as to capture those 'golden lights' that were enhanced under these conditions. Continuing, he said: 'I should think myself guilty of neglect, were I not, among those who pursue this method, to mention Mr. Etty; whose unwearied perseverance of application, and steady method, well deserve to serve as an example to his fellow-students.'[3] From the beginning, a friendly relationship had established itself between the two men, and Etty tells in his Autobiography how Fuseli had first encouraged him: 'When one night in the "Life", Fuseli was visitor, I threw aside the chalk and took up my pallet, set with oil-colour, and began to paint the figure. "Ah, there", says Fuseli, "you seem to be at home"; and so I truly felt.' Indeed, Etty's reputation was made above all as a colourist, but his notebooks for 1814–16 contain warnings such as 'Let your principal attention be to the *Form*: for without *that*, the best Colouring is but a chaos'. And again, '*Drawing* is the soul of art', a familiar aphorism in the academies of Europe and not peculiar to Ingres alone.[4] At this time, Etty was still groping his way,

---

[1] *Literary Gazette*, No. 83, IV, Saturday, 28th January, 1860, pp. 122–3, contains an obituary notice, *The Late George Franklin and Etty*, from which these remarks have been drawn. The article was brought to the author's notice by a reference in the *Whitley Papers* (British Museum). Franklin's picture collection was sold at Christie's, 2nd January, 1860: among it were some Etty's as well as his own work.

[2] Anderdon's annotated *Catalogues of the Royal Academy Exhibitions*, LX, 1828 (British Museum). Ir. Thomas H. Etty also possesses a small painting by Franklin. Between 1828–47 he exhibited eight pictures at the British Institution, and nine paintings at the Academy, 1825–45.

[3] Gilchrist, *op. cit.*, I, p. 96. It has not been possible to find a record of this report in the *Royal Academy Council Minutes*, but Gilchrist saw the original MS., which had been presented to Etty by Fuseli's executors, among Etty's own papers.

[4] N. Pevsner, *Academies of Art Past and Present*, Cambridge, 1940, p. 151, quotes, for example, from S. L. Dury's speech at the opening of the Cassel Academy in 1777: 'Drawing is the soul of painting.'

and he reminds himself 'to paint with one colour at a time, in Flesh, or at most with two:—'twill give a cleanness and clearness of tint. And let each layer of Colour be seen through. Or, in other words, manage it so, by *scumbling*, that the tints underneath appear. It will give depth, and a fleshiness of effect, impossible to get by *solid* colour.' When drawing from the Life, 'avoid that slovenly and unartist-like method, of scrawling over your paper or canvas with a variety of confused and unmeaning lines'. The general character of the figure is to be seized and recorded with the greatest economy and truth of line. Then the pencil outline is to be gone over and strengthened with a dark oil colour, usually Vandyck brown but sometimes yellow ochre mixed with crimson lake. This is usually enough for one sitting.

Next, comes the actual painting: the palette is set with black and white and a little Indian red. 'Mix up your tints,' he writes, 'a little black and red for the shadows, keeping them in the first colour warmer than you see them, for scumbling over. The next tint is an union of the three colours, making a sort of iron-grey; which must melt tenderly, at the edges only, into the adjoining tints. The next in gradation is black and white; the next, lighter still, until you come to the local colour (a little red and white), and next that, the high light, which, *he says* [perhaps Fuseli is the authority quoted], you may paint an inch thick if you like. The next thing is, to *lay them in*, beginning with the shadows: which put in square and decided, yet tenderly melting at the edge.' Half-tints must be kept smooth, whilst the highlights may be impasted. Form must never be lost under a welter of meaningless colour, and the work should be done by careful, deliberate stages, always keeping to a strict pattern. This is the academic method *par excellence*, and the *Male Nude with a Staff* [pl. 5*b*], already mentioned, a typical result. But this is still rather stiffly painted, and may date from soon after Etty's discovery of the technique of glazing, a discovery made, according to Gilchrist, early in 1816. Experimenting with various media, Etty notes that 'Copal-varnish, passed over a milled-board figure, etc., makes pleasant ground, when oiled out', and 'Saccharum, turpentine, and raw oil, make a pleasant vehicle when your picture is rubbed over with it'.[1] Then comes the vital point: 'It has hitherto been my practice to paint over, and consequently lose, those subtile and beautiful demi-tints and half tones, (which give so much lustre, beauty, and fleshiness to Colour), that result from one coat of colour, Indian red and white, or any other flesh tint, painted over the milled-board: and which, once lost, cannot be regained.' This realized, he resolves in future to modify his system so that during the first and second sittings he outlines and paints in the figure as previously, but then for the third and final stage he brushes over the whole a thin layer of copal varnish 'to secure' the body colours of black, white and red. When the varnish has dried, 'glaze, and then scumble on the bloom; glaze in the shadows, and touch on the lights carefully, And it is done'.

This was the foundation of Etty's method, but it was to undergo several changes

[1] The Etty notebooks from which Gilchrist quotes (*op. cit.*, I, pp. 53–8) are missing, and the accuracy of Gilchrist's dating cannot be verified from a study of the original MSS.

'*Saccharum*' is an archaic (and inaccurate) description of the siccative, sugar of lead (lead acetate), much favoured by Etty and, incidentally, by Reynolds. The word occurs in Reynolds's own memoranda, some of which may be found in B. R. Haydon's *Autobiography and Memoirs*, II, Appendix III, pp. 857–8, under the heading *Serres Varnish*.

during his lifetime as he became increasingly skilled and more knowledgeable. Sir Charles Eastlake, discussing the Flemish and Venetian use of colour, perceived that 'the English painters cannot be said to be exclusively wedded to one or other; but undoubtedly Sir Joshua Reynolds, with all his enthusiastic admiration for Rubens, preferred in his own practice, the Venetian method. It appears that, even in the latter part of his life, Sir Joshua was in the habit of lending, for beginners to copy, a head painted only in white, black and red: the shadows being of course lighter than they were ultimately to be, in order that the final glazings might be duly transparent . . . Many of you may remember that Mr. Etty in his Academy Studies (which, assuredly, were not deficient in final richness and force) began in the same manner.'[1] Often, however, Etty did adopt a Flemish technique, particularly in the latter half of his career. Moreover, he was a much sounder craftsman than Reynolds, shunning the curious formulae with which Reynolds experimented in his own pictures. Etty, perhaps warned by Reynolds's example, can only occasionally be detected using bitumen, to name but one snare. But although he seems to have been slow in grasping the advantages of his medium, and although it mortified him to realize that he had been painting for nearly eight years before discovering the magic of glazing in half-tints, this discovery should be related to a more general historical process. In the work of Wilkie and Mulready, as well as of Bonington, one may detect an increasing interest in this technique during the early 1820s and subsequently.

Thus, at the age of thirty-five, Etty was on the threshold of a distinguished career. Technically competent, his confidence strengthened by a degree of recognition and success, besides some regular patronage, Etty was perhaps in the best frame of mind to benefit from a prolonged stay abroad. Although full of ideas for future pictures, he needed an opportunity to widen and deepen his knowledge of those Italian and French masters whose work seemed most in accord with his own ideals. Instead of the hurried glimpses of previous occasions, he was to enjoy a long enough stay to be able to absorb and reflect upon his impressions, testing his reactions to a particular stimulus not once, but many times. Only thus could he fully realize his own powers and give coherent expression to his personal artistic convictions and conceptions.

[1] Sir Charles Eastlake, P.R.A., *Sixth Discourse to the Royal Academy*, London, 10th December, 1863, p. 18.

CHAPTER FOUR

THE GRAND TOUR: 1821-1823

'AT last I am in Rome. We arrived here this day week, Saturday, in the evening. We were told it was as much as our lives were worth to enter Rome at this hot season, but I had vowed in my heart ere I left my country that I would reach Rome should it cost me my life.' [1] Thus, it was a rather more determined Etty who set off upon this second Italian tour—a tour which was to prove far more successful and rewarding than its predecessor; so much so that Etty always looked back upon this part of his life with great pleasure and a certain nostalgia. This time he went with his friend Richard Evans, a fellow student under Lawrence; and Evans, better acquainted with Italy, was invaluable as a guide, a fact Etty gratefully acknowledges when writing home to Walter and Sir Thomas Lawrence. Almost all the letters that he sent to these two men, and to Thomas Bodley, survive, providing a detailed record of his wanderings and of his friends. They are long and rambling and it is impossible to quote them at length: Gilchrist, who valued them as much for their revelation of the writer's personality as for their documentary importance, did not hesitate to edit and prune wherever necessary.

The two artists left London on 23rd June, 1822, and, crossing the Channel by the new steam-packet service, arrived three days later in Paris, where they stayed over a fortnight. Besides revisiting Derveaux, the colourman, they made the usual round of public galleries and an excursion to Versailles. Also the biennial exhibition of modern French painting was then on at the Louvre. Etty's attention was naturally drawn to the large history pieces there, although his admiration for these was countered by contempt for the portraiture. Writing to Lawrence, he said: 'In the Luxembourg, which you have seen, I think Guérin, Regnault, etc. the best. Amongst the old masters in the Louvre Rubens's Luxembourg pictures look, I think, more splendid than ever; and with all its losses [*i.e.* of Napoleon's loot, now returned to former owners], the Louvre is yet a fine and splendid national gallery. I wish we had anything like it in England.' [2] That Rubens's *Marie de Médicis* series should have appeared yet more splendid is proof enough of Etty's tacit admiration for Rubens in 1816, while it is

---

[1] Letter to Walter Etty, 'Rome, Saturday August 18, 1822' (York City Reference Library).
[2] *See* Appendix I, *Letter 5*, dated Rome, 12th October, 1822, *Royal Academy Collection of Autograph Letters*, IV, p. 18. *Also* Gilchrist, *op. cit.*, I, p. 105, Letter to Walter Etty, 28th June, 1822.

D   35

interesting that he now adds the name of Guérin to the list of contemporary French painters whose work most attracted him. Nearly six years previously Delacroix had entered Guérin's studio, and he too was beginning to hold Rubens in high regard. His *Dante and Virgil*, exhibited in 1822, aroused fierce criticism because of its Rubensian treatment, and it is surprising that Etty should not have noticed the work of his French contemporary and remarked upon it.

After a pause at Dijon, only long enough to see the picture gallery there, the two men went into Italy over the Simplon (as in 1816) and arrived at Milan six days after leaving Geneva. The two days' stay in Milan was used to visit the Brera Gallery and to view Leonardo's *Last Supper*; then on to Piacenza and to Parma, where they were delighted by the Correggio frescoes in the cathedral. At Bologna, Guido Reni's *Pietà*, and the Carracci paintings in the museum were particularly noticed. The journey from Milan to Florence took nearly sixteen days, travelling by cabriolet; dust and fierce heat were the worst enemies in what was said to be an abnormally hot summer. The two students, Joseph Bonomi (the younger) and Elton, whom Etty had met in Paris, wisely postponed their journey south. Despite these discomforts (shared this time), Etty seems to have been far more alive to his surroundings than before, being able to appreciate those landmarks and paintings made familiar to him, by name at least, during his Academy training. Florence was a little cooler, and in just over two days Etty had visited the Uffizi, sketched in the Accademia del Disegno and savoured the delights of the Pitti Palace. It was here that he admired Titian's portrait of *La Bella*, as well as Rubens's *Horrors of War*, and the *Ulysses and Nausicaa*; for although he had 'paid his respects' at Michelangelo's tomb, yet, significantly, it was the Venetians and the Flemings who most deeply stirred him. Finally, on 10th August, climbing the brow of a hill they found on the other side Rome itself spread before them, bathed in the golden light of a summer evening.

Etty's expectations of what Rome would look like had been tempered by the descriptions of previous visitors, and it is noticeable that he never expresses quite the same affection for Rome as he does for Venice, which undoubtedly held him more completely under its spell. The day after their arrival was Sunday, and in the company of two English officers who travelled with them from Florence, Evans and Etty visited St. Peter's. The magnificence of the basilica and its setting suitably impressed them, although Etty disliked the façade designed by Carlo Maderna, and felt that in its west front, at least, St. Paul's, London, was superior. Eastlake, by nature an intellectual, had also disapproved of the façade, but he had analysed its defects with scholarly precision, and he expressed his views with a lucidity which was denied to Etty.[1] On the Monday, they saw the *Stanze* frescoes, and quickly followed this visit to the Vatican by another to the Sistine Chapel. Writing to Lawrence, Etty dilates upon the splendours of the Sistine ceiling, which far exceeded his greatest hopes, and he speaks of Michelangelo's 'beautiful and almost Venetian color'. To Walter he makes no secret of the fact that for him Michelangelo ranks above Raphael, although 'both are Kings, and must rule alternately'.[2] He also tells his brother that he has met Canova through a letter of introduction from Lawrence. Only a few weeks later Canova was dead.

[1] Sir Charles Eastlake, *Contributions to the Literature of the Fine Arts* (Second Series), London, 1870, p. 62.
[2] Letter to Walter Etty, 'Rome, Saturday August 18, 1822' (York City Reference Library).

Among other gossip to Lawrence he notes that Domenichino was then much admired in Rome, an admiration understood but not fully shared by Etty, who preferred Guercino's *Sta. Petronilla* in the Capitoline, considering the latter to have those restrained golden tones and that depth of colour most suitable for history pictures. In fact, this picture recalled for him not only the work of the Carracci, but also Sir Joshua Reynolds's *Death of Dido*.[1]

When he had been in Rome only a fortnight, Etty decided to go out to Naples. He went alone, as neither Evans nor Joseph Gott, the sculptor, another friend, found it opportune to leave Rome, despite the prevalence of malaria, a risk they were prepared to accept. At Naples he was entertained by Henry Vint, who allowed the artist to stay for nearly a month at his villa on the Piazza Falconi. Vint was now forty-four and had married Martha Elizabeth, the daughter of William Redmore Bigg, R.A. Whilst in Italy he collected some antiquities, although statements that he was an ardent collector are apparently untrue. He was elected a Fellow of the Society of Antiquaries, and was Mayor of Colchester from 1841 to 1844. Etty's time was well spent sketching the remains of Herculaneum and Pompeii preserved in the museum and the *Tauro Farnese*, besides studying Correggio's *Marriage of St. Catherine* and Titian's *Danaë*. From where he was staying he could enjoy a magnificent view of the Bay of Baiae nearby, and of Vesuvius. One of his most vivid memories was a night ascent of the volcano made in the company of a guide and a sailor; how Etty revelled in the awe and splendour of the situation may be gathered from the account he wrote to Walter soon after. But his emotions were tinged with melancholy, for once again Etty was hopelessly in love: this time his affections had been stirred by a young cousin, Mary, whose portrait he had painted a few days before leaving for Italy. It might be easy to depict him as the lonely hero of the romantic novel, except that there is never any element of tragedy, only, it must sometimes be confessed, of bathos. It is also possible to recapture some idea of the young artist as he then appeared to others, for he shared a coach from Naples to Rome with Robert Comyn and William Macready, the actor. Macready described him as 'a short thin young man with very light hair, his face marked with the small-pox, very gentle in his manner, with a shrill and feeble tone of voice, whom we found a very accommodating and agreeable travelling companion, and whom through all his after-life I found a very warm friend'.[2] Once back in Rome he explored the city more thoroughly, and went out to Frascati and Tivoli. But he also began to make copies after various old masters, a practice he continued throughout his stay abroad. Among the paintings copied may be listed Titian's *Sacred and Profane Love* and *The Education of Cupid*, and Van Dyck's *Crucifixion*, all in the Borghese Palace; Veronese's *St. John the Baptist Preaching* and his *Rape of Europa*.[3] The choice is interesting, and fully reflects Etty's predilection for the Venetian school. At the same time, however, he made many pencil sketches from Michelangelo's Sistine Chapel ceiling frescoes and *Last Judgment*,

[1] According to Gilchrist, *op. cit.*, I, p. 133, Etty had made several copies of Reynolds's *Death of Dido*. None have yet been traced.

[2] *Macready's Reminiscences, and selections from His Diaries and Letters*, ed. Sir Frederick Pollock, Bart., London, 1875, I, xvi, p. 266. Robert Comyn was later knighted; an Indian judge, he acted as Chief Justice of Madras from 1835–42.

[3] *See* Appendix II for a list of paintings which appears to record all those pictures which he intended copying. The Borghese *Crucifixion* is only attributed to Van Dyck (*see also* Catalogue No. 6).

and these included details from the *Deluge* and studies of the *Ignudi* and *putti*—the latter certainly providing Etty with suggestions for the poses of many of his own 'cupids'.

Still unhappy, he had thought of returning home and had set off for Venice, arriving there on 17th November; but once his uncertainties had been resolved, the wiser counsel of his brother prevailed and he remained in Venice for more than seven months instead of the ten days he had originally intended. Not that he had lacked company in Rome, for a small band of English artists worked there, including Joseph Severn, Seymour Kirkup, Charles Eastlake, John Gibson and Gott, besides Evans; there were also, of course, a number of English residents not only in Rome, but in Florence and Venice. He travelled alone to Venice, going through Perugia and Arezzo, pausing for wo days at Florence, and then on over the Apennines in bitterly cold weather to Bologna. At the next city, Ferrara, Etty 'saw and kissed with poetic veneration the old arm-chair in which Ariosto sat and wrote his *Orlando Furioso*'.[1] He shuddered in the dungeon where once Tasso had been held captive, and recalled how, five years before, Byron, after having visited it, had been inspired to write his *Lament of Tasso*. The artist's homage to the poets now paid, he went on to Padua and Fusina, until Venice was reached at last. Here he was to find his second home: as he wrote at the end of his life 'dear Venice—Venezia, cara Venezia! thy pictured glories haunt my fancy now! Venice, the birthplace and cradle of colour, the hope and idol of my professional life ... I felt *at home most in Venice*, though I knew not a soul. I had good letters however ... Mr. Eastlake kindly gave me a letter to Harry D'Orville, our Vice-Consul, Hoppner our Consul were both friends to me.'[2] So indeed they were, for D'Orville arranged that Etty should stay in his own house, and enjoy specifically English comforts instead of the rigours of Antonio Bertuzzi's lodgings near the Accademia.

'Rome', wrote Etty to his brother, 'is the place for a sculptor I think—Venice for a painter to see the power of color and Chiaroscuro';[3] and to Lawrence he confided that he found it 'not a little strange' that Venice, containing so many works by painters greatly admired in England, should be so neglected by British travelling students. The more so, he thought, since the technique of oil painting was brought to such perfection there, and thus from that point of view must be of greater help to the vast majority of artists who used that medium rather than fresco. This opinion, he afterwards found, was shared enthusiastically by Lawrence himself, and Etty urged some of his own fellow students to visit Venice, lending such weight as he could to the President's advice.[4] Of modern foreign painting, he considered the French school as leading the rest of the Continent, and he was unimpressed by the then famous Vincenzo Camuccini. Canova, of course, he did like, and he remarked that the Venetians were particularly pleased by Lawrence's generous donation towards the monument of their fellow citizen. In fact, Lawrence was esteemed throughout Europe at the time, and Etty was proud to be able to claim him as his former master. The arrival of Lawrence's portrait of *George IV* at the Vatican had provoked great admiration and attention; so much

[1] Letter to Walter Etty, Venice, 6th December, 1822 (York City Reference Library).

[2] Autobiography, *The Art Journal*, XI, London, 1849.

[3] Letter to Walter Etty, 'Rome, Saturday August 18, 1822' (York City Reference Library).

[4] *See* Appendix I, *Letter 6*, to Sir Thomas Lawrence, dated 'Venice, March 26, 1823', *Royal Academy Collection of Autograph Letters*, IV, p. 4.

so, that the great number of applicants wishing to copy from it, and obtain the 'new manner', had caused special regulations to be enforced limiting its use for that purpose. As in Rome—and to a greater extent—Etty spent much of his time in Venice copying from the old masters, particularly Titian, Veronese, Tintoretto and Paris Bordone, as well as Carpaccio and Bonifazio.[1] Those pictures of which he possessed 'memorials' (as he called his copies) included Titian's *Assunta* (then in the Accademia, now returned to the Frari Church), Tintoretto's *Last Judgment* (Accademia), Bordone's *Fishermen presenting the Ring to the Doge* and Veronese's *Clemency of Darius*. He also expressed the greatest admiration for Titian's *St. Peter Martyr* altarpiece, in S. Giovanni e Paolo—a picture which he could have seen at the Louvre in 1815. (Forty-four years later it was destroyed by fire.) This by no means exhausts the list, and Etty divided his time between working from pictures in the Accademia during the mornings, and painting from the Life in the evenings. He also got to know very thoroughly Tintoretto's Scuola di San Rocco paintings, and a typical example of what Gilchrist described as 'a mere Artist's-*abstract* of colour, Composition, etc.', survives at York Art Gallery. It is a tiny study of Tintoretto's *Ecce Homo*, in the Sala dell'Albergo, and is a brief yet vivid notation of the main features and colours of the picture.

The idea of making these 'memorials' was not new, and of course it was (and for that matter still is) an artist's only way of obtaining a permanent and reasonably accurate record of the colours used in a particular painting, however good an engraving of it might exist. Although Reynolds, in his *Second Discourse*, condemned detailed repetitive copying as of no lasting value to the student, he did not exclude the practice altogether, but suggested that 'those choice parts only be selected which have recommended the work to notice. If its excellence consists in its general effect, it would be proper to make slight sketches of the machinery and general management of the picture.' Such sketches were to be kept by the student as a continual guide for his own style. Etty rightly considered it well worth while spending time gathering together a collection of these studies, and was quite prepared to forgo sending any original work to either the British Institution or Royal Academy exhibitions of 1823. In reply to his brother's enquiries on this point, he wrote: 'You say it would be easy to send something for the Exhibition. Perhaps it would, easier than paint it: situate as I have been, engaged, not only in seeing the immensity of things to be seen in Art, but in making memorials of a few of the best. If one spent all the time in painting originals, one might as well, nay better, be at home. Eastlake has been seven or eight years abroad. I do not know whether he would not better have been at home; incline to think he would, the greater part of the time. And others think so too.'[2] Eastlake had wanted to join Etty in Venice, but was far too busy with commissions which would keep him occupied for over a year, and which he could best accomplish at Rome. A slight note of regret appears in Etty's letter when he mentions that before leaving England, Eastlake had painted 'a very clever Historic picture', but that now he had turned to landscapes, 'figures of Costume, Banditti etc.', but which were admittedly well painted, with a good feeling for colour, and in popular demand. Apparently Etty, in common with some others, had not yet fully grasped the particular bent of Eastlake's talent, although four years later Etty,

[1] *See* Appendix II.
[2] Gilchrist, *op. cit.*, I, pp. 163–4; letter to Walter Etty, 30th January, 1823.

at least, was to acknowledge the scholarly qualities of this future P.R.A. Lawrence probably realized Eastlake's abilities early on, and relied upon him as a kind of unofficial agent in Rome. Eastlake's letters to Lawrence of this period are in strong contrast to those of Etty. The main topic was the formation of a British Artists' Academy in Rome, and Eastlake's gifts for administration were already apparent. Yet other subjects, equally significant, occur: in a letter of 15th August 1822, Eastlake mentions the recently published (1817) *Life of Titian* by Ticozzi; he has also been discussing the Venetian painting technique with Pietro Palmaroli, a picture-cleaner and chemist well-known to Lawrence, and he encloses Palmaroli's formula for a new kind of vehicle using Cyprus balsam instead of oil for glazing.[1] Clearly, Eastlake was concerned with more than picturesque banditti.

The opulence of the Venice Academy and the many facilities it offered to a student greatly impressed Etty, and he described to several friends its two rooms of Antique casts, the picture gallery, its Schools of Perspective, of Design and of Engraving, besides the inevitable *Scuola del Nudo*. In the Life School he made a great reputation for himself with his brilliant oil studies. The Italian *professori* were extravagant in their praise: Mattini (or Martini) was delighted with Etty's succulent flesh painting; San Dominichi thought him 'un genio proprio'; and others nicknamed him 'Il Diavolo' because of the speed with which he painted. Famous people were brought to see this 'English Tintoretto', including the Patriarch of Venice, and Rossini, who was then in Venice to supervise the production of his opera *Semiramide* at the Teatro della Fenice.[2] As a final mark of esteem the Venetians elected Etty an Honorary Academician. This honour was shared, most appropriately, by his master Sir Thomas Lawrence, and Etty had the pleasant task of bringing Lawrence's diploma back with him to England and delivering it in person. The difference in value of this distinction to both men was neatly phrased by Etty, who wrote to Lawrence that 'by electing you, they honored their own body: by electing me, they honored only myself'.[3]

By 7th June Etty was contemplating a move from Venice, and he tells his brother of the fruits of his labours, 'Thirty studies in oil after the Venetian School, and Twenty in oil of Academic figures'.[2] These included thirteen 'reduced copies' from Veronese, nine from Tintoretto, three from Titian and two from Bonifazio. Leaving this precious harvest in the care of a Venetian family, he went south to Florence, with the particular intention of copying Titian's *Venus of Urbino* in the Uffizi. His route lay through Vicenza, where he stopped to see Veronese's *La Cena di San Gregorio Magno* at the Sanctuario di Monte Berico; then on to Verona, spending a few hours looking at the Roman arena, 'Juliet's tomb', and Veronese's *Martyrdom of St. George* (S. Giorgio in Braida). At Mantua, remembering some advice of Lawrence, he stayed a day to study

---

[1] Letter to Lawrence, dated 'Rome, Aug. 15, 1822', *Royal Academy Collection of Autograph Letters*, IV, p. 14. The series of letters, 1822–8, are most important for the evidence they provide of Eastlake's growing interest in the history of art; so also is Lady Eastlake's *Memoir* attached to the second series of Eastlake's *Contributions to the Literature of the Fine Arts*, London, 1870.

[2] Gilchrist, *op. cit.*, I, pp. 162–3; letters to Walter Etty, 13th and 30th January, 1823; letter to Thomas Bodley, August-September 15th, 1823 (York City Reference Library). Stendhal, *Vie de Rossini*, Paris, 1864, pp. 297, 321.

[3] *See* Appendix I, *Letter 7*, to Sir Thomas Lawrence, dated 'Paris, Nov. 14, 1823', *Royal Academy Collection of Autograph Letters*, IV, p. 52.

Giulio Romano's frescoes in the Palazzo del Tè, and the Castello. For entertainment of another kind, he attended a play in the modern amphitheatre built by the French in honour of Virgil. In many of his letters home, Etty slips in odd scraps of information he has gleaned about a town and its associations, for although he could not pretend to any formal learning, he was by now quite widely read and had built up a good general knowledge, mainly by his own efforts and greatly to his credit.

Evans was awaiting Etty in Florence, and the two stayed together for almost all the rest of the tour. To copy Titian's *Venus of the Tribune* (as it was then called) was not an easy matter, as the deputy director of the Uffizi, Baron Montalvi, at first opposed Etty's intention of copying it full-size. Armed with letters to both English and Italian officials in Florence, Etty achieved his purpose after ten days' delay, and began to paint what is perhaps one of his finest copies, and certainly the only one he executed the size of the original. Much pleased with his work, he gave instructions for it and another copy from a Titian in Rome (probably the *Sacred and Profane Love*) to be insured for £100 upon their arrival in England.[1] Wilkie, writing to Collins two years after his Florence visit of 1825, recalled his impressions of Titian's Uffizi *Venus* in these words: 'With us, as you know, every young Exhibitor with pink, white, and blue, thinks himself a Titian; than whom perhaps no painter is more misrepresented and misunderstood. I saw myself at Florence his famous Venus, upon an easel, with Kirkup and Wallis by me. This picture, so often copied, and every copy a fresh mistake, is what I expected it to be; deep, yet brilliant, indescribable in its hues, yet simple beyond example in its execution and its colouring. Its flesh (oh, how our friends at home would stare!) was a simple, sober, mixed-up tint, and apparently, like your skies, completed while wet. No scratchings, no hatchings, no scumblings, no multiplicity of repetitions, —no ultramarine, lakes, nor vermillions, and not even a mark of the brush visible; all seemed melted into the fat and glowing mass, solid yet transparent, giving the nearest approach to life that the painter's art has yet reached. This picture is perhaps defective in its arrangement, but in its painting quite admirable. Now, can nothing like this ever be done again? Is such toning really not to be reproduced? I wish to believe the *talent* exists, and am sure the *material* exists. But we have now got another system, our criterion of judging is changed: we prefer a something else, or, what is still more blinding, there is a something else that we mistake for it.'[2] Evans had urged Etty to copy this picture, 'never copied as it ought to be', and if Wilkie's remarks do nothing else, they at least show quite clearly that Etty's mastery of the Venetian technique was all the more outstanding at that time, since his copy must be considered among the most competent. It is tantalizing that no comment by Wilkie on Etty's copy seems to have survived, yet he surely knew of it.

At the end of July, Etty bade farewell to Florence for the last time and with Evans turned northwards. Two more months were spent in Venice: more copies were made, still more sightseeing undertaken—a valedictory tour, in fact, of his beloved city. A

[1] Letter to Walter Etty, dated 'Florence, Via Maggia, No. 1922, July 28, 1823' (York City Reference Library).

[2] Wilkie Collins, *A Memoir of William Collins, R.A.*, 2 vols., London, 1848, I, pp. 289–90; letter from Wilkie to Collins, dated 'Geneva, 26th Aug. 1827'. Wilkie was in Italy during the latter part of 1825, and remained abroad until 1828.

passport dated 8th October, 1823, is counterstamped for Verona, Paris and England,[1] and the next day they left Venice just as the autumn rains were beginning. From Verona, a two-day excursion was made to Mantua, such were its attractions for Etty, and so struck had he been before by Giulio Romano's frescoes in the Palazzo del Tè. Several pencil sketches were made, and some hint of Etty's conception of classicism is provided by his descriptions of the *Camera di Psyche*: '. . . how novel, how classical, how every way extraordinary, it is quite a treat to find a series of Pictures that treats classical subjects in so learned, so antique a style—after being deluged with nothing but Saints, Martyrs and Virgin Maries [*sic*] by thousands, the imagination revels with delight in his poetic landscapes, his giants intimidate, and his females, tho voluptuous in the extreme, have an air of greatness truly Roman; what foreshortening and effects in the ceiling! with what breathless caution his Acis and Galatea eye the sleeping Polypheme! . . . There are some in another of the rooms over the door, of the Lapithae and Centaurs rushing out and engaged in battle; without exception the most beautiful knots of composition I ever saw. If Michel Ange and Raffaelle are before him—'tis only they. He and Poussin seem to me the only men who have painted antiquity. With great reluctance I left these charming works; the subjects are so congenial to me, so every way satisfactory in what he attempts.'[2] However, he had hopes of getting a set of engravings of the *Camera di Psyche*, then in preparation, as soon as they were published. Eastlake's opinion of Giulio Romano counterbalances Etty's lyricism, for the former considered most of his Mantuan work as being 'decidedly bad'. This is exactly the reaction one would expect from the severe academic mind nurtured on an entirely different conception of classical art and literature.

Throughout Etty's Italian sketchbooks are scattered many landscape studies made while travelling between towns [pls. 14*a*, 14*b*]. They have no pretension to great artistic merit, but are noteworthy as evidence of Etty's continuing interest in this genre. Often they are little more than hastily scribbled outlines of the elements of the scene before him, and are usually drawn in soft lead pencil: one may be of a road winding between hills, with squat-roofed farm buildings half-hidden among the trees; another is of a church; yet another a panorama of Florence; and, a few pages further on, there is one of Siena. There are also more careful topographical studies of Venetian landmarks such as the Bridge of Sighs and the Rialto; on another page there is a small sketch of a gondola. In one sketchbook alone, it is possible to find drawings of this type mingled with studies of antique sculpture, of Michelangelo's figures of *Night*, *Day* etc. on the Medici Tombs, and a detailed outline study of, for example, the figure of Abraham from Titian's *Abraham Sacrificing Isaac*. Occasionally, one even comes across diary entries and rough drafts of letters: so it is not surprising that the loss of a sketchbook, even if temporary, should cause Etty so much distress.[3]

The journey was continued, and in Switzerland Etty had hoped to see once more

---

[1] Passport in the City Art Gallery, York. Also a letter to Walter, dated 'Mantua, Monday Night Oct. 13, 1823' in Anderdon's *Collectanea Biographica*, XXXIII, 1853, ff. 33–91 (British Museum).

[2] *See* Appendix I, *Letter 7*.

[3] *Sketchbooks I and II*, and '*Cash Book*', City Art Gallery, York, are the relevant sources. On his way from Bologna to Florence, Etty had lost an Italian grammar book containing on its blank pages studies made in Rome from Michelangelo and Raphael. After much fuss and anxiety it had been retrieved.

his friend D'Orville, who was now staying at Vevey to convalesce after chronic ill-health. But D'Orville had left the day before; so on again to Geneva, and thence, after four days' and three nights' travelling, to Paris, where Etty and Evans arrived on 31st October. The horrors and discomforts of coach transport are again described by Etty in meticulous and bitter detail to Walter. Nevertheless, at one stage he and Evans had seriously considered coming home from Verona over the Tyrol, visiting Munich and its gallery, then going by boat down the Rhine to Antwerp. But they had left Italy too late in the year, and winter was upon them to discourage the idea, lack of money apart.[1] Seventeen years were to go by before Etty was able to carry out this plan of a journey to the Netherlands.

In Paris they overtook D'Orville, besides meeting several other Englishmen, mostly artists; but Etty was also introduced to the English Chaplain of Paris, Dr. Luscombe, who afterwards became a staunch friend. At first Etty intended to cross to England at the beginning of December, but, as in Venice, he dallied making copies and collecting prints. His stock of the latter was substantially increased by the purchase of several albums—*Ancient Designs of Costumes, The Luxembourg Gallery, Heathen Mythology*, etc.—to which were added fresh supplies of colours and, two most important items, a lay-figure and brushes. For the brushes, he again visits Derveaux, whom he described as living 'up three pairs of stairs in one of the dirtiest holes in Paris with two or three dogs, and some birds, and last not least, his son and wife who materially aid and assist him'. Fully aware of his supremacy as a brush manufacturer, the old man required coaxing, but Etty was fortunate to obtain fourteen dozen of his best grade, plus two or three dozen more of lesser quality—a lifetime's supply, as he told his brother. To Monsieur and Madame Huot he went for his lay-figure, they being equally renowned for their product, and among the customers on the waiting-list was John Jackson, R.A. the portrait-painter.[2]

At that time the Louvre remained open only four days a week, but undaunted by this restriction or the cold weather, Etty began a small copy of Veronese's *Marriage at Cana* and Poussin's *Le Déluge: L'Hiver*, exacting tasks which kept him busy most of November and the early part of December. On Christmas Day, he dashed off a short note to Walter telling him that he had delayed his homecoming so as to be able to make a 'memorial' of a 'glorious Water-nymph of Rubens' he had long admired.[3] This was almost certainly one of the figures from the *Landing of Marie de Médicis at Marseilles*. During March and April of the following year, Delacroix also studied Rubens's *Médicis* paintings and he too made a copy of *Les Sirènes* (Etty's 'water-nymph[s]'). In the *Journal* for these months, his visits to the Louvre and elsewhere are recorded, and one typical entry is the following: '*Vendredi 19 mars.*—Passé une excellente journée au Musée avec Édouard [Guillemardet]. Les Poussins! Les Rubens! et surtout *le François Ier* du Titien! Velasquez.' Later that month he is again studying Poussin, and with the

[1] Letters to Walter Etty, dated 'Hotel de Dusseldorf, Rue des Petites Augustines, Quai Voltaire, Paris, Sunday, Nov. 9, 1823' and 'Saturday, 15th Nov., 1823' (York City Reference Library).

[2] Letter to Walter Etty, dated 'Hotel de Dusseldorf . . . Paris, Sunday Night, Dec. 7' (York City Reference Library).

[3] Letter to Walter Etty, dated 'Paris, Christmas Day, 1823' (York City Reference Library). This copy was exhibited at the Seventh Old Masters Exhibition, Burlington House, 1876, No. 235; canvas, 51 × 37 in., lent Sidney N. Castle.

aid of a stool he examined a Veronese, probably the enormous *Marriage at Cana*.[1] It is remarkable how closely the two artists are linked by their mutual interest in the same old masters; for a short time the careers of the English and French younger generation of painters run parallel, the French even deriving inspiration from their English brethren. Etty gives some glimpse of this situation when he writes to Lawrence: 'In France too, they seem beginning to think *we can paint a LITTLE*! numerous English engravings are everywhere met with in Paris—our Vignettes by Stothard, Smirke, Westall, etc., are not only admired, but imitated. Wilkie is much in request—and much admired—but it is yet lamentable to see the narrow nationality of their school—Titian, Coreggio, Paolo, Rubens, throw down their pearls before them in vain—the beans and husks of their [own] school are preferred far before them—*The Entry of Henri Quatre into Paris* by Gérard, is multiplied a thousandfold . . . while its noble and magnificent pendant Paolo Veronese, has not a single devotee except me.'[2]

It would be entirely false to suggest that Etty stimulated Delacroix's interest for Titian and Rubens, since both men discovered the qualities of these masters independently of each other, and put their knowledge to use in different ways. Yet it can be shown that Delacroix's convictions were strengthened by what he saw of the work of his English contemporaries both in 1824 and, more important, in 1825.

Before leaving Paris, Etty had been asked by Lawrence to provide him with some notes on the Michelangelo and Raphael drawings in the Louvre. He had previously excused himself from another commission—to do a copy of Titian's *Christ Crowned with Thorns*—also for the President; even the indefatigable Etty was tired of such work, having brought back with him more than fifty copies of varying sizes and subjects. His comments upon the Louvre drawings interest us more as a revelation of the man rather than of some unknown or unsuspected quality in the works themselves.[3] To this extent he differed from Eastlake, whose opinions about a work of art were backed by wide experience and connoisseurship: Eastlake had an enquiring mind and he made voluminous notes about the contents of nearly all the European public and private collections, besides many minor pieces in less familiar places. What became a matter of course for Eastlake was for Etty an infrequent practice. This is not to suggest that Etty's remarks are valueless; nor is he unobservant. But he reacts with zest to whatever appeals strongly to him and ignores or soon forgets that which does not. He was by instinct selective and subjective; Eastlake attempted, often successfully, to be encyclopaedic and objective. This contrast in outlook is brought into sharpest focus when one remembers that Eastlake was most successful as the first Director of the National Gallery: Etty excelled as one of the great artistic virtuosi of his time.[4]

[1] *Journal de Eugène Delacroix*, ed. André Joubin, Paris, 1950, I, pp. 61–5, and 294 (note 1). Alfred Robaut, *L'Œuvre Complet de Eugène Delacroix*, Paris, 1855, dates the copy of *Les Sirènes* to 1828 (No. 260), but provides no evidence for this date. R. Escholier, *Delacroix*, Paris, 1926, I, pp. 52, 63, reproduces an oil sketch and a watercolour study of the *Débarquement*, and these might even date from 1822.

[2] *See* Appendix I, *Letter 7*.   [3] *See* Appendix I, *Letter 8*, with the Notes appended.

[4] Samuel and Richard Redgrave, *A Century of British Painters*, Phaidon ed., London, 1947, p. 474, describe Eastlake as one of the 'few exceptional painters who have served the art they loved better by their lives than by their brush'. In 1841 Sir Robert Peel had proposed a consultative committee of eminent artists to advise his fellow-Trustees of the National Gallery upon important purchases. Among those whom he invited were Etty and Eastlake.

CHAPTER FIVE

ACADEMIC HONOURS: 1824-1830

ETTY returned to England early in January, 1824, and at once began to prepare for that year's Academy exhibition. Time was short, but he concentrated on one work, the subject of which had been in his mind long before he went to Italy. This was the *Pandora Crowned by the Seasons* [pl. 16]. As early as 1820 he had sent to the British Institution a highly finished study for a *Pandora*, and it seems that he had intended to paint a bigger canvas for the Academy: there is an unfinished picture in the City Art Gallery, Birmingham, which is almost twice the size of the finished painting. The abandoned Birmingham picture differs in composition from the later work, notably in the changed poses of Vulcan, Venus and Pandora herself. All the changes made have resulted in a much more compact and balanced composition, but it can hardly be said that Etty has mastered the art of concealing art, and the mechanics of the composition are a little too obvious. He has used what was to become a favourite device of his, the diamond shape, slightly flattened top and bottom, which encloses the principal figure or group of figures. Often, in his preparatory sketches, he has placed his figures within a network of criss-crossing diagonal lines, and it is possible to follow the evolution of some of his larger pieces from the first sketches (sometimes hardly more than cryptic notations) through to oil studies and the final product. A good example of his rapid pen sketches is that showing an intermediary stage of the *Pandora* composition.[1] Although more controlled and accurate than a Fuseli or a Romney pen drawing, it undoubtedly continues in that tradition. The Tate Gallery has a small oil study [pl. 19a].

The picture itself is made up of a curious blend of elements. With an almost relief-like effect, the figures seem to be projecting from the flat surface of a backdrop, rather than standing freely in space. The analogy with sculpture is not inappropriate if one recalls the bas-reliefs of John Gibson; for although as a painter Etty evokes none of the slightly austere qualities found in Gibson's work, a tendency to elongate the female form is common to both artists. Flaxman's *Hesiod* (published in 1817) would also have provided Etty with enough prototypes, particularly plate 4, *Pandora Attired*, and the importance of these series of engravings cannot be overemphasized, as they were to inspire several other paintings by Etty. However, there is another element, almost antithetic, which springs directly from Rubens. The device of placing a figure so that part of it should

---

[1] *Sketchbook II*, p. 109, City Art Gallery, York.

touch the picture frame is applied to Vulcan, whose right foot presses down hard upon the bottom edge of the frame. Etty need only have gone to Dulwich to see an example of this in the *Samson and Delilah* by Rubens's pupil Van Dyck (a picture mentioned by Fuseli in his *Fourth Lecture*, although not because of that particular feature).

There are still links with *The Coral Finder* in the *Pandora*, particularly the group of Venus and Cupid on the left; but the handling of the paint is far more subtle and assured. Where before the flesh painting had been rather dry and hard, it is now softer and more liquid, giving a sveldtness quite new in Etty's work. To this is added a sparkling richness of colour, and there is hardly any of the stridency which mars the *Cleopatra*. The general tone of the picture is cool, an effect produced by the large areas of cold white clouds, and the absence of any dark shadows on the main figures. On the right he has painted a 'Venetian' orange and blue sunset sky, a cliché he quite often used in later years. Pandora has a pale pink robe, and the pale radiance of her figure contrasts with the ruddier hue of the three Graces. The two on the left are in green, red and golden yellow robes, while the third wears an orange mantle over a royal blue dress. The value of Etty's experience abroad may be judged by the success with which he has harmonized these strong positive colours.

The *Pandora* was much praised: by purchasing the picture Lawrence bestowed the final token of approbation. But a more popular reaction seems to have been grudging admiration not unmixed with philistinism. One contemporary critic wrote:

'There is a captivating style of Painting that is not natural, and yet blends with it so much poetic inspiration and celestial beauty, that we are irresistably compelled to admire in despite of our more calm judgment. *Mr. Etty has a style of his own.* It is nothing earthly, yet his drawing is beautiful, and his imagination exquisite.

'We sincerely wish we could induce him to be a little more terrestial in his ideas, and we doubt not of his becoming one of the greatest ornaments of the English School. His work has all the beauties of which we have been speaking, and is quite as full of what we consider the errors of his style.' [1]

Presumably the writer would have preferred Etty to paint subjects drawn from everyday life, like those chosen by Wilkie and Mulready. Not everyone shared this view, and William Carey (as might be expected) found much to praise and nothing to blame. He awarded laurels both to Lawrence for his patronage of living artists and to Etty, whom he called '*that inspired Lyric Painter*'. Sometimes Carey's admiration almost embarrasses with its unrestrained fervour. [2]

Prompted by his friends, Etty moved from Stangate Walk to more spacious apartments in Buckingham Street, where he was to remain until his retirement. The transition was not as smooth as Gilchrist would have us believe, and Walter received a 'wretched letter' from his brother, dated 29th June, 1824, in which Etty pours out all his doubts and agony of mind. [3] The overriding fear was of the extra expense the

[1] Charles M. Westmacott, *Descriptive and Critical Catalogue* (of 1824 Royal Academy exhibition), extract found in Anderdon's *Catalogues of the Royal Academy Exhibitions*, LVI (British Museum).

[2] William Carey, *Observations on the Probable Decline . . . of British Historical Painting, from the Effects of Church Exclusion of Paintings*, London, 1825, pp. 126–7. Like Haydon, Carey felt it to be the duty of the state to encourage young artists by purchasing their works, and putting them in a national gallery.

[3] *See* Appendix I, *Letter 9*; a slightly shortened version was quoted by W. T. Whitley, *Art in England 1821–1837*, pp. 80–1.

change involved ('the servant alone costing more than the whole of the other together'), expense which he felt he could never meet: the idea of remaining a permanent burden on his brother distressed him beyond all else. It has been said that Etty was by nature optimistic, but he had his moments of black despair. Fortunately, the outlook brightened considerably towards the end of the year, and on 1st November Etty was elected A.R.A. This was the first time he had put up for election, and William Allan, Wilkie's candidate, was his strongest rival. When the results of the final ballot were declared, Etty received 16 votes to Allan's 7 and won a convincing majority.[1] *The Times*, when reviewing an exhibition of copies at the British Institution, singled out for especial praise Etty's copy of Tintoretto's *Esther before Ahasuerus* (now in the Royal Collection). Concerning his election the reviewer makes the caustic comment that 'as matters are conducted at the Academy, this cannot be as an honour conferred on Mr. Etty: if it were, he had deserved and should have obtained it long ago'.[2]

The years 1825–40 undoubtedly form Etty's 'heroic' period, and although more paintings were produced, for example, in 1835–49, yet quality and inventive skill became markedly less consistent during the last nine years of his life, and the number of major works decreases. At the Academy of 1825 appeared the first *grande machine*— *The Combat: Woman pleading for the vanquished—An ideal group* [pl. 17]. It was the first entry in the catalogue and attracted much attention and not a little praise. As with the *Pandora*, Etty seems to have had ideas for *The Combat* even in 1821, but the conception must have gained in power as a result of the Italian experience. In this painting, Etty has sought to give pictorial expression to an abstract virtue, Mercy, and it is interesting that he has dispensed with any underlying story, drawn either from history or from mythology, to give point to his theme. This is a new conception of history painting or, perhaps more accurately, a new twist to an old idea. Certainly it comes within Etty's own purpose to reveal (as he later wrote) 'some great moral on the heart', but while attempting to idealize his figures, he relies almost entirely upon a literal transcription of his studio models. This seems to be one of the fundamental contradictions in his conception of the 'ideal' and is symptomatic of the confusion of purpose then prevailing in European academic painting. For although the picture has certain classical elements reminiscent of similar combat scenes in the metopes of the Elgin Marbles, yet the spirit underlying the whole is rather one of tempestuous romanticism. The drama of the struggle is heightened by its setting, a wild and desolate seashore; and the superhuman figures owe more to Michelangelo than to the Carracci. It may be argued that David's *Sabines* is a dramatic work, but the drama is of a different order, since there the passion is rigidly controlled, whereas in the Etty there is the unbridled ferocity of a baroque composition like Rubens's *Horrors of War*.

Although as it now stands *The Combat* represents no particular incident of history or of literature, yet one preliminary oil sketch provides a clue to its inspiration [pl. 21*b*]. The attacker in this study wears what appears to be a lion's skin over his head, which would identify him as Hercules. This sketch has further interest as another indication of Etty's methods at this time. Action and composition are uppermost in his mind, and

---

[1] *Minutes of the General Assembly of the Royal Academy*, III, pp. 416–17. A letter from Henry Howard, R.A., dated 2nd November, informing Etty of his election, is now in the City Art Gallery, York.

[2] *The Times*, 4th November, 1824.

he has paid little attention to anatomical accuracy or minute detail; but the vigour of the sketch, both in handling and inspiration, has survived in the finished painting. A very necessary improvement in the composition has been made, and in place of the sharp diagonal line from bottom left to top right, Etty has twisted the pose of the vanquished warrior so as to unite the figures in a closely-knit group. The figure of the pleading woman has been criticized, but the pose, even if a little awkward, is correctly drawn and there does not seem to be any such deliberate distortion as often appears in the female nudes by Ingres. Deprived of this boldly conceived *motif* the picture would lose half its dramatic force.

The critics were pleased, and *The Times* considered the work 'a masterly effort, and though defective in some respects, it realizes a union of the florid beauties of the Venetian school with much of the sober dignity and power of the Roman school'.[1] This last remark seems fairly apt, and *The Combat* does indeed unite the qualities of, say, Titian's *Cain Slaying Abel* (Sta. Maria della Salute, Venice) and Annibale Carracci's fresco *Remus Slaying the Cattle Thieves* in the Palazzo Salem, Bologna—both works likely to interest Etty when he was gleaning ideas for his own painting. The criticism is itself a reflection of a more conservative tradition which regarded the Carracci as the correct standard by which all academic painting should be judged. Much space was also devoted to the works of Mulready, Landseer, Wilkie, Henry Pickersgill and Ward, but Constable, a much greater figure, was hardly discussed at all. *The Combat* was the largest picture so far produced by Etty, and its size must have daunted many prospective purchasers, since it was left to John Martin to keep a rash promise he had made when seeing the painting in the studio: after the exhibition Martin bought the picture for 300 gns., but it was far too large for a private house, and he later sold it to the Royal Scottish Academy. William Carey seized upon Martin's act of patronage—'the calm resolve of his own strong mind'—and used it as a stick with which to strike at public apathy towards contemporary British art in general, and at the almost invariable preference for things foreign, or 'the Anti-British prejudice'.[2]

Admiration for Etty's *Combat* might also have come from another source, for Delacroix arrived in England towards the end of May, and would certainly have seen the work on exhibition. His first general impressions of English painting were not altogether favourable, but 'ils ont des peintres admirables dans les proportions moyennes. L'envie de briller davantage les ôtera de la route qu'ils suivent. Ils feront de grands tableaux qui ne seront plus à la portée des particuliers.'[3] This last is a particularly apt comment, although Delacroix had in mind Hilton's *Christ Crowned with Thorns* (recently bought by the British Institution) rather than Etty's *Combat*. Among his English acquaintances were Lawrence, Wilkie, the Fielding brothers and Etty, from all of whom he received courtesies which he afterwards recalled with great pleasure when writing to Théophile Silvestre in December 1858.[4] Etty would undoubtedly have delighted in showing his

---

[1] *The Times*, 3rd May, 1825. For other criticisms, *see* Whitley, *Art in England 1821–1837*, pp. 87–8.

[2] William Carey, *Some Memoirs of the Patronage and Progress of the Fine Arts in England and Ireland*, etc., London, 1826, pp. 166–8. *See also* Thomas Balston, *John Martin*, London, 1947, pp. 84–5.

[3] *Correspondance Générale*, Paris, 1935–8, I, pp. 157–8. Letter to Soulier, 6th June, 1825.

[4] *Op. cit.*, IV, pp. 57–8.

French visitor whatever paintings happened to be in his studio, and in exchanging ideas within the limits imposed by language difficulties. But there is nothing to suggest more than this professional acquaintanceship, for although the two painters met several times, no further contact was made after Delacroix had written a farewell letter to Etty on leaving England the next August.[1] When Etty visited France in later years he never availed himself of Delacroix's invitation; he may even have forgotten all about him.

The *Self-portrait* of 1825 is a unique document of its kind for this period [pl. 20]. Although it is an idealized classical profile portrait (even its oval shape is reminiscent of a cameo) it shows a degree of introspection, one might almost say of melancholy, which places it with similar works of the French romantic school. The same sombre background shrouds the figure and increases the sense of mystery and remoteness surrounding the personality of the subject. These qualities may also be found in the unfinished *Self-portrait* by Lawrence, where full-face, he stares out inscrutably at the spectator. Unlike Lawrence, Etty has used rich pigments, and the creamy flesh tones are contrasted sharply with the thickly impasted white collar which tails off into a very delicate glaze at the back of the neck. Below this comes the red and blue cravat, painted in almost pure tints, and this is counterbalanced by the black fur band of the dark brown cloak with its brass fastening. Curiously enough, irrespective of his natural colouring Etty has given himself black hair, as if to complete the harmony of alternate lights and darks. The portrait reflects both the great qualities and the unfulfilled aspirations of the artist.

Although *The Combat* was not bought until after the exhibition, its merits had brought the artist to the notice of Lord Darnley, who commissioned Etty to paint another large picture—the subject of which it was agreed should be the *Judgment of Paris* [pl. 22]—at a price of £500. The result of Etty's labours was shown at the Academy of 1826, when it was deservedly admired for its 'brilliant and harmonious colouring, combined with graceful grouping and careful execution, such as no artist of the present day can equal'.[2] It is to Etty's credit that he has succeeded in painting a hackneyed subject so as to make it appear fresh and vibrant. No other English artist of the time could produce that same blend of technical skill, imaginative power and, not less important, conviction. To some extent, this picture also represents the logical conclusion of an academic tradition, and although it would be wearisome to dwell at length on the pedigree of its iconography, certain points should be noted. The composition of the picture quite clearly derives from a Flaxman engraving of the subject [pl. 23a], published in his *Iliad* series of 1793 and well known to Etty.[3] There are variations, of course, but the poses of Minerva and Juno are particularly close to the Flaxman, even to the extent of borrowing the same headgear of plumed helmet and coronet. That Etty was also well aware of the two Rubens *Judgment of Paris* paintings in the Prado and the National Gallery is obvious from a preliminary sketch in the British Museum which contains the *motif* of a flying

[1] *See* Appendix I, *Letter 10*, dated 'Londres, le 24 aout 1825' (York City Reference Library). This letter was first published by me in *The Burlington Magazine*, XCIV, March, 1952, p. 80.

[2] *The Times*, 29th April, 1826.

[3] *See* Appendix I, *Letter 4*, where he specifically mentions Flaxman's *Iliad* and *Odyssey* engravings as in his possession.

putto about to place a crown of flowers upon the head of Venus [pl. 24*a*]. This drawing, incidentally, again demonstrates Etty's method of composing his groups within clearly defined diamond-shaped sections. It is also probable that he knew of either Mengs' *Judgment of Paris* (Hermitage) or a Poussin prototype, which has a satyr peeping from between the tree-trunks. Finally, it seems more than likely that he possessed a specimen of the archetype for all these compositions, Marcantonio Raimondi's engraving of Raphael's *Judgment of Paris* [pl. 23*b*], as a study for the figure of Paris repeats fairly closely the general pose of the Raphael Paris. Other similarities are no less obvious. The fact that one can discern several prototypes for Etty's picture in no way detracts from the beauty and grandeur of his work. It is most sensitively painted, particularly in the plumage of the peacocks and in the landscape background, while the idea of placing the strong yellow of Paris's cap against a deep plum-coloured mantle suspended between the trees adds a brilliancy to the whole comparable only with Poussin. Unfortunately, Lord Darnley seemed dead to its virtues, and for a long time it remained stored in the painter's studio. After repeated requests, £400 was paid, but not until 1834 was the account settled with Lord Darnley's heir and executor, and then £25 short of the original fee. Exasperated by such dilatoriness, Etty was prepared to cut his losses rather than go to law.[1]

The English artists' urge to equal and if possible to surpass both in size and subject the work of rival schools, commented upon by Delacroix, was certainly admitted by Etty, and his next epic picture, *Judith and Holofernes* showed him to be aiming high. On the back of a sketch for this painting, he had written 'Honour and glory to the next Exhibition!—We must keep the foreigners from fooling us!'; and, more solemnly, the story of Judith had been chosen to epitomize the ideals of patriotism and devotion to one's country and people, and to God; for, unlike *The Combat*, this second epic had a specific event, based upon the *Apocrypha* story, with which to point the moral. Enough has been said already about Etty's conception of history painting, but one other fact emerges. In the *Judith* Etty deliberately chose to depict the moment just before the actual beheading, because it seemed to him a more interesting moment psychologically, and it avoided 'the offensive and revolting butchery, some have delighted and even revelled in'. He was perhaps guided in this choice by Fuseli, who in his *Fifth Lecture on Painting* had suggested that an artist should shun scenes of unpleasantness and choose the moment *before* a martyrdom or decollation.[2]

It is difficult to discuss any of the three *Judith* pictures in detail, for their condition is such as to preclude more than a general idea of the composition of each. But oil studies for the central picture exist, and there are also a number of small pencil sketches [pls.24*b* 25*a*]. One oil study is particularly interesting, and its vigorous brushwork, combined with great brilliancy and purity of colour, has led to its being mistaken for the work of Géricault [pl. 25*b*]. Red, white and gold are the dominant colours, but it is noticeable that Etty has resorted to bitumen in an attempt to increase the intensity of his shadows, an unhappy idea which has contributed to the decay of all the final *Judith* pictures, as well as of some other paintings of this period. The figure of Judith, with sword uplifted,

[1] Gilchrist, *op. cit.*, I, pp. 233–5. Letters to Walter Etty, dated 3rd June and 1st July, 1834 (York City Reference Library). The painting, after several changes of ownership, was sold for £1,000 in 1848.
[2] Gilchrist, *op. cit.*, I, p. 237. Fuseli, *Lectures on Painting*, London, 1820, pp. 220–1.

is a little too squat in the oil study, and this, with other minor discrepancies, has been rectified in the final version. It seems that Etty had first planned that Judith should hold the sword in a more horizontal position, but changed his mind after realizing the increased dramatic force to be gained by making Judith hold the sword almost vertically. More canvas had then to be added to the top edge of the picture. As a composition, the *Judith* would appear to break fresh ground, yet it is tempting to see some link between this and a similar work by Veronese, *Judith about to slay Holofernes*, now in the Ashmolean Museum, Oxford.[1] Whether Etty knew of this painting is now impossible to prove. Something of the quality of the Etty picture may also be seen in a finished study for the head of *Judith* now at York. Here, the conception of the thrown-back head, revealing the vast column of a neck, seems almost repellent taken thus from its context; it is certainly rather overpowering.

The *Judith* was very favourably received, and *The Times* devoted long paragraphs to praise of this painting, which it was said had been painted in the short space of four months. It was suggested that a church or chapel would be a suitable home for this scriptural subject (Hilton's large *Crucifixion*, at the same exhibition, was destined for a church in Liverpool). As Etty and Hilton are praised so also is Constable whose *Chainpier at Brighton* is here considered as one of his best works, and he is now hailed as the first landscape painter of the day. Alfred Chalon, writing to Thomas Uwins in Italy, was also enthusiastic: 'The Exhibition was a good one; its principal features, Hilton's *Crucifixion*, an immense picture in three compartments . . . to be copied in glass for a church, and Etty's *Judith and Holofernes*, also a large picture, very forcible in colour and effect. . . .'[2] Hardly any attention was paid to Etty's other painting, *The Parting of Hero and Leander* [pl. 26], which although considerably smaller has quite as much power as the *Judith*. It is brilliantly coloured: Hero is clothed in white and orange, with a scarlet ribbon in her dark hair, and Leander wears a plum-coloured loin cloth. The figures are set against a deep ultramarine sea and sky, and the cool reflected moonlight on Leander's body cleverly balances the flood of light from the open doorway. The subject has provided Etty with every opportunity to display the knowledge gained in the Life School, but this has been transmuted into a painting whose mood is of tender romanticism, heightened by tragic pathos.

Among the younger exhibitors that year was Eastlake, whose *Isadas the Young Spartan*, commissioned by the Duke of Devonshire, had been sent from Rome. There, incidentally, exhibited in Eastlake's studio, it had been praised by Guérin. It also pleased Etty, who wrote to congratulate Eastlake upon his success. He went further, and told Eastlake that he had put down his name on the list of candidates for associateship of the Royal Academy. 'If I have done wrong', he wrote, 'you must scold me. But joking apart, I hope they will elect you. It is with men like you, of genius, and classic erudition, that its first ranks ought to be filled, then we might hope for something better in our Catalogue than "Portrait of a Gentleman"—"Portrait of a Lady with a favourite Spaniel", whole length of a Race Horse, ditto of a Poodle, etc., etc. . . .' He then goes on with the news of various

---

[1] This painting, one of a series of six *Judith* pictures, was once in the Methuen Collection (*vide* Ashmolean Catalogue, No. 455), and was presumably still in London up to 1816, but it did not re-appear until 1904, when it was exhibited at Burlington House (No. 38).

[2] *A Memoir of T. Uwins, R.A.*, London, 1858, I, p. 183; a letter of 10th October, 1827.

friends, and ends by urging Eastlake to visit Venice.[1] Eastlake was elected on 5th November, 1827, and writing to Uwins he told him that his name 'had never been inscribed before and it is even more gratifying to my feelings than the honour itself, to recollect that it was set down by the generous friendship of Etty, without consulting me, and he wrote to me about two months since to tell me of it, and *apologize* for doing it '.[2] These letters need no comment, unless it is to recall Etty's remarks of 1823, when he seemed less appreciative of Eastlake's abilities.

Early in February 1828, Etty was himself promoted to full Academic rank, and his chief rival this time was Constable, for in the preliminary round Etty had 16 votes to Constable's 6, and when the final votes were cast Etty received 18 and Constable 5; a decisive victory and, most appropriately, Etty succeeded to the place of Flaxman. As the President's candidate Etty's chances of election had been greatly enhanced, and few would deny that he fully merited the honour; but it was unfortunate that Constable, an even more deserving candidate, should have to wait for his reward until the next year.[3] Etty's joy knew no bounds and he wrote in boyish triumph to Walter and to Thomas Bodley. The news must also have comforted his mother, who was by now in failing health. But if Etty was at last secure within the Academy, criticisms of his work began to hint at impropriety, a charge first made six years before but not renewed until now. The cause of the trouble was his *Venus now Wakes, and Wakens Love* [pl. 27b], exhibited at the British Institution in 1828. Its painterly qualities were not overlooked: 'The drawing is free and flowing; the line of beauty is admirably observed throughout; and the colouring, though rich, is perfectly natural. The subject is, however, handled in a way entirely too luscious (we might, with great propriety, use a harsher term) for the public eye.' [4] The critic obviously refused to accept the lily as a token of purity in this instance, and it must be admitted that the heavy, Rubensian figure of Venus would shock a generation accustomed to Howard and Flaxman. Neither is the oversweet sentiment of the final version much to modern taste; nor does the curious distortion of the right thigh occur in the wonderfully fresh study for the figure of Venus now in the collection of Mr. A. W. Bacon [pl. 27a].

Etty sent three works to the Academy of 1828: an almost life-size portrait of the Earl of Normanton's two children—*Guardian Cherubs* [pl. 32], as it was rather fancifully called; a larger work which had no formal title, but which has since been labelled *The World Before the Flood;* and *Venus, the Evening Star.* The first was of course commissioned, but Etty was fortunate enough to sell both the other pictures by the end of the exhibition, the Marquis of Stafford buying *The World Before the Flood* for 500 guineas, and Mr. Digby Murray the *Venus.* It was not until late in his life that Etty would again find himself in such a pleasant situation for any length of time. Yet *The World Before the*

---

[1] The text of this letter is made up from two sources; Lady Eastlake's *Memoir* in Eastlake, *Contributions to the Literature of the Fine Arts* (Second Series), 1870, p. 112; and cuttings from the Catalogues issued by Maggs Bros., the booksellers (No. 1896 in the Catalogue for Summer, 1914), among the *Whitley Papers* (British Museum); last advertised in 1932, but the present owner is unknown to Maggs Bros.

[2] *A Memoir of T. Uwins, R.A.,* I, pp. 297–8; letter dated 'Rome, Nov. 28, 1827'.

[3] *Minutes of the General Assembly of the Royal Academy,* IV, pp. 42, 43, 9th February, 1828. *The Letters of John Constable, R.A. to C. R. Leslie, R.A., 1826–1837,* ed. P. Leslie, London, 1941, pp. 5–10. Letters dated 5th January and 8th February, 1828.

[4] *The Times,* 4th February, 1828.

Flood [pl. 108] was successful not because of any striking originality, but rather as a maturer version of its predecessor, *The Judgment of Paris*. All the elements are there, including a harpist and one of the negro warriors first seen in the *Cleopatra*, but with a bigger cast and a different story. To pursue the theatrical metaphor still further one might say that the production this time is more lavish, and certainly more skilful, for the actors, in performing their parts, blend together more harmoniously to form a pleasing chorus dance. The stage scenery remains almost the same as that for the *Judgment of Paris* set in 1826, and for the choreography, Etty seems to have relied, in part, upon that used in Poussin's *Bacchanalian Revel Before a Term of Pan*, a picture which had been bought for the National Gallery only two years before. Newspaper critics, in some cases, contented themselves by repeating the pious platitudes with which they had praised Etty's work of the past two years: *The Times* reviewer, after taking exception to the colouring 'in some instances exaggerated: for example, one nymph has orange-coloured vertebrae, which is carrying the reflex a little too far', thought that the picture had great merit, 'and augments the hope . . . that time and study will make Mr. Etty such a painter as England may be reasonably proud of'. But the *Gentleman's Magazine* complained of an excess of 'that voluptuousness which his favourite Titian indulged in', and ends with a sarcastic reference to the purchaser, 'The picture will serve to accomodate the *private* Titians of that nobleman.' [1] An admiring critic in the *News* was nevertheless amused by the costumes, 'One lady, though she has walked out of doors quite naked, has taken care to have her hair curled by Truefitt, and wears a very handsome turban from Madame Maredan's.' [2] But perhaps the most uncompromising comments come from Haydon, who wrote in his *Memoirs* 'The whole Exhibition was lamentably deficient. Constable and Jackson are the only colourists left. Why are there no historical pictures? Hilton has had no commissions, Etty has had no commissions, I have had no commissions. Why are there so many portraits?'—a question which received the obvious answer. [3]

To add to Etty's triumphs that year, the British Institution voted him the sum of £100 as a public acknowledgement of his artistic abilities and as an encouragement to further success. In passing, it may be noted that the British Institution since its foundation in 1806 had already done much to promote British history painting; even so, this did not prevent the Academicians discussing plans of their own to this end in July, 1809. Joseph Farington, in his *Diary*, noted some of these projects. [4] Flaxman had proposed annual payments of £400 to be divided equally between two Academicians for two history pictures. In August, Martin Archer Shee had suggested that £1,000 be

[1] *The Times*, 6th May, 1828; *Gentleman's Magazine*, XCVIII, June, 1828, pp. 538–9.

[2] W. T. Whitley, *Art in England 1821–1837*, pp. 145–6, who also refers to the other criticisms. Pigot's *London and Provincial Directory*, 1828–9, lists three hairdressers named Truefitt: Francis Trufitt, of 1 New Bond Street, established in 1805 and probably the best known; his brother Peter, who set up in opposition in 1819, of 20/21 Burlington Arcade; and William, also in the Burlington Arcade. Madame Maredan was a fashionable milliner in Hanover Square.

[3] B. R. Haydon, *Autobiography and Memoirs*, London, 1926, II, p. 443. It seems strange that he should omit the names of Turner and Etty from his list of colourists.

[4] Joseph Farington, *Diary*, pp. 4406–7, 4435, 4442, 4575 of the British Museum typescript of the Windsor Royal Library manuscript; entries for 2nd July, 3rd, 4th and 19th August, 1809; 26th June, 1810.

awarded once every two years to one history painter, 'thereby calling forth all his powers'. Fuseli immediately picked upon the difficulties of selecting the artist, and Flaxman's idea of using either seniority or a system of rotation decided by drawing lots was felt to be unworkable. When Lawrence was approached by Lord Castlereagh about state patronage of paintings for public buildings, by providing an annual fund of £2,000 or £3,000 from the Exchequer, he thought established artists would be unwilling to risk the consequences of public competition. However, by June 1810 it was known that the Chancellor of the Exchequer had refused to grant £5,000 for such a purpose. The merits of the British Institution's system were probably that it prevented the Academy from securing a monopoly of all the awards for history painting, and further, the British Institution aimed also at patronage on several levels of artistic activity. Its main weakness was undoubtedly its financial instability.

As soon as the exhibition pictures were finished, Etty had to begin his R.A. Diploma work and, ever conscientious in these matters, he delayed taking his holiday in York until the end of August; by then he had completed most of the work and had only to paint in the draperies, landscape and minor details, all of which could be done at York since no models were needed. Thus, in October Etty was able to present his *Sleeping Nymph and Satyrs* [pl. 30], and fulfil his obligations according to the Academy laws. Few Academicians have sent in as their diploma piece work of such quality. Roger Fry said that in it 'we see him ingeniously fitting together a *pastiche* of a Poussinesque design with a careful and brilliant study of a nude model, but the two elements do not fuse. His nude refuses to become a nymph, and his satyrs remain mythological and are left in a different world.'[1] This last comment perhaps begs the question, but there can be no doubt of the inspiration underlying this picture. Poussin's *Sleeping Nymph Surprised by Satyrs*, of which there is an engraving by Mme. Soyer,[2] certainly provides a close parallel, the more so, since Etty has used a typical Poussin device of filling the picture space with only three or four figures; in colour too, the picture is nearer to Poussin than the Venetians. Yet above all, Titian's *Venus of the Pardo* (Louvre) comes to mind, and, in noting the resemblance, a difference of conception is no less obvious. Instead of idyllic calm, Etty has produced a feeling of dynamic tension, the satyrs struggle with each other, and the nymph is no longer in a smooth, self-contained pose, but is spreadeagled with her body sharply twisted on its own axis. Perhaps it is just this tension which Roger Fry found so disturbing.

In December Etty received his diploma, and along with Robert Smirke, Senior, Abraham Cooper and William Collins succeeded the retiring members on the next year's Council, as well as joining the list of Visitors.[3] He also obtained a picture he had long coveted, a *Bacchanalian Revel* by Jordaens, taken instead of a year's fee for instructing James Mathew Leigh, the son of its owner. This was almost the only time Etty accepted a pupil: he seems to have followed Lawrence's practice of providing a room in his own house for the student's use, and promising to instruct him on occasion.[4] Leigh was for-

[1] Roger Fry, *Reflections on British Painting*, London, 1934. Republished 1951, p. 187.
[2] A fragment of a copy of this picture was bequeathed to the National Gallery in 1831 by the Rev. Holwell Carr.
[3] *The Times*, 13th December, 1828.
[4] A letter from Leigh, then in Paris, to Etty, dated '19th of the early darkning days, year of the Arts

bidden to enter Etty's own studio except when invited to do so by the master. Except for a few odd references in Etty's letters, little is known about the artist: he seems to have exhibited at the Academy rather infrequently between 1828 and 1849.

Early in January 1829 Etty drove a bargain with the Scottish Academy of Fine Arts (later to become the Royal Scottish Academy), who had repeatedly asked him to lend his *Judith* for exhibition in Edinburgh. After failing to sell the picture either at the R.A. or afterwards at the British Institution exhibition of 1828, Etty agreed to let the Scottish Academy have the *Judith* for 300 guineas, although he had asked 500 guineas in 1827. At the same time, Etty offered to paint two pendants for the *Judith*, in furtherance of his original scheme, for 100 guineas each. The deal was settled, and the Scottish Academy in effect obtained three pictures for the price of one. Nevertheless, it was a noble gesture on the part of the Scots, whose academy had been founded only in 1826, and Etty was touched by the warmth of their feelings towards him. By securing the *Judith* the Scottish Academy also ensured the success of their own exhibition, in face of some stiff competition from their rivals the Edinburgh Royal Institution, who had Wilkie's *Penny Wedding* as the chief attraction. By May 1829 Etty had received the full amount due to him for the *Judith*, with the assurance of another commission ahead. The same year Etty was made an honorary member of the Scottish Academy, and this brought the number of his honorary distinctions up to three; in 1824 the Venetian Academy had conferred membership upon him, and in the same year the Charleston Academy of Fine Arts similarly honoured him.[1]

Etty only showed one painting at the British Institution that year, *A subject from Ovid's Metamorphoses*, about which it was remarked, 'Another of this artist's astonishingly luxuriant pictures. What a depth of feeling is expressed in those eyes. It represents a pair of lovely figures standing in the water embracing. The drawing is excellent; the colouring very good; but the drapery is so cast as to be useless.' [2] The Academy received two pictures of a more serious nature, *Benaiah* and *Hero, having thrown herself from the Tower at the sight of Leander drowned, dies on his Body* [pls. 34*b*, 31]. Of the two *Hero expiring on the body of Leander* (to give it a less unwieldy title) is the more interesting; *Benaiah* is but a variation on the theme of *The Combat*, and although it displays the artist's great skill and anatomical knowledge, it is difficult to feel any great enthusiasm towards this idealization of valour. Etty has used the pose of the slain man in the *Benaiah* for part of his figure of the dying *Hero*, a bold piece of foreshortening which adds enormously to the tragic force of this painting. Equally unconventional is the composition as a whole, with its strong diagonal axis broken only by Leander's outstretched hand and softened by the curving line of Hero's body. The method of painting has also changed to some extent, and the palette is an unusual one for Etty: for, except on the

1830', is in York City Reference Library. He asks for Etty's opinion of setting up an *atelier* in Paris to be run by English students, but inviting French instructors to attend. A Jordaens *Triomphe de Bacchus et de Silène*, answering to the description given in Gilchrist, passed through the Palais des Beaux-Arts, Brussels, Bougard Sale (lot 135), 9th May, 1932, and again appeared at Charpentier, Paris, 20th March, 1953.

[1] The Charleston Academy of Fine Arts is almost certainly the South Carolina Academy of Fine Arts, organized in Charleston in 1816. This Academy flourished until 1830, when it was disbanded; a satirical obituary notice appeared in the *City Gazette*, 22nd July, 1830. Its place was taken by the Carolina Art Association, founded in 1857 and still flourishing.

[2] *Gentleman's Magazine*, XCIX, March, 1829, p. 251.

bodies and draperies, all is very thinly painted, and the dank sand at the foot of the tower gleams with moisture—an effect achieved by allowing the dull ochre-coloured underpainting to show through. Hero is clad in a sombre robe of bluish purple, the shadows of which are almost black, and traces of bitumen may be detected here and in other shadows on the bodies. Almost the only points of bright colour are the gold bracelet and a silvery-green cloth around Leander's legs. Even so, Etty has not been afraid to use a strong red in the shadows of the ears, nostrils and hands of his figures. Etty has caught brilliantly the atmosphere of sullen calm after storm, it is almost dawn and wisps of angry lead-coloured clouds are dispersing across the dark cobalt sky. As in *The Storm* of the following year, Etty has deliberately attempted an experiment on a 'principle of attaining harmony of colour by neutral tints'.[1] Rightly, he always looked upon *Hero expiring* as one of his best works, and in it he has given expression to a fundamental human emotion by the action of his figures alone. Anderdon thought it worthy of a place in the National Gallery when he saw it again at the Society of Arts in 1849[2] and even Turner seems to have emulated Etty when he, too, painted a *Parting of Hero and Leander*, begun in 1828 and exhibited in 1837.

In February Etty had been shocked by the news of a disastrous fire in York Minster, but this sad event was soon overshadowed by a far more grievous personal bereavement: on 30th July his mother died suddenly at Thomas Etty's home in Hull, and after hurrying back to York Etty arrived in time for the funeral. A little later he wrote six verses inspired by the memory of his mother which, although quite undistinguished as poetry, are a touching record of his love and piety.[3]

Etty's attachment to the Life School of the Academy has become legendary: it marked him out from his fellow Academicians even during his lifetime and at first his colleagues remonstrated with him, suggesting that attendance, other than as Visitor, was both unnecessary and unprofessional. Constable certainly shared this view, and in a note to Leslie of 1831 remarked, 'Sass—the inexorable Sass—and the imperturbable Etty are never absent; they set an excellent example to the Modles [sic] for regularity. I presume not to hold them up as examples in any other respect.' Etty calmly ignored such protests, and once offered to resign rather than give up the practice, adding, 'It fills up a couple of hours in the evening, I should be at a loss how else to employ.' While not agreeing with the Academicians' contention that Etty's action might detract from the dignity of the office, this last remark does seem an admission of the narrow professionalism which all too often was allowed to dominate his life; for even if one shunned society these 'couple of hours' would be used by most men to enrich their minds and experience. Gilchrist also noted that Etty now read far less widely than in his student days.[4] Whatever ill-effect this narrowing of interests may have had upon the artist is partly offset by such masterly studies as the *Male Nude with Upstretched Arms* [pl. 36*b*], which seems stylistically to date from this period. Like the study for the Venus, in *Venus now Wakes*,

[1] Gilchrist, *op. cit.*, I, p. 286.

[2] Anderdon, *Catalogues of the Royal Academy Exhibitions* (British Museum), LXI. By an odd twist, it was the companion picture, *The Parting of Hero and Leander*, which eventually entered a national collection.

[3] Obituary notice in the *Gentleman's Magazine*, XCIX, 1829, part ii, p. 189. The verses are in a notebook now belonging to Mr. Jacobus J. T. Bosch.

[4] C. R. Leslie, *Memoirs of the Life of John Constable, R.A.*, ed. Shirley, 1937, pp. 257–8. Gilchrist, *op. cit.*, I, p. 247; and P. G. Hamerton, *The Portfolio*, 1875, VI, p. 149.

and Wakens Love, it is painted with a rich, creamy pigment, fairly cool in tone, and is of a quality and finish which puts it among the best of his studies. With fluent ease he has caught a most complicated pose and turned it into an extremely satisfying composition.

As has been remarked earlier, Etty wanted fame as a history painter; but he still produced portraits frequently and during 1825–30 had painted at least five of different sizes, almost all of friends like Mrs. Cicely Bulmer, Mr. North and Thomas Bodley. The portrait of *Thomas Bodley* was painted in 1825, is a half-length picture, almost full-face, and depicts Bodley dressed in a cloak and set against the background of a rocky sea coast. It has great dignity and vigour, and it is a pity that the picture cannot now be found. Of about four years later is the portrait of *Miss Emma Davenport* [pl. 45*b*], daughter of a family well acquainted with Etty. The somewhat amorphous treatment of the lower half of the figure is explained by an anecdote, for it appears Etty had insisted that the sitter should wear a blue dress and ruffle to which she objected, hence the blue dress material was only draped over her and the artist had to reconstruct as best he could. But the head is painted with great success and spirit, and it is worth comparing the subtle charms of this portrait with the slightly *gauche* painting of *Miss Catharine Etty*, done some eighteen years earlier.

During the autumn of 1829 Etty devoted much of his attention to the scheme to restore York Minster. He had subscribed £30 to the restoration fund, and was anxious that all should be done that was possible to heal the ravages suffered by his beloved Minster. When it became known that plans were being made to move the screen back from its original position, Etty, with Sydney Taylor, Lewis Cottingham (the architect) and Stothard, led a vigorous protest campaign on behalf of the majority of the subscribers against the Dean and Chapter, who were being advised by Sir Robert Smirke. Answering a letter from Etty, Smirke, while assuring him that nothing would be undertaken which was contrary to the general wish, agreed that the idea was to set back the screen so as to reveal the pillars of the tower, and that 'by the removal they wod. be enabled to gain the desirable object of opening to full view the magnificent East Window, as the organ could then be placed in the two side aisles'.[1] Opposition was so strong as to prevent the plan from going ahead, for the time being, at least.

Early in the new year Lawrence died, and Etty felt as if his world were falling about his ears: 'My Dear Mother and my Dear Master both lost in six short months,' he wrote to Bodley.[2] The poignancy of the loss was increased for him by the knowledge that Lawrence had been dying at the moment when Etty, returning from the Academy, had enquired after the President's health from a servant boy at his door, and had gone away cheered by a reported improvement. After the funeral came the inevitable question 'who will succeed him to the President's chair, it is impossible to anticipate: Beechey, Etty, Hilton, Howard, Phillips, Pickersgill, Shee, Wilkie, and others are already spoken of by their respective friends. We have certainly a proud list to choose from, independently of sculptors and landscape-painters, who, we know not why, are not so much mentioned as likely candidates.'[3] When Shee was elected by a large majority, Etty was loyal in support of the new president, but Haydon, not

---

[1] Robert Smirke to Etty, 18th September, 1829 (York City Reference Library).
[2] Letter to Thomas Bodley, 27th January, 1830 (York City Reference Library).
[3] *The Times*, 11th January, 1830.

unsurprisingly, had nothing but bitter contempt for the Academicians' choice, and considered that Wilkie, already an artist of European reputation, should have been given the office.

Of the three paintings Etty exhibited at the Academy in 1830, only two were new subjects, for the third, *Judith Going Forth*, was a continuation of the *Judith* series. At first, this picture, hung prominently in the Great Room, was praised by *The Times* in the general notice of the exhibition, but in a more detailed criticism the reviewer either underwent a change of heart, or was replaced by another critic, since in a more general and prolonged attack on the privileges enjoyed by Academicians, Etty's works, along with those by Ward, Turner and Rossi, were mercilessly slanged. Nothing pleased: the proportions of the figures, the colour, and Etty's lack of taste were the chief complaints. It was also objected that Etty had shown Judith with her face turned from the spectator, an innovation stoutly defended by the artist. 'It is a principle with me, as far as lies in my power, to endeavour to make my heroes or heroines act as they would do if placed in similar circumstances in reality; without thinking or caring which way they turn their faces: endeavouring to forget all consciousness of Art . . . I have a strong feeling that, under the dangerous part she was then playing, her first feeling and anxious care would be, how far the guards were insensible of what she had done.' Further, he had considered 'how much may sometimes be gained by leaving something to the spectator's imagination. It seemed to me the natural and spontaneous mode of feeling and telling the story.' [1] This, perhaps, more than anything shows how far Etty had moved away from the neo-classicism of an earlier generation. But his 'realism' consists primarily of what he considered to be a literal interpretation of an event remote in time; and this conception of realism must not be confused with that of, say, Courbet, who often chose his subject-matter from the minor, but recurring, themes of everyday life, and then invested them with a quality of timelessness. This distinction between the two interpretations will become even clearer from a study of Etty's later work.

The other two paintings were no more favourably received. *Candaules, King of Lydia, showing his Wife by stealth to Gyges* was deservedly criticized, then more on account of its subject, although now it may certainly be reckoned of poorer artistic quality than *The Storm* [pl. 34*a*], exhibited at the same time—although even this was accounted a 'sad failure' by the otherwise favourably disposed *Gentleman's Magazine*.[2] Like the *Hero* of 1829, *The Storm* is very sombre in tone and for the most part thinly painted, but the two figures stand out against a deep red cloak which billows out behind them (a too obvious device, perhaps), while the man is draped in a rich golden brown robe; the woman is perfunctorily clothed with some ultramarine drapery over her knee, and these, with the white sail, provide almost all the positive colour there is in the picture. In the top right-hand corner are about eighteen strips of various colours, which suggests that Etty had evolved a very careful colour harmony. Once again there is the strong diagonal composition reminiscent of Géricault's *Radeau de la Méduse;* but the subject as presented by Etty does not move us very deeply. As so often happens with his work, it is the painting as such which attracts, rather than the moral it may contain.

[1] Gilchrist, *op. cit.*, I, p. 287. *The Times*, 1st and 4th May, and 12th, 20th and 23rd July, 1830.
[2] *Gentleman's Magazine*, C, May, 1830, p. 444, and June, 1830, p. 542.

CHAPTER SIX

'A DECENT COMPETENCY': 1831-1835

However unsympathetic Etty may have been towards political reform and revolution whether at home or abroad, he reacted to a tense situation with great gusto. On a visit to Paris in 1830, he found himself walking straight into the battle during the 'Glorious Three Days' of the July Revolution; and the vivid account of his experiences written to Thomas Bodley soon after his return suggests that he might well have made an excellent journalist, had he not lacked completely an understanding of the wider implications involved, essential to a good political correspondent.

After paying a visit to Bodley at Brighton on the way, Etty had arrived in Paris by early July. There he found other relatives, Walter's wife and her daughters Jane and Patty, as well as his pupil Leigh, two of the Bulmer family, Bishop Luscombe (an old acquaintance) and Mr. Isaac Brandon: together these formed an English outpost to make life easier for the artist, who confessed to not liking Paris as well as once he did. As a storm raged outside, he wrote to his niece Betsy, 'The thunder peals louder and louder: as if God spoke in anger to the gay and giddy multitude of Paris (and all of us indeed), as they crowd to the theatres, balls, and *cafés*. What a place it is! If I had a daughter, she should *not* be educated here. Pleasure and amusement are the idols.'[1] (This from the man who but a year earlier had been attacked for impropriety and lasciviousness in his paintings!) Betsy was Etty's unmarried niece, and she had been with him as housekeeper since 1824, remaining a loyal companion until his death. She was afterwards married twice, first to a chemist, Stephen Binnington in May, 1850, then on his death, to Mr. Ince. Etty always had a strong affection for Betsy, and his letters to her reveal a fatherly solicitude for her well-being; as he grew older and more infirm, his dependence upon her increased, while she, for her part, did all that could be expected in ministering to her uncle's needs and habits.

In this same letter, Etty speaks of his visits to the Louvre; already he had begun the first of five copies accomplished in that hectic month. The subject was Giorgione's *Fête Champêtre*, and Etty completed the copy on 13th July [pl. 35*b*]. Like the Uffizi *Venus* copy, it is done in great detail, although this time only two-thirds the size of the original. It

---

[1] Gilchrist, *op. cit.*, I, p. 290: letter to Elizabeth Etty, Sunday, 11th July, 1830. Perhaps the unfavourable reference to a Paris education was an indirect criticism of Walter, whose daughter Jane Elizabeth was at school there (a fact recorded in Etty's letter to Thomas Bodley, 13th July, 1830, York City Reference Library).

has been done with great skill and understanding but is perhaps more thinly painted, especially in the foreground, than its Venetian prototype. Another of his copies was of Titian's *Supper at Emmaus* and yet another of Jacob van Ruisdael's *Fresh Breeze: Sea Coast*. What the other two copies were is unrecorded. Delacroix, it will be remembered, had copied the *Fête Champêtre* just six years before.[1] Caught up in the political unrest as an unwilling spectator, Etty insisted on continuing to paint in the Louvre even during some of the worst moments of the Revolution; and it is somewhat amusing to see him wandering around the Paris streets, quite regardless of his own safety, slightly bewildered and yet genuinely moved by the scenes of bloodshed and fervour. He afterwards admitted that it was an experience that he would not have missed, but certainly one he would not want to repeat. On 31st July he managed to salvage his five copies from a cupboard in the Louvre where a porter had thrust them three days earlier. Then, escorting his friends, he made for England at the earliest opportunity. A plan to visit Brussels and Antwerp was wisely abandoned.

After the alarms of France follow those which touched him more nearly. Despite an initial defeat, the Dean and Chapter of York Minster renewed their attempts to get the Screen moved, and there followed a pitched battle between the two factions. Etty again roused his friends and wrote long letters to London, Edinburgh and Yorkshire papers; some of the county families came to the aid of the 'Preservers', until finally, in February, 1831, the day was won and the Screen saved from destruction. The campaign had taken up much of Etty's time and energies, but no sacrifice seemed too great when the welfare of the Minster was threatened.

In a notebook of about this date occurs the following declaration: 'It appears to me then that virtuous happiness being our lawful aim in life, that having Academic Rank and Fame the next thing to be considered (if God approve) is to seek that Decent Competency which shall make my latter days comfortable and happy, which I hope if it please Him, to be able to do by the time I am fifty—by occasionally mixing with my historic picture a Portrait or two, and to vary and extend my sphere—a classic Landscape or two so that if I can get about 100 a year I may be enabled to retire to my dear native city and spend my latter days in peace.'[2] Written when he was about forty-three, after a prolonged struggle for recognition, it shows him quietly reflecting upon his prospects and demanding little of the world save peace and security. It may sound dull and unambitious, yet in the same notebook a little before this quotation, he wrote, 'If it please Almighty God to bless my exertions I may . . . do great things with his blessing and powerful aid—without it nothing.' Although Etty still clung to history painting as the *ne plus ultra*, he now began to give more prominence to lesser works: age, and the need to pay off debts and provide for himself, slowly force him into painting increasingly trivial pieces.[3] To this potentially dangerous state of affairs was added the hazard of

[1] *Journal de Eugène Delacroix*, ed. Joubin, Paris, 1950, I, p. 75.

[2] From a notebook in the possession of Mr. Jacobus J. T. Bosch.

[3] Gilchrist, *op. cit.*, I, p. 358, quotes a note from Walter Etty of 26th May, 1831, to his brother, which was a financial statement; and an identical note occurs in Etty's own '*Cash Book*' (City Art Gallery, York). £3,937 had been paid out on William Etty's behalf, and £3,133 received, leaving a debt owing to Walter of £804. Nothing could give so clear an idea of the extent to which Walter had helped his brother, nor, as may be seen from subsequent entries in the '*Cash Book*', how William was prompt to settle his debts whenever the opportunity arose.

unintelligent patronage, especially on the part of dealers, who debauched Etty's imaginative capacities and diverted his attention to painting sentimental simpering nymphs and cupids. It was to be Etty's tragedy that he allowed himself to become exhausted by such work, leaving him quite literally neither physical nor mental strength for 'great things'. Any suggestion that the next twenty years of his career was a period of unrelieved gloom and decay would, however, be quite false. Often when it is least expected there flash out those gleams of brilliance which redeem his reputation; only now the scale and subject have altered.

'Took Room in Soho Square The 18th October 1830'; and then follow details of payments to his landlord Hookham. This room is no doubt identical with that later referred to as the 'Academy Soho-Square', and it seems more than likely that Etty may have rented an extra studio at this time, which he retained at least until 1839. The same notebook also contains the timetable followed most days by the artist. Rising at seven, he would breakfast at eight and begin painting either at nine or ten o'clock, depending upon whether he entertained a visitor to breakfast, and would continue work until four, at which hour he dined. This meal finished an hour later, would be followed by a walk, and at six he would be at the Academy. Sometimes he stayed the full two hours in the Academy Life School, but often he divided his time equally between the Academy and the Saint Martin's Lane Life Class. By ten he had returned home and, after drinking a nightcap of tea ('two Cups only'), he retired to bed at midnight or thereabouts. He seems to have laid down for himself a strict daily routine, even to the extent of fixing the amount of tea or wine he should drink with each meal. Some nine years later he decided to abstain from wine altogether, perhaps on medical advice or as an act of self-discipline. When a victim to asthma in later years, the journey to the Academy on a foggy evening would often be quite agonizing for the ageing Etty, and for one so abstemious it must have been doubly hurtful to be accused by some ignorant passer-by of drunkenness, as gasping for breath, he groped for support.[1]

The Academy exhibition of 1831 shows Etty attempting a new type of subject-matter. This was the *Window in Venice, during a Festa* [pl. 37a], a simple yet ingenious composition and much freer in technique. The rich brocaded dresses have been dashed in with thick layers of paint, and there is rather less subtlety of glazing on these parts, since the artist has relied upon a much bolder method of modelling. The curiously shaped fingers on the left hand of the woman in the foreground are probably the result of bad restoration, since a study for this picture had no such distressing feature. It would not be inaccurate to call this picture the secular equivalent of a Venetian *sacra conversazione*, but besides this more obvious parallel, the work also recalls paintings by Bonington in a similar vein. The picture was bought by Robert Vernon for £120, the same man buying the *Candaules* of a previous year; and Vernon may be taken as one of the first of a new type of patron upon whom Etty was to rely so much as time went on. Although Vernon's history is well known, it is perhaps worth remembering that while he made no claims to an extensive knowledge of Old Master paintings, being gifted with a good eye for pictures he found great pleasure in patronizing the leading artists of his day—and by his business acumen as an Army contractor he had sufficient wealth with which to indulge his tastes. On his death in 1847, the National Gallery, in accordance with his will, chose

---

[1] Gilchrist, *op. cit.*, II, pp. 182–3.

160 pictures from his collection—almost all by English artists of his own lifetime. Eleven Ettys became national property in this way.

The other paintings exhibited that year included the last of the *Judith* series, *The Maid of Judith waiting outside the Tent of Holofernes*; *Nymph Angling* [pl. 37*b*, as *Love's Angling*]; *The Shipwrecked Mariner*; and *Sabrina*. The Maid of Judith was said to be 'very well-executed; but the subject is hardly worth the labour that has been bestowed upon it. One picture representing the principal event in this history would have been enough.'[1] Churlish perhaps, but not unjust. The *Sabrina* [pl. 38*b*], illustrating lines in Milton's *Comus*, 'Sabrina fair, . . . The loose train of thy amber dropping hair', has a curious dream-like quality about it, an effect heightened by the ambiguous positions of the four main figures, who apparently form a tight parallelogram floating in space, while ghostly figures hover in the sky. Sabrina's pose is not unlike that found in Michelangelo's *Leda* group, and it may be that a *Nude Female Study* [pl. 38*a*, as *Leda*], now in the collection of the Earl of Sandwich, was made with this picture in mind. Etty would also have had an opportunity of studying Rosso Fiorentino's large cartoon after Michelangelo's *Leda*, for it had been presented to the Academy by William Lock the Younger in 1821. However, there is a marked difference in conception between the solidly modelled figure done from the Life, with its robust spontaneity, and the slim, elegant creatures in the *Sabrina*. This inconsistency may be explained by the gradual change in Etty's use of his Life studies. Until now it seems that he had used the studies made from his models as guides throughout the process of painting a finished work, whether large or small. This was so in his Diploma work, in his *Manlius* and in *The Combat*, to name but three examples; but in a notebook for this period occur the remarks 'Models from MEMORY' (*c.* 1830) and 'Fill your Memory with Natural Attitudes' (*c.* 1835–39), or again 'Mem. Not to Copy after this year [1830?] either Pictures or . . . but Design from Memory . . .'.[2] Etty was now relying much more upon a store of memories and ingrained knowledge of the human form when he actually composed and painted his figures. Such a method could result in greater freedom of invention without any loss of formal skill; for although in the same book he wrote, 'FORM Antique and Fine Nature; COLOR Venetian and Nature; Chiaroscuro Correggio, Rembrandt, Rubens and Nature. "Nature supreme over all",' he appears to have realized that in representing the human form, the ultimate result is an idealization of many images and impulses received during the course of the work. What emerges conforms less to a particular aspect of the model than to a preconceived notion of what the model ought to look like. Accidents of pose, colouring and physical type are incidental, a fact which he had partially grasped in 1816, when he wrote of concentrating upon 'the more general lines of the Figure', and of seizing upon some 'leading trait'.[3]

It would be rash to assume that all the Academy Life School students of 1831 were aware of this philosophical ideal; and an emphasis upon truth to Nature (in the narrower sense) might have been encouraged by Constable's innovation of placing the model in the pose of Eve, and surrounding her with a Garden of Eden composed of evergreen branches brought from the grounds of his house at Hampstead. The novelty

[1] *The Times*, 6th May, 1831.
[2] Notebook belonging to Mr. Jacobus J. T. Bosch. The underlinings are Etty's.
[3] Gilchrist, *op. cit.*, I, p. 55.

was much admired both by the students and by Etty, who, as Visitor in 1832, arranged a much more ambitious *tableau vivant* consisting of several models with full *décor* of antique remains, two altars, blazing tripods, fruit and flowers, to illustrate the subject of *Venus Sacrificing to the Graces*.

More than ten years after he had made the first study for this picture, Etty completed what is still one of his best-known works, *Youth on the Prow, and Pleasure at the Helm* [pl. 39]. Exhibited at the Academy, it was greatly admired for Etty's usual qualities of fine colour and poetic fancy, but despite these virtues, it must be confessed that the picture is singularly inept; and with its inconsistencies of scale and composition it recalls the *Cleopatra*. Although both paintings were conceived at about the same time, it is quite surprising that after so many years Etty should have produced such an immature work. Constable's acid comments on this picture are not entirely unmerited; yet the savage frenzy of the notice which appeared in the *Morning Chronicle* of 8th June, makes it now seem only the more amazing that such prurience should be provoked by so harmless a work. Another picture, also of the 'bumboat' class, was Etty's *Phaedria and Cymochles, on the Idle Lake* [pl. 43a], very lush in colour and sentiment. Here, for the first time, he exploits the erotic effect of juxtaposing Phaedria's naked flesh and the gleaming metal of Cymochles's armour. This device recurs quite frequently, but is of course, not peculiar to Etty. The picture was bought for £105 by Wynne Ellis, Esq., M.P.[1] Ellis, an advanced liberal ('radical' might be too strong a description), had entered politics after establishing himself as one of the largest silk mercers in London, and he was one of several Whig politicians among Etty's patrons.

The third picture exhibited at this year's Academy, like the *Youth on the Prow*, was also a development of a sketch dating from 1822, and is described by Gilchrist as a commissioned work but for whom intended is not disclosed. Its title was grandiloquent, *The Destroying Angel and Daemons of Evil, interrupting the Orgies of the Vicious and Intemperate* [pl. 44], and it was further noted as 'A finished sketch of that class of compositions called by the Romans "Visions", not having their origin in history or poetry.' This explanation provoked some smart remarks from *The Times* critic who progessed himself unable 'to understand what class of composition that is which originates neither in history nor poetry—no doubt Mr. Etty does; but as far as we can comprehend his picture, which is much more intelligible than his language, it represents a quantity of able-bodied demons, who appear angry at the ladies for having stayed out so long, and who are come to fetch them home accordingly'.[2] Nevertheless, it is conceded that the picture has great power, and as a sketch, its incomplete background may thus be excused. Although the idea for this picture lay dormant in Etty's mind over ten years, the result could hardly illustrate better his attempts to 'Design from Memory'. Using his accumulated knowledge of the human figure, Etty has here presented us with an assembly of Life studies, but studies at one remove, so to speak, from the Life academy. The point perhaps becomes more obvious when one notices the recurrence of certain poses, such as the extremely foreshortened figures in the front of the picture or the dancing 'maenad' behind the demon holding aloft a torch; and having noted them, compare them with

[1] *'Cash Book'* (City Art Gallery, York), entry for 30th August, 1832. *See* also *D.N.B.*, VI, for further details of Wynne Ellis.

[2] *The Times*, 24th May, 1832.

The World Before the Flood, Hero expiring, or even *Cleopatra.* The two central figures are reminiscent of a *Venus and Adonis* group, but this time apparently in the guise of Paris and Helen, whilst the avenging angel seems to be inspired by the figure of the soldier in Tintoretto's *Massacre of the Innocents* (Scuola di San Rocco). At one time the picture had been catalogued as a 'Last Judgment'.

It is a sobering thought that this picture is perhaps the nearest English equivalent to Delacroix's *Mort de Sardanapale;* for although Etty claimed (perhaps rashly) that the *Destruction of the Temple of Vice* had cost him months of arduous study and was a work into which he had thrown his whole soul, it fails to capture our imagination for long, if at all. William Carey would have found such a conclusion quite unsupportable: indeed, writing under his pseudonym 'Ridolfi', he addressed three letters to the editor of the *Yorkshire Gazette,* in which he extravagantly praised this painting and Etty's work in general. After rambling off into long descriptions of the picture, Carey suggests that Etty has fully proved himself a master of technique and 'is not, therefore, any longer called on for a similar display on *ideal* subjects. . . . It is now in his interest, and will be to the advantage of the British School, to devote his pencil wholly to the field of legitimate history'; and it is to the poets Shakespeare, Milton, Thomson and others, that Etty should turn for inspiration.[1] Thus history painting had been finally debased to 'poetry on canvas', and this conception was to dominate the minds of many private patrons for at least a generation.

After his Scottish tour and visit to the Lake District of the previous year, Etty's holiday took the customary form of a stay in York, and he arrived there from London in September. He was pleased to see that the city walls and Bootham Bar were being repaired, for these had been the objects first of attack by the City Corporation and then of defence by Etty and his friends, who wanted them to be restored wherever possible. Nor were Etty's restoring activities confined to York, as in the February of the following year he spoke in support of a plan to repair St. Alban's Abbey and in the same year became a member of the Committee of Restoration controlling the preservation of the Lady Chapel of St. Saviour's, Southwark.[2] He had, in fact, begun to acquire some reputation as a defender of antiquities, if not as an antiquarian, and he could always rely upon the support of his friend Lewis Cottingham, elected in May 1832 a Fellow of the Society of Antiquaries. During this stay at York in 1832, he was fêted by many of the local dignitaries, and at last began to receive some modicum of recognition in his native city. But dinner-parties did not absorb all his energies, and he found time to paint an excellent portrait of *James Atkinson* [pl. 42], a well-known, if somewhat eccentric surgeon and a founder member of the Yorkshire Philosophical Society. Elected to honorary membership of the Society in 1829, Etty had become a warm friend of Atkinson, and in this portrait he has captured the rugged humour and strong intellect of his sitter. Deep and cool in tone, broadly yet finely painted, this portrait

---

[1] *Ridolfi's Critical Letters on the Style of Wm. Etty, Esq., R.A.* . . . *etc.,* pp. 33–4. These letters, of October and November 1832, with additional notes, were published privately in London in 1833, and 500 copies were printed, all for gratuitous distribution. The cost of this enterprise was borne by Henry Payne (letter from Payne to Etty, 8th February, 1833; York City Reference Library).

[2] *Gentleman's Magazine,* CIII, February, 1833, p. 170, contains an account of the meeting at the Thatched House Tavern, London. St. Saviour's is now Southwark Cathedral. Gilchrist, *op. cit.,* I, pp. 343–4.

shows Etty again using his favourite device of a very dark reddish-brown background, only relieved by the plum red damask of the chair-back and the dark green tablecloth. Atkinson's fresh complexioned face, fluffy grey-white hair and white shirt contrast dramatically with the sombreness of his black coat and dark surroundings. His hands are painted with a freedom of style akin to that used in the hands of a late self-portrait by Courbet, the *Courbet à Sainte-Pélagie*. The picture won the whole-hearted admiration not only of York society, but also of Wilkie, who thought it one of the finest in England.

Etty sent four paintings to the Academy exhibition of 1833, only three of which need be dealt with in detail. *The Lute Player* [pl. 43*b*] is a more elaborate variation of the *Window in Venice*. Although it is small in scale and hardly more than a study, the delicate glazes on the women's dresses, and the great deftness with which he has brushed in the modelling of the fingers and hands give an extremely vibrant effect. But nearly two years later Etty painted a second *Lute Player* (Tate Gallery) [pl. 48] in which all the glittering brilliance of his technique is brought to perfection. In this picture the negro servant's dress has been painted so thinly that the pigment, dragged over the surface of the panel, allows the grain of the wood to show through and produce the texture suggestive of a coarser fabric, in contrast with the satins and silks of the other figures. Still more interesting is the fact that glimpses of the underpainting seen through the lute player's cap show Etty to be using the typical Rubens device of washing streaks of thin brown paint over a grey undersurface. It is understandable that Sir E. L. Bulwer (later Lord Lytton) should remark, after examining a work of this kind, '. . . the prevalent characteristic of the English school of painting at this moment is the MATERIAL. You see bold execution and glaring colours, but there is an absence of sentiment—nothing raises, elevates, touches, or addresses the soul, in the vast majority of our artists. I attribute this, indeed, mainly to the little sway that Religion in these days exercises over the imagination. It is perfectly clear that Religion must, in painting and in sculpture, inspire the most ideal conceptions; for the artist seeking to represent the images of Heaven, must necessarily raise himself beyond the earth.'[1] Nor does he mean only the Christian religion, but Religion in its more general metaphysical sense. Then follows a brief appraisal of the more famous living British history painters, during the course of which he says, 'Etty, practised in the colours of the Venetian painters, if not strictly of the Historical School, can be classed in no other. His beauties are in a vigorous and fluent drawing, and bursts of brilliancy and light, amidst an imitative affectation of the errors as well as excellence of the Venetian School.'[2] Already, it would seem Etty is beginning to lose slightly his reputation as a history painter, although to be fair, it should be added that in this essay Bulwer sets out to laud John Martin as the great painter of the day, or at least 'the most original genius of his age'.

Presumably *Hylas and the Nymphs* [pl. 47*a*], also exhibited in 1833, would not have completely satisfied Bulwer as a history piece either, despite its classical subject. Yet this is among the most ingenious of Etty's compositions, and it is surprising just how well the two halves of the picture hold together. The group of Naiades surrounding the slightly effeminate figure of Hylas, immediately suggests the *Youth on the Prow* and Rubens's

[1] Sir E. L. Bulwer, Bart., *England and the English*, London, 1840 (1st edition, 1833), Chap. IX, 'The State of the Arts', pp. 497–8.
[2] *Ibid.*, p. 502.

'Water Nymph' from the Marie de Médicis paintings; but what emerges most clearly is Etty's ability to suggest the landscape setting without needing to particularize. Also, he has again achieved a harmony by neutral tints, and the distraught figure of Hercules is almost entirely in monochrome. Unfortunately, he has resorted to bitumen in an attempt to increase the richness of his shadows, with the usual harmful results. Even Etty could succumb to this temptation at times.

His third picture was of a subject from Spenser, *Britomart Redeemes Faire Amoret* [pl. 46]. Like the *Phaedria and Cymochles* it is richly coloured, but darker and more resonant in tone, and Etty has captured something of the exotic fancifulness of his Elizabethan source. A brilliant crimson and white plume waves from Britomart's helmet; her glistening armour reflects the orange-red hue of Amoret's robe, and the vivid emerald green of the enchanter's *culotte*; even the architecture, with its exaggerated curves and bloated forms, heightens the sensuous effect of the whole painting. How very different from Stothard's *Britomart taking off her helmet and revealing her sex*; yet in both paintings the artists have chosen a moment of dramatic surprise.[1] Where Etty borders on melodrama in much gentler mood Stothard conveys a feeling of rapt suspense and poses his figures with more deliberate sophistication.

During the same year the church of St. Edmund the King and Martyr, Lombard Street, underwent some repairs, and Etty painted two panels for the carved wooden reredos. This reredos follows the usual seventeenth-century pattern of four side bays, the outer two of which contain panels of the Lord's Prayer and Creed, whilst the inner two in this example, have paintings of Moses and Aaron on the left- and right-hand side of the altar respectively. The panels are quite large, $52\frac{3}{4} \times 23\frac{1}{2}$ inches, and although obscured by dirty varnish, they are in good condition and quite impressive. *Aaron* [pl. 49] is the more successful of the two pictures, and the figure, unlike that of the *Moses*, does not suffer from seeming to be cramped into too small a space. But both figures have great vitality and appear caught in mid-action; Aaron swings a censer, and Moses, holding the blossoming rod, moves forward with his left hand outstretched as if presenting Aaron to the people. Unfortunately, the right hand and arm of Moses appear distorted, as Etty has not sufficiently shown the extent to which they are held away from the body. Both figures are set against a Vandyck brown background, and in the *Moses* there is a faint outline of the floor space. As befits the semi-monumental character of the pictures, Etty has modelled the robes and limbs of the two prophets with thick, vigorous strokes, which tend to conceal the fact that a considerable amount of detail has gone into the heads of both, and Aaron's vestments are most carefully, yet broadly treated. The *Aaron* glows with colour, the gold patterning on the priest's white under-robe gives an effect as of damask, while his red surcoat has a broad viridian green hem; these colours are given added richness by the white headdress and the golden censer and chain. The heavily impasted jewelled breastplate, even in its present condition, still glistens and catches the light. The *Moses* is less brilliantly coloured, for subdued bottle-green robes conceal a red under-tunic; but orange-yellow flames spring from his temples. The Etty family had close connections with the church of St. Edmund the King. The names of the

[1] This picture, painted in 1786, was No. 52 in the Old Masters' Exhibition, Burlington House, 1881, when it belonged to J. C. Robinson, Esq. It was lot 23 in the Northcliffe Sale, Christie's, 20th April, 1923.

artist's uncle William and his wife Elizabeth, their children, and those of Etty's brother Walter and his wife and family, appear frequently in the parish registers from 1773 until 1830, and probably beyond. It is not inconceivable that Etty may have painted these panels as a gift to the church, or at most, for a nominal fee.

This is a convenient place to introduce Etty's self-appointed mentor and fertile source of gratuitous advice, Thomas Myers, junior. An enthusiastic admirer of Etty, he had begun writing to him in 1832, and besides quoting extracts from newspaper criticisms supplemented by his own comments, he advised Etty upon subjects and authors which he thought were both congenial to the artist, and likely to take the public's fancy.[1] Thomas Myers was a tenacious but not unpleasant character, and Etty seems to have borne him with humour and patience. His letters are not entirely valueless, for they hint at the tastes of some of the wealthier patrons, although it is difficult to decide just how accurately. One delightful idea that occurred to Myers was as follows: 'Let me', he writes, '. . . recommend you to take some of your female faces—I wish you could get their figures too!—from *our aristocracy*—Mrs. Lane Fox, Lady Ellenborough, Lady Harrington etc. You might do this *quietly*—& it, certainly, would raise the demand for your works—both with those who did & those who did not, find out the likeness. There is fashion even in Beauty, in some degree.'[2] He also suggested that Etty should exhibit at the Brussels Salon, following John Martin's example and success, but he seemed not to realize that Martin had been invited to send a picture by King Leopold.[3] In another letter, of 26th December, he reiterates his plea that Etty should paint a *Fall of Phaeton*, to illustrate Book V of Lucretius, which he thinks should be the size of Turner's *Childe Harold's Pilgrimage—Italy* (1832, Tate Gallery), and which would attract the attention of Sir Robert Peel. On 21st September he had quoted at length lines from William Wordsworth's *Boy* and Thomas Moore's *Girl* (*Irish Melodies*), as subjects likely to please the young Princess Victoria at the next year's British Institution exhibition, since these were two of her favourite poets!

Gilchrist underrated Myers's influence, and wrote as if Etty was never inspired to act upon any of his suggestions. To some extent he had been dishonest, for while it is true that Etty ignored much of Myers's advice, it seems more than likely that he was responsible for Etty painting his gigantic *The Sirens and Ulysses*. When Myers was staying with Mr. Jee, a brother-in-law of the late Lord de Tabley, he learnt that Lord de Tabley had intended to give Etty a commission, but had died before being able to do so. (By his death not only Etty but many other British artists had been deprived of a most liberal and enthusiastic patron.) Two subjects had been considered, one, *Thetis ordering the Nereids to descend into the Sea*, taken from Book 18, line 177, of Pope's translation

---

[1] Thomas Myers, an Etonian, was admitted to Lincoln's Inn on 15th January, 1824. He was entered as 'Thomas Myers, jun., late of Oriel College, Oxford (aged 20), only son of Thomas Myers of Tilney Street, May Fair, esq.' He was called to the Bar on 24th January, 1831, but apparently did not attempt to practise law. Myers's letters to Etty are now in the City Reference Library, York: the first dated letter is of 25th July, 1832, the last is 4th May, 1844. Gilchrist refers to him, although not by name, *op. cit.*, II, pp. 75–6.

[2] Thomas Myers, jun., to Etty, 23rd December, 1833. This was no new idea, for example many of the female nudes which appear in the work of the Fontainebleau School were portraits of court ladies.

[3] Thomas Balston, *John Martin*, London, 1947, p. 111. *The Fall of Nineveh* (1829) was the painting shown in Brussels.

F

of Homer's *Iliad*; the other, *The Sirens*, also from Pope's Homer, this time Book 12 of the *Odyssey*. After passing on these details, Myers continues, 'Flaxman has designed *both* subjects, in outline, in his Illustrations of Homer, published by Longman. *See them too*. He has considerably overcome the difficulty of the lower parts of the figures of the Sirens being those of fish.'[1] Etty seems to have been quick to take the hint, for Gilchrist notes that *Ulysses* was 'projected in 1834', but suppresses all mention of Lord de Tabley and of Myers.[2]

Towards the end of 1833 Etty painted an extremely fine portrait of *Miss Elizabeth Potts* [pl. 45*a*], which was exhibited at the Academy the following year. Once again, the sitter's parents were friends of the artist, although he was first introduced to them by Thomas Bodley; in any case, Miss Potts was a most attractive subject and Etty has done full justice to her charms. Half laughing at himself, he once asked to be remembered to 'the young lady with tresses like the moon! stilts again'.[3] The portrait combines all the glittering richness of *The Lute Player* with the stone archway composition first used in the *Window in Venice*, and again Etty has masked its shape with pale silvery-green vine leaves and a plum red curtain. Against a warm, golden brown background, Miss Potts, with blonde hair, blue eyes and fresh complexion smiles serenely beyond the spectator, as she sits in all her finery of gold bracelets and brooches. Clad in a white dress she seems to radiate light, and Etty has achieved a silvery, gossamer-like effect in his treatment of the transparent muslin sleeves, which envelope but do not conceal the arms, so delicately have they been glazed over. The dress itself is thickly impasted, with much use of the palette knife evident but never uncontrolled, for bluish-grey shadows give solidity to the bodice and shoulders. Her hands are suggested with great sensitivity rather than firmly outlined, and Etty seems quite deliberately to have focussed more sharply upon the head and shoulders, with full regard to the total optical effect thus gained. The head is gracefully tilted, and where the falling tresses cast a shadow on the left side of the face, Etty has brushed in strong Indian red—just as on the other side of the neck and cheek, in shadow but lit by reflected light, he has obtained a translucent effect by rubbing the wet pigment until the canvas shows through underneath, and then glazing thinly over the whole surface. He has also introduced markedly greenish areas into some of these shadows, especially those on the neck, a practice also used by Turner in his *Jessica* of 1829. Some emerald green drapery clasped in her hands, a few flecks of very pale pink and blue in her sash, and a Spanish comb thrust into the *chignon* perched on the back of her head, complete a most exotic painting, and yet one which is extremely cool in tone. The only weakness is the poor articulation of the right arm with the body.

A work of such mature splendour ought to have attracted praise enough, but *The Times* only thought it 'Very admirably painted; somewhat gaudy, and not in pure taste; but its faults are more than outbalanced by a very fine picture, the work of the same hand, *The Cardinal*.' With greater gallantry, the *Gentleman's Magazine* preferred *Miss Potts*.[4] Etty received 65 guineas for this picture. Elizabeth's father, Thomas Potts of

[1] Thomas Myers, jun., to Etty, 14th January, 1834, from Thaxted Vicarage, Essex. Sir John Fleming Leicester, 1st Baron de Tabley, died in 1827, aged 65.

[2] Gilchrist, *op. cit.*, II, p. 52.

[3] Letter to Thomas Bodley, 'Saturday Dec. 8, 1832' (York City Reference Library).

[4] *The Times*, 6th May, 1834; and *Gentleman's Magazine*, London, I (New Series), June 1834, p. 630.

Clapham Common, also interests us as the early patron of William Edward Frost, R.A.; and writing to Bodley on 19th December, 1832, in answer to a request for help, Etty recommends that 'young *Frost*, (Mr. Potts protégé) would be very likely to do it well and reasonable—he is a very clever modest lad—only mind and don't tumble in with a Frost'.[1] The 'it' referred to was a portrait of Mrs. Grote. As early as 1825, when Frost was only fifteen years old, he had been introduced to Etty who advised him to study at Sass's School in Bloomsbury. Again through Etty's help, Frost was enabled to work in the British Museum, and by 1829 he was accepted as a student in the Academy Schools. Etty seems to have been his chief adviser, and although he was never a pupil of Etty in the strict sense (as was James Leigh), his work is strongly influenced by that of the older master.[2] Even at its best it is only a pale reflection of Etty's style, but a number of Frost's paintings are still mistaken for Etty's or are sometimes hopefully promoted to that status. In November, 1938, an album of Frost's pen and watercolour drawings was exhibited as being by Etty. They are mainly groups of nude male and female figures, and are altogether much freer and more exaggerated in style than any by Etty [pl. 51*a*]. Proof of their real authorship exists in a decorative frontispiece to this album, signed 'April 13, 1835 W. E. Frost', which was acquired by Lord Methuen [pl. 51*b*]. These drawings, which had been removed from their original binding, are now dispersed: some belong to the Fogg Museum and the Witt Collection, some are still in private collections, while others have appeared frequently in the sale rooms during the past four years masquerading as Ettys.

Of the three pictures sent to the British Institution in 1834, that of *Christ Appearing to Mary Magdalen* [pl. 54*b*], was first intended as an illustration for *The Sacred Annual for 1834*. This was a spurious publication put out by John Turrill, the publisher of Robert Montgomery's epic poem *The Messiah* of 1832. Seizing a chance to profit by the popularity of this work, Turrill decided to produce it under a new guise two years later, embellished with twelve hand-coloured lithographs after paintings specially commissioned from Martin, Haydon, Etty and others.[3] Apparently Etty was so dissatisfied with the final engraving that he sent the original oil sketch to the British Institution to vindicate himself. The picture is rather loosely composed, and for the most part thickly painted in dark blue-greens and reds. The angels, sketchily brushed in with white, and the dark stormy landscape complete a painting strongly akin to the later work of Tintoretto. This 'sketch' (as it was originally called) has further interest when compared with another *Christ Appearing to Mary Magdalen* painted more than six years later by John Prescott Knight, R.A. [pl. 54*a*].[4] In composition, Knight's painting is almost identical with Etty's, but in reverse. The soldier has been omitted, and instead Christ

---

[1] Etty to Bodley, 19th December, 1832 (York City Reference Library), and Gilchrist, *op. cit.*, I, p. 354. Again in 1835 Etty recommends 'young Frost of Wandsworth' to Bodley (letter to Bodley, 29th March, 1835; York City Reference Library).

[2] *The Art Journal*, London, 1st June, 1849, p. 184.

[3] Balston, *John Martin*, London, 1947, pp. 153–4, gives a detailed and amusing account of the whole enterprise. It has so far proved impossible to see *The Sacred Annual for 1834*; the British Museum's copy was destroyed during the second World War.

[4] City Art Gallery, York: panel, 27¾ × 36 in. This picture was bought at Appleby Brothers, London, in December, 1952, as a work by Etty. For details of its re-attribution to J. P. Knight, R.A., *see* City of York Art Gallery, *Preview*, VII, 28, October, 1954, p. 291.

points to the city of Jerusalem. It is more tightly compressed and as a composition is perhaps more forceful than Etty's picture. The Knight *Christ Appearing to Mary* is much cooler in tone, and has been painted over a priming of Indian red, a method hardly ever used by Etty after the early 1820s. Perhaps the quality distinguishing it most from an Etty is its preciseness of form and composition. The Magdalen is also of a female type rarely met with in Etty's paintings.

Several paintings begun towards the end of 1833 and in the early part of 1834 were not finished in time for that year's Academy show, because Etty fell ill soon after February and continued to be a semi-invalid well into June. The nature of the illness is not definitely stated, but it seems to have been a complete breakdown, and in his misery he wrote to some friends of his inability to finish, 'I know not how much work: full in my sight,—staring me in the face. Yet I feel scarce the strength of a kitten. A severe cough, sore throat, hoarseness, low fever, and soreness all over, deprive me of all interest and pleasure in my pursuit, . . .' [1] By the middle of June he went to convalesce at York, and rented a small cottage on the Mount, just outside the city walls and opposite a mill once occupied by his father. In August he was touring the countryside with his friend John Brook as guide, visiting Poppleton, Gilling Castle, Duncombe Park and Kirkdale. They passed through Lastingham, John Jackson's birthplace, saw his altarpiece of *Christ in the Garden of Olives* in the parish church, as well as a tablet there to the memory of the artist, who had died but three years before. They afterwards called on his mother. Continuing their journey they went first to Rievaulx Abbey and then to Byland Abbey, both delighting Etty with their beauty and idyllic setting, for he always responded to the charms of the picturesque; indeed, he devoted much of his spare time to defending it, whether in the form of ancient fortifications or shop fronts in the older parts of York. The past possessed a romantic appeal which was shared by many of his generation, Sir Walter Scott's *Waverley Novels* are an enduring expression of this form of romanticized antiquarianism, just as in August, 1839, the Earl of Eglington's famous Tournament provided a brilliant, if fleeting, revival of sumptuous medieval pageantry. Most of the summer and autumn were spent by Etty either in York or making sorties to nearby beauty spots in the company of friends, and it was not until early December that he returned to London.

Robert Vernon had again patronized Etty this year by purchasing his picture of *The Persian* [pl. 52], when it was exhibited at the British Institution. This type of picture or 'costume piece' is one of a long sequence of similar works in which Etty has painted simply a head and shoulders study of a man, dressed the figure in a cardinal's robe or a soldier's cuirass, and given some appropriate title. The earliest example of this seems to be *The Jew's Head*, exhibited in 1827 at the British Institution; although the title has been queried, and the painting may be a portrait of an actor in the part of Shylock. Perhaps it is Macready, for there are points of resemblance between the Etty and John Jackson's portrait of *Macready as Virginius*. Of the same class, but more specific in subject is *The Warrior Arming* [pl. 53], exhibited at the Academy of 1835. Etty had begun work on this painting as early as September, 1833, and from the start had had in mind the story of Godfrey of Bouillon, although only at the Society of Arts exhibition was it

[1] Gilchrist, *op. cit.*, I, p. 3. Almost the whole of Chapter XVIII is given over to an account of Etty's illness and convalescence.

called *Godfrey de Bouillon the Crusader arming for Battle*. It is typical of the new interest in medieval history that Etty should turn for guidance to Thomas Keightley's *The Crusaders*, first published in 1834. Curiously enough, however, in a letter to Bodley of 9th September, 1833, Etty quotes a long section from Chapter 23 of this book, 'The Leaders of the Crusades': either Etty received an advance copy, or it was first serialized in some periodical. Keightley's book gives an account of the Crusades based mainly upon Tasso's *Gerusalemme Liberata*, and says of Godfrey of Bouillon that 'His exterior also was agreeable; his features were handsome, his hair a light brown, his person tall, and he was equally strong and active in his limbs'.[1] About this time too, Etty had begun to acquire pieces and even complete suits of armour and chain mail—both for their own sake and, of course, to provide stage properties useful to his art. In connection with this new interest, he carried on some correspondence with Sir Samuel Meyrick, himself a keen collector and then regarded as a great authority on the subject. At least one letter survives from Meyrick to Etty, of 19th February, 1838, in which he discusses the various methods, both European and Oriental, used to clean armour; and also refers to recent sales of armour at Gwennaps.[2]

The picture of *Godfrey de Bouillon* is a most accomplished work, sparkling with colour but not gaudy. The armour is very freely painted and the greenish-blue metal gleams with a multiplicity of reflected lights. As if to offset the coldness of the armour, Etty has painted the plume of the helmet (resting at the left of the picture) a strong crimson, a colour recurring in the negro servant's white turban where it is mingled with streaks of peacock blue. By contrast, Godfrey appears pensive and unaware of his splendour; his beard, perhaps once a lighter colour, is now almost blackened with the effects of bitumen, but one can still see how Etty has used the brush handle to scratch into the wet paint to give an effect of stranded hair. On Godfrey's head is a dull plum red cap, a red ribbon supports the gold crucifix about his neck, and his page lifts a scarf of grey and gold over his master's shoulders. Although both figures are solidly modelled, there is hardly any attempt to define the space in which they stand, and this crowding together of the compositional elements is not unlike that met with in Mannerist portraiture of the mid-sixteenth century; only now, a romantic nostalgia has replaced the neurotic tension which so often marked the work of the earlier period. It must also be remembered that the cult of medievalism was not confined to England. Delacroix had admired the novels of Scott, and often chose subjects based upon events in *Ivanhoe* and *Quentin Durward* (and, be it noted, from Tasso's *Gerusalemme Liberata*). Five years after Etty had painted *Godfrey de Bouillon*, Delacroix had finished the first of his *La Prise de Constantinople par les Croisés*. But Delacroix applied his mind and heart to reading the literature and interpreting the events of the past with a sustained passion and imaginative power far surpassing that of his English counterpart. Although it would be wrong

---

[1] Thomas Keightley, *The Crusaders; or Scenes, Events, and Characters from the Times of the Crusades*, London, 1834, new ed. 1847, p. 24. According to the *D.N.B.*, X, this book was 'Published under the Direction of the Committee of General Literature and Education, appointed by the Society for Promoting Christian Knowledge'.

[2] Letter from Sir Samuel Meyrick to Wm. Etty, R.A., 19th February, 1838 (Victoria and Albert Museum Library). In a letter to Bodley, 17th November, 1837, Etty also speaks of a 'very kind reply to my letter to Sir Samuel Meyrick'.

to call Delacroix humourless, it is difficult to imagine him writing letters to a cousin in mock-medieval idiom such as Etty sent to Bodley at this time.[1]

This year, too, Etty more than made up for his meagre showing at the Academy of 1834; for in addition to *The Warrior Arming*, he sent seven other pictures, the most interesting of these, though not the most noticed, being *The Bridge of Sighs* [pl. 60a]. Enthralled by the macabre associations of the Ponte de' Sospiri, Etty has depicted the moment after an execution has taken place, when the body of the criminal was about to be carried away and dropped into the Lagune. Like Byron before him, Etty visited the Venetian *Prigioni* in May, 1823, and drank in the lurid stories retailed by the guide —stories robbed of much of their glamour since the researches of Ruskin. But the inspiration did not fail the artist, who painted a work of great dramatic force. It is interesting to compare two preparatory sketches, done on the spot, with the finished picture.[2] At first only concerned with accuracy of architectural detail, he afterwards altered his viewpoint, and in the painting the architecture is invested with a Piranesi-like grandeur with walls towering up on each side of the canal. In the shadows, the grey stone takes on a warm ochre hue, in the moonlight it gleams coldly against an intense velvety blue night sky. The two men carrying the corpse are seen silhouetted against the light from an open doorway, the red headdress of one of them showing up brightly in the surrounding darkness. Nowadays, Etty would have found himself designing stage *décor*, and it is not surprising that this picture should have appealed to the actor Macready. When *The Bridge of Sighs* was advertised for sale again in June 1840, Macready called first upon Etty (who was, however, in York at the time), then upon Colnaghi, agreeing to give £40 for it if Colnaghi would negotiate the purchase. The deal was concluded and Macready wrote, 'I do not grudge the money for it. It is to me poetry on canvas. The story of that gloomy canal and its fatal bridge is told at once; there is a history before you and a commentary upon it in the single star that is looking down upon the dark deeds below.'[3] Etty greatly admired Macready, and had been anxious that he should secure the picture.

Three of the pictures shown this year provoked a storm of righteous indignation that quite eclipsed the other Ettys also on view. The three were: *Venus and Her Satellites; Wood Nymphs Sleeping; Satyr bringing Flowers,—Morning;* and *Phaedria and Cymochles on the Idle Lake.* This last was a further instalment of the story portrayed in the painting of 1832, and if the earlier picture may be taken as a guide it is understandable that at the time some exception should be taken to its successor. The *Wood Nymphs Sleeping* [pl. 55] is quite different in character, and yet it too did not escape some scathing comments. Although fairly small, the picture is quite monumental in scale and cleverly constructed, although the rather awkwardly posed sleeping nymph on the left seems slightly out of scale with the other two figures. Etty has sought a far bolder solution here than in his Diploma picture, so closely allied to it in subject and treatment. Not only is the brush-work freer, but the whole work has been carried out with greater *panache* and assurance. If this painting could cause an uproar, what would have been the reaction had Etty shown his *Sleeping Nymph and Satyrs* in 1828? Presumably it would have been declared

---

[1] One long letter and a note, of this kind, undated but *c.* 1834, are in the City Reference Library, York.

[2] *'Cash Book'* (City Art Gallery, York).

[3] *Macready's Reminiscences*, ed. Pollock, II, pp. 161–2. Entries for 24th and 25th June, 1840.

well painted though exceedingly indelicate and quite unfit for public exhibition; for so, at least, the *Wood Nymphs Sleeping* was considered by the critic of the London *Literary Gazette*.[1]

The somewhat larger *Venus and Her Satellites* (more properly a *Toilet of Venus*) [pl. 56] received the longest and harshest attacks. Yet it was not the subject that aroused anger, but its presentation: *The Times* critic wrote of Etty that 'This painter has fallen into an egregious error. He mistakes the use of nudity in painting and presents in the most gross and literal manner the unhappy models of the Royal Academy for the exquisite idealities in which Titian and other masters who have chosen similar subjects revelled. . . ,[2] Enemies of both Constable and Etty found support in a long and venomous tirade contained in *The Observer*, which said of the *Venus* '. . . A brothel on fire, which had driven all the Paphian nymphs from their beds into the courtyard would be a modest exhibition compared to him, for they would at least exhibit *en chemise*. Several ladies we know were deterred from going into the corner of the room to see Leslie's, Webster's and other pictures of merit there, to avoid the offence and disgrace Mr. Etty has conferred on that quarter'[3]. Such prim hypocrisy represented an extreme view, and not everyone shared it, for Thomas Myers wrote to Etty that 'Curiously enough, *Phaedria* "first", & *Sighs* "next", have been reviewed in the *Morning Post*; so favourably that I do not copy the Critiques, lest I should corrupt & seduce your "native modesty"! They have almost turned my head: what would they do to yours, that created the Pictures?'[4] Besides, Etty was able to sell the *Venus*, after refusing one offer, to the Rev. Edward Pryce Owen for just under 300 guineas. Etty took the picture to its new owner when he stayed with Owen that August at his home in Shropshire. There he also painted a portrait of Archdeacon Bather for the local clergy. Owen had bought *The Cardinal* exhibited the previous year, and the artist felt happy that his paintings were in the hands of an appreciative owner, especially the *Venus* which was particularly dear to him.[5] Owen was himself a talented amateur topographical draughtsman and engraver, and had contributed illustrations to his father's *History of Shrewsbury*, which appeared in 1825. Two volumes of engravings, the fruits of his travels abroad, were later privately printed in 1846 and 1855. The figures in the *Venus* fall into a smooth elliptical composition, with those of Mars and a Raphaelesque Homeric musician acting as *repoussoirs*, similar to the formula used in the *Judgment of Paris*. Here, however, the arms and bodies of the figures form a sinewy internal pattern, rather more complex than before; once again Etty has sealed off the space in which his figures are placed, and there is only the faintest hint of some recession provided by the temple columns and a glimpse of landscape. Blond in tone, the painting is suffused with light, and the white-clad Venus acts as a focal point around which the darker colours of her attendants' robes are assembled. The woman holding Mars's shield has an amethyst robe, while the three Graces form a pattern of

[1] *Literary Gazette*, 1835, p. 314.

[2] *The Times*, 23rd May, 1835.

[3] *The Observer*, 10th May, 1835. *See also* Whitley, *Art in England 1821–1837*, pp. 299–300.

[4] Letter from T. Myers, jun., Aldeburgh, 18th May, 1835 (York City Reference Library).

[5] From information contained in three letters from the Rev. E. P. Owen to Etty of 20th and 22nd July, and one of *c*. December, all 1835 (York City Reference Library). Gilchrist, *op. cit.*, II, p. 31. The portrait of Archdeacon Bather was later engraved by S. Cousins, and published by J. Eddowes, Shrewsbury, 1836; *see also* letter from Etty to Bodley, 7th June, 1839 (York City Reference Library).

yellow, pink and ultramarine; the musician's brown mantle balances the more sombre tones of Mars's armour. A very fine study for the figures of the three Graces was acquired by the Metropolitan Museum, New York, in 1906 [pl. 57b].

The second and more finished version of *The Lute Player* [pl. 48], exhibited at the British Institution earlier in the year, is interesting *vis-à-vis* Turner's painting of the *Burning of the Houses of Lords and Commons*, hung in the same room. Apparently not even all the usual brilliance of Etty's palette could equal that of Turner's, and it was remarked how pallid the one looked by comparison with the other. *The Spectator* commented, 'Turner's wonderful picture . . . throws into shade *The Lute Player* by Etty—a group of fair damsels at a window, attired and surrounded with drapery of the most gorgeous hues; but which look as if mud had been the vehicle of the pigment. The brilliancy of Turner's picture is not owing to the more fiery hue: if there be any doubt of this, a glance at Chalon's picture of the same scene, taken from Parliament Street (273) will suffice.' [1] One other painting begun in 1833 and completed for the R.A. of 1835 should also be mentioned, *Preparing for a Fancy-Dress Ball* [pl. 58], which shows two ladies of the Williams Wynn family dressing up in Italian costume. The figures are three-quarter length, done life-size, one woman seated and the other standing to her right. It is a continuation of *The Lute Player* tradition, but this time incorporating portraiture.

Before returning from holiday that year, Etty paid a visit to Manchester where he looked in at the Art Exhibition, and, once recognized, became the centre of attraction. One of the cotton trade magnates showed the artist round his mill, and Etty, usually so conservative by instinct, was moved to wonder at the whirling machinery which accomplished so much, and seemed 'almost endowed with intelligence'.[2] Thrilled as he was by such novelties, he confessed himself glad to escape from the grime and bustle of Manchester into the pure, clear air of York. While at Manchester, however, he made the acquaintance of a wealthy new patron, from whom he received a commission to paint a hundred-guinea picture. This man was Daniel Grant.

[1] A. J. Finberg, *The Life of J. M. W. Turner, R.A.*, Oxford, 1939, p. 352, quotes the criticism at length.
[2] Gilchrist, *op. cit.*, II, pp. 33–4.

CHAPTER SEVEN

FRIENDS AND CRITICS: 1836–1840

IN June 1835 Archibald Keightley, Sir Thomas Lawrence's executor, sold the whole of his fabulous collection of old master drawings to Messrs. Woodburn. This followed a prolonged and exasperating struggle to carry out the terms of Lawrence's will. Early the next year Woodburn's began to exhibit some of the masterpieces from the collection and, in so doing, provoked a last despairing effort by the Academicians to get the drawings purchased for the nation. Like his colleagues, Etty had been quick to see the unique opportunity that had presented itself as soon as the terms of Lawrence's will had become known; but the lamentable story of government apathy and inaction is all too familiar, and it is only necessary to recall some of the efforts made by Etty to arouse public interest before it was too late. The Academy had already voted £1,000 towards the sum of £18,000 needed to buy the collection, and Etty reminds his readers of this in a letter to the *Morning Herald*, 25th February.[1] On 8th June he allowed his studio to be used by a committee of Academicians and other friends who discussed an eleventh-hour plan whereby Parliament might still be prevailed upon to acquire the collection. Wilkie wrote to Etty beforehand, pledging his support but asking to be excused attending the meeting; while C. R. Cockerell, addressing Etty as 'My zealous and valiant friend', promised to put down £20 and to obtain a further ten subscriptions.[2] But all their efforts were to no avail: the drawings were gradually sold off and dispersed. At the Michelangelo exhibition organized by the British Museum in 1953, nearly one hundred of the drawings on view were originally owned by Lawrence, and thus were the public reminded of the superb quality of only part of the collection.

William Beckford commissioned a work from Etty this year, *Adam and Eve at their morning orisons*. Beckford apparently held Etty's work in high esteem, and in this particular painting the artist went to great trouble in searching for models appropriate to his subject. Gilchrist describes some of his difficulties; it seems that Etty wanted a model from whom he could paint the whole figure of Eve, not, as he more often did, making up a figure from the good points of several nude studies. In this picture 'Etty aimed at perfection of Form, and at showing that he could paint a naked man and

---

[1] In a letter to John Sydney Taylor, former editor of the *Morning Herald*, 19th February, 1834.

[2] Letter from Sir David Wilkie, R.A. to William Etty, R.A., 7th June, 1836; Letter from C. R. Cockerell, R.A. to Etty, 10th June, 1836; both in York City Reference Library. *See also* Gilchrist, *op. cit.*, II, pp. 38–43; and Whitley, *Art in England 1821–1837*, pp. 276–80.

woman expressive of pure and devotional feeling'.[1] The picture was first called *Adam and Eve at their Morning Prayers*, and it was probably due to Thomas Myers that Etty changed the title slightly and quoted *Paradise Lost*, Book V, line 140, when the painting was shown at the Royal Academy in 1837.[2] If in Beckford's picture the figures were meant to express 'pure and devotional feeling', that of *The Prodigal Son* [pl. 61b] exhibited at the British Institution in 1836, could scarcely be surpassed as an expression of wretchedness and repentance. It seems characteristic of Etty that, given a theme requiring but few figures, he could concentrate his powers and produce a work of great emotional force. *The Combat*, the two *Hero and Leander* paintings and the Diploma picture all have this quality in common; but the attempt at *terribilità* in the *Destruction of the Temple of Vice* was not entirely successful largely because of its diffuse, overcrowded composition. The dark tone and colours of *The Prodigal Son* accord with the subject and, as in the *Hylas*, Etty varies the texture of his paint considerably in different parts of the picture. Many drawings exist for both the pigs and goat, sometimes of a whole animal, but more often of a snout, a head, or a limb; almost all have been done with soft lead pencil. *The Athenaeum* of April, 1839, describing the sale of this and other Etty paintings from Mr. Stewart's collection, spoke of it as being in his 'blackish-florid style'.

John Harper the architect had organized a loan exhibition at York in the summer of 1836, to which Etty sent eleven pictures, some painted that year and others of earlier date which he had persuaded their respective owners to lend for the occasion. Four portraits were supplied by York citizens. The exhibition paid its way, but the lack of enthusiasm was such as to discourage further attempts of this kind for several years. However, Etty sold his picture *A Family of the Forests* [pl. 68] to the Harpers for £50. When exhibited at the Academy it had not found a purchaser. The picture charms by its simplicity and fluency; the artist has created his own world of make-believe, but just fails to capture that quality of timelessness implicit in the subject. One is never allowed to forget that the figures are, after all, neatly groomed studio models, carefully posed complete with curtain and stage landscape.

Another painting first shown at York in 1836 was *Mars, Venus and Cupid* [pl. 50b]. Here, the most impressive figure is certainly that of Venus, and it seems unfortunate that a finely painted work (in the technical sense), should be made to appear slightly comic by the introduction of a glassy-eyed Life Guardsman acting the part of Mars. Far more appealing is the painting of *Venus and Her Doves* [pl. 57a], which had been commissioned by Daniel Grant. There can be little doubt that Titian's *Sacred and Profane Love* was uppermost in Etty's mind when he composed this picture, although in colour it is less markedly Titianesque, for the two female figures contain bluish tints in the shadowed parts of their flesh and the cheeks of the Cupid are too ruddy by comparison with the sallow complexion of an Italian youth. Bitumen has spoilt much of Venus's golden brown robe, and its effects are also apparent in the hot browns and lime greens of the landscape. In the far distance are blue mountains shimmering in a heat haze, a favourite *motif* with Etty.

[1] Gilchrist, *op. cit.*, II, p. 45.
[2] Letter from Thomas Myers, jun., to Etty, 3rd April, 1836 (York City Reference Library). It is an indication of Myers's persistence that between 3rd April and 1st May he had written to Etty no less than six letters, nearly all of some length.

It has often been assumed that Constable rather despised Etty both as a man and as a painter; but although Constable often made caustic remarks about Etty's pictures, his respect for him increased once they had ceased to be rivals for Academic honours. In 1828 he had written to Archdeacon Fisher about Etty's *World Before the Flood*: 'Etty has a revel rout of Satyrs and lady bums as usual, very clear & sweetly scented with otter [*sic*] of roses—bought by an old Marquis (Ld Stafford)—coveted by the King (from description), but too late.'[1] A man of intelligence and earthy wit, he could see the comic side to Etty's high seriousness, and it was not malice which prompted him to tell Leslie of a letter Etty had sent him about a model. 'The next week I have a little girl aged 17. She is *procured* by Etty our grand "*curator*"—and I am to have her maiden "sitting" on Monday week—his note is amusing in which he announces his decision—

Dear Constable

A young figure is brought to me—who is very desirous of becoming a model—She is very much like the Antigone *and all in front memorably fine*.

Yours etc
W. Etty'.[2]

Ten months before, Constable had prepared a syllabus for his four lectures at the Royal Institution, and wrote to Etty: 'My Dear Etty, I send you a Syllabus of my lectures—I shall be flattered if you could be present at any one of them as it would be a sanction to my endeavours to extend the knowledge of Art, perhaps you can find our [?legal] friend I think he would like to come—I mean Mr. Mirchouse—at any rate I put a "friend" on the card of admission.

I am Dear Etty always truly Yrs
John Constable

To Wm. Etty Esq.'[3]

Then in March 1837, at the last meeting of the Life School in Somerset House, when Constable was Visitor, Etty had presented him with a life study. 'You might eat it,' Constable is said to have remarked, smacking his lips. Constable had become popular in the Life School, and many were grieved by the news of his death on the last day of that same month. Etty was among the artists forming a committee to organize a private subscription, by which it was hoped to raise the 300 guineas needed to purchase Constable's *Cornfield* for the National Gallery; others on this committee included Dominic Colnaghi, John Sheepshanks and John Murray. A printed circular dated July 1837 was sent by Etty to Thomas Bodley with a letter urging him and his friends to help; the picture 'is a beautiful one calculated to do him honor, and to be an ornament to our National Gallery. It is in fact a *National* picture, being painted by one of our nation. . . . Constable is English—truly English.'[4] Happily, this venture succeeded

---

[1] R. B. Beckett, *John Constable and the Fishers*, London, 1952, pp. 257–8; letter of 11th June, 1828.

[2] *The Letters of John Constable, R.A. to C.R. Leslie, R.A., 1826–1837*, ed. Peter Leslie, London, 1931, pp. 164–5; letter of 25th February, 1837.

[3] This letter, now in York City Reference Library, is undated, but Constable's Syllabus is dated 23rd April, 1836, the first lecture being given on 26th May, 1836.

[4] Letter to Thomas Bodley, 5th August, 1837, with circular and preliminary list of subscribers enclosed (York City Reference Library). Etty sent 3 gns., as did A. E. Chalon and Clarkson Stanfield; Chantrey, Leslie and Wilkie gave 5 gns., Cockerell and Eastlake 2 gns.

and honour was done to a man who, when alive, had often been passed over and maligned.

The *Cornfield* was thus added to the small core of paintings then forming the national collection, and in April, 1838, the new National Gallery building in Trafalgar Square was formally opened to the public. These premises were also shared by the Royal Academy who had already moved into the eastern wing the previous year. At this Summer Exhibition of 1837, the first to be held in their new home, one of the chief attractions was Etty's enormous *The Sirens and Ulysses* [pl. 63] a painting almost ten by fifteen feet in size, hung in the centre of the East Room, the best room in the gallery. How the idea for this picture was suggested to Etty has been noted in the previous chapter, and a comparison between Etty's work and Flaxman's *The Sirens* (plate 19 of *The Odyssey*, 1805) [pl. 62a] is striking evidence of this relationship. But although the Flaxman engraving provides the starting point, Etty has evolved a picture of markedly individual character. A preliminary pencil study shows that he had once thought of placing the Sirens on the right-hand side of the picture, with each Siren looking out towards the boat; in the final version he has reverted to Flaxman's composition, but changed the poses so as to give more depth and coherence to the group. It is however curious that Etty, given the advantages of his medium, has sacrificed some of the three-dimensional effect possible by deliberately emphasizing the figure of Ulysses and placing him at eye-level; whereas Flaxman adopted the reverse process and, despite the limitations of an outline engraving, has defined the spatial planes of his picture far more clearly. In scale, too, Ulysses's figure is disproportionately large by comparison with those of the rest of the crew; and both he and the group of seamen struggling to bind him to the mast are caught in the glare of a lightning flash, thus heightening this disparity. The result is comic rather than heroic.

Etty worked upon the *Sirens* with great care, but once the final composition was clear in his mind he painted with great rapidity, beginning in November 1836 and finishing by April of the following year. He was perhaps one of the first English artists of his time to visit public mortuaries and study from corpses in varying stages of decay, thereby gaining first-hand knowledge before painting the grisly remains of the Sirens' victims. (Ford Madox Brown, when painting his *Prisoners of Chillon* [1856], visited the dissecting rooms of University College Hospital. But also in this method of getting details Etty had preceded him, for he had sought the aid of Robert Liston the surgeon while painting the *Entombment of Christ* in 1843. In France, of course, Géricault had painted the heads of guillotined criminals, and several of these studies still survive.) Etty's insistence upon accuracy of detail in such matters naturally shocked many of the public, and the average reaction to his picture is probably recorded more or less faithfully by the critic of the *Spectator*, who considered it 'a disgusting combination of voluptuousness and loathsome putridity—glowing in colour and wonderful in execution, but conceived in the worst possible taste'.[1] Less squeamish and far more appreciative, the *Gentleman's Magazine* devoted a long section of its review to Etty's work, which it considered the finest he had ever painted, and of a subject well suited to his abilities. 'Mr. Etty avails himself of the assistance of a model in all he undertakes. Nature is his handmaid, and

---

[1] *The Spectator*, 6th May, 1837; *see also* Whitley, *Art in England 1821–1837*, p. 334, who quotes this criticism as well as one of the same tenor from the *Observer*, 4th June, 1837.

to her he has recourse, whatever may be the theme upon which he is employed, so that the accuracy of his details may be safely taken upon trust; it might otherwise be imagined that the proportions of the principal figure in this picture were a little extravagant. We are surprised to hear exceptions taken to the subject of the work, as there are certainly few passages in Homer, or any other author, ancient or modern, to which the talents of the painter or sculptor could be more legitimately addressed.' [1] Thomas Wright, of Upton Hall near Newark, the early biographer of Richard Wilson, R.A., and himself an amateur artist and patron of Etty, thought that if the National Gallery's newly acquired picture of the *Brazen Serpent*, by Rubens, had been exhibited before or at the same time as the Royal Academy exhibition, there would have been very little criticism levelled at Etty about voluptuousness and livid flesh. [2] Unfortunately, the 'glowing colour' of the painting is at present largely obscured by dirty varnish; so that only an imperfect idea can be obtained of, for example, the orange loin cloth of the seaman hoisting sail nearest the mast, and of the vivid red sweat cloth adorning the brow of his shipmate. The flesh of the Sirens is cool, butter colour by comparison with the warm, bronzed flesh of the sailors, but the whole picture lacks the sparkle usual in Etty's work. When painting the sea in the *Sirens*, Etty asked Bodley for the sea study he had made at Brighton the previous Summer; this was but one of a group of studies made there at various seasons over a period of several years. [3]

The vast size of the *Sirens* weighed heavily against its chances of finding a purchaser, and it was not sold until October of that year. While in Manchester, Etty was entertained to dinner by Daniel Grant who asked him to name a price for this picture and *Samson and Delilah*, a painting of the same year, which had been sent first to the Royal Academy, and then to the exhibition at Manchester. Surprised by the sudden chance of selling his pictures the artist suggested £300 as the lowest price he could be expected to accept for both of them. He had already refused an offer of £100 from Mr. Owen for the *Delilah*, and had previously set a nominal price of £300 upon the *Sirens* alone. Grant, although complaining of business losses running into one or two hundred thousand pounds, had taken £300 with him that morning to the Heaton Park Races, of which sum he had lost a mere £25 by the end of the day. He tempted Etty with £250 in cash, and after much heart-searching the painter reluctantly accepted the offer. The episode was typical of the new patronage: on the one hand there was Grant the wealthy, speculative industrialist; on the other, Etty, an exceptionally bad business head, anxious not to have unsold pictures cluttering his studio, and always mindful of Haydon's precarious financial position. Daniel Grant had scarcely examined the *Samson*, and had not even seen the *Sirens* previous to buying both pictures! [4]

---

[1] *Gentleman's Magazine*, VII, June 1838, pp. 628–9.

[2] Letter from Thomas Wright, Esq. to Etty, 25th October, 1837 (York City Reference Library). Another of Etty's friends the Rev. E. P. Owen, was probably responsible for this picture's later being called a Homeric paraphrase on 'The wages of sin is death'.

[3] Letter to Bodley, 21st January, 1837 (York City Reference Library). In the margin Bodley has noted that this was the first study of its kind by Etty. Gilchrist erroneously dates this letter to 1835 (*op. cit.*, II, p. 28), but the paper has a watermark *1836*. Three *Seascapes* belong to Mrs. Anne Marie Borenius (*see* Catalogue).

[4] Letter to Walter Etty, 5th October, 1837 (York City Reference Library) contains the whole story of the transaction.

A *Samson and Delilah*, canvas, 32 × 39 in., is in the possession of Mr. R. W. Alston Curator of the

Soon after this meeting with Grant, Etty was writing to Betsy of his hopes concerning a commission for an altarpiece to be painted for a Roman Catholic chapel at Everingham. The building was in the hands of John Harper, who had hoped to persuade the patron, Mr. Maxwell, to interest himself in an altarpiece instead of a stained glass window.[1] The commission was not given, although Etty had gone so far as to prepare sketches and had quoted the modest sum of £300 as a maximum, although the commission would require some twelve months' work. The artist's attitude towards Catholicism had completely changed over a period of twenty years, and he now professed himself 'in his heart's core deeply and sincerely of the Ancient Faith—*Catholic:*—not of the Daniel O'Connell school, but that of Alfred, St. Augustine, St. Bernard, St. Bruno, and Fénélon; not forgetting Raphael, Michael Angelo, and a host of other great and good men'.[2]

The position of the Roman Catholics in England had also changed, and after 1829 they were permitted more freedom. A reforming spirit was also at work within the Anglican church, seeking to re-establish its intellectual integrity and spiritual authority. The appeal made by the Oxford reformers to the doctrine of apostolic succession provided a link with the ancient Latin Church attractive to a man of Etty's temperament. He could also number among his friends several Roman Catholics, including John Rogers Herbert, R.A., Clarkson Stanfield, R.A., and not least Augustus Welby Pugin. Pugin was received into the Roman Church in 1833 (the year of the first of the Oxford *Tracts for the Times*), and like Etty, his love of Catholicism was partly based upon an aesthetic ideal. The first mention of Etty in Pugin's diary is a note 'August 15, 1837 saw Mr. Etty', followed by two other brief references: 'April 28, 1839 Mr Etty'; 'November 9, 1841 went to Mr. Etty's'.[3] Etty's words to John Harper that 'Architecture, Painting, Music, Sculpture, all owe their second existence to the Catholic Faith' echo Pugin's own sentiments; but it should always be remembered that Pugin's acceptance of Catholicism was based upon deep religious conviction, which found its more immediate expression in his passion for medieval art. Nevertheless, Etty underwent some struggles with his conscience, and clear indications of his difficulties may be found among his diary entries between 1839 and 1845: 'I am *not* a Protestant—because a Protestant is one who protests *against* the Catholic Religion—but being in Mind and Heart a True Friend and Believer in the Holy Catholic Faith I pray God to direct me in the way I should go.' And later, 'My heart and mind I feel to be more Catholic than anything else—but I do not turn Catholic at least at present for several reasons, amongst which are the following: Auricular Confession: Being Shut out of those glorious Minsters that they have erected, and obliged to worship in those poor Chapels, which they are banished to, at least for the present—Cousin Thomas Bodley; and

---

Watts Gallery, Compton, Surrey. Unfortunately it does not quite agree with Gilchrist's description of the 1837 picture, containing only eight, not *nine* figures, and its subject seems to be taken from Milton's *Samson Agonistes*, ll. 951–9, rather than from *Judges*, XVI (Society of Arts Catalogue, 1849, XXII). Stylistically too, it is untypical.

[1] Letter to Elizabeth Etty, 'York, Sunday, 8th October 1837' (Jacobus J. T. Bosch Collection).

[2] Gilchrist, *op. cit.*, II, pp. 69–71.

[3] I am very much obliged to Dr. Phoebe Stanton for this information, which has been taken from unpublished material in her possession.

Friends' objections—I wish—I wish—I wish——' He once wrote a strong letter to Walter Etty demonstrating that 'we are indebted to the Catholics for most that is great or good which our Ancestors have handed down to us'.[1] But Etty was too old to uproot himself and endure the isolation that would result from a change to Rome; and he obviously found himself unable to accept all the practices that such conversion would involve.

As late as 1847 the problem still nagged at his mind, and he sought Eastlake's advice, who wrote: 'My dear Etty In reply to your "momentous question"—"whether in my opinion the Roman Catholic or Protestant Faith is best adapted for promoting the Happiness and best Interests of the Human Race"—I have no hesitation in saying that I think the Protestant Religion is best adapted for such purposes. On the other hand, & with reference to another part of your letter I cannot but admit that the arts have flourished most under the inspirations which the Catholic Faith prompted & the dignified encouragement which it held forth. Still, I think it would not be right to attribute all the excellence of art to that influence only, for in Catholic countries now— in Italy & in Spain for instance—the arts have sunk although the religion is unchanged, & although the mere demand for some works of art, consecrated to Religion, is still great.' In answer to the wider problems involved, Eastlake refers Etty to a book then just published by Longman, *From Oxford to Rome: and how it fared with some who lately made the journey*. 'I know it only from Reviews but I think, from the passages I have seen, that it may contain an *experimental* answer to your question. Ever sincerely yours C. L. Eastlake.' Etty replied the next day, thanking Eastlake for his kind and prompt answer, but it is obvious that he found Eastlake's sober, scholarly views slightly dispiriting. Nevertheless, he bought the book and promised to read it.[2]

Etty was not alone in his search for an answer to the questions of whether the Roman Church was not then still the more sympathetic and liberal patron of the arts, and whether the Protestant churches could ever employ artists (especially painters) on a similar scale. R. N. Wornum wrote a long article in *The Art Journal*, May, 1850, which he entitled *Romanism and Protestantism in Their Relation to Painting*.[3] After noting the Church's early antagonism towards the pictorial arts during the second and third centuries A.D., because of their pagan associations, he pointed out that this hostile attitude changed once it was realized how powerful a weapon for propaganda lay to hand. This

---

[1] From a diary belonging to Mr. Jacobus J. F. Bosch; and an undated letter to Walter Etty (c. 1840–?), City Reference Library, York.

Etty's old friend, Bishop Luscombe, is described in the *D.N.B.*, XII, as holding 'high church principles'. He was one of the founders in 1841 of the *Christian Remembrancer*.

[2] Letter from C. L. Eastlake, R.A., to W. Etty, R.A., '12 Novr. 1847' (York City Reference Library). Letter from W. Etty, R.A., to C. L. Eastlake, R.A., 'Nov. 13, 1847' (Victoria and Albert Museum Library).

The book, *From Oxford to Rome*, 'By a Companion Traveller', had run to three editions even in 1847. It was written by Elizabeth F. S. Harris, herself a disillusioned convert to Rome, apparently with the intention of warning Anglicans against succumbing to the lure of Roman Catholicism: she suggested that those who desired to see the English Church regain the spiritual force it had in Pre-Reformation days should not ape blindly the Roman Church of later times.

[3] *The Art Journal*, XII, 1st May, 1850, pp. 133–6. R. N. Wornum, art critic and connoisseur, was appointed 'Keeper of the National Gallery in December, 1854, on the recommendation of Sir Charles Eastlake.

change took place in the fourth century, partly as the result of the work of such powerful advocates as St. Gregory of Nyssa and St. Gregory of Nazianzus, both fathers of the Eastern Church. Wornum then argued that the process repeated itself when the Protestants rejected the arts because of their strong links with Catholicism. This apparent deadlock could easily be resolved, since both Protestant and Catholic shared a common tradition, and there were many Biblical subjects that could be depicted without touching upon those doctrinal points peculiar to the Roman Church. It was an ingenious thesis, and a brave attempt to overcome the psychological problem raised by associating religious art with a particular sect. Faith, Hope and Charity are universal Christian virtues, and illustrations of their works or practical examples would be an inspiration to all. Wornum drove home this argument with the remark, 'Every virtue belongs to this category, and as an example of how a Protestant can treat such matters we may refer to Etty's great pictures lately exhibited at the Society of Arts, which are, and were expressly designed to be by the painter, illustrations of the practical operation of the several virtues represented; and how infinitely superior to cold abstract impersonations: the drama against allegory.'[1]

Another of Etty's friends was his physician, Mr. R. Cartwright of Bloomsbury Square, and in 1838 the artist presented his picture of *The Good Samaritan* [pl. 62*b*] to him as a whimsical tribute to Cartwright's professional attendance during Etty's long illness five years before. The painting had been sent to the British Institution in 1838, where it seems to have gone almost unremarked. As might be expected, the painting is everywhere fluent and accomplished; again Etty has used a thin brown underpainting, over which he has deftly brushed in the figures of priest and Levite, producing an effect most often found in the works of Breughel or Rubens. By contrast with these shadowy grey figures, the Samaritan appears substantial and is clothed in rich green, red and white robes; his noble head, Rembrandt-like in its strongly contrasted chiaroscuro, is of a type frequently seen in Etty's work of the last two decades. Here it has been used to convey a sense of deep compassion which avoids becoming mawkish. (Delacroix, when deeply moved by a subject, would also sometimes neglect the mechanics of his composition, yet still produce a work of strong emotional power. Nevertheless, he succeeds in overcoming the difficulties of representing *Le bon Samaritain*, as may be seen from his painting of that title of 1852 in the Victoria and Albert Museum. Etty's picture is not flattered by such a comparison.)

Some idea of English reactions to contemporary French painting may be gained from an extremely perceptive criticism of the Louvre exhibition that appeared in *The Times*, 5th April, 1838. Its author signed himself 'D.D.', and after making the usual criticism that French artists were generally unable to handle colour harmoniously, he remarked upon Delacroix, Decamps and Roqueplan as brilliant exceptions to this censure.[2] Two

---

[1] *The Art Journal*, XII, 1st May, 1850, p. 135.

[2] This particular and persistent English criticism of French art only emphasized a negative quality. It quite overlooked the fact that the French artist often far surpassed his English rival in his ability to compose a picture with a lucidity and cohesion that was the direct result of a discipline instilled during his training as a student, since French academic tradition regarded colour as subordinate to composition. Later in this article, *The Times* correspondent acknowledged the superiority of the French as anatomists, but failed to mention the reason for this circumstance.

of Delacroix's pictures, *Médée* and *Les Convulsionnaires de Tanger*, were regarded as the most outstanding things in the exhibition, and the critic spoke warmly of the character of 'greatness' which marked his work. Only the subject-matter of *Les Convulsionnaires* was found a little disagreeable; other qualities in the work were highly praised. Above all, it is significant that Etty was compared, not with Delacroix as is now fashionable, but with Roqueplan.[1] 'If the reader can fancy Etty and Watteau mixed up together, he may have some idea of this delightful artist.' The luscious colour in Roqueplan's *Vandyck à Londres* was only to be found again in 'some of the glorious sketches of Mr. Etty'. Thackeray, writing a year later, also paid tribute to Delacroix's paintings which he said bore 'the stamp of genius on all of them,—the great poetical *intention*, which is worth all your execution'.[2]

In 1838, Etty's work already begins to show signs of unevenness and, although the average number of pictures sent to each Academy exhibition now increases, one may detect an almost proportionate deterioration in quality. The factors contributing to this decline have been noted earlier, but perhaps the part played by dealers, and at this moment Richard Colls in particular, now becomes more evident. Colls was the first dealer to become interested in his work, when in 1835 he bought Etty's *Wood Nymphs Sleeping*, and he alone, among the professional dealers, bought direct from the artist, establishing something like a monopoly of his output. By 1844, Etty was only selling to Colls, or to a very few old friends and patrons. It is significant, too, that in 1836 he had refused to finish studies for Colls until the *Sirens* was completed. At least three of the paintings sent to the R.A. in 1838 display signs of a failing hand, *A Bivouac of Cupid and His Company, Somnolency* and *Il Duetto*. Critics were quick to notice this, and the *Gentleman's Magazine* wrote of the *Bivouac* [pl. 69] that it was a 'clever thing . . . though a repetition of some of his former works. The artist's manual powers are superior to his invention.'[3] Perhaps even this last assertion might be questioned, for the picture has been executed in a rather slipshod, facile manner, and much of the flesh modelling appears flaccid as well as damaged by bitumen. Only occasionally, as in the painting of the metal ewer and fruit has Etty maintained his usual standard of clear, crisp technique.

Another critic, soon to become distinguished as the author of *Vanity Fair*, writing his first exhibition review for *Fraser's Magazine*, also felt the artist to have slackened off that year. 'I don't know whether the Duke has this year produced anything which one might have expected from a man of his rank and consequence. He is, like great men, lazy, or indifferent, perhaps, about public approbation; and also, like great men, somewhat too luxurious and fond of pleasure. For instance, here is a picture of a sleepy nymph, most richly painted; but tipsy looking, coarse, and so naked, as to be unfit for appearance among respectable people at an exhibition. You will understand what I mean. There are some figures, without a rag to cover them, which look modest and decent for all that; and others, which may be clothed to the chin, and are yet not fit for modest eyes to

[1] Camille-Joseph-Étienne Roqueplan (1803–55), landscape and genre painter. Pupil of Baron Gros and of Abel de Pujol, influenced by Bonington, his fellow pupil under Gros.

[2] Wm. M. Thackeray, *Fraser's Magazine*, December, 1839, p. 682, where he discusses the collections of the Louvre, Luxembourg and École des Beaux-Arts.

[3] *Gentleman's Magazine*, IX, June, 1838, p. 632.

gaze on. *Verbum sat*—this naughty "somnolency" ought to go to sleep in her night-gown.' [1] Perhaps Thackeray was justified here in his criticism, but in the next paragraph, he writes a sensitive appraisal of Etty's second *Prodigal Son*, which was bought by William Beckford. [2] He remarked that 'It is a grand and touching picture and looks as large as if the three-foot canvas had been twenty.' The satirical element is never far away in Thackeray's reviews, but it is often tinged with schoolboy humour as when he invented a mock hierarchy consisting of 'Duke' Etty, 'Baron' Briggs; 'Daniel, Prince Maclise'; 'H.M. King Mulready'; 'Lord' Landseer, and 'Archbishop' Eastlake! He also called the new National Gallery a 'little gin-shop of a building', thus swelling the ranks of those who found its appearance unpleasing.

After the hard work involved in a large picture like the *Sirens*, some slackening off may be forgiven, especially if it is soon followed by a portrait as fine as that of the solicitor *John Brook* [pl. 59], an intimate friend of the painter. John Brook was a man of strong and generous character, and a distinguished member of his profession. He had held several important legal offices, and at the Coronation of George IV in 1820, he acted as staff-bearer to the Earl Marshal of England. His interests were wide, and this portrait was painted for the York Musical Society in October, 1838. At the same time Etty made a copy of it for Brook's family. Like the *James Atkinson* it is robustly painted; slightly warmer in tone than the earlier portrait, it also contains more variety of colour. The figure is set against the usual dull red background, but this time Brook's dark blue jacket with its brass buttons and gold fob, the red and green title labels on the calf-bound books, and Brook's chestnut hair all make for a more sonorous effect. The fresh-complexioned face and hands are thickly painted, yet their plasticity is suggested with deceptive ease. Instead of the more familiar Indian red, Etty has used a dark crimson in the shadows around the mouth and nostril. John Brook was sixty-eight when Etty painted him, and the artist has done full justice to this sturdy old man, whose shrewd grey eyes gaze thoughtfully upon a private world of memories.

It was during this stay in York that Etty began a campaign to establish a School of Design in his native city. In October, 1838, he read a paper on the *Importance of the Arts of Design* to the Council of the Yorkshire Philosophical Society, in support of a plan to establish a 'School of Drawing and an Exhibition Room on the Manor Shore'. At the request of the Council he repeated this lecture for the public on 5th November. Although he read it rather badly, the subject-matter caught the interest of his audience. As might be expected, he began with a lengthy *apologia* for the Fine Arts generally, and painting in particular; after which he outlined a scheme whereby the Hospitium (now the Roman Antiquities Museum) could be used as a depository for carved stone fragments in the lower half of the building, with the top part devoted to a school and exhibition room. The school was to be of practical value to young men engaged in arts and trades in the city. [3] Nothing came of this scheme, but a modified version of it was adopted later, after

---

[1] *Fraser's Magazine*, June, 1838, p. 763. ' "Strictures on Pictures", A letter from Michael Angelo Titmarsh, Esq. to Monsieur Anatole . . . Hercule de Bricabrac, Peintre d'Histoire, rue Mouffetard, à Paris.'

[2] This picture is still not located, but it seems to have followed the general pattern of the 1836 version.

[3] Letter to Walter, 26th October, 1838 (York City Reference Library). *Yorkshire Gazette*, 10th November, 1838, gives a three-column report of the speech. The *Art Union*, I, December, 1839, pp. 182–3, contains a much abridged account of another lecture *The Arts of Design* given by Etty in York a year later.

Etty had persisted in his efforts and enlisted the support of the government. The school was opened in September, 1842.

A subject which had been maturing in the artist's mind since 1834 now began to take definite shape. This was the *Pluto Carrying off Proserpine* [pl. 64], exhibited at the Academy the following year. Early in 1835 he had written to the dealer Colls, 'There is a subject I hope to paint, before I am much older,—after my own heart, and I think of your sort. This is to be strictly *entre nous*. . . . One does not like to be anticipated: as I *have* been, . . . It is one I have often thought on, lately indeed, composed *en groupe: Pluto carrying off Proserpine*.' For as Etty realized, the theme was most suited to his gifts, '*There*, are beauty, action, masculine vigour;—landscape, sky, motion, agitation, flowers, and freshness;—the consternation of her attendant Nymphs scattering their flowers in their fear and flight: matter enough to make a fine Picture.' [1] Thus at York he began sketches for the final painting, making studies from 'cream-coloured horses', and upon his return to London he continued his researches into horse anatomy by visiting the wharf of his friend Mr. Wood, a merchant in the City. About this time Etty painted a small sketch for the composition, in which are all the main elements of the final picture. The sketch also shows a cupid flying over the horses' heads, and this feature was also in the finished picture, the The Times critic noted that a 'young Love, in flame-coloured taffeta, floats over all'. [2] This feature, and that of a fourth horse on the furthest side of the composition, appear to have been painted out by 1934, although a photograph of 1892 shows the picture as it must originally have been. Etty worked on the composition again after the Academy exhibition, but it is very unlikely that he would have introduced quite such sweeping and clumsy alterations. On 7th January, 1839, he started to draw the outlines of the composition in charcoal upon the canvas, and after three months of steady progress the picture was almost complete. The finishing touches were applied in April, when the artist bought flowers, grass, sedges and moss from Covent Garden for guidance as he painted in the foreground. Even so, the picture was finished only just in time for the Royal Academy exhibition, and during the varnishing days Etty worked still further on certain details that had been criticized. His diary entries for this period make interesting reading: 'April 25th, To Royal Academy, to meet the ideas of the Noodles.—May 1st, The Noodles at me again: . . . begin to put in white and gold draperies.—May 2nd, Last day of varnishing. Took off the thick paint, and restored the transparent.' [3] Such was Etty's angry contempt for his critics.

Although the *Pluto Carrying off Proserpine* is boldly planned, the composition is somewhat forced and does not flow easily. Etty has relied too heavily upon a few stock poses with the result that his figures fail to express alarm and terror convincingly, and the spectator is not deeply moved. But if the artist's inventiveness has not served him well in this respect there is still much to admire, particularly the three prancing horses and the kneeling figure on the left of the picture. This figure has been broadly brushed in, although that part of the face in shadow is most thinly painted, with much of the underpainting still visible. Some red, yellow and blue flowers strewn from their basket over the ground have been suggested by a thick, whipped-up impasto which contrasts with the heavy, chunky strokes used in the delicate pink drapery wrapped around the thighs of the kneeling woman. The group of Pluto and Proserpine perhaps owes a little

[1] Gilchrist, *op. cit.*, II, pp. 28–9, 96. [2] *The Times*, 7th May, 1839. [3] Gilchrist, *op. cit.*, II, p. 98.

to Charles LeBrun's design for a *Rape of Proserpine* sculpted by F. Giraudon in 1680 for the Garden of Versailles, but Etty has flattened the group so that it is seen almost as a bas-relief, the figures moving across the picture rather than receding into it.[1] This is by now a familiar Etty practice, for even the nymph falling over backwards (taken from an earlier composition, *A Bivouac of Cupid*) does not break the limited recession of the composition. The figure of Pluto was drawn from an Indian model, Mendoo, who apparently often posed for Etty at this time.

The press took up in public criticisms that had earlier been voiced privately. *The Times* printed a long and flippant notice, and in *Fraser's Magazine* Thackeray rather foolishly wrote that 'A great, large curtain of fig-leaves should be hung over every one of this artist's pictures, and the world should pass on, content to know that there are some glorious colours painted beneath.' [2] Bearing in mind Etty's remarks to Colls expressing a fear of being anticipated, it is interesting to note that J. M. W. Turner also sent in a *Pluto Carrying off Proserpine* to the same exhibition, and it seems quite possible, if non-proven, that a certain amount of rivalry existed between the two artists. Turner's work suffered no better fate at the hands of the critics, for although his *Fighting Téméraire* was acclaimed by Thackeray, the same writer stigmatized his other pictures as 'pert caricatures of nature, or mad exaggerations'. Despite his great admiration for many of Turner's achievements, Etty also failed to appreciate his later works, some of which he called 'fiery abominations'.[3]

An altogether different criticism appeared in the *Art Union*, and was occasioned by another of Etty's pictures at the 1839 Academy exhibition, the *Diana and Endymion*. It deserves quoting in its entirety: 'Mr Etty is not conspicuous in this exhibition, as he ought to be. His powers are of the very highest order, and though he is seldom happy in the selection of his subjects, he has qualities which make some amends for his defects. With most amazing genius, with industry, perhaps, unparalleled, with a thorough knowledge of the "machinery" of his profession, he is rarely successful with the mass, simply because he aims to satisfy the judgment rather than to touch the heart. Now this, we submit, is neither politic nor just. It is the noblest privilege of art to inform and gratify universally; to make the more elevated class of subjects familiar and easily understood, and not so as to paint as to be "caviare to the general". We are not of those who raise a silly and impure outcry against his painting the "Human Form Divine"; but we join with those who protest against his so continually selecting themes that excite no sympathy and rouse no generous emotion. His powers are great, his capabilities greater, and we, therefore, the more deeply grieve at finding him very frequently doing as little good for mankind as the priest who preaches his sermon in Latin.' [4] The *Art Union* was a new magazine edited by Samuel Carter Hall, its first issue appearing on 15th February, 1839, and it may therefore be taken as representing the views of a younger generation of critics and connoisseurs. This is perhaps the first warning that Etty was becoming an anachronism and losing touch with the trends of his age. The *Art Union* critic has only partially sensed this, and gives no clear indications as to the subjects he thinks should be treated by the artist, but it is significant that Etty relied far less upon classical

[1] An engraving was made of this marble group by B. Picart.
[2] *The Times*, 7th May, 1839; *Fraser's Magazine*, June, 1839, p. 743.
[3] Gilchrist, *op. cit.*, II, p. 216.   [4] *Art Union*, I, May, 1839, pp. 67–71.

mythology as a source of inspiration during the last ten years of his life. The conception that a work of art should serve some moral purpose remained unchanged, but the language used to express that purpose most certainly did change. It was a gradual process, for at the Academy in 1850 F. R. Pickersgill could exhibit a *Rape of Proserpine* (closely based upon Etty's painting) and a *Samson Disarmed*, and be warmly praised: at the same exhibition, Millais's *Christ in the House of His Parents* was fiercely criticized for its starkness and uncompromising realism; it was even regarded as blasphemous by some sections of public opinion.[1] Millais was nine years younger than Pickersgill, but both admired Etty, and Pickersgill's work of the 1840s and 1850s was strongly influenced by Etty's style, as indeed was that of Millais for a brief period.

Etty almost invariably surprises at the very moment when one begins to think that he has little else new to produce. In September 1839 he painted the first of a series of still-lifes, *Pheasant and Peach*. Still-life as an incidental trapping had appeared often enough in his earlier work, but it now assumed an independent status, and between 1841 and 1848 he exhibited no less than six pictures in this *genre*. This is not without wider historical significance, for excepting the work of minor painters such as Edward Coleman (*fl.* 1813–48), George Lance (1802–64) and William Duffield (1816–63), no English artist of note had ever paid serious attention to the *genre* until Sickert, with the New English Art Club, introduced a taste for it from France during the 1890s. Coleman, Lance and Duffield worked in the tradition of the Dutch seventeenth-century masters, and their pictures display little originality.

Etty's still-lifes are not easy to date stylistically, but the *Flower Study* [pl. 70a] may probably be dated to the latter half of 1839. A comparison between this painting and the still-life of flowers in the foreground of the *Pluto Carrying off Proserpine* reveals some similarity of treatment, the blossom and foliage in both are touched in with broad, thick strokes of pure luminous colour. The *Pheasant and Peach* mentioned by Gilchrist may well be the same picture as that now called *Still-life; Dead Pheasant and Fruit* [pl. 82a], in the York Art Gallery. The composition of this painting is striking for its apparent haphazardness; the bird has been thrown down upon the table among some grapes, an apple and a pink-flecked white rose. Although colour is the chief unifying factor of the whole composition, yet the forms do fall into a pattern, the plan of which becomes more obvious as one realizes that the head, tail, wings and claw form two diagonals running across from each corner of the picture. An entirely new element is the dramatic presentation of the subject-matter; the abruptness with which one is confronted by the objects of still-life distinguishes it immediately from the work of two centuries earlier. This same quality is no less apparent even when Etty imitates some of the *clichés* of Dutch still-life painting such as the inclusion of a partially-peeled lemon, the rind of which is left to curl down decoratively over the edge of a glass or table. The *Still-life with Lemon, Peaches and Grapes* (York Art Gallery) demonstrates this point, as does another picture, *Still-life with Glass* (Gabriel Collection) [pl. 71], where the Dutch tradition has been followed more carefully, yet transformed, nevertheless, by an extremely personal and advanced technique.

Another still-life in the Gabriel collection, *Still-life with Stone Jar*, shows Etty painting objects seen as if in the open air. Here, the silver bowl of fruit and the stone jar are

[1] *The Times*, 4th, 6th and 9th May, 1850; Charles Dickens, *Household Words*, 15th June, 1850.

placed on the stone coping of a wall, and set against the sky with a glimpse of the sea and horizon on the left. The picture is everywhere thinly painted, the composition flat and a little ambiguous. Richly coloured, although deliberately restricted in range, the plasticity of the objects only becomes apparent when the picture is viewed in an oblique light and from a short distance. It is only then that the full beauties of the bloom on the peaches and the luminous atmosphere may be appreciated. Finally, the *Still-life with Ewer* [pl. 70*b*] must surely demonstrate his peculiar facility for seizing upon an object and so presenting it to us that we seem to be looking at it through a magnifying-glass and as a detail of a much larger picture. Sometimes, by staying too close to his model Etty has produced a slight distortion (*e.g.* the figure of the woman in *The Combat*), but here he seems to have turned this possible failing to advantage. The fact that in the summer of 1839 and 1840 he received lessons in perspective from George Belton Moore suggests that he may have felt himself ill-equipped to deal with spatial problems in his pictures.[1]

It was in September, 1839, that Etty began to shape his ideas for the last of his monumental undertakings, the three *Joan of Arc* pictures, and at the end of the first week the three pictures had been roughed out on paper. Previously, he had toyed with the story of Thomas à Becket, and had studied books and armour in the British Museum with this in mind. One notebook has three pages covered with notes taken from Sharon Turner's *The History of England during the Middle Ages*, and contains a sketch for a *Martyrdom of Thomas à Becket*.[2] Nothing came of this, however, and by August, 1840, Etty had already prepared canvases for the *Joan of Arc* paintings. He recorded their sizes in his notebook as follows: 'Joan of Arc. Centre Picture—15 by 9 ft. 9 inches. Sides —6 ft 6. by 9 ft 9 inches.'[3] It is perhaps somewhat surprising that three paintings of such dimensions are now missing, but the history of their career belongs to a later chapter, for they were not completed until 1847.

Works exhibited at the British Institution and Royal Academy in 1840 reflect the increasing difficulty Etty experienced in preparing finished 'exhibition' pictures. When he repeats old formulae he is more or less successful; his attempts at new subjects are less happy. This becomes clear from a comparison between the *Mars, Venus, and attendant derobing her mistress for the bath* and *A subject from the Parable of the Ten Virgins*. The latter picture is remarkable if only for the curious architectural features introduced; upon seeing them one critic was reminded of the entrance to a 'modern station-house', and another asked who could have been the models employed by the artist.[4] The *Andromeda—Perseus coming to her rescue* completed the number sent to the Royal Academy, and is perhaps the most interesting picture [pl. 82*b*]. It is superbly painted in a Rubensian technique and sparkles with brilliant translucent colours. Against this must be set a

---

[1] Gilchrist, *op. cit.*, II, pp. 102 and 114. The 'Mr. Moore' was George Belton Moore (1806–1875), painting and drawing master at the Royal Military Academy, Woolwich, and at University College, London. Author of *Perspective, its Principles and Practice*, London, 1851.

[2] *Sketchbook VI*, City Art Gallery, York. *See also* Gilchrist, *op. cit.*, II, p. 107; Sharon Turner, *op. cit.*, London, 2nd ed., 1825, I, pp. 275–7.

[3] From a notebook belonging to Ir. Thomas H. Etty, *c.* 1839–43. In a notebook of 1830–9 (Mr. J. J. T. Bosch Collection), Etty seems only to have considered doing one painting, measuring $13\frac{1}{2} \times 11$ feet.

[4] *The Times*, 6th May, 1840. Anderdon, *Catalogues of the Royal Academy Exhibitions*, (British Museum), LXXII, 'A large life-size group—not very pleasing. Who were the Models?'

certain crudeness in the conception of the subject, particularly the unpleasant effect produced by the contorted pose of Andromeda. Perseus is mounted on a rocking horse, and the vulgar theatricality of the picture stultifies any attempt Etty may have made to capture a sense of urgency, or to convey the nobler qualities implicit in the story. Nevertheless, the picture has been painted with complete self-assurance, and a unified, consistent pictorial expression has been the result.

In May that same year, Etty was startled to hear of a second fire which had gutted the nave of York Minster. He felt as if he had suffered a deep personal loss, and was unable to work for several days. A visit to York comforted him slightly, when he saw that the damage was not so extensive as first he had feared. Needless to say, he was quick to speak and act in support of the restoration fund begun soon afterwards.

Four months later he went with his niece Elizabeth for a ten-day tour in the Low Countries. Rubens was the chief attraction, but the shortness of his stay only permitted a fleeting glimpse of the picture galleries, palaces and churches of Ostend, Bruges, Antwerp, Brussels, Aachen, Cologne and Bonn. They returned home through Rotterdam after travelling down the Rhine from Bonn. It was really more a pleasure trip, although Etty did buy some studio properties including a dress and red wooden clogs; some shot from the field of Waterloo, and a medal of Rubens. The first two items were used in a picture *The Flemish Courtship* begun in 1842 and shown at the following year's Academy exhibition. No correspondence seems to have survived from this visit abroad; in any case, so much of the time must have been spent travelling that there would have been few opportunities for writing letters.

CHAPTER EIGHT

PROSPERITY: 1841–1845

ONE of the most interesting aspects of the last nine years of Etty's career is the speed with which his personal fortune increased. Old debts to Walter Etty and Thomas Bodley had been fully discharged, and the artist was now in a position to invest his earnings. At first, knowing his lack of business ability, his friends Edward and John Harper set up an 'Etty Fund' on his behalf. They paid into the bank a few sums of money which they and other friends owed the artist, and this they converted into 3 per cent Bank Stock. Thus in 1841 Etty (much to his delight) had £300 so invested, and by 1845 he was able to write in his notebook, 'The Last Day of November 1845 my stock in the Reduced 3 per Cents was £8500.' [1] A quite considerable sum, but at his death Etty owned just twice as much—£17,000—in funds. That he was able to put away such a fortune is symptomatic of a new stage in the evolution of British patronage, and is closely linked with the rapid success of self-made men like Joseph Gillott the steel pen manufacturer, whom Etty met for the first time at Birmingham in 1843. [2]

During this period Etty was involved in the early struggles of the School of Design, to whose Council he was appointed in 1840. Opened in London in 1837, the Normal School of Design was the result of recommendations made by a parliamentary commission set up two years before to investigate 'the best means of extending a knowledge of the arts and of the principles of design among the people (especially the manufacturing population) of the country'. [3] Ten years later another parliamentary commission had to report the complete failure of the system to achieve its aims. This failure could hardly be put down either to lack of enthusiasm on the part of its Director, William Dyce, or of councillors so conscientious as Etty. The fault lay rather in a system which ignored the need for combining practical instruction in industrial skills with more formal artistic training. In 1838 Dyce tried to begin a course in weaving: he had to abandon the idea after two years for lack of students. The School suffered another

---

[1] From a notebook belonging to Ir. Thomas H. Etty.

[2] Gilchrist, *op. cit.*, II, p. 160. The first letter to survive from Etty to Gillott is dated 30th October, 1844, and is addressed to Gillott's secretary G. Hawkesworth. In it Etty makes an open arrangement to see Gillott whenever the manufacturer should be in London.

[3] N. Pevsner, *Academies of Art Past and Present*, Cambridge, 1940, pp. 247, *et seq.*, for an account of the School.

reverse in May 1843, when Dyce resigned the directorship following a disagreement with the councillors over the amount of time he should devote to teaching. Just before this Etty had written to Gladstone strongly protesting against the dismissal of Dyce, and reminding him that every practising artist needed to refresh his inspiration.[1] He also dwelt upon the difficulty of finding in his place someone as well qualified as Dyce.

Each of the six pictures Etty sent to the Academy in 1841 represent different aspects of his art, and they are widely ranged in subject. Perhaps the outstanding one was *The Repentant Prodigal's Return to His Father* [pl. 72], which was also acclaimed as one of the best pictures in the exhibition. The central group of father and son is nobly conceived and certainly conveys the emotional and spiritual force of the parable; but the composition in general does not cohere quite so effortlessly as it might. Etty makes little attempt to conceal the structure of his paintings, and the familiar diamond-shaped plan is here made obvious by devices such as the stick in the foreground leading the eye of the spectator back to the discarded cloak on the left, where the outstretched arm of the elder brother aligns with one side of the upper triangle. Similarly on the right, where the man bending over an iron-bound chest also acts as a cornerstone for that half of the picture. Like the *Andromeda* of 1840, much of it is thinly painted and the whole is flooded with a brilliant light in a way which anticipates the harshly-lit early work of the Pre-Raphaelites. Although it is a religious subject Etty has introduced a group of rejoicing dancers made more familiar in another context as the three Graces. The humourless art critic of the *Art Union*[2] took exception to their presence, but he seems not to have realized that the artist had combined the actual homecoming of the prodigal son with the secondary theme of the elder brother's return from work in the fields.

Almost the same size as the *Repentant Prodigal* but very different in subject is Etty's second Academy picture, *To Arms, To Arms, Ye Brave!* [pl. 73]. It compares most closely with the 1835 *Toilet of Venus*, and in some ways acts as a sequel to that picture. Once again, Etty has divided his picture into a strict pattern of diagonals, with the figure of Mars as a central pivot. The grouping of Mars and Venus is almost an exact paraphrase in reverse of Prud'hon's *Venus and Adonis*, now in the Wallace Collection, and Etty must have been familiar with Normand's engraving of this picture.

In July, he paid a second visit to Belgium, landing at Antwerp. The whole tour lasted ten days, and Etty went to Malines, Ghent, Bruges, and left from Ostend. At Malines, he saw Rubens's *The Miraculous Draught of Fishes* and *The Beheading of St. John the Baptist* in the Cathedral of Notre Dame. It should be remembered that Etty had still to complete the three *Joan of Arc* compositions, and would have looked at the large *Draught of Fishes* triptych with particular interest, seeking guidance for his own work. He must also have found inspiration in the two magnificent altarpieces at Antwerp Cathedral of *The Raising of the Cross* and *The Descent from the Cross*. During his stay he went twice to a Trappist monastery ten miles outside Antwerp, remaining overnight

---

[1] MS. draft of a letter (incomplete) from Etty to W. E. Gladstone, dated 'Palm Sunday' but no year given; the paper bears watermark *1843* (York City Reference Library). Apparently the Council's decision was taken when Etty was unable to attend several meetings because of finishing pictures in time for the Academy exhibition. *See also* Redgrave, *A Century of British Painters*, Phaidon ed., London, 1947, pp. 481–5.

[2] *Art Union*, III, May, 1841, pp. 75–9.

the second time. He also purchased a Trappist monk's habit, and from the Capuchin monastery at Bruges he obtained a Capuchin monk's robe. His impressions of monastic life were useful data for the *Joan of Arc*, and inspired several minor pieces such as *The Cardinal*, *Head of a Monk*, and *Study of a Man's Head*. These three works are now in the Victoria and Albert Museum.

The remainder of Etty's summer holiday was spent in and around York. He went on a two-day sketching tour with John Harper to Bolton Abbey, and there painted *A Landscape View of the Strid Bolton Abbey, Yorkshire* [pl. 74]. This oil study may have been done directly from the subject *en plein air*, and Etty's debt to Constable is manifest. Perhaps the tree forms are less solidly painted and the space less clearly defined than they would have been in a comparable Constable, but Etty's powers as a colourist are more than sufficient to produce a charming and spontaneous result. Lincoln, Beverley and Hull were also visited, and in a letter to John Sydney Taylor Etty remarked that Beverley and Hull would make a page for Pugin's *Contrasts*; at York, the new bells for the Minster had not yet been hung and only the squeak of the railroad could be heard.[1] In the same letter Etty wrote 'what ostentatious Temples the Methodists are building after the Pagan model in York and Hull—lofty . . . porticoes, Ionic columns thick as leaves that strow the brooks, candelabras of gilded brass crimson linings to the pews and cushions, organs! Hull is truly the hot bed of dissenters and chapels lay thick as hail.' Etty had never had much reason to love Hull.

This letter to Taylor was written while Etty was the guest of John Harper at his home in St. Leonard's Place, York, and it was probably then that he painted his host's portrait. (He had stayed at the Harpers' in 1839, but the portrait belongs to a later phase of Etty's style.) The *John Harper* [pl. 75*a*] must take a very high place in the list of distinguished portraits from Etty's hand. It combines intimacy with grandeur, dramatic force with tenderness, and these seemingly contradictory qualities are balanced one against the other to produce a work of serene vitality. Like the still-lifes of this period, the portrait is painted with masterly freedom, is dark in tone and without any tinge of flashiness. Harper's tanned complexion, dark grey-blue eyes and chestnut hair give a sombre brilliancy to the whole picture. The dark wine-red shadow in the nostrils is a characteristic finishing touch.

An interesting series of 17 pen drawings of female nudes dates from the period 1839–41. Two drawings *Standing Model* and *Seated Model turned to left*, are inscribed 'Nov. 1840' and 'June 1841' respectively, and another is dated 1839. All are done in sepia ink and are marked by a scratchy, yet quite firm and sensitive line. That of the *Sleeping Female Nude* [pl. 76*b*] is drawn with a pleasant superficial grace and delicacy; another, *Back view of stooping female nude* [pl. 77], shows rather less understanding of form, although Etty's crisp notation of the surface modelling links him, momentarily, with sculpture rather than painting. He has chosen an unusual viewpoint, and has delighted in the more abstract monumental qualities of the human figure. Also belonging to 1841 is a pastel drawing of *Mlle. Rachel, the French Tragedienne* [pl. 75*b*]. Mlle. Rachel came to London in May, 1841, and gave performances at Covent Garden and at Her Majesty's Theatre. William Macready was among the first to welcome her, and it seems most likely that he was responsible for getting her to sit to his friend Etty. Although this por-

[1] Letter to John Sydney Taylor, 4th September, 1841 (City Art Gallery, York).

trait is a relatively slight work, it is nonetheless of extreme sensitivity and perception, echoing Macready's description of the actress. Meeting her for the first time he wrote: 'She is a very engaging, graceful little person, anything but plain in person, delicate and most intelligent features, a frank, a French manner, synonymous to pleasing.' [1]

Macready's *Diaries* are a fascinating record of London society of the period, and of his numerous acquaintances. After his first meeting with Etty in Italy in 1822, Macready did not see him again until May, 1837, when they were both guests at a dinner party given by Samuel Warren. Two years later Etty's name figures among the list of visitors at Macready's home, when the artist met Charles Dickens and his wife. Again, in April, 1840, 'Dickens called for me, and we went together to Lord Northampton's. Saw there Babbage, Maclise, Etty, Pickersgill, Horner, Jerdan, Stanfield, Lord Aberdeen, Archbishop of Canterbury, Cartwright, Sir H. Ellis, Sir Richard Jenkins, T. Hook, Dr. Dibdin, Sir D. Wilkie. Walked home with Dickens.' [2] Daniel Maclise, R.A., related to Gilchrist how Etty had been too shy or diffident to participate in many social functions, and that he would often sit silent at a dinner party. Nevertheless, he could be a warm host, especially to his artist friends and to students, with whom he was always very popular.

The largest picture which Etty showed at the Royal Academy of 1842 was *The Dance*. Begun in the autumn of 1841, it was inspired by Alexander Pope's translation of lines from Homer's *Iliad* describing the Shield of Achilles, 'A figured dance succeeds: a comely band / Of youths and maidens hand in hand. . . .' The picture was praised; but, noted *The Times* critic, 'It is not highly finished. Indeed, it is a very sketchy picture, but full of vigour; the figures move, and all is animation.' [3] This lack of finish is further aggravated by a slackness in the composition, which contrasts unfavourably with, for example, *The World Before the Flood* (1828). In December, 1847, a plaster cast of Flaxman's bas-relief *The Shield of Achilles* was specially made for Etty with the permission of his former patron Joseph Neeld, who then owned what must have been either one of the bronze or plaster casts taken from the original plaster in the possession of Messrs. Rundell and Bridge, the goldsmiths, who had commissioned the work in 1818. Silver gilt and bronze versions had been sent to the King, the Dukes of York and Northumberland, and others. This cast Etty then presented to the York School of Design. He was certainly familiar with Flaxman's relief before he painted *The Dance*, and it may well have inspired his own work.[4]

A visit to his friend the Reverend Isaac Spencer early in the autumn of 1842, resulted in a fine landscape sketch of his host's grounds '*The Plantation*', Acomb [pl. 78a]. This beauty spot had great attractions for him as a retreat from the noise and bustle of

[1] *The Diaries of William Charles Macready*, ed. William Toynbee, II, p. 134, entry for 5th May, 1841.
[2] *Ibid.*, I, pp. 395, 503, entries for 20th May, 1837, and 25th March, 1839; II, p. 57, entry for 11th April, 1840.
[3] *The Times*, 3rd May, 1842.
[4] Among the engravings sold at the Etty Sale, Christie's, 14th May, 1850, was lot 929, 'Flaxman's Shield of Achilles'. Lots 943–7 in the same sale were folio volumes of Flaxman's illustrations to *Dante, Acts of Mercy, Odyssey* and *Iliad, Hesiod*, and *Æschylus*. Plaster casts of the *Shield of Achilles* were in the collections of the Royal Academy, Sir Thomas Lawrence (this was bought by Rundell at the Lawrence Sale, Christie's, 6th July, 1830, lot 68), and C. R. Cockerell (presented to University College, London).

London, and he often returned to it in his last years. Probably of the same date and place is another *Landscape* [pl. 79] which is of great interest as one of his largest and most finished works of this kind. Here perhaps is the token fulfilment of a youthful desire to paint landscape referred to by his biographer Gilchrist. The picture is composed of delicate harmonies of lime greens and darker greens, relieved by the browns of trees beginning to change to autumn colours. Grey, red-ridged roofs in the foreground reflect the tints of a cloudy pale blue sky; and the trees sway gracefully, their leaves and branches rippled by a light breeze. Somewhat different in style is the *Landscape with House* [pl. 78*b*]. The subject is not easy to identify; it could be 'The Plantation', or perhaps the house of his friends Mr. and Mrs. Singleton of Givendale. It recalls the landscape of *The Strid, Bolton Abbey*, and is particularly striking for the direct, vigorous manner Etty has chosen to depict the scene. The house, with its buff-coloured stone walls and pink roof, is partially screened by tall dark green poplar trees; once again, Constable is the source of inspiration.

Despite pressure from dealers to produce small, easily saleable works, Etty managed to carry forward the *Joan of Arc* paintings. By 5th October he had begun 'to get in the great lines' of the composition, and a month later, full-scale preparatory sketches in charcoal had been completed on all three canvases.[1] In this same month (November), he proposed, and the Council of the Royal Academy accepted, a new bye-law 'providing that no half length portraits of the size of life be in future hung below the line, excepting only that of the Sovereign'.[2] His object was to prevent mediocre portraits being hung in places on the line worthy of better pictures. The resolution was passed unanimously.

The *Joan of Arc* still had to give way to work for the annual exhibitions, and in 1843 Etty sent six pictures to the British Institution and seven to the Academy—the largest number of new works ever sent by him for exhibition in one year. Those at the British Institution included a landscape *On the Thames (Chelsea)*, painted from the balcony of Mr. and Mrs. George Bulmer's house at 2 Belle Vue, Chelsea; and a *Sketch for a large Picture of Christ Blessing Little Children. A subject intended originally for St. Margaret's Church, Brighton.* This picture does not seem ever to have been worked up into a finished painting, and St. Margaret's Church is now scheduled for deconsecration, but it is not unreasonable to suspect that Thomas Bodley, Etty's cousin in Brighton, may have had some share in first promoting the idea. Etty quickly sold all his pictures this year, and those at the Academy had been spoken for when still in the artist's studio. The *Entombment of Christ* became the property of the Rt. Hon. Henry Labouchere, M.P., and *The Infant Moses and his Mother* was bought by the Rt. Hon. Sir James Wigram; a third picture *In the Greenwood Shade*, remains unlocated. The landscape in this painting is described by Gilchrist as the fishpond at Givendale, and Etty seems to have combined his powers as history and landscape painter, albeit on a small scale. Nevertheless, at the behest of dealers, Etty was succumbing to the practice of converting minor studies into exhibition pictures, and the *Art Union* critic wrote: 'No. 169 *In the Greenwood Shade* . . . A female figure lying on a flowery bank, and with her a winged child, whom we must

---

[1] Gilchrist, *op. cit.*, II, pp. 138–9.

[2] *Minutes of the General Assembly of the Royal Academy*, V, p. 13, 7th November, 1842; *Minutes of the Royal Academy Council*, IX, p. 290, 26th November, 1842.

presume to be Cupid; the figures lie in shade, canopied over, as it were, with the boughs of trees. We can suppose this no more than an accidental study, wrought into a picture, and, like all such works—the *capita mortua* of the studio. . . .' [1]

By now the pattern of Etty's final development has been established, and the clue to his large fortune disclosed. Thomas Uwins, R.A., surprised that Etty died so wealthy, nonetheless explained that 'he [Etty] was taken up by dealers, and they can make a man's fortune. The dealers can no longer get a market for their Raphaels, Correggios, and stuff, manufactured in their backshops, and smoked into the appearance of antiquity; to do any business at all, they must go to living painters, and the man they take up becomes popular. The old nobility and land proprietors are gone out. Their place is supplied by railroad speculators, iron mine men, and grinders from Sheffield, etc., Liverpool and Manchester merchants and traders. This class of men are as much in the hands of dealers as the old black collectors were formerly. But they do not love darkness, and therefore will only deal with their contemporaries. The voluptuous character of Etty's works suits the degree of moral and mental intelligence of these people, and therefore his success!' [2] Uwins's rather sweeping condemnation of the new class of patron does scant justice to the perception and taste of men like Sir Robert Peel, Gillott and Vernon, who were often far in advance of their times. Furthermore, he has given only part of the general story, for he does not mention state patronage, which by then was in an experimental stage.

In November, 1841, a Royal Commission was appointed with the idea of promoting and encouraging the fine arts of the United Kingdom, and having particular reference to the decoration of the new Houses of Parliament with large 'historical' works. On 25th April, 1842, the Fine Arts Commission issued details of the competition and inviting artists to submit cartoons illustrating subjects taken from British history. These cartoons were to be done life size, and were intended as an exacting test of the competitors' abilities to design on a grand scale. Etty was among those appointed by the Commissioners in the following year to act as professional judges of the competition pieces, and on 24th June, 1843, he wrote to Eastlake (then Secretary to the Commission, and the only artist holding an official post), listing the cartoons in order of merit. [3] In his opinion, the artists entitled to the three first prizes of £300 were: John Callcott Horsley, for *St. Augustine Preaching to Ethelbert and Bertha*; C. W. Cope, for *The First Trial by Jury*; and John Zephaniah Bell, for *The Cardinal Bouchier Urging the Dowager Queen of Edward IV to give up from Sanctuary the Duke of York*. Of these, only Cope won a first prize; Edward Armitage and G. F. Watts (both of whom Etty had listed among the second prize winners) sharing with him this honour for their cartoons of *Caesar's First Invasion of Britain* and *Caractacus led in Triumph through Rome*. Horsley and Bell were each awarded a second prize of £200.

Before the competition results were announced, Etty was himself commissioned by the Prince Consort to paint one of the eight lunettes for the new summer pavilion in the

---

[1] *Art Union*, III, June 1843, pp. 159–78. This review also has a description of Etty's *Flemish Courtship*, exhibited that year, but now missing.

[2] *A Memoir of T. Uwins, R.A.*, London, 1858, I, pp. 124–5, letter to John Townshend, dated 'Kensington, Jan. 14, 1850'.

[3] Letter to Sir Charles Eastlake, 'Midsummer Day 1843' (York City Reference Library).

grounds of Buckingham Palace. This was on 8th May: he and Sir William Ross were the last to be asked; the other Academicians already named were C. R. Leslie, Clarkson Stanfield, Daniel Maclise, Thomas Uwins, Charles Eastlake and Edwin Landseer. Prince Albert chose fresco as the medium, a technique revived by his compatriots Peter von Cornelius and Johann Friedrich Overbeck some twenty years before in Rome. Even in England fresco was not entirely unknown, and a notice had appeared in *The Times*, 15th June, 1833, calling attention to Mr. Lane's fresco painting of the *Holy Family with a Doctor of the Church*. On 28th June, 1833, a letter from 'Scotus' of Edinburgh, refuted the idea that Lane's work was unique and cited John Zephaniah Bell's work on the ceilings of two of the public rooms in the newly built Muir House, Edinburgh. Thomas Barker (of Bath) had also painted a fresco of the *Massacre of Scio* on the wall of his private house at Bath, but the date of this work is not yet clearly established.[1] Etty was very reluctant to accept the commission, pleading unfamiliarity with fresco technique, and he experienced considerable difficulties during the whole of the time he spent working on the decorations. In June he wrote for advice to William Dyce, but he did not profit much from the very detailed information supplied by his colleague.[2]

John Milton's *Masque of Comus* had been decided as the subject from which the eight artists were to illustrate various episodes, and Etty chose the lines 'Circe with the Sirens three, Amidst the flowery-kirtled Naiades'. All July was spent struggling with the fresco, at the end of which he found it as intractable as ever. Maclise recalled how Etty would retouch upon the dry plaster of a previous day's work—with disastrous results, for the paint was never absorbed and would flake off.[3] He tried to do with fresco as he did with oil, and could not adapt himself to an entirely opposite process. His conception of the subject survives in a large oil painting *Circe and the Sirens Three* [pl. 80], now in Australia. Although this picture must have been done later than the fresco, it is likely to have followed the original plan fairly closely. But the composition, charming though it is, lacks the compactness and monumental scale so necessary for a large decorative design. The problem of how to fill the empty space above the reclining figures has not been solved satisfactorily, and Circe seems to emphasize this fault by her raised arm and wand. After a six-month interval, Etty was again at work on the fresco in February, 1844, and was advised by Maclise to give more precision to his details in an effort to suit the taste of the Prince Consort.[4] Lady Eastlake (then Miss Rigby) gives an interesting account of the scheme in her *Journals*. After a visit in March, 1844, she wrote: 'Walked to Buckingham Palace. . . . There is an artificial mound [in the garden], on which stands a little Chinesey box, divided into three or four small rooms; the centre an octagonal apartment, each side with a half circle devoted to one artist. The subjects are from Comus; Eastlake's is beautiful—he is the Raphael of England. Etty's next best in composition, and the nearest to real fresco effect. The others over-finished, and look-

---

[1] *Art Union*, III, 1841, p. 69, where the fresco is discussed, gives no precise information on this point. The fresco is still extant at Doric House, Sion Hill, Bath, and I am indebted to Mr. T. S. R. Boase for calling my attention to it.

[2] Letter from William Dyce, 20th June, 1843 (York City Reference Library).

[3] Gilchrist, *op. cit.*, II, p. 152.

[4] *Ibid.*, II, p. 165, Gilchrist does not name Etty's adviser, but strongly implies that it was Maclise.

ing no better on wall than they would have done on canvas. Prince Albert is to fill up the spaces beneath himself.'[1]

Dissatisfied with his previous attempts, Etty wrote to Colonel Anson, Prince Albert's Private Secretary, offering to paint a second subject of *Hesperus*. He also asked to be allowed to paint it in the peace and comfort of his own studio, fixing the picture in place afterwards. Tireless in his efforts to please, he left a sketch of his new composition at Buckingham Palace for the Prince's approval. In order to vindicate himself publicly, however, Etty sent to the Academy a large and finished oil painting of *Hesperus*, 'painted the size of the intended Fresco' [pl. 81]. This is undoubtedly a much more successful composition, and although sweeter in sentiment it has some of the monumental qualities of the 1826 *Judgment of Paris*; but there is also a fluency and easy grace not apparent in the earlier picture. The colour is much lighter in key, and pallid, slightly astringent hues of orange and chrome green characterize this and much else of Etty's later work. Complimented upon his *Hesperus* by the Prince Consort at the Academy dinner, Etty's hopes for a second chance were raised but never fulfilled. The first fresco proving unsuccessful and unacceptable, it was ordered to be removed and William Dyce was commissioned to paint a new one in its place. Dyce thus found himself in an unenviable position, and he wrote to Etty explaining the situation and seeking his generous understanding of the affair.[2] Meanwhile, Etty had received his fee of £40 as promised under the terms of the commission. The reward was not exactly on a princely scale, and Etty lost heavily on this venture.

The treatment accorded Etty by the Prince Consort angered several men, including William Thackeray who wrote some long and scornful attacks on the fickleness of royal patronage in *Fraser's Magazine*.[3] One suspects that Thackeray's biting sarcasm was directed at royal parsimony partly because it was an issue which could be used to express a more general dislike for the Prince. This dislike was shared by many Englishmen at the time, and was based to some extent upon a natural distrust for a foreigner as yet hardly known to the public. Any false move he might make was seized upon and used against him. Thus *Punch* could publish a doggerel verse which ran:

> I will not toil for queen and crown,
> If princely patrons spurn me down;
> I will not ask for royal job—
> Let my Maecenas be A SNOB! [4]

Thackeray wrote: 'What victims have those poor fellows been of this awful patronage! Great has been the commotion in the pictorial world . . . regarding the fate of those

[1] *The Letters and Journals of Lady Eastlake*, London, 1895, 2 vols. I, pp. 117–18. *See also* Lewis Grüner and Anna Jameson, *The Decorations of the Garden-Pavilion in the Grounds of Buckingham Palace*, London, 1846, for coloured engravings of the scheme as finally executed.

[2] Gilchrist, *op. cit.*, II, pp. 169–70.

[3] *Fraser's Magazine*, May 1845, pp. 583–97, *The Royal Academy of Arts, Its State and Prospects*.

[4] Quoted by Thackeray, *Fraser's Magazine*, June 1845, p. 719, in his review of the current Royal Academy summer exhibition. Prince Albert married Queen Victoria on 10th February, 1840; it was in 1844 that he began to effect stringent economies in the running of the royal household and entirely re-organized its management. He did not become better known to his people until the 1851 Great Exhibition.

frescoes which royalty was pleased to order, which it condescended to purchase at a price no amateur would have the face to offer . . . Think of august powers and principalities ordering the works of such a great man as Etty to be hacked out of the palace wall—that was a slap in the face to every artist in England. . . .'[1] Eastlake's sketch for the *Comus* decorations was exhibited at the Academy in 1845; where Thackeray criticized it as a 'prim', 'laboured' and lifeless composition. Eighteen years later, when tempers had cooled, G. F. Watts praised the Prince's attempts to encourage fresco painting, considering it a duty which should have been performed much earlier by the Royal Academy.[2]

Etty had stopped work on the Garden Pavilion fresco in order to pay what was to be his last visit abroad. On 16th August, 1843, accompanied by his friend John Wood, he left London for France. He wanted to see the places connected with the life of Joan of Arc, and during his fortnight's stay he travelled to Rouen, Paris and Orléans. Pensively, he wandered around the market place at Rouen, once the scene of Joan's martyrdom; in Paris he remarked upon the street improvements, the extensions to the Louvre and the Spanish pictures there; but it was Orléans that stirred him most. From here he wrote letters which show him re-living the story of Joan; few medieval buildings remained, but those still standing were enough to fire his imagination. After two days and a night at Orléans he returned to Paris, and visited Bishop Luscombe again. Three small oil studies were made of Louvre pictures—a Titian, a Veronese and a Carpaccio. Excursions were also made to Saint Denis, and to Versailles where he admired Horace Vernet's large battle scenes. Etty by now had warmed to France and he returned better in health, for 'French living and wines well agree with him'.[3]

Earlier that year he had the delightful surprise of meeting his youngest brother Charles, whom he had not seen for over thirty years. Charles Etty had risen to the rank of captain in the merchant service, and then in 1831 had set up as sugar-planter at Wonolangan, Java. His enterprise was extremely successful and he had come home to buy large quantities of new machinery for his factory. He remained in England for two years, and did not sail away until the end of July, 1845, never to return to the peaceful retirement in York he had once planned.[4] The portrait of *Charles Etty* [pl. 84] was painted by his brother William sometime during this stay, and it provides a vivid record of this resourceful and robust character. Compare this portrait of him with another done by his brother over thirty years before, and it will be seen that there is the same directness of style underlying both works. When Charles went back to Java he took with him

[1] William Thackeray, *Fraser's Magazine*, June, 1845, pp. 718–19. Richard Colls, the dealer, paid Etty £40 for the frescoes which he obtained from Lewis Grüner, the Superintendent who had charge of them during the time they were stored in a shed in the grounds of Buckingham Palace. William Wethered bought them from Colls for £400, only to experience the greatest difficulty in selling them after two attempts in 1856 and 1858. The Pavilion was dismantled in 1928: *see* John Steegman, *Consort of Taste*, London, 1950, p. 205 (note).

[2] *Report of the Commissioners to inquire into the present position of the Royal Academy*, H.M.S.O., London, 1863, p. 332, extract from the evidence of G. F. Watts, Minute 3132 (17th April, 1863).

[3] Gilchrist, *op. cit.*, II, pp. 154–9.

[4] He died at Wonolangan, 4th December, 1856, aged 63. The sugar refinery was in operation until the Japanese invasion of Java 1942–3. From information supplied by Ir. Thomas H. Etty: also Gilchrist, *op. cit.*, II, pp. 148, 176–7, 205.

a pictorial reminder of the meeting of the five surviving brothers held at York on 8th September, 1844. This was William's painting of a stone monument bearing the initials of the brothers and an inscription 'Let Brotherly Love Continue' [pl. 94*b*]; a pilgrim's staff, water gourd and wreath lean against the stone; beyond is a view of York Minster at sunset. A milestone indicates that York is one mile distant and the base of the monument is inscribed 'for Charles 1845'. There is a touching *naïveté* about this memento symbolizing much that was dear to Etty, giving yet another glimpse of his character.

Although Etty met Joseph Gillott in 1843, this new Maecenas did not begin to buy his paintings until 1845. Or, more accurately, the first receipt to survive is dated 23rd April, 1845, when Etty acknowledged Gillott's payment of £340 for 'various Copies, Studies, and Works'.[1] After this, the rate of buying quickens considerably, and on 1st November, 1845, he acquired five Etty studies for £147, besides confirming a deal with Colls for Etty's 1838 *Bivouac of Cupid* (£438), an *Ablution* [*sic*] *of Cupid* (£105), *Warrior* (£65), *Joan of Arc* (£50, obviously a study for one of the final pictures): making a total of £805 thus spent. A week later, Gillott made a payment direct to Etty of £1,000 on account for three pictures he had commissioned from him: 'The Choice of Paris 600Gs; Circe and the Syrens 350Gs; Venus Cupid & Psyche 200Gs.'[2] At this stage, Gillott was only just beginning to build up his collection and his account books make interesting reading, for it is possible to follow through many of the stages by which he obtained his pictures. Sometimes it was direct from the artist; but more often through dealers and collectors such as George Pennell of Birmingham, F. W. Hooper of Leamington, Thomas Rought, William Wethered (a tailor in Conduit Street), Henry Wallis, and Colls—all of London. Often, too, he would exchange and barter pictures, and being well versed in commerce he usually managed to strike a good bargain. Although he did buy some old masters, Gillott was justly famed for his patronage of J. M. W. Turner, John Linnell, William Müller and other contemporary English artists. His wealth derived from a revolutionary idea he himself had perfected for using pressed steel in the mass production of metal pen nibs. Ingenuity and shrewdness were mingled with generosity and homeliness in his character—qualities that endeared him both to his friends and his workmen. By founding a benevolent society for his employees, and ensuring good working conditions in his factory, he joined the ranks of the earlier 'paternal capitalists' such as Josiah Wedgwood and Robert Owen.

Gillott seems to have brought out certain aspects of Etty's personality which previously had lain dormant. A certain boisterous schoolboy humour, a delight in elaborate puns and heavy wit, characterize much of the correspondence between the two men. These elements may be found in a few of the letters to Walter Etty and Thomas Bodley, but never to the same extent. The friendship soon ripened, and by the end of 1845 Etty signs himself as a 'partner' in the firm of Gillott & Company—as well he might, considering the amount of business conducted between the two men.

[1] Etty-Gillott correspondence, Nicholas Gillott collection, Birmingham.

[2] From Gillott's *Memorandums of Sales & Purchases Pictures etc.*, (May, 1843—November, 1846), an account book belonging to Nicholas Gillott, Esq. Bernard Denvir has published a few of the more light-hearted Etty letters in his article on Joseph Gillott as a collector, *The Connoisseur Year Book 1958*, 'Pens and Patronage', pp. 71–7.

CHAPTER NINE

RETROSPECT AND RETIREMENT: 1846-1849

'Went to Etty, who is very thin, very asthmatic—will not, I fear, last very long: he is *revelling* in colour and in form, but is in some parts of his larger picture deficient in expression, though in other parts most powerful and most happy.' [1] This gloom-tempered verdict was given by Macready in April 1846; the 'larger picture' was Etty's second *Judgment of Paris*, then on exhibition at the Academy. Both this and the *Circe and the Sirens* were adversely criticized by *The Times*—a not unusual occurrence, it might be said, at any rate until 1844, when Samuel Phillips became art critic for the newspaper. Phillips, who had been a political writer for the *Morning Herald*, soon became well known in his new capacity, and his appointment, made permanent in 1845, marked a new stage in art criticism. More space was given to the subject, with a corresponding increase in the quality of writing. Although not a highly original critic, he was both perceptive and informed, so that his opinion is of value. It is with genuine regret that he had to call attention to the weaknesses in colour and composition of the two Etty paintings. [2] A fine *Study of a Peacock* for the *Judgment of Paris* partly retrieved the artist's reputation.

The extent and rapidity of this deterioration of Etty's powers is most strikingly revealed by a comparison between his *Fairy of the Fountain* [pl. 87], finished in the latter part of 1846, and *Musidora* painted in 1844 but exhibited at the British Institution at the beginning of 1846. The firm modelling, clear colour and strong composition of the earlier picture only emphasize the deficiencies of its successor. The curious title and incongruity of scale between the tiny figure on the right and the female nude are explained in a letter to Gillott (dated 4th September, 1846): '. . . I have abandoned the idea of the broken fragment of marble bas-relief, and make the little urchin "the fairy of the fountain!" which will be prettiness indeed, she is looking towards it, so that he will be standing on vapour which seems rising from the fountain—a little fay, . . .' There are at least four versions (and several copies) of *Musidora*, the first being shown in 1843 at the Academy, where it was bought by George Knott for 70 guineas. All of them show the nude figure in the same pose, but there are slight variations in the treat-

[1] *The Diaries of William Charles Macready 1833–1851*, ed. William Toynbee, London, 1912, II, p. 335, 7th April, 1846.
[2] *The Times*, 6th May, 1846. *See also* chap. 3, note 7.

ment of the landscape background, which is itself based on the pool in the grounds of 'The Plantation' at Acomb. When exhibited in 1843 and 1846 both paintings were entitled *The Bather*, '*At the doubtful breeze alarmed*' [pls. 85a, 88], and the subject is inspired by some lines in James Thomson's *The Seasons: Summer* which describe how Musidora is surprised by Damon when bathing in a woodland stream. It is possible too, that Etty knew Thomas Gainsborough's *Musidora* (Tate Gallery), when this painting was still in the collection of Robert Vernon.

During July, 1846, Etty visited his friend A. W. Pugin at Ramsgate. Writing to Walter Etty and to Gillott, he described Pugin's 'Gothic Castle' set in golden corn-fields, with green seas beyond and azure skies above—'music and masses within, and larks singing without'.[1] He attended Mass in Pugin's private chapel, accompanied by Clarkson Stanfield and J. R. Herbert. 'I wish,' he told Walter, 'you could enjoy this place a while—it is wonderful the admirable way in which every thing is done, so solid, good, and truly comfortable, without nonsense and frippery. He is a marvellous man, there is only one Pugin. We have been up to the Tower today you did not see that the last time you were here—such a view. . . . Pugin is building a Church and Cloisters around. Here he will have a little Town.'[2] Etty met Pugin as early as August, 1837, and his admiration for him had kindled quickly, for in May the following year he attended the ceremonial opening of the Roman Catholic chapel of St. Mary, Oscott College, Birmingham, largely the work of Pugin. A full pontifical High Mass was celebrated and such a splendid and elaborate service had been unknown in England for some three centuries; Pugin was joint master of ceremonies. Lord Shrewsbury was the most distinguished layman present, and Etty must have been one of the very few non-Roman Catholic members of the congregation allowed to attend. At the time of the Ramsgate visit Pugin was absorbed in designing the new Houses of Parliament, in co-operation with Sir Charles Barry—an architect later unfairly condemned by Etty as a 'Destructive', because he pulled down old Westminster Bridge.

Back in London, Etty one day encountered J. M. W. Turner in the street and was asked by him about his apartments in Buckingham Street. Having heard that Etty was planning retirement to York, he had begun to covet his rooms with their commanding view over the Thames; 'I suppose', wrote Etty to Gillott, 'Queen Ann Street West since the storm (which put his pipe out sadly) seems to be too dilapidated to be agreeable— he came and looked and longed—and then departed wishing me well wherever I went or wherever I staid, and said he should be sorry to lose me.'[3] Etty did not retire until 1848, but it is not surprising that Turner should envy him his rooms when one reads a description of them in J. T. Smith's *A Book for a Rainy Day*: 'Should my reader's boat ever stop at York Watergate, let me request him to look up at the three upper balconied windows of that mass of building on the south-west corner of Buckingham Street. Those, and the two adjoining Westminster, give light to chambers occupied by that truly epic historical painter, and most excellent man, Etty, the Royal Academician, who has fitted up the balconied rooms with engravings after pictures of the three great masters, Raphael, Nicholas Poussin, and Rubens.

[1] Etty to Gillott, Sunday morning, 12th July, 1846 (Nicholas Gillott Collection).
[2] Etty to Walter, Sunday morning, 12th July, 1846 (York City Reference Library).
[3] Etty to Gillott, 7th September, 1846 (Nicholas Gillott Collection).

'The other two windows illumine his painting-room, in which his mind and colours resplendently shine, even in the face of one of the grandest scenes in Nature, our river Thames and city edifices, with a most luxuriant and extensive face of a distant country, the beauties of which he most liberally delights in showing his friends from the leads of his apartments, which, in my opinion, exhibit the finest point of view of all others for a panorama.'[1] Etty had the top floor of a five-storey house which had been built on the site of Samuel Pepys's old home, and still stands today. When Etty first moved to 14 Buckingham Street in 1824 he leased the 'lower floor' (presumably Gilchrist meant the ground and first floors), but two years later the upper storey became vacant, and Etty seized the opportunity to obtain the more attractive position, even although it meant incurring some financial loss by forfeiture of his previous lease.

Throughout the rest of 1846 and the early part of the following year Etty worked hard to complete his last great work, the three *Joan of Arc* pictures. Chronic ill health hampered his efforts, and the strain of painting three large canvases was often almost beyond his strength. Dealers were told firmly not to expect any minor pieces during this period, although Etty did send three works to the British Institution. One of these, *An Israelite Indeed* [pl. 83b], bears a strong resemblance to the *Godfrey de Bouillon* of 1835, and the two paintings make an interesting comparison. The later work shows how much looser Etty's brushwork had become; there is also, perhaps, a greasiness in the handling of the paint and a formlessness in the modelling which betray the artist's failing hand. And yet, as will be seen, there are other paintings of this time which equal the best of his earlier years. In his quest for accuracy of detail in the *Joan of Arc*, Etty sought advice from several friends and authorities including James Robinson Planché. Planché was a dramatist, theatrical manager, and expert on heraldry—later becoming Somerset Herald. He recommended the painter to read Millin de Grandmaison's *Antiquités nationales* (1799), and Bernard de Montfaucon's *Les Monumens de la Monarchie Francoise* (1729–33) for guidance over armour and harness of the time of Charles VII.[2] To revise his knowledge of horse anatomy Etty also went on sketching expeditions to Astley's and Tattersall's. By the middle of April, 1847, the three paintings were ready for the Academy exhibition.

It will be recalled that the central picture measured 15ft. by 9 ft. 9 in. and the two flanking canvases 6 ft. 6 in. by 9 ft. 9 in.[3] When exhibited the subjects were described thus: '123 left *Joan of Arc, on finding the sword she had dreamt of, in the church of St. Catherine de Fierbois, devotes herself and it to the service of God and her country.* 124 centre *Joan of Arc makes a sortie from the gates of Orleans, and scatters the enemies of France.* 125 right *Joan of Arc, after rendering the most signal services to her Prince and people, is suffered to die a martyr in their cause.*' Joan was shown in the triple rôle of saint, patriot and martyr. A fuller account

---

[1] John Thomas Smith, *A Book for a Rainy Day, or Recollections of the Events of the Years 1766–1833*, ed. W. Whitten, London, 1905, p. 305. No. 14 now bears a plaque commemorating the tenancies of Pepys (1684–1700) and Robert Harley, Earl of Oxford (1661–1744) in the old house; of Etty (1824–49) and Clarkson Stanfield (1793–1869) in the present one.

[2] Planché to Etty (undated) *c.* 1846/7, written from the Royal Olympic Theatre (York City Reference Library). *See also* Gilchrist, *op. cit.*, II, p. 222. An English edition of Montfaucon's *L'Antiquité expliquée et représentée en figures* (Paris, 1719), publ. by Humphrey, 1721, was among the books in the Etty Sale, May, 1850.

[3] *See* chap. 7, p. 88 and note 3.

of the inspiration and intention of the pictures occurs in a letter Etty wrote to Richard Colls, 5th May, 1847, which the latter had duplicated so as to sell copies of it with the sets of engravings executed by C. W. Wass. The idea first came to the artist over seven years before, when he was in Henry VII's Chapel at Westminster Abbey. He thought of Joan as the Judith of modern times, and conceived the picture in the form of an epic, with a beginning, a middle, and an end. (The multiple of three times three seems to have had some special attraction for Etty!)

Since the pictures themselves have disappeared, perhaps the best idea of their composition and general effect may be gained from Samuel Phillips's exhibition review in *The Times*: 'On entering the great room, a picture by Etty, divided into compartments, and illustrating three epochs from the life of Joan of Arc, instantly arrests the attention. . . . The character of the heroine under these different circumstances is preserved with extraordinary skill. In the church we have the single-minded enthusiasm of the inexperienced girl; in the conflict with her enemies, where she is scattering death around her, there is still the same consciousness of high purpose; so that every blow she deals seems to be the act of one by whom nothing is done in anger, and with whose will no human emotion could interfere; while, on the pile, her task completed, and the animal vigour by which she has been sustained in her career no longer needed, her entire spirit seems to be concentrated in the trance of martyrdom. This last compartment would be painful if it were more than part of a grand whole, for the eagerness of the monk [Father Avenel] holding up a crucifix at the last moment, while yet he can venture near, the bursting up of the flame and smoke, which in another moment will remove the victim from sight, and the crowd of eager faces (among which one female head is alone discernible, and that turned away) impart an intensity of action to the scene the impression of which is not easily subdued. Amidst all these merits there are faults, and some glaring ones, although they are none of them such as to interfere with the sentiment of the work. The routed and half naked soldiers in the sortie look more like Saracens than the people of any other country, and it is quite clear that the colossal horse upon which Joan is mounted could never have emerged from the very moderate sized castle in the back ground.' [1] Ten days after this was written, it was announced that C. W. Wass and R. Colls had bought the paintings at the artist's price of 2,500 guineas; and in August Etty was reported to be putting the finishing touches to the pictures which by then were on show at Colls's premises in Bond Street. Wass had undertaken to engrave them, but first ambitious plans had been made for a provincial tour followed by showings in Paris and elsewhere on the Continent. [2] The projected tours did not take place. Only a few prints of the Wass engravings were issued, and it is not improbable that the failure of the *Joan of Arc* paintings to win popularity contributed to Wass's bankruptcy in May 1852. [3] The three paintings became separated, and passed through the sale rooms several times, quite often being bought in for very small sums. The original purchasers could only have regained a fraction of their original outlay.

J. H. Anderdon records that the Hon. Mrs. Norton was the model for Joan in the

[1] *The Times*, 1st May, 1847.

[2] *Ibid.*, 11th and 17th May, 19th August, 1847. Gilchrist, *op. cit.*, II, p. 225, notes that William Wethered was also one of the joint shareholders in the *Joan of Arc* speculation.

[3] *The Times*, 19th May, 26th November and 24th December, 1852.

third picture which depicted her martyrdom. 'The third No. 125 was at Manchester at the Great Exhibition in 1857.—the Honble Mrs Norton related to the Director as he attended her thro' the Gallery her having stood to the artist as Model for his Martyr.— the lady appears to have acted some sense of distress and suffering and to have indulged in some contortions which Etty rebuked, reminding her of the gentle Endurance required of a Sainted Martyr!—to this overacting of the heroine may fairly be attributed the failure in the resemblance. N.B. This last of the three pictures was in the collection of a Mr. Cox on the walls of Messrs. Fosters Gallery for sale in Mar 1861, and a most ugly affair it was.'[1] A small oval head and shoulders portrait of *The Hon. Mrs. Caroline Norton* now belongs to Lieut.-Colonel William Stirling [pl. 90]. It shows a strikingly handsome woman looking half left, with her head tilted back slightly so as to display a slender neck. A white lace ruff is caught together at the front by a brooch on which is inscribed the word 'Salve'.

Useful as these written descriptions are, they give little idea of the actual disposition of the elements within each picture. Nevertheless, the general composition of the central panel is indicated by a small but lively pen sketch now in the Victoria and Albert Museum [pl. 89b]. In this appear figures marching from a castellated gateway across a drawbridge; the mounted figure carrying a battle standard in their midst is presumably Joan of Arc. Another hastily executed watercolour sketch in the Bradford City Art Gallery seems to represent a burning pyre, with a figure in monk's habit crouching in front of it, while in the foreground appears a turbulent crowd of spectators and to the right is a mounted soldier. This is perhaps a preliminary study for the martyrdom of St. Joan, and may be only a detail since the figure of the saint is not clearly distinguishable. A sheet of pen and ink studies of the figure of Joan at the stake has survived, and she is shown looking heavenwards clutching a crucifix to her bosom [pl. 89a]. The pose agrees with a woodcut illustration of the subject published in a London journal soon after Etty's death. Although it is a little pathetic that of the original grand scheme only a few meagre snippets should remain, yet it is doubtful whether the *Joan of Arc* paintings, had they survived, would have added much lustre to Etty's fame.

In the summer of 1847 Jenny Lind paid her first visit to England, and was an instant success at her first appearance at Her Majesty's Theatre as Alice in *Roberto il Diavolo*. Not quite twenty-seven, she was at the height of her operatic career when she sat to Etty for her portrait. As with Mlle Rachel, so it seems likely that William Macready was also responsible for introducing the artist to this new sitter. However grave the defects of Etty's large-scale work may have been, none of these weaknesses spoil his portrait of *Miss Jenny Lind* [pl. 91b]. Indeed, this is one of the most interesting records there is of the singer; although the artist may be guilty of a little flattery in the representation of his subject, for she had somewhat plain features and a broad snub nose whereas in the portrait her nose is made to look slim and elegant. Someone who knew her well described her thus: 'She had two great powers in her face; one of stiffening it, and the other of resolving it, so to speak; I mean of imparting all sorts of active expressions, chiefly of the arch and comical sort to it. It was sometimes perfectly motionless and stiff as to be almost corpse-like, but not without a certain grandeur, an expression of determined obstinacy, stubbornness and hauteur. Then when she changed to active expres-

[1] Anderdon, *Catalogues of the Royal Academy Exhibitions*, LXXIX, 1847 (British Museum).

sion, she had all sorts of odd uses of her eyes, looking from underneath and from the corners of her eyes, and so on, and was excessively arch; and one expression chased another just like the waves over the sea.' [1] Etty has suggested exactly these qualities in his portrait of her. Apparently unaware of the pet dog pawing her, she remains slightly aloof, yet a smile hovers around her mouth and there is a hint of amused curiosity in her gaze. The picture is most delicately painted, particularly the hands which are touched in with exquisite ease.

Another painting of about the same time is the *Portrait of an Unknown Lady* [pl. 91a]. This is very similar in style to the *Miss Jenny Lind*, and it is notable that Etty maintained a high standard of portraiture even to the end of his life. The contrast between his *Bather* series of 1843–5 and *The Fairy of the Fountain* has already been discussed, and this change in style is also reflected in his portraiture. *The Children of Henry and Ann Wood* [pl. 92], completed in August 1845, should be compared with the two later portraits of about 1847. It will be seen that within the space of two years Etty has changed from a smooth, flowing brushstroke, to a broken, hatched stroke—a difference most obvious in the flesh painting of the three pictures. Probably contemporary with the *Wood Children* is the triple portrait of *Mrs. William Wethered* [pl. 95], although it was not exhibited until the R.A. show of 1849. The slightly incongruous centre portrait of Mrs. Wethered, with her hair falling loosely about her shoulders, may be explained by her having acted as a model for Etty's *Joan of Arc*. Etty was much attracted by the idea of a triple portrait, for he also painted *The Hon. Mrs. Norton and her Sisters* [pl. 93], which may date from 1847. This is a glittering, colourful painting; the youngest, flaxen-haired girl wears a pale cerulean blue dress, her sister is in white, and the other sister has a black dress with a small red, blue and green floral design, and her black hair is set off against a green curtain in the background.

Late in December 1847, Etty took a step nearer retirement when he gave up his seat on the Council of the Royal Academy. Thoughts of retirement had been in his mind for some time, and in August 1844 he had written to Betsy '. . . I now want but little of 5,000£ hurrah!—bless the Lord—we if all be well shall soon have our 156£ per Annum, whatever wind blows—and a Cottage in York. . . .' [2] The 'cottage' was bought two years later, in April, 1846, for the sum of £1,100. It was a substantial two-storey house in Coney Street, and near enough the banks of the River Ouse for its back windows to command a pleasant prospect up river. Etty was not able to move in immediately, as certain alterations had to be made which included the building of a bow window on to the painting room overlooking the river. These were supervised by his friend James Atkinson, and in June 1848 Etty retired to York. But he retained his old rooms in Buckingham Street, and his removal to York was not completed until September that same year.

Among the seven paintings sent to the Academy exhibition of 1848 was *A Group of Captives: 'By the Waters of Babylon'* [pl. 96]. Inspired by Psalm 137, its mood perhaps reflects Etty's own sadness at having to exile himself from London. Modest in scale, the painting is nevertheless an impressive swansong, although it was not intended as the

---

[1] *Letters of the Rev. J. B. Mozeley, D.D.*, ed. by his Sister, London, 1885—quoted by Edward Wagenknecht, *Jenny Lind*, Boston and New York, 1931, pp. 98–9.

[2] Letter to Elizabeth Etty, Thursday, 1st August, 1844 (Jacobus J. T. Bosch Coll.).

chef d'œuvre among his pictures that year. A colossal *St. John the Baptist*, with the text 'Him that crieth from the wilderness, Repent ye!', attracted most attention and it was welcomed as a change from the long series of female nude studies of recent years. Phillips, writing in *The Times*, expressed the hope that Etty would continue the new line of subject begun the previous year with the *Joan of Arc*, for 'The public were taken by surprise at this new production of historic art, and were curious to know whether Etty intended to maintain the position so suddenly seized. The *St. John* of the present exhibition shows that he will keep to his post. The expression of the countenance and the commanding gesture evidence the sublime conception of the artist. The flesh reveals his wonderful power of colour, and the upper part of the figure is admirable. But descending from the girdle those deficiencies so well known in the smaller works begin to be manifest. In the left leg there is a slovenliness in the drawing which recalls the old inattention to detail, and the ground is more unfinished and smudgy than is consistent with a perfect picture. The attempts and conceptions of Mr. Etty are very great, but he does not quite abandon the preparatory aspect.' [1] The landscape sketch of *Givendale, Yorkshire*, exhibited in 1848 is probably the small picture of Givendale Church now in the York Art Gallery. It is very close in style to the background of '*By the Waters of Babylon*'. John Ruskin, in his review of the exhibition wrote: 'Little else that could be called colour was to be seen upon the walls of the Exhibition with the exception of the smaller works of Mr. Etty. Of these, the single head, *Morning Prayer* (No. 25), and the *Still Life* (No. 73), deserved, allowing for their peculiar aim, the highest praise. The larger subjects, more especially the St. John, were wanting in the merits peculiar to the painter; and in other respects it is alike painful and useless to allude to them.' [2]

Robert Vernon had died in 1847, and in December 160 paintings had been selected from his collection on behalf of the nation. By October of the following year these pictures were on exhibition to the public at the National Gallery, but it was not long before strong complaints appeared in the press about the way in which the works were hung. They had been condemned to the gallery cellars, where they were crowded together in the rooms beneath the central stairs, and to the inconvenience of poor lighting were added the damaging effects of dust and the public's elbows. [3] *Punch* called the Vernon Collection the 'National Cellar-ius', and it was not until April, 1850, that the pictures were removed to Marlborough House, where a private view was held on 1st August, 1850. The collection contained some of the best and most representative examples of the modern British school of painting and with the exception of the Turner Bequest, was one of the largest bequests of its kind to the nation during the nineteenth century. Eleven Ettys became public property in this way.

Once in York, with the excitement of settling into new quarters passed, Etty began to miss greatly the Life School of the Academy, as indeed the models had lamented the going of one of their most regular patrons. [4] The problem was solved when the artist

---

[1] *The Times*, 2nd May, 1847. The *St. John* was bought by the Rev. Isaac Spencer for £450 in May 1849.

[2] J. Ruskin, *Modern Painters*, II, Addenda, IV, Cook & Wedderburn ed., p. 340.

[3] Four letters on the subject were printed in *The Times*, 30th October, 8th, 10th and 11th November, 1849.

[4] Writing to the Board of Trade 16th August, 1847, resigning from the Normal School of Design's Council, Etty had pleaded for improved 'accommodation and instruction in the Female School' (*see* N. Blakiston, *The Burlington Magazine*, XCIX, Feb., 1957, p. 58).

obtained locally models of both sexes who would pose for him. He had feared that this might cause a scandal in York, but such was not the case although he encountered some opposition when he tried, successfully as it happened, to introduce study from the male nude to the York School of Design. The practice was continued until the death of John Patterson, the Master of the School. During the winter, Etty also painted several studies from Madame Wharton, who visited York with her *Poses Plastiques*. It was during these first three months of retirement that Etty composed the autobiographical notice which was published in *The Art Journal* early in the following year. 'They were going to do it', he explained to Wethered, 'and I thought I could do it better than a man who knew nought about it.' [1]

An exacting task which fell to Etty's lot in 1849 concerned the big retrospective exhibition of his work organized by Henry Cole for the Society of Arts. Upon being invited to advise on the selection of pictures, the artist made it a condition that his nine great works should be included, and although the Royal Scottish Academy readily agreed to lend its five history pieces, the Royal Manchester Institution was persuaded to part with the *Sirens and Ulysses* only after strong assurances had been given regarding its safety *en route*. The *Joan of Arc* paintings were close at hand and presented less of a problem. One hundred and thirty-three pictures were collected together at the Adelphi, representing all aspects of Etty's artistic career from 1820 to his most recent work. It is remarkable that nothing was included of the period 1810–19, and one is left wondering whether this omission was deliberate or whether the works were simply not available. The private view was held on Saturday, 9th June, 1849, and the exhibition must have provided a most attractive spectacle; it remained open until 25th August. Prince Albert, as President of the Society of Arts, visited the exhibition and formally congratulated Etty, but warmer admiration came from fellow artists and friends.

During the course of the exhibition, Etty experimented with the idea of having an English translation of Homer's verses of the Sirens' Song set to music and performed in the room adjoining that which contained his *Sirens and Ulysses*. We are not told who composed the music, but the result does not seem to have been very successful. The exhibition got off to a slow start and although later quite well attended, it did not prove a financial success. It was the second of a series which had begun the year before with an exhibition of works by William Mulready, R.A., and which were promoted 'In Aid of the Formation of a National Gallery of British Art'. The Mulready exhibition had shown a modest profit, but the Society lost heavily on its successor, and expenses were only paid by the diversion (with the donor's consent) of £500 given in 1837 by Mrs. Acton, the widow of Samuel Acton, an architect member of the Society. The money was originally intended to found prizes for subjects related to architecture and architectural design. [2] One imagines that the cost of transporting the *grandes machines* would have cut deeply into the Society's resources. The daily press reacted to the exhibition in various ways, *The Times* containing no mention at all, the *Observer* praising it, and the *Morning Post* devoting a column and a half to it—almost all of it condemnatory. [3]

At the last Academy dinner Etty was to attend it was noticed how shrunken he had

---

[1] Etty to William Wethered, York, 13th December, 1848 (*Whitley Papers*, British Museum).
[2] Sir Henry Trueman Wood, *A History of Royal Society of Arts*, London, 1913, p. 379.
[3] *Observer*, 10th June, 1849; *Morning Post*, 11th June, 1849.

become, and how quickly the slightest exertion tired him. In early August he suffered a severe attack of rheumatic fever, but he rallied and managed to visit the Society of Arts several times before his exhibition closed. When the morning came for it to be dismantled and dispersed, Etty stood in the midst of his life's work and sadly bid adieu to it all.

The anxiety and strain of the past few months had left him quite exhausted, and he returned to York a prematurely aged man. But he still retained all his mental faculties and he forced himself to continue working on a large picture, *The Grecian Bridal Procession* (12$\frac{1}{2}$ ft. by 7$\frac{1}{4}$ ft.), begun earlier that year. The subject was again taken from Homer; the highlights had been laid in with white chalk, and the figures outlined in black charcoal, 'the musicians go before the Bride; two maids at her side. Other figures follow'.[1] The picture was never finished; the canvas was sold at the artist's sale and all traces of the old composition obliterated by a new design.

The end came quickly, hastened by an imprudence on Etty's part. One evening he left off his flannel undergarment before retiring to bed, the next night—3rd November—he succumbed to an unusually fierce attack of asthma, and already crippled with rheumatism his condition gradually worsened, so that by the 10th (Saturday) he was confined to his bed in a room next to the studio. On the following Tuesday towards evening, he realized that he was dying. Looking out across the River Ouse at the setting sun, he spoke serenely of death as a great mystery: 'wonderful! wonderful! this death!' He died at a quarter to eight that same evening.[2]

Ten days later, Etty was buried in St. Olave's Churchyard, York, after a public funeral attended by a large number of civic dignitaries and citizens as well as many relatives and friends. It had been Etty's wish that he should be buried in York Minster, but in his Will he had made no provision for payment of the statutory fees, and York seemed too preoccupied with its own financial worries following the collapse of George Hudson's railway kingdom to consider either waiving the rules or setting up a public subscription.

Six months after Etty's death, a sale of all his studies, books, painting materials and miscellaneous studio effects was held at Messrs. Christie & Manson (as they then were). It began on Monday, 6th May, 1850, and continued until the Friday of that week, the remaining two days of the sale being held on Monday and Tuesday of the following week. A total of 1,034 lots was disposed of, and the sum of £5,186 16s. 6d. realized. Among the lots were 60 copies after other masters, including that of Titian's *Venus of the Tribune* which was bought by 'Francklin' [*sic*] for 70 gns., and more than thirty unfinished paintings as distinct from academy studies, of which latter there were nearly 800. There were also two suits of armour, one Milanese and the other Bavarian. Several small studies for the *Joan of Arc* were sold, but are now lost. The sale attracted a lot of attention and was well attended. Anderdon wrote that 'This was a wonderful Sale to see—Christie's 2 Rooms encumbered by Millboards and Sketches of canvas each displaying forms of man and womankind—heaps.'[3]

In his last years Etty had become famous and even wealthy, yet what was his influence upon succeeding generations of British artists? It must be admitted that he could not

[1] Gilchrist, *op. cit.*, II, p. 295. [2] *Ibid.*, II, pp. 293–7.
[3] Anderdon, *op. cit.*, LXXX, 1850 (British Museum).

claim to have founded a school of painters. He had a number of imitators perhaps, usually of the second rank and among whom may be included George Baxter, Edward Calvert, W. E. Frost, B. Hubbard, F. R. Pickersgill, John Phillip, R. A. (some of whose oil nude studies come close to Etty in colour, although harder in modelling), Rothwell and John Wood. However much he was admired and respected by many of the younger men, the unevenness and aimlessness of his later work prevented him from becoming the leader of a new school of realist painters. Holman Hunt has given an interesting account of the situation when, as a student, he was himself searching for a 'perfect guide'. Writing of the years 1844–50, he said, 'What I sought was the power of undying appeal to the hearts of living men. Much of the favourite art left the inner self untouched. . . . Etty, after twenty years of failure and irrepressible effort, had in his full prime become the rage. His "Syrens", "Holofernes", and the diploma picture will always justify his great reputation; but in my youth he had lost the robustness he once had, and at last he composed classic subjects with the tawdry taste of a paper-hanger. He retained a consummate mastery over brush and paint, with a richness of tints and tones that ranked him among the famed colourists of the world; but the paintings of his advanced age cloyed the taste by their sweetness, and his forms bore evidence of being copied with little fastidiousness from town models, distorted by the modiste's art.' [1] It is sad to think that such great talent should never have fulfilled its early promise.

Sir John Millais was another artist who in his student days had formed himself on Etty's example. His first oil painting *Cupid Crowned with Flowers*, of 1841, bears all the marks of Etty's style, and this influence continues right through Millais' early work, as may be seen in *Pizarro Seizing the Inca of Peru* (1845) and again in *Cymon and Iphigenia* of 1847. Two years later, however, all trace of Etty's style has gone, unless one can claim that the brilliant colour in *Lorenzo and Isabella* is his Venetian legacy to his compatriots. Millais' son spoke of Etty as being the only man of the old school whom his father had really admired.[2] It must be put to Etty's credit that he was able to inspire (if only briefly) a number of the younger talented men of his day; men as diverse in outlook as Millais and G. F. Watts. Perhaps if one seeks an heir to Etty it should be Watts. He of all men was the most capable of designing on a grand scale and often more successfully than Etty, and he too, had learnt much from the sixteenth-century Venetians. Both were didactic artists—Watts far more so than Etty, and certainly he was more self-consciously the moralist. But whereas Etty was pious and optimistic, Watts was a gloomy sceptic. This is not surprising when one considers the very different upbringing of the two men and recalls that not only did a generation separate them, but that one lived on until the turn of the century.

The history of Etty's life and work is tantalizing to behold, since he appears to have been the victim of his own ambition to become a history painter. An aim which was almost always at odds with his limited, but genuine talent. Schooled in the traditions of eighteenth-century classicism as taught by Reynolds, Fuseli and Opie, Etty also looked to the French academic painters of his day for the most flourishing example of grand-scale history painting. At the same time, however, he had been attracted to the Venetians

[1] W. Holman Hunt, *Pre-Raphaelitism and the Pre-Raphaelite Brotherhood*, London, 1905, I, pp. 49–50.
[2] J. G. Millais, *The Life and Letters of Sir John Everett Millais*, London, 1902, I, p. 46.

and to Rubens not only because of his training at the Academy, but also by an innate sympathy for these colourists. His admiration was shared by Delacroix and there is a brief moment when both artists pursue a similar course. Yet Etty is neither the Ingres nor the Delacroix of the British School, and any attempt to equate him with either of these men would be both irrelevant and to misunderstand his peculiar artistic personality. For although much of the best of his work still appears startlingly fresh and advanced for its time, Etty could never shake himself quite free from an outmoded classicism. As a result, his imaginative powers became sterile and atrophied, the impetus of his earlier years was lost and he became not a prophet, but a grand glittering relic of a past age. Even so, British painting would be infinitely poorer if bereft of the work of one of the greatest figure painters it has so far produced. Despite his many shortcomings, Etty has left a rich and diverse artistic legacy, the scope of which is only now being fully understood.

APPENDIX I

LETTERS

Most of the letters reproduced below are published for the first time, and are intended to supplement the main part of the book. Those letters which have been used by Gilchrist in his *Life of William Etty, R.A.*, usually in part only, are noted as such, and the appropriate reference given. All letters are fully transcribed, with only such minor corrections of punctuation and spelling as were necessary to avoid confusion. Beyond this, no full-scale editing has been done.

LETTER 1[1]

My dear Walter,

I was afraid you would think I was lost, I have been so long writing to you. I set off this morning after I left you, it rained a good deal in the morning, sometimes very heavy, but in the afternoon it cleared up, and proved a beautiful day the country on all sides looked extremely well: we arrived at Stamford about 8 in the evening, where I stayed all night, and in the morning visited Burleigh House, which is just a pleasant walk from Stamford, thro' the Park, saw the House and Pictures, the last are very numerous filling upwards of twenty rooms, many very fine ones. At night I set off for York where I arrived on Friday night at six. I found all our friends in tolerable good health, my mother very hearty, looks as young as she did the last time I saw her, and says she never was happier but my poor father is very much altered indeed, stoops a great deal, and cannot hold a limb still, however, he eats pretty well and walks almost every day to John's if the weather allows; they have a snug little cottage in the garden which just accomodates them and no more, so I sleep at John's, where I have painted his eldest daughter, Kitty, (who by the bye, is grown a tall genteel girl, 'tis a pity she is now from school, serving in the shop and making spice) I have painted my mother too; and begun my father but it is almost too much for him poor man; he is weak and sitting in one position cramps him, & he stoops so much it is a difficult task, but I hope I shall accomplish the head; I have begun John's second daughter too, so having been pretty well employed must be my excuse for not writing sooner; and having had another picture hunting excursion on Sunday when John and I and his daughter Betsy took gig and went to Castle Howard, and saw the Park, House & Pictures, which pleased me as well I think as well as any I have seen,

---

[1] This letter is discussed in chap. 2, pp. 18, 19. It is now in the British Museum (Add. MS. 38794E, ff. 94/5). On the verso, it is addressed to: 'Mr. Walter Etty / No. 3 Lombard Street, / London'; and Walter has written: 'Wm Etty / York / 19 June 11' (*i.e.* 1811), indicating that the letter was carefully filed. Many of these letters to Walter bear similar inscriptions noting the date and writer with business-like accuracy.

particularly the celebrated three Marys, by Carracci, which after some difficulty I got to see, fine Portraits by Vandyck, Sir Joshua etc.

After I have finished at York, which I expect will be about Monday, I shall go to Hull, where I think I shall take a lodging for a week or two, and finish anything I may have to do there, then come back to York, as my Father and Mother wish it, that I may take up my freedom.

John has been making wonderful improvements in Walmgate indeed; you see no traces of the dirty tumble-down old houses that used to be there, and in their stead have risen neat good houses, with a spacious yard behind and divided from the garden by a wall and iron pallisadoes, at the entrance and in the garden is the cottage, and they have a slip of garden to themselves. The buildings have cost John more than was calculated on by 3 or 400£ consequently he is not so fluent in cash as he could wish I dare say at this moment, but he thinks he can weather it without selling any of his houses.

I mentioned your intention to my parents respecting the 20£ a year which they were very thankful for, but said they did not wish for any such thing, but if you should think proper at any time to send them a pound note or two, they should be very well satisfied, they said, God be thanked we have money enough, if we could but get it when due, the thing is, Tom is so straitened with paying a guinea and a half a week, and John with the buildings, that they cannot pay it when it is due so they become straitened too.

My father thinks a little Rum and water or Rum and Milk when he goes to bed makes him rest better, and nourishes him; if you could conveniently send them a few bottles it would be acceptable. All accounts agree they are much better in health than when they left Hull.

Respecting Mr. Lawrence's [here the seal has been torn away, but perhaps the missing words are 'payment I . . .'] leave it to you to do as you think most advisable. If you should be passing the Royal Academy will you call in and tell Samuel Strowger I wish him or Levell to take the 2 Queens marked E on the back to Mr. Lawrence's.

Now to come to the grand finale we heartily congratulate you on the birth of your daughter and happy to hear so good an account of mother and child; may she inherit the virtues of both her parents, and she will be an ornament to her sex.[1]

Your Affectionate Brother,
Wm Etty

Feasegate, York,
Wednesday Night
   June 19.

LETTER 2[2]

Dover Monday Jan. 2

My Dear Walter,

When the clock of the Horse Guards was striking six we started, the moon was shining, the morning mild and fine, I mounted the roof and kept it all day, except when I run on before, which I did when the coach stopped to warm myself, in this way I proceeded very pleasantly, the sun seeming to smile benignant on my enterprise (this part of the country must be very pleasant in summer, for even now it had its charms) in short I passed a very pleasant day, we dined at Canterbury, had an indifferent dinner, but a good appetite having breakfasted at

---

[1] This child was Jane, born 15th June, 1809; but she did not survive long, dying on 5th April, 1812. *See* William Brigg, *The Parish Registers of St. Edmund the King and Martyr, Lombard Street, London, 1670–1812,* pp. 43 and 125.

[2] British Museum, Add. MS.38794 E, ff. 96–7.

five. They charged me a pretty good price too. After that got inside, and proceeded to Dover where at Potovins, the King's Head, I took up my quarters had tea, and slept till the morning dawned of a day *not quite so pleasant* as the last. I took a walk before breakfast, reconnoitred the town, cliffs, castle etc. walked to the pier head, and listened to the waves as they beat on the shore. The wind promised fair, we breakfasted, after that wrote to York, went with our baggage to the Custom House, got it passed and changed the remainder of my notes for Louis D'or and francs by this time it poured with rain, the wind turned against us, and the Captain talked of staying till to-morrow, as he had only a very few passengers, however, he got the others to give him a guinea each, and if I liked to give him a half guinea extra I might go as the diligence only allowed him half a guinea, as I was anxious to go, and if I had staid it would have cost me the half guinea at the inn, so I consented, so after running here and there, sometimes after the Capt. sometimes to the Beach, the Custom-house, the inn, and I don't know where, in a most unpleasant cold rainy day, neither umbrella or great coat, we went to the beach where a boat with the luggage was waiting, as the vessel was riding in the roads. "Now Gemmen", says an old weather beaten amphibious animal "if you want to go aboard, you must pay me for your passage", pay what for, says I, I have paid my passage, all the way to Paris, "that there's nothing at all to me, this here my boat, so if you like to pay 4*s*. a piece, you may go, if not, here she goes, shove her off, so I and a French gentleman wandered about the beach in the rain for a considerable time waiting for Capt. Harris of the Poll packet, the vessel that was to take us, at last he came about two and the remainder of the passengers, and his mate, others remonstrated in the same way, but it was of no avail, we were all obliged to pay, so away we went, mounted the packet, and set sail. Adieu!

Kingston Hotel, Calais, Tuesday morng.

Here I am, my dear Walter, metamorphosed in the course of 24 hours into a foreigner. Thank God, such days are seldom as that of yesterday. Except to see my dear Friend, and England I think old Neptune will never catch me on his dominions again, I was so ill. We set sail as I told you the wind was tolerably fair, the day promised to clear up I felt well, and had assured myself I should do well, but how futile is human hope, as we got out the horizon grew thick and heavy, and seemed surcharged with rain, which came rapidly towards us, the wind increased, and the rain fell heavy. I went below, but the closeness and the unpleasant smell soon sent me up again, I stood in the companion a short time, taking advantage of part of an umbrella, however, I began to feel a little comical, and left it to get more in the air, still getting worse and worse, so I thought I would try the experiment of closing my eyes by which the giddiness arising from passing objects rapidly is in some measure removed and consequently one cause of sickness, so there I lay, exposed to the wind, the rain and the surge, for several hours, the Capt. and passengers repeatedly admonished me to go below as I should catch my Death of cold, but, cold, sick, wet and shivery as I was I thought I should be more sick below, so laid still, by this time the wind increased amazingly, and the sea frequently reminded us of the power it possessed to annoy us, the rain fell heavily, and whenever I opened my eyes the sea was foaming like cream by us, and notwithstanding my experiment my sickness increased, and the night closed fast upon us. At first, the passengers laughed, and joked, and talked, but by this time most of them were sick or silent, some seemed even worse than myself, in this state of suffering we endured some hours at last the Capt. began to ask if the man forward if he saw the Calais light, bye and bye the man cries "I think I see it on the weather bow Sir". How long will you be in going Capt. was now asked, "about an hour Sir" the reply. About an hour passed, he was asked again "about an hour Sir" was again the reply. All this I heard as I lay, and prognosticated no good from it. He was asked again, "it is impossible to say Sir" he cried, I began to think we should have to stay on board all night, however, bye and bye thank heavens the Capt. cries don't you smell the smoke of Calais? "Ah Ah" echoed a French courier "nous scentons la fumé". We tore away and neared Calais rapidly, at last we cast anchor, hung out a light for a boat, no boats came, we waited in anxious expectation some time, and began to think we should have to stay on board all night, however, soon we heard the noise of cheering in the distance, "they are coming" cried the passengers joyfully, at last they came, and after a vast deal of talk, got most of us on board, we had a great way to go before we landed, in the boat, and here my sickness increased, again, at last we got into smooth water, and were towed up the harbour, charged 6s a piece for taking us on shore, where I landed with no little satisfaction I assure you about nine at night where men were waiting from the hotels. Cold and wet as I was, I yielded to the tempting offer of an English hotel where I found a good fire a l'Anglais, had some tea, bed warmed, and forgot in sleep this horrible day. Today Tuesday, is frosty and fine, I have been walking about town and to the Diligence and custom-house, have got port paper and passport signed by the Mayor, and intend starting for Paris all well, about two.—Allons! Messieurs. I like what little I have seen of France already the scene is novel and interesting, I will tell you more bye and bye. Give my love to Martha, Jane and Thomas.

> Believe me
>   My dear Walter,
>   Yours most Affect^ly
>   Wm. Etty

[on verso]
Mr. Walter Etty,
Lombard Street
London
[Postmark: 7 Jan. 1815
          Dover 72]

[Note in Walter's writing:
  'Wm. E.
  Dover 2 Jan 1815
  Calais 3 ,,   ,,
  Recd. 7th.
  Ansd. —

Memo:
Lodge Letter of Credit with Perrigeaux & draw
Money as wanted—£100—
Name of agents Calais & Dover Mr. Chester.']

LETTER 3[1]

My dear Walter,

I have a few words to say to you, which I find I can do in this way better than any other —I have two ambitions, to the accomplishment of which the efforts of my life shall be applied —the first is to become a good man—the next a great painter—in progress for the latter you know it is my fixed determination to proceed to Italy—I have therefore a simple but important question to pose to you—it is this—Whether you think it would be advisable (supposing for a moment I could meet with an amiable girl with some property of her own) to take her with me as a wife, to be the companion of my bosom in a foreign land, to soothe my lonely hours, and by making me enamoured of home, preserve me from the effects of vice, and the contagion of example? or whether—I should proceed alone, equally unincumbered, and *unfriended* and take my chance for the remainder?

---

[1] British Museum, Add. MS. 38794 E, ff. 98–9.

You will easily discern from the tenor of this, that my heart is not at present entirely my own—but as I know your answer will be the result of deliberation, acting on wisdom matured by experience, it is my determination to abide by its choice.

I am ever

My dear Walter

Your Affectionate and Grateful Brother

Wm Etty

Surry-Street
Wednesday Morning.

[On verso, in Walter's writing:
'Wm. Etty
24 July 1816']

LETTER 4[1]

Dear Walter,

   Mr. N. Hardcastle called on me day before yesterday relative to one of his Copies—and asked me to go down to dinner there one day this week—I said Friday—so I am going tomorrow afternoon—yesterday I was invited to dine with Mr. Arnould at Peckham, I availed myself of a Greenwich coach to get down at the end of Peckham-lane and so walk on—and five minutes after Mr. Hardcastle's carriage happened to pass me going to Peckham with two of the Miss Hardcastles in it, who very kindly stopped and set me down at Mr. Arnould's door—so I was launched in style at the Doctors!—so far in explanation. During conversation Miss Emma H. expressed a wish to see my Flaxman's Iliad and Odyssey—and as they are very fond of prints I have sent Franklin to beg you will send by him *your large Folio—with the 8 Poussins* and the other selected Prints from my collection, and you shall have them all carefully returned.

   Mr. Wothen, of Gloucestershire, called on me yesterday—they are people of the first consequence there, (I think one of them is an M.P.) recommended by Mr. Bolton of Liverpool has seen my Pictures there, and is desirous I should paint him, complains that he has lately sat to one Stuart, who has tormented him with *twenty* sittings and made a daub of him at last. Mr. Arnould is likewise going to sit to me, so that I am not to be idle, they are determined.

   The Hardcastle's are anxious to visit the Exhibition on *Monday,* will you send me by Franklin a bottle of your *Port* and one of *Madeira*—as I should wish to shew some return to the many civilities I have received from that worthy family.

Yours truly

Wm. Etty

Thursday

LETTER 5[2]

13 Piazza Fiametti, Rome,
October 12, 1822.

   At last, my dear Sir Thomas, the spell is broken, and I am in Rome! To write from *such* a place to the most distinguished painter in Europe, requires considerably more talent in epistolary correspondence than I possess, however, as you wished it, I will endeavour to give you a sketch of our movements: We set off from London on the 23rd. June, on the 26th. we

---

[1] British Museum, Add. MS. 38794 E, ff, 100–1. The letter bears no date, but has a watermark '1817'.

[2] *Royal Academy Collection of Autograph Letters*, IV, p. 18. Letters 5, 6, 7 and 8 were known to Gilchrist, and he has quoted quite extensively from each letter in chapters 6, 7, 9, 10 and 11 of his book. This collection of letters was in the keeping of Lawrence's executor Archibald Keightley, and was afterwards made over to the Royal Academy.

arrived in Paris where we staid upwards of a fortnight; the biennial exhibition of the French school was open at the Louvre, and to say the truth, their efforts were highly creditable to them, were they even of less merit than they are; it was thought not so good as generally, but really many were highly respectable, history of course I mean, the less said of their portraits, God knows, the better—large, immensely large, were some of their pictures, and in their attempts at least they set us a good example. In the Luxembourg which you have seen, I think Guerin, Regnault, etc. the best. Amongst the old masters in the Louvre Ruben's [*sic*] Luxembourg pictures look, I think, more splendid than ever—and with all its losses, the Louvre is yet a fine and splendid national gallery—I wish we had anything like it in England. In Paris, we met two fellow students, Elton, a painter, and Bonomi, the sculptor, on their road to Rome, but they prudently did not venture it as soon in the season as we.

At Dijon is a gallery of ancient and modern Pictures, and an Academy with casts after the antique—we passed by Geneva and the Simplon into Italy, and a stupendous barrier indeed it is, which I hope you have seen, as I know you admire the grand and the terrible—we visited the Isles Bella [Isola Bella] and Madre on the Borromaen Lake [*sic*], and arrived at Milan in 6 days from Geneva—we staid a day or two and saw the Gallery, the remains of the Last Supper, of Leonardo, etc. at Piacenza we saw a few pictures in the churches, during the few hours we remained there—at Parma we were much delighted with the Correggios, and at Bologna with the large Picture of Guido—the dead Christ, Marys, etc. . . . and pictures of Carracci etc. in the Museum. I perhaps here ought to tell you that we entered Italy in the middle of the hottest summer, some of the oldest Italians have known, we, of course, had our share of its many *pleasures* (however, with all its drawbacks it is yet a glorious country)—the rivers were dried up, the roads dusty in the extreme, and one might almost have said with Satan, "Oh! Sun, to tell thee how I hate thy beams! It has, I am persuaded, left a lasting and *warm* impression on both our minds. From Bologna to Florence the Fair is the next stage—at Florence we found the air more temporate, (from the vicinity of the mountains, I suppose) and a day or two's respite was desirable, which we employed in seeing the Gallery, as well as the Pitti Palace, the Studio, the tomb of our noble Friend MichelAngelo, churches, etc. What a lovely portrait of a Lady there is in the Pitti Palace, it is of the most divine colour, the dress of a Laky color, slashed with blue, and embroidered with gold delicately—her hair, "flowing gold"—a gold chain on her neck—oh! it is indeed sweet! A fine Picture of Rubens Mars rushing to Battle, the opening of the Temple of Janus, & some Venetian Pictures.

On Wednesday the 7th of August, we left Florence for Rome, by vetturino; we agreed with him to take us in four days instead of 5, the usual time for them, we were consequently up at 3 or 4, and travelling till mid-day, under a burning sun, without a cup of coffee or tea to refresh us, it was dreadful, and almost more than nature could bear—we got out and were obliged to cut down branches of trees to put over the top of the cabriolet, the sun had such a penetrating power, so we looked like "Birnham Wood coming to Dunsinane". At last on the Saturday evening the 10th August, when we reached the brow of a hill—Rome spread out its towers on the plains beyond, backed by noble mountains, now of a hot purple, and rosy hues: the fields, owing to the long drought, were burnt to the color of dust, and formed a striking contrast to the verdure of England—we arrive in the Porto del Popoli and hail the tutelary genius of Rome! to a man of your own splendid imagination, I am apprehensive the first impressions of Rome would scarcely accord with those "sights such as youthful poets dream", at midnight "by some haunted stream"—but I had lately heard some tolerably correct descriptions, and had consequently lowered somewhat my expectations; and I don't know that I can say I was disappointed. St. Peter's was the first place I was taken to; what a magnificent effect has that noble colonnade, the fountain, obelisk, and the façade of St. Peter's itself, but I don't like the effect of the statues on it and the clocks,—and indeed I think in the upper part by no means so good as our St. Paul's, but the interior how different to it, what a golden light breaks in, what a saintly purity pervades the whole! what noble monuments of Canova's talent! if any temple is worthy of the Deity, surely it must be this. With awe and reverence I enter the Sistine Chapel and hail its mighty Author! Great Heavens, what a Ceiling that is, and the Last Judgment too, however blackened by time and smoke; the ceiling far exceeds my expectations; what composition, what daring defiance of all difficulty, without mentioning its grand air and drawing—qualities we all know it possesses amply—what masterly light and shade, what beautiful and almost Venetian colour! M. Ange & Raffaelle have been much libelled I have heard the coloring of both abused—for it frequently seems to me nearly all that it should be.

What a congregated mass of art and splendor is the Vatican! it is almost overpowering. Domenichino is much admired in Rome, and justly too, I think, tho' I confess he does not *touch* me as some do—there is a fine painting by him, which you have seen no doubt, in the Borghese Palace, Nymphs of Diana contending for the prizes, it is full of novelty and beauty, tho' not so glorious in color as such a subject would admit of—a large picture by Guercino in the Capitol struck me a good deal, the subject I don't know [Sta. Petronilla], except that a lover is watching the disentombment of the corpse of his mistress, whilst her spirit is kneeling above to Christ in heaven; it struck me as "the proper tone of historic color" as much, or even more than that of the Carracci, so well recommended by Sir Joshua—its tremendous depth without black, its richness without gaiety, its deep toned shades and golden subdued lights, reminded me of one of the best of Sir Joshua's own picture's color, his Dido.

How fine, now, in October, is the Landscape round Rome, and Naples too; the Coast and Bay of Baiae and the Elysian fields how beautiful! I have climbed the cinders of Vesuvius too, at midnight, by torchlight, and approached as near the crater as the guide said was prudent—for it was vomiting immense showers of red hot stones with the explosion of artillery, without a short distance—as I walked all the way up from Portici, the fatigue was immense, I shall never forget it. I went alone to Naples, Mr. Evans having his engagements to attend to; he has been very good in showing me about Rome and other places, and I may safely say, I have seen about twice as much as I should have done alone—for he is an excellent cicerone. He unites with me in our best wishes for [your] happiness and welfare. When I went to Naples —I rather wished Mr. Gott to accompany me as he seemed half-inclined, however his anxiety to get on determined him to remain in Rome, as he had got up a model of Venus and Adonis, very beautiful (as well as some smaller sketches,) with which he wished to proceed; I thought he would have to see Naples some time, and he would by that means be away from Rome at a critical season, however, when I asked him for his final determination he declined it; he stayed in Rome, unfortunately, and caught the fever, and has been exceedingly ill, and low in spirits occasionally in consequence. He is now, I am glad to say, very much better and has again commenced his group, for to add to his misfortunes, when he had got it in a very forward state—he, being ill, intrusted its removal to persons, who were recommended to him as capable of it, and they broke it all in pieces! He has it all in consequence to do all over again, and has some idea of making some change in the subject. He begs me to offer you his most respectful remembrances and trusts you will excuse his not having written, as his illness has prevented him having that pleasure. Mr. Kirkup also desires his respects and kind remembrances. I could say much more but that my paper and the clock both tell me I must now bid you Adieu and Farewell!

Believe me,
My Dear Sir Thomas,
Respectfully and Affectionately yours,
Wm. Etty.

APPENDIX I

Saturday night.
Sir Thomas Lawrence etc etc.
[Postmark: Oct. 29, 1822]

LETTER 6[1]

Venice, Casa di Signor D'Orville,
Vice Console Inglese
March 26, 1823

Dear Sir Thomas,

For some time past I have been intending to write to you to tell you where I was, what I was doing etc. but as is usual with me, postpone writing as long as is possible, and oftener longer than I ought I am sorry to say. When I left England I intended being back in about Six Months, only wishing to have a *look* at the great works in Rome, Venice, etc. in that case I should have been at home before Christmas, *but Venice detained me*, and my six months will be a year; however, I trust it will be of benefit to my (pictorial) health; I have been in Venice near 5 months, making a number of memorials of some of the fine things (in the Academia principally as yet). I came here on the 17th. Nov. intending to look around me for ten days, but I saw so many things capable of giving me lessons that I determined to stay the winter, and endeavour to profit by what I saw—it seems to me not a little strange that a place abounding with such specimens of Venetian art, and containing such lively and interesting remembrances (living and dead) of that school we admire so much in England, should be so neglected by our general travelling students, when we recollect too that the great works here are in the same vehicle as that now in use, (and not fresco) it seems reasonable to think that they must convey more *applicable* lessons (in the *technic* I mean, and I suppose that is generally what is wanted by copying) than most others. I am not a little glad, on comparing notes with Mr. Hoppner our consul, to find my thoughts on this head agrees in a great measure with one much more competent to decide—he tells me your opinion of Venice as a school of art was very favorable.

There is here a very good Academy, you know, the way in which the Antiques are arranged and lighted, is novel and beautiful, and the life (del Nudo) and the other departments seem admirably arranged with regard to leading students thro' all the elementary stages of art—but Painting, (Color) that rainbow vested dame, seems to have deserted the modern school of Venice, and I must say I think she has made herself most at home amongst you, even in our much-abused cloudy climate, and of late years has been observed to make some of her most brilliant scintillations not far from Russel-square. Painting, on the continent, indeed, I am sorry to say, what I have seen, seems more or less dilutions of the French "manière". The efforts the French make are indeed great, and much that is desirable is mixed up with much that is bad, but there is an agreable choice of subject, a daring excursion into the realms of history and poetry, a knowledge of drawing, and of details, and *sometimes* in color very respectable (tho' not often) altogether, that leaves an impression of power on one; but when we have seen French art—we have seen the best (at least that I have seen) of continental art. I confess that I do not very much admire the famous Camuccino [Camuccini], in saying this, I must bear testimony at the same time, that I consider him a man of very considerable talent, but its not being of that stamp I am in the habit of looking for, I am in all probability a prejudiced judge; there is however, much excellent study in his works but there is a want of that "vis animi" about his works, which I like to see. The Venetians, admirers of Canova, are much pleased with your munificent donation to his monument—I understand it is about 3 times as much as the whole Congress of Verona contributed!

---

[1] *Royal Academy Collection of Autograph Letters*, IV, p. 4.

APPENDIX I

Mr. Evans is still at Rome, but expects soon to be done there, and then he stays a short time in Florence, and afterwards comes here. I hear your picture of the King is so much admired, and so numerous are the applicants to copy from it to attain the "new manner" that they are obliged to restrict it to certain regulations. I did not see it, it was come—tho' not opened when I left Rome. We have had an extraordinary severe winter here for Italy, quite as cold and unpleasant [as] an English one, and indeed, more so, for at home you have better means of guarding against it. Venice, on a cold rainy, or a snowy, day, with water, above, below, and on all sides round, and sometimes coming up in the streets is then no very comfortable place you may think; I have painted in that large marble hall of the Academy till my pencil has been ready to drop from my fingers with cold; but the worst is over and Spring, thro' tarrying long, is coming, like a lusty bridegroom, redolent in youth to visit his earthly spouse, and his caresses are even now, very warm. I suppose this will reach you about the time you are enjoying the "otium cum dignitate" after your yearly labors, for I suppose you will have about sent in your pictures for the Academy. I shall not this year have any mortification on that head, for tho' it was as good a place as I deserved, (and I am not unaware of your kind exertions on my behalf,) yet still it is mortifying to think, after having studied so many years as I have, and with such application, that a Picture that I had spent three months about, and carefully studied each part from nature, should be judged worthy of no better place than that of being placed by the floor, to be hid by the legs of the spectators of a neighbouring and celebrated picture and reflect its colour on their boots, had it been out of such a crowd I should not have heeded so much, but I am convinced more than half would have no idea such a picture existed; tho' not so extensive a composition, perhaps it was a more complete picture than Cleopatra—I took at least more pains with the parts—and it had a decidedly worse place, and as I hope I don't retrograde—I shall hope that my places won't. However I beg to thank you for the interest you took in it; I cannot help thinking when I looked at *even* some of the member's pictures, that some mismanagement must have existed somewhere that year—but I am speaking treason perhaps—so "enough" no more of that.

You I am sure must have been much struck with the Tintorets here, in the Madonna dell'Orte Academy, Ducal Palace etc., his Last Judgment, his small St. Agnes, and his Crucifixion etc. what a glorious group that is at the foot of the Cross; really for composition, for pathos, for appropriate and harmonious composition of hues, and great executive powers, I have never seen it excelled, and rarely equalled—the poetry of his Last Judgment. The hues of this, the teeming richness of its composition, figures whirled in all possibilities of action and foreshortening—and then the sweet and carefully painted small picture of St. Agnes occasions a degree of astonishment at his powers that does not easily subside. Paolo Veronese's "Tent of Darius" is a beautiful assemblage of tones and hues.

The church of St. Sebastian, where his ashes rest, you have seen no doubt. There, and the tomb of Titian I have, you may be sure, made a pilgrimage to; I don't know where Tintoret reposes, (at present), I must learn—I'm sure if a *few masses* would do their *souls* any service, I would pay for them, but I think they must be too well situate to need them. By the bye— don't you admire the beautiful picture of *Parigo Bordone* of the Fisherman presenting the ring to the Doge—the pretty subject of Bonifaccio, the *rico Epolone*, or bad rich man—both in the Academy—there is a painting by Carpaggio, (before Titian) very rich in the draperies, from which Titian borrowed I think something. All these names tho' great here, are hardly known among us, I have memorials of these, as well as the grand Assumption of Titian, and others. I have given some of the students at Rome notice of your opinion of Venice, and several talk of coming, but I suppose not immediately. Wherever I go in Italy, I hear of you, and I am not a little proud that I can boast of having been your pupil.

APPENDIX I

Pray make my kind remembrances to Mr. Fuseli, when you see him, I hope he is well, and may you long enjoy your health and the elevated station which you fill,

believe me,

Dr. Sir Thomas, is the sincere wish of your
friend and pupil
Wm. Etty.

Sir Thomas Lawrence, Knt., P.R.A. etc. etc. etc.
   65 Russel Square
      Londra
Inghilterra
[Postmark: April 14, 1823]

LETTER 7 [1]

Hotel de Dusseldorf, Rue des Petites
Augustins, Quai Voltaire, Paris.
Nov. 14, 1823.

Dear Sir Thomas Lawrence,

Had I not been for these six months past expecting to move towards home, I should have written to you before, but the desire of possessing a memorial of *this* Picture and *that* Picture to put in my Painting Room, and guide my Practice, (as I cannot purchase originals) seduces one, and time glides rapidly and almost insensibly away, ere we are aware of it. But it is almost over, and I must now think of making something of my own.

I am making a sketch of the Marriage of Canaan by our old friend Paolo Veronese, but the Louvre is only open 4 days a week and the weather being excessively cold keeps one back; but in about three weeks from this time I hope to have the pleasure of seeing you; and presenting you with something that I think will be pleasant to you: I bring (for your already well and justly honored brows) another wreath of laurel, laurel grown in the country of Titian and Canova! In plain language I bring for you your diploma making you an Honorary Member of the Imperial and Royal Academy of Venice. They did themselves the honor of electing you about 7 months ago. Perhaps it may diminish the value of that distinction to you, when I tell you, that at the same time they conferred that degree on me, your pupil. But the difference is this, by electing you, they honored their own body—by electing me, they honored only myself. However it was on their part, on both sides, very handsomely and honorably done; and when you were proposed, I understand it was with acclamations unanimously carried. I did not apprise you of this fact before because I expected myself to be the bearer of the intelligence ere this, but now I make no doubt you know of it. It is delightful to hear in every part of Italy the favourable idea of English art your works and name have left, they yet talk with rapture of them, and I have met a number of persons, who seemed proud to say they knew you, or had seen your works—in Venice particularly—the admiration of your works, and gratitude for your munificence go hand in hand.

In France too, they seem beginning to think *we can paint A LITTLE*! Numerous English engravings are everywhere met with in Paris, our Vignettes by Stothard, Smirke, Westall, etc. are not only admired, but imitated. Wilkie is much in request, and much admired, but it is yet lamentable to see the narrow nationality of their school—Titian, Correggio, Paolo, Rubens, throw down their pearls before them in vain. The beans and husks of their school are preferred far before them—The Entry of Henri Quatre into Paris by Gerard, is multiplied a thousandfold, it is copied as a Picture, it is copied in all its parts, its heads are drawn in

---

[1] *Royal Academy Collection of Autograph Letters*, IV, p. 52. Reprinted in part by George Somes Layard, *Sir Thomas Lawrence's Letter-bag*, London, 1906, pp. 181–3.

lithography, water, chalks, and I don't know what while its noble and magnificent pendant Paolo Veronese—has not a single Devotee except me. It is annoying to me to see our countrymen and countrywomen come with book in hand—or valet de plan by their side pointing out its wonders, come and stare with silent and stupid admiration at this work, admiring it because they are told it is fine, (for it is the work of the idol of the French School), when we have amongst our artists so many who do better; that Gerard has considerable merit I am very ready to allow, and even the picture in question has points that are admirable, but altogether I think it detestable. How any man with Paolo and Rubens at his elbow could mix up such a nauseous draught of color! I cannot help thinking yet that Guerin and Regnault are two of their first men. The Students and young men I fear study better than ours, they have indeed more facilities for studying the figure, the consequence is, they have generally more power in drawing, when I have said this, I have given them I think the greater part of their merit—they are (with exceptions doubtless) in general—noisy, boyish, dirty, and frequently rude, (perhaps without intention) but I do not much like them, and what is worse than all, I understand from long residents here, that their moral character is at a very low ebb; indeed, so I should think. I am sorry to speak severely on them, but I think I am not so far wrong—they have in some respects *great* merit, but speaking in general—I think they don't appear to such advantage as before I had been in Italy.

They possess advantages we are strangers to, in study as well as encouragement. The Government I understand has just ordered Fifteen Historical Pictures—"They manage *these* things better in France", as Sterne says. Gerard is to paint the Triumphal Entry of the Duke de Angouleme. There are two portraits of Actresses just published here in Lithography after two by Gerard—very clever—and an evident imitation of something he has seen of yours, at least Mr. Evans and I thought so. I joined Mr. Evans at Florence after being a long time in Venice and he in Rome. We came with a Mr. Wallace of Florence to Venice and staid there two months or more; from dear Venice we came to Paris, staying a few days in Verona and two in Milan. I made a little slight sketch of the St. Giorgio Picture there, but the advanced state of the season, the very dark days we had there during the latter rains, prevented its being very satisfactory. The rivers in Italy have been much swollen, and a good deal of damage done in consequence. There was a good deal of snow in the Simplon when we passed, however, we got over pretty well, but we feel the season very keenly here now, with thick fogs, and frost, and other agreeables. Mr. Evans leaves today or tomorrow, and will be the bearer of this; I wish I had completed what I wish, that I might go too, as the season is late, as I long to see my dear Brother, my friends, and my country.

When I went to Florence I made a finished copy of the Venus of Titian in the Tribune; and when on the road (recollecting what you said to me of Giulio Romano) I went to Mantua, and found your eulogism on him amply deserved. Indeed, so delighted I was, that when at Verona I went again to Mantua with Mr. E. and staid another day or two. That Chamber of Psyche—how novel, how classical, how every way extraordinary, it is quite a treat to find a series of Pictures that treats classical subjects in so learned, so antique a style—after being deluged with nothing but Saints, Martyrs and Virgin Maries by thousands, the imagination revels with delight in his poetic landscapes, his giants intimidate, and his females, tho voluptuous in the extreme, have an air of greatness truly Roman; what foreshortening and effects in the ceiling! with what breathless caution his Acis and Galatea eye the sleeping Polypheme! What beautiful composition, what a boundless fancy; his monsters, how monstrous! His fauns, his satyrs, how truly the beings of antiquity and bacchic revel. There are some in another of the rooms over the door, of the Lapithae and Centaurs rushing out and engaged in battle; without exception the most beautiful knots of composition I ever saw. If Michel Ange and Raffaelle are before him, 'tis only they. He and Poussin seem to me the only men who have painted antiquity. With great reluctance I left these charming works; the subjects are so congenial to me, so every way satisfactory in what he attempts; but I am glad to find a series of outlines are about to be published of these in the Camera di Psyche (in Mantova) they are drawn, but not yet completed in the engraving, when they are, I will certainly have them if it is possible and I think you will, or I am mistaken.

I suppose you have seen the statue of Venus which is here, which was discovered or brought here to the Louvre very long ago—(I believe Mr. Chantrey has a Cast). Don't you think it very noble and beautiful, the head and neck very great and dignified, and the whole seems to me of very superior order. How I envy them the possession of the Luxembourg Gallery, what a foundation it would be in England for the foundation of ours. However, it is written, "thou shalt not covet another man's goods" so we must suppress such longings, and be satisfied. I am glad to hear something of a National Gallery is projected, it must surely take place, or we must give place in that respect to every polished nation in Europe. I am sorry to hear a report that our old friend Mr. Fuseli is very ill I hope and trust ere I return he will have recovered; we shall not easily "look upon his like again". Should you see him pray make him my respectful remembrances, and accept the same yourself, with my warm wishes for the recurrence of many healthful and happy years, to add yet more largely to the delight of mankind, and your own gratification in our dear Art.

I remain
Dear Sir Thomas Lawrence,
Ever respectfully and Affectionately,
Your Friend and Pupil,
William Etty.

LETTER 8[1]

London, Wednesday, Morng.

Dear Sir Thomas,

I arrived here last night, and intend myself the pleasure of calling on you about nine tomorrow morning (Thursday) to take my chance of finding you at home, when I shall have the pleasure of presenting you with your Diploma and Letter from the Academy of Venice.

I have written from Paris a letter to the Count Cicognari, the President, and accounted for your not having yet acknowledged the receipt of it, by my prolonged stay abroad, and assured him of your favourable sentiments towards the Academy, and of your kind acceptance of the Compliment.

I have made a few notes on the Drawings of Raffaelle and M. Angelo in the Louvre according to your request, I fear they will hardly be of use to *you*, who know them well, but I have endeavoured to fulfill the Commission to the best of my ability.

With regard to the Copy of Titian, I hope you will excuse my not having made that, I really am *tired* of copying, and had I any other means of possessing memorials of our great friends of Venice and Flanders without it, I should not have spent so much time in it as I have; but I thought it was of little use, my being abroad, did I not avail myself of what was around me, and postpone painting anything original till I got home; besides, I feel that I ought (if possible) to get something done for the Exhibition now, years are rolling over my head, I ask myself "what have I done?" so my Ambition steps in and says "something you *must* do". I consent, and determine to try. And I trust that God will give me health and power to do something ere I die that may be worth remembering.

I hope I shall find you quite as well as when I left you, tho' I am sorry to hear you have

---

[1] *Royal Academy Collection of Autograph Letters*, V, p. 3.

been but poorly; and with a happy new year, hope you will have many returns, and brighter days for Painting than today is (in the City).

Ever affectionately
Your friend and Pupil
Wm Etty

16 Stangate-Walk
Westminster Bridge.

P.S. You must expect to see your Diploma with its seal broken. Nothing escapes, hardly, the rapacity and rudeness of the *Douaniers*. On the frontiers of France they opened it.

Notes on the Drawings of Michel Ange and Raffaelle in the Louvre.[1]

Of the *first* of these great Names there are but two small sketches, one a Hand drawn with a few bold and powerful dashes with a pen and ink, but full of intelligence of the bones and very masterly.

The second is a Drawing in Red, Head of a Satyr, in which he has indulged a little in caricature.

Raffaelle.

The Collection of Raffaelle are more numerous.

They consist of 18 Drawings—some of the first class;

The three first (in my opinion) are: The Atila, the Culumny of Apelles, and the Alexander and Roxana.

The first I mention is the Atila. The drawing is on a lightish paper, washed with bistre, and heightened with white, with all the careful and sweet detail of a miniature, with the most perfect comprehension of the form and character of the individual part. It is perhaps unnecessary for one to enlarge on those great qualities you know the picture possesses, of its noble conception of its grand taste of design, of the striking light in which the painter places the powerful influence of the church, of his religion, and apostolic interference, in making them arrest the progress of a host of barbarians, rushing from a mountain gorge like a flood, or a devouring flame, towards that Eternal City they were anxious to destroy. How perfectly flying and how finely drawn and draped are the two Ministers of Heaven, how grand and graceful his horsemen, how well they sit their steeds, what spirit in the horses, what fine Drawing in the Warriors on foot in the foreground, turning round to look at the Vision that spreads dismay thro' their legions—their desolating spirit he has shown a town in flames in their track—and not the least interesting part is a group of horse and foot on the left which in the picture has been left out to put in Leo X and his Court.

The Calumny of Apelles, is of another *genre*, and is perhaps equally great with the last— Atila is Homeric—this of the Spencer [*sic*] class—allegoric and poetic. In a gloomy temple Credulity (with the ears of an ass) sits enthroned; Ignorance and Suspicion, are her Counsellors, Ministers and Whisperers, she receives Calumny, introduced by Envy a starved, haggard, and squinting wretch, shivering in rags, and misery. Calumny is the figure of a woman finely and richly apparelled—and her friends, and handmaids (who dress her) are Fraud and Artifice; Calumny, ushered in by these friends, advances to Credulity's throne, armed with a blazing torch, dragging an innocent victim who lifting up his hands and eyes to Heaven implores assistance. Pale Repentance comes behind, tearing her hair looks at last back on the bright figure of truth who naked enters in a flood of light and illumines the whole!

Whether I look at the perfection with which the allegory is carried thro'—the fine moral of

---

[1] *Ibid.*, IV, p. 51.

the design, its poetic fancy, the noble and fine arrangement of the great lines of its composition, (a principle he had studied well from M. Angelo), the inimitable truth and perfection of each individual character, whether formed by the action of bad or malevolent passions, stigmated by ignorance or enlightened by truth—I must say I think it one of the finest of his Drawings, and one of his most characteristic, poetic, and interesting works. It is not [*in*] quite so good preservation as the one preceding—it is drawn with a pen washed with bistre, and has been heightened by white, most of which is gone.

There are three others by Raffaelle, next in merit they are these—one in Red Chalk of Venus and Psyche very truly and sweetly drawn, apparently from Nature.

Another sketch in Red Chalk evidently done from his Fornarina, the study for the Virgin in the celebrated Holy Family in the Louvre, (so finely engraved by Edelinck), the arms and the lower limbs nearly all naked, and a slight indication of the infant reaching towards her.

And last, not least

A drawing, the outline begun in black lead, drawn with pen and washed with bistre, the natural and pretty action, and sweet expression is delightful the drapery broad and beautifully folded.

There are various other fine Drawings 1 or 2 by Giulio Romano, some by Correggio, Rubens, Carracci, Ligorii, Buonaccorsi, Poussin, Etc.

LETTER 9[1]

14 Buckingham Street,
Tuesday Morning.

My dearest Walter,

After all the trouble you have had, and all the expense that has been incurred, it may seem like ingratitude and flying in your face—to feel as I do—but believe me—I am here truly wretched—could I have foreseen one quarter of the unhappy feeling that has possessed me and yet paralyses me I would never have thought of leaving a place where I was truly happy, healthy, and had a mind at peace—could I even ever like this place equal to my last which is impossible—the idea of the heavy expense, (the servant alone costing more than the whole of the other together) weights down my mind, and utterly unnerves me—O forgive me! forgive me. I entreat you—I will never do any thing to disgrace you, or give you uneasiness after this, but I feel my happiness, and my health are gone, attached from the first to that dear place, where I have made some of my happiest efforts—because my mind was at peace, and I had an easy rest—and a situation that could banish those clouds of melancholy that now hang over my mind—I feel that in leaving it I have lost almost everything dear to me, except yourself. —It was a distance that insured my health by rendering a walk to the Academy necessary, surrounded by spacious Gardens and the river the air is purer—I have scarcely had a night's rest since I have been here—my stomach revolts from food that used to be grateful to me—in short I am truly unhappy in mind and body—Had I listened to my own feelings more than officious people who persuaded me, I ought to be in another situation I should yet have been happy—here it is impossible—the slow returns of a painter devoted to my line of art I am sure can never meet it even were my mind at peace—how can it—miserable as I am—as I feel I must ever be here—O! let me go back! I entreat you! on my knees I would entreat you! to where I painted my Cleopatra my Maternal Affection, and my Pandora,—there I can live— here I am dead to Art and everything—at an expence that I dread to contemplate, I have no wish but to live and die in Lambeth, a name ever dear to me, because I have there been truly

---

[1] British Museum, Add. MS. 38794 E, ff. 109–10. Quoted also by W. T. Whitley, *Art in England 1821–1837*, pp. 80–1, but in shortened form.

happy, more so than ever I was, or shall ever be again unless I go back. If you will, I will spare no exertions to get on in my dear Art—I will work my fingers to the bone but I will repay you some time or other all I owe you, except the grateful obligations, I feel, which I fear are more than ever I can repay—for God knows I should think my dear Walter, my life too little in return for what you have done for me—I am now much in debt, with you and the idea of that, with the heavy outgoings of the present rooms—quite oversets me—together with the thoughts of the happiness I have left—O I should have thought of it before I grant—but I could not forsee what I have felt and still feel—and must ever feel here—O pardon my weakness—my dear Walter—but my nerves are aspen like. Grant me but this, and in my whole shall I endeavour to repay you—I shall never be happy till you do—I feel it impossible—I declare I never was *so* unhappy—so long together, and I hope I never shall be so again—I don't wish to live in splendour, I wish to be great as a Painter, to live virtuous and happy—is all I wish. Let me then go while 'tis yet in my power! I conjure you, by the Love I bear you, by all your desires for my welfare—for I fear the effects of a refusal—I feel sensible that it would have some bad effect on my health, which God knows, is not strong—or what would be worse, my mind, which when so affected, is oppressed with a gloom indescribable.

O Grant it me! and I will yet live to be happy, and I trust to make you so too, at least I will spare no pains to try to do so—

> Pity and forgive me
>> My Dear Walter, I can't help it
> and believe ever your Affectionate Brother,
>> William Etty.

Mr. Walter Etty
31 Lombard Street.

> [Note on verso written by Walter:
> 'Wm. Etty
> 29 June 1824
> wretched Letter']

LETTER 10[1]

Londres, le 24 aout 1825.

Monsieur,

J'eprouve un vif regret d'être obligé de quitter l'Angleterre sans avoir eu le plaisir de vous revoir. Mon depart a été beaucoup plus precipité que je ne pensais, et ayant été quelque temps en Essex d'où je suis arrivé depuis peu de jours, je n'ai pu m'acquitter d'un devoir tout agreable pour moi, Veuillez donc en recevoir mes excuses aussi bien que Monsieur Calvert que j'avais rencontré et qui avait bien voulu m'inviter à le voir. Si vous venez a Paris, je me trouverai heureux si je puis vous y être utile en quelquechose.

Agreez, je vous prie, l'assurance des sentiments distingués avec lesquels j'ai l'honneur d'être,

> Monsieur,
>> Votre devouè serviteur
>> E. delacroix
>> Rue du Houssaye No. 5
>> a Paris

---

[1] The letter is in York City Reference Library. It was published by me in *The Burlington Magazine*, XCIV, March, 1952, p. 80, where its more general significance was also discussed. It is transcribed verbatim, and Delacroix's use of accents has been somewhat casual.

APPENDIX I

Voudrez vous m'excuser de vous ecrire en Français, j'aurais été incapable à mon grand regret de m'exprimer dans votre langue.

—Etty Esqre.,   [Note in Etty's writing:
                                                  'Lacroix
                                                      24 Sept. ("Sept" deleted)
                                                      Aug. 1825'.]

APPENDIX II

A LIST OF PAINTINGS FOUND IN SKETCHBOOK II

(This list, on p. 48, probably records those paintings which Etty either copied, or at least intended to copy during his stay abroad in 1822–3.
*Indicates that Etty has ticked off works thus marked.)

Miracle of Saint Marc'—Tintoret*
Assumption—Titian*
St. John—St Francis Santa Caterina—Paul Veronese*
Dives & Lazarus, Bonifaccio*
Fisherman before the Senate Paris Bordone
Circular Ceiling—Paul Veronese*
Venus and Cupid—School of Ditto*
Holy Family, Bassan*
Holy Family Bonifaccio*
Presentation in the Temple—Carpathius Victor*
St. Francis and Catherine—Bonifaccio*
Adam & Eve by Tintoret*
Santa Christina,—Paolo Veronese

Digger—Tintoret
Puller—Tintoret
and Sundry Bits of Ceilings

Europa Paolo Veronese*
Marriage [*sic*] of Bacchus & Ariadne ⎤
Peace and War   ⎬ *Tintoret
Three Graces   ⎦
Triumph of Venice*
Liberality— ⎫
Modesty—   ⎬ Paolo Veronese*

Darius's Family by Paolo Veronese*
Sant Pietro Martyr—Titian*
Pesaro Family Titian*
Organ Presentation Paolo Veronese
Group at the Foot of the Cross—Tintoret*
Ceiling of a Sacrifice Paolo Veronese*

Crucifixion. Tintoret*
Presentation in the Temple—Tintoret
Triumph of Venice Paulo Veronese*
Battle Bassan*
San Sebastian Paulo Veronese*
Marriage of [sic] Canaan—Tintoret*
Two Angels—Paulo Veronese*
Hercules, Venezia and Ceres Paolo*

Florence
Venus of Titian
Cardinal Bentivoglio Vandyck

Rome
Profane Love Titian
Three Graces Ditto
St. John—Paulo Veronese
St. John etc.—Paulo Veronese
Europa Ditto
Vandyck's Cross—
Leg of Potipha's Wife
        Original sketch.

(It will be noted that there are forty-seven separate items, most of which can be identified quite easily. There appears to be some duplication, e.g. Veronese's *Triumph of Venice* occurs twice, otherwise the list tallies well with those works Etty mentions in his various letters home. *See also* Chapter Four.)

CATALOGUE

EXPLANATORY NOTES

The works, which are numbered consecutively, have also been divided under subject headings, with cross-references where they are appropriate. A few important works have been included whose provenance is known up to within the past fifty years, although they are at present unlocated. Oil studies and drawings are discussed with the pictures to which they refer, but a concise list of drawings is also provided.

Space and considerations of general utility have made it necessary to select only a small number from the hundreds of nude studies which are scattered throughout many private and public collections. The selection has been made with two guiding factors in mind: firstly, the need to obtain studies representative of all periods of the artist's career, within the limits imposed by the difficulty of dating precisely these works; secondly, to choose works only of the highest quality. It is thus hoped to provide a reasonably sure framework with which to assess the merits of uncatalogued paintings of this type. The same plan has been followed in choosing studies for reproduction in this book.

All measurements are in inches: height precedes width. All paintings are in oils, unless noted otherwise. Sale references are to those held at Messrs. Christie, Manson & Woods, Ltd., London, unless stated to the contrary. Similarly, all exhibitions were held in London, where no specific location is given in the text.

The following abbreviations have been used:

A.C.	Arts Council.
A.R.A.	Associate of the Royal Academy.
Autobiography	William Etty, R.A., *Autobiography*, published in *The Art Journal*, XI, 1849, pp. 13, 37–40. This was in the form of a letter to a cousin, John Clark, dated 28th October, 1848.
B.C.	British Council
B.F.A.C.	Burlington Fine Arts Club.
B.I.	British Institution.
Etty	Arts Council Exhibition Catalogue by Dennis Farr, *William Etty*, 1955 (2nd ed., with supplement).
Gaunt & Roe	William Gaunt, M.A. & F. Gordon Roe, *Etty and the Nude*, Leigh-on-Sea, 1943.
Gilchrist	Alexander Gilchrist, *Life of William Etty, R.A.*, 2 vols., London, 1855.
Inscr.	Inscribed, *i.e.* by the artist.
N.A.C.F.	National Art-Collections Fund.
P.R.A.	President of the Royal Academy.
P.R.I.	President of the Royal Institute of Oil Painters.
R.A.	Royal Academy; Royal Academician.
R.I.	Royal Institute of Oil Painters.

CATALOGUE

R.S.A.	Royal Scottish Academy; Royal Scottish Academician.
S.A.	Society (now Royal) of Arts: William Etty Retrospective Exhibition, opened 9th June, 1849.
York	City Art Gallery, York: Etty retrospective exhibitions held 1911 (20th February–8th April), 1948 (January), and 1949 (*Centenary Exhibition* 13th November–31st December).

CATALOGUE

RELIGIOUS

1 [pl. 49] AARON
Panel, 52¾ × 23½.
Lit.: George Godwin, *The Churches of London*, London, 1839, ii, p. 4.
    This, and the *Moses* (*v. sub.*) were painted for the reredos of St. Edmund the King and Martyr, Lombard Street, in 1833.
St. Edmund the King and Martyr, London.

2 AARON, THE HIGH PRIEST OF ISRAEL
Canvas, 54 × 44.
Coll.: Purchased from the Artist for 100 gns. by Joseph Gillott (Gillott *Account Book*, p. 8, 10th April, 1848); sold by Gillott to Thomas Rought £375, 15th July, 1854 (*loc. cit.*, p. 66); Thomas Thompson, Bowness-on-Windermere, formerly of Sunderland, who bequeathed it to Sunderland, 1895.
Exh.: R.A., 1848(215); York, 1911(124).
Lit.: Gilchrist, ii, pp. 243, 341.
Museum and Art Gallery, Sunderland.

3 [pl. 34*b*] BENAIAH
Canvas, 120 × 157.
Coll.: Purchased from the Artist by the Royal Scottish Academy, December, 1831, and presented to the National Gallery of Scotland, 1910 (No. 188).
Exh.: R.A., 1829(16); B.I., 1830(444); R.S.A., 1831(VIII); S.A., 1849 (VI); *International Exhibition*, 1862(337).
Lit.: Autobiography, pp. 39–40; Waagen, *Art Treasures*, iii, 1854, p. 271; Gilchrist, i, pp. 103, 266, 285, 334, 353, 356, ii, p. 336; Rinder & McKay, *The Royal Scottish Academy, 1826–1916*, Glasgow, 1917, contains detailed information about the protracted negotiations for this picture, for the three *Judith* paintings, and for *The Combat*; Gaunt & Roe, pp. 64, 77 (repr. pl. 9).

Repr.: The Art Journal, 1905, p. 60; *The Magazine of Fine Arts*, I, November, 1905–April, 1906, p. 113.
    The exploits of Benaiah, one of King David's captains, are described in II *Samuel*, xxiii, 20–3: 'He slew two lion-like men of Moab.'
National Gallery of Scotland, Edinburgh.

(*a*) Canvas, 23 × 30.
    Coll.: James Brownleigh Hunter, Diddingston, Edinburgh, from whom purchased by York, 1927 (No. 70/1927).
    Exh.: York, 1911(115); York, 1948(22); York, 1949(78).
    City Art Gallery, York.

(*b*) Pencil, 7½ × 9, on notepaper postmarked 'Nov. 3, 1828'.
    Coll.: J. P. Knight, 1870; P.D. 180 C, Portf. 252F/5/7652/16.
    Victoria and Albert Museum, London.

4 THE CARDINAL
Millboard, 9⅞ × 7½.
Coll.: John Sheepshanks Gift, 1857 (No. 72).
Exh.: R.A., 1844(146); S.A., 1849(LII), lent Sheepshanks; Whitechapel, Spring, 1905(69).
Victoria and Albert Museum, London.

5 [pl. 54*b*] CHRIST APPEARING TO MARY MAGDALEN AFTER THE RESURRECTION
Canvas (enlarged by ¼ to ¾ strips on all sides), 15¾ × 26.
Coll.: Commissioned by John Turrill to be engraved as an illustration for *The Sacred Annual for 1834*, Turrill paid Etty £25 (*Cash Book*, entry for August, 1833); afterwards acquired by Robert Vernon; Vernon Gift to the National Gallery, 1847 (No. 362). Transferred to the Tate Gallery, 1929.
Exh.: B.I., 1834(283) *A Sketch made for the Sacred Annual.* 'As Mary, weeping by the tomb remained / ... / Back she turn'd her eye of

tears / And there stood Jesus'—Montgomery's *Messiah*. Whitechapel, *British Art 1830–1850*, 1920(41).

Engr.: S. Sangster, *The Vernon Gallery*, 4th Series [1853?], No. 3, and *The Art Journal*, 1853, p. 171, as *The Sepulchre*.

Lit.: Gilchrist, ii, pp. 1, 2, 337; Thomas Balston, *John Martin*, London, 1947, pp. 153–4.

It has so far been impossible to find a copy of *The Sacred Annual* to compare the original engraving with the painting.

Tate Gallery, London.

6 CRUCIFIXION

Paper mounted on canvas (relined), 26½ × 39½ (semi-circular top). Enlarged on all sides.

Coll.: Anon., 8.2.1902(133), bt. Short 14 gns.; F. E. Sidney (*c.* 1909), but not in either of the Sidney Sales, 1937–8. Bought at a London sale-room *c.* 1942 by Captain A. Coumandareas, who presented it to the Cathedral.

Repr.: Sir Walter Armstrong, *Art in Great Britain and Ireland*, London, 1909, p. 219, pl. 401.

A worked up copy from the *Crucifixion* attributed to Van Dyck (Borghese Palace) and probably identical with lot 381, Etty Sale, 1850: 'The Crucifixion, after Van Dyck', bt. Smart £11. Begun 1823 (*see* Appendix II).

The Greek Cathedral Aghia Sophia, London.

7 DAVID

Millboard, 21 × 18.

Coll.: (?)Anon., sold 19.7.1890(102), bt. Innes 23 gns.; Miss A. N. May (until 1938).

Exh.: York, 1949(32).

Lit.: *Bulletin & Annual Report of the Russell-Cotes Art Gallery & Museum*, XVII, 3, September, 1938, p. 30 (repr. on cover).

Painted *c.* 1810–12, the subject may also represent a bowman.

The Russell-Cotes Art Gallery and Museum, Bournemouth.

8 DAVID

Panel (painted circular top), 33½ × 19¾.

Coll.: Thomas Thorpe, junr., of Alnwick; Rev. William Tudor Thorpe; Thomas Alder Thorpe; R. A. F. Thorpe, sold 2.8.1951(225), bt. in 5 gns.

Exh.: R.A., 1841(519); S.A., 1849(LXXII).

Lit.: Gilchrist, ii, pp. 118, 274, 339; *York Preview* 24, October, 1953, pp. 256–7.

The Royal Academy catalogue contained a quotation from *Psalm* lvii, v. 9, as printed in the *Book of Common Prayer*: 'Awake [up] my glory; awake, lute and harp; I myself will awake right early.'

Brigadier R. A. F. Thorpe, Bamburgh Castle, Northumberland.

9 THE DISCIPLE

Millboard laid on panel (painted oval top), 19½ × 15⅜.

Coll.: Robert Vernon Gift to the National Gallery 1847 (No. 361). Transferred to the Tate Gallery, 1929.

Engr.: J. C. Armytage, *The Vernon Gallery*, 3rd Series, 1853, No. 36, and *The Art Journal*, 1853, p. 196, as *The Disciple*.

In the Tate Gallery *Concise Catalogue of the British School*, 1953, referred to as a *Study for a Head of Christ*. A *Head of Christ* was in the Edward Harper Sale, 16.4.1853(76), bt. Wallis 50 gns. Another painting, *The Saviour*, was lent by C. W. Wass to the Society of Arts, 1849 (LXII), and described as shown at the British Institution, 1844(1), *Study of a Head*.

Tate Gallery, London.

10 [pl. 44] THE DESTROYING ANGEL AND DAEMONS OF EVIL, INTERRUPTING THE ORGIES OF THE VICIOUS AND INTEMPERATE. 'A finished sketch of that class of compositions called by the Romans "Visions", not having their origin in history or poetry.' Paper mounted on canvas, 36 × 46.

Coll.: Purchased from the Artist for £130 by Henry Payne, The Newarke, Leicester 1832; sold anon., 18.3.1854(121), bt. Sir Joseph Whitworth, Bt., 770 gns., who presented it to Manchester 1882.

Exh.: R.A., 1832(215); *Art Treasures*, Manchester, 1857(605); *National Exhibition of Works of Art*, Leeds, 1868(1175); *British Art*, Manchester, 1934(86); Salford, 1938; York, 1949(49); R.A., *First Hundred Years*, 1951–2(242); *Art Treasures Centenary Exhibition: European Old Masters*, Manchester, Oct.–Dec., 1957(209).

Lit.: *Autobiography*, p. 40; Gilchrist, i, pp. 103, 345–6, 362–3, ii, pp. 275–6, 337; Gaunt & Roe, pp. 77–9 (repr. pl. 17).

Commissioned as early as 1822 for 60 gns., it was not finished until ten years later. In February, 1824, Etty was having the paper laid on canvas by Mr. Macdonald, a colourman (MS. letter to Walter, 16th February, 1824; British Museum Add. MS. 38794 E, ff. 102–3). Two MS. letters from Henry Payne to Etty 16th February and 4th August, 1832 (York City Reference Library) refer to the transaction. The painting is described as a *Last Judgment* in the Manchester Art Gallery handbook, 1905, but previously Etty had called it *The Destruction of the Temple of Vice*. An 'outline

study' for *The Destroying Angel* was in the Etty Sale, 1850(655), bt. Hamilton £3 7*s*.
City Art Gallery, Manchester.

(*a*) Pencil, $2\frac{3}{8} \times 5$.
Coll.: J. P. Knight, 1870; P.D. 180 C, 252F/3/7650/114.

(*b*) Five pencil studies, $12\frac{1}{4} \times 14\frac{1}{8}$, on verso folded sheet of a London Institution pamphlet dated 21st November, 1831.
Coll.: as for (*a*), Portf. 252F/5/7652/42.
Victoria and Albert Museum, London.

(*c*) Pencil, $9 \times 7\frac{3}{8}$, on outside of letter from T. Bodley to Etty, 10th December, 1832.
Coll.: G. H. Scott (until 1954).
Appears to be re-planned composition of the Royal Academy picture, but no other oil painting of the subject is recorded.
City Reference Library, York.

11 EVE
Panel, $21\frac{3}{4} \times 15\frac{1}{4}$.
Coll.: William Wethered, sold 27.2.1858(68) *Eve Listening to the Serpent*, bt. Rippe 39 gns.; H. A. J. Munro of Novar, sold 6.4.1878(19), bt. Hooper 9 gns.; A. A. Wolmark.
Exh.: Montage Gallery, James Street, W.1, 1951.
Lit.: W. E. Frost, A. R. A. & Henry Reeve, *Catalogue of the Collection . . . of the late H. A. J. Munro of Novar* [n.d.], No. 560.
Painted *c.* 1840–5. A painting entitled *Eve Listening* was in the John Nussey Sale, 17.6.1861 (56), bt. Deacon 6 gns.
Alfred A. Wolmark, Esq., London.

12 EVE
Panel, $31\frac{1}{2} \times 21\frac{1}{2}$. Strips added of between $1\frac{1}{2}$–2 to top and left side, with three large sections added along the bottom edge.
Coll.: H. Fantin-Latour; Mrs. Edwin Edwards, who presented it to the Louvre, 1904 (R.F. 1539).
Probably painted *c.* 1835. The Louvre catalogue it simply as *Étude de femme nue dans un paysage*, but the woman holds an apple in her right hand.
Le Musée du Louvre, Paris.

13 EVE AT THE FOUNTAIN
Panel, 26×20.
Coll.: Painted for £30 for Richard Colls; William Wethered, sold 27.2. 1858(64), bt. Colls 51 gns.; Anon., sold 12.5.1860(89), bt. Gambart 70 gns.; C. F. Huth, sold 19.3.1904(51), bt. Agnew 32 gns.; with J. Leger & Son, 1948–1949, from whom purchased by Doncaster, September, 1949 (No. P. 221, Styles Bequest Fund).
Exh.: R.A., 1844(371); S.A., 1849(CXIII); *Old Master Paintings*, Leger Galleries, May–June, 1948(37); York, 1949(23).
Lit.: Gilchrist, ii, pp. 173, 340.
A similarly entitled work appeared in the J. C. Grundy Sale, 27.2.1852(133), bt. Grundy $5\frac{1}{2}$ gns.
Art Gallery and Museum, Doncaster.

14 [pl. 62*b*] THE GOOD SAMARITAN
Canvas, $21\frac{5}{8} \times 26\frac{1}{4}$ ($\frac{3}{4}$ strip added on right side).
Coll.: R. Cartwright, Bloomsbury Square, London; H. A. J. Munro of Novar, sold 6.4.1878(22), bt. Agnew 160 gns.; Edmund Crompton Potter, Rusholme House, Manchester, sold 22.3.1884(20), bt. Vokins 120 gns.; Anon., sold 17.5.1945(73), bt. Bode 10 gns.; with Leggatt Bros.; Lord Fairhaven.
Exh.: B.I., 1838(233); S.A., 1849(XLI); *Art Treasures*, Manchester, 1878(230); York, 1949 (11).
Lit.: Autobiography, p. 40; Gilchrist, ii., pp. 80, 338; W. E. Frost, A.R.A. & Henry Reeve, *Catalogue of the Collection . . . of the late H. A. J. Munro of Novar* [n.d.], No. 156.
Inscribed in ink on verso of canvas: 'Painted by Wm Etty R.A. And presented by him to his Friend R. Cartwright, Esq., in Testimony of his sense [*sic*] of his unremitting Attentions to Wm Etty, during a long and painful illness. March 1839.'
The Lord Fairhaven.

(*a*) Canvas, $11\frac{1}{2} \times 21$.
Coll.: (?)Etty Sale, 1850(497) *The Good Samaritan*, bt. Grundy £8 5*s*.; (?)Bryant, sold 23.6.1865(46), bt. Slee $2\frac{1}{2}$ gns.; Cuthbert Britten Slee, sold 25.3.1901(6), bt. Pickering 1 gn. Present location unknown.

15 [pl. 96] A GROUP OF CAPTIVES: 'BY THE WATERS OF BABYLON'
Millboard laid on panel, $23 \times 26\frac{1}{2}$.
Coll.: Purchased from the Artist by William Wethered; Joseph Gillott from Wethered for £200 on 25th February, 1848, and he gave Etty £30 to enlarge it (Gillott *Account Book*, note, p. 8); not in Gillott Sale, 1872, but sold to Henry Wallis, 14th May, 1853 (*loc. cit.*, p. 62); Richard Newsham Bequest, 1883.
Exh.: R.A., 1848(188); S.A., 1849(XLVIII); Leicester Fine Art Society, December, 1849; Birmingham Society of Artists, 1852(111) *The Hebrew Captives*, lent by Joseph Gillott; Whitechapel, Spring, 1905(52); York, 1911(167);

Leeds, 1911; R.A. *First Hundred Years*, 1951–2 (235); A.C. *Etty*, 1955(37).
Lit.: Gilchrist, ii, pp. 240, 242, 341.
Repr.: Illustrated Catalogue of Preston Art Gallery, 1939, No. 218, pl. 37; Gaunt & Roe, pl. 61.
Version: Richard Nicholson Sale, 13.7.1849 (192) 'By the Waters of Babylon', bt. Wass 73 gns. Not located.

From Psalm cxxxvii: 'By the rivers of Babylon, there we sat down; yea, we wept, when we remembered Zion.' Etty has used the version printed in the *Book of Common Prayer*.
The Harris Museum and Art Gallery, Preston.

16 'HE WAS DESPISED AND REJECTED OF MEN'
Panel, 26½ × 20½.
Coll.: John Wood (in 1849); Messrs. Stapley, Uckfield, Sussex (by 1937), from whom purchased by George Barlow.
Exh.: S.A., 1849(LXXXIX).
Lit.: Gilchrist, ii, p. 341.

The title is a paraphrase of part of *Isaiah* iii, 3: 'He is despised and rejected of men; a man of sorrows, and acquainted with grief.'
George H. Barlow, Esq., Tunbridge Wells, Kent.

17 HEAD OF A MONK
Canvas, 12 × 10½.
Coll.: The Rev. Chauncy Hare Townshend Bequest, 1869 (No. 1390).
Painted *c.* 1841–2.
Victoria and Albert Museum, London.

18 AN ISRAELITE
Canvas, 13½ dia.
Coll.: John Elliot Bequest, 1917.
Exh.: York, 1949(26).
Williamson Art Gallery and Museum, Birkenhead.

19 [pl. 83*b*] AN ISRAELITE INDEED
Millboard, 26¼ × 19¾.
Coll.: John Miller, Liverpool, sold 21.5.1858 (155), bt. Gambart 40 gns.; John Torr, M.P.; G. Beatson Blair Bequest, 1941.
Exh.: B.I., 1847(39); S.A., 1849(CXIX).

A similarly entitled work was in the William Wethered Sale, 7.3.1856(120), bt. Hooper 55 gns.
City Art Gallery, Manchester.

20 JOAN OF ARC, ON FINDING THE SWORD SHE DREAMT OF, IN THE CHURCH OF ST. CATHERINE DE FIERBOIS, DEVOTES HERSELF AND IT TO THE SERVICE OF GOD AND HER COUNTRY
Canvas, 117 × 78.
Coll.: This, and the other two *Joan of Arc* paintings were purchased jointly from the artist by Richard Colls, William Wethered and Charles

W. Wass for £2,500 in 1847. The three pictures later became separated: this was in the two William Wethered Sales 7.3.1856(150) *Joan of Arc finding the Sword*, bt. in 225 gns., and 27.2.1858(109), bt. in 115 gns. Possibly the same picture later belonged to Charles Reade, sold 18.5.1885(244) *Joan of Arc*, bt. Bolton 20 gns.; Anon., sold 27.7.1891(54) *Joan of Arc*, bt. Lesser 29 gns.; H. S. Ashbee, sold 19.11. 1900(85) *Joan of Arc at the Tomb of Saint Denis* [*sic*], 118 × 78, bt. Maple 14 gns.
Exh.: R.A., 1847(123); S.A., 1849(VII) lent by C. W. Wass and William Wethered.
Engr.: C. W. Wass *c.* 1851 and published by E. Gambart. (The set of three Wass engravings were lent to the York exhibition, 1911(59, 60 & 61) by Mr. George Benson, but prints can no longer be found.)
Lit.: *Autobiography*, pp. 39–40; *The Art Journal*, August, 1851, p. 224; Gilchrist, ii, pp. 97, 107– 108, 114, 117, 124, 125, 138–9, 154, 156–8, 166, 172, 210, 213, 218, 220–30, 234, 271, 322, 341.
(*a*) Millboard, 18 × 15½.
Coll.: York Art Gallery, 1927 (No. 82/1927).
This is a full-face, head and shoulders study for Joan as she stands holding a sword hilt in her right hand and looks up.
City Art Gallery, York.
(*b*) Watercolour, ex-coll. James Orrock & Sir James Linton, sold 25.4.1895(110) *Joan of Arc at the Tomb of Saint Denis*, bt. Green 27 gns.

21 JOAN OF ARC MAKES A SORTIE FROM THE GATES OF ORLEANS, AND SCATTERS THE ENEMIES OF FRANCE
Canvas, 117 × 180.
Coll.: either Colls or Wass; sold ('From a Country House in the North of England') 2.3.1934(108) *Jeanne d'Arc*, unstretched 120 × 180. 'The frame and stretching are sold with the picture.' Bt. Smith 5 gns.
Exh.: R.A., 1847(124); S.A., 1849(VIII).
Engr.: C. W. Wass *c.* 1851.
Lit.: as for above.
(*a*) [pl. 89*b*] Pen, brush and ink, 3⅝ × 5.
Coll.: J. P. Knight, presented to Victoria and Albert Museum, 1870, P.D. 180 C, Portf. 252F/1/7650/17 recto.
A preliminary sketch showing Joan on horseback with foot soldiers grouped around her marching out across a drawbridge, banners are flying and on the left is a castellated gateway.
(*b*) Pencil, as for (*a*), Portf. 252F/1/7650/28 verso.

Sketch similar in detail to (*a*) but with four superimposed studies of Joan on horseback.

(*c*) Pencil and wash, $5\frac{1}{8} \times 8\frac{9}{10}$. Postmarked 'Dec. 7. 1846'.
Coll.: as for (*a*), Portf. 252F/5/8752/13.

Shows a confused *mêlée* of fighting horse and foot soldiers on the right; a castle gateway on left.

(*d*) Sixty-two studies of horses, some in pen and wash but mostly in black crayon, average size $9 \times 7\frac{2}{5}$.
Coll.: as for (*a*), Portf. 252F/7/7654/1–73 (some misc. studies of human skeletons make up the other eleven items).

Probably made in connection with the *Joan of Arc*. Sheets are watermarked 1843 (7654/61, also inscr. 'Nov. 9. 1845'); 1845 (7654/64); and 1846 (7654/70).
Victoria and Albert Museum, London.

22 JOAN OF ARC, AFTER RENDERING THE MOST SIGNAL SERVICES TO HER PRINCE AND PEOPLE, IS SUFFERED TO DIE A MARTYR IN THEIR CAUSE
Canvas, 117×78.
Coll.: Either Colls or Wass; Thomas Todd; William Cox, sold Foster's, 26.3.1861(126), bt. in; (?)W. Ramsden, sold 14.1.1893(127), bt. Lesser $7\frac{1}{2}$ gns.
Exh.: R.A., 1847(125); S.A., 1849(IX); *Art Treasures*, Manchester, 1857(349).
Engr.: C. W. Wass *c.* 1851.
Lit.: as for above.

A woodcut illustration of this picture was published in an unidentified journal soon after Etty's death (Print Room, British Museum).

(*a*) [pl. 89a] Pen, $4\frac{3}{8} \times 7\frac{1}{4}$, shows several poses of Joan at the stake.
Coll.: Bernard Evans, R.I.

(*b*) Pen, $4\frac{1}{2} \times 7\frac{1}{2}$, Coll.: as for (*a*). *Recto:* Five slight sketches of head and shoulders of Joan at the stake, clutching a crucifix to her bosom. Also studies of armour, helmets, gauntlets, and mace. On *verso:* many sketches of women's heads, are recognizably the head and shoulders of Joan as on *recto*.
H. G. Simpson, Esq., Bristol.

(*c*) Watercolour, and pencil, $4\frac{1}{4} \times 3\frac{3}{4}$.
Coll.: Purchased by Bradford 1920.

Shows what appears to be a blazing pyre with soldiers grouped around its base.
City Art Gallery, Bradford.

Various other oil and pencil studies have passed through the sale rooms: *e.g.* R. Nicholson Sale 13.7.1849 (164) *Joan of Arc*, a study, bt. Farrer 37 gns., and (174) *A Study of Joan of Arc*,

bt. Read 62 gns.; Sir Robert Rawlinson, K.C.B., sold 18.5.1903(126) *Joan of Arc* (on panel), bt. Rawlinson 4 gns.; and probably sold again 22.1.1912(271) *A Study of Joan of Arc at the Stake*, panel, $18\frac{1}{2} \times 14$, bt. Gray 3 gns.; (?)sold Robinson & Foster 16.4.1953 (133). *See also* Etty Sale, 1850(607, 609, 744, 745 and 786).

Many sketches for Joan of Arc were lent by R. W. Anderson & Sons to York, 1911(1 & 3), and Dr. E. C. Carter lent a *Joan of Arc* (83) priced at £50.

None of the original three large canvases has been traced.

23 JUDAS ISCARIOT
Millboard laid on panel, $16\frac{1}{2} \times 12\frac{1}{2}$.
Coll.: C. Hargitt; Edward Hargitt, London, sold 22.2.1896(62), bt. O'Dea £1 12s.; Sheffield Art Gallery, Graves Gift 1937 (No. 257).
Exh.: (?)B.I., 1843(80) *Head of Judas; Yorks. Fine Art & Industrial*, York, 1866(125); Sheffield, 1934(257); A.C. *Yorkshire Artists 1600–1900*, Leeds, 1946(13); York, 1949(62).
Lit.: Gilchrist, ii, p. 339.
Graves Art Gallery, Sheffield.

24 JUDITH
Canvas, 120×157.
Coll.: Purchased from the Artist by the Royal Scottish Academy, January, 1829, and presented to the National Gallery of Scotland, 1910 (No. 186).
Exh.: R.A., 1827(12); B.I., 1828(445); R.S.A., 1829(177), and 1831(I); S.A., 1849(I); *International Exhibition*, 1862(353); York, 1911(179). On long loan to York, 1922–50.
Lit.: D. E. Williams, *Life and Correspondence of Sir Thomas Lawrence, Kt.*, 1831, ii, pp. 470–71; *Autobiography*, pp. 39–40; Waagen, *Treasures of Art*, 1854, iii, p. 271; Gilchrist, i, pp. 235–8, 254, 260–4, ii, pp. 275, 278, 336–7.

The centrepiece and first of the three paintings based on the Apocryphal *Book of Judith*: 'Then she came to the pillar of the bed which was at Holofernes' head, and took down his faulchion from thence. And approached to his bed, and took hold of the hair of his head, and said—Strengthen me, O Lord God of Israel, this day!'

(*a*) *National Gallery of Scotland, Edinburgh.* Millboard, $7\frac{3}{4} \times 6\frac{1}{2}$.
Coll.: Sir James Linton, P.R.I., who presented it to the Royal Scottish Academy 1891.
Exh.: York, 1911(85) *Sketches for 'Judith' Series of Pictures.*

The board is divided into two roughly equal sections, with composition studies top and bottom. The lower sketch shows Judith with her arm held at a less acute angle than in the finished painting; she is also placed nearer the centre. The upper sketch is closer to the finished work.

(*b*) Millboard, 7⅝ × 10¼.
Coll.: as for (*a*).
Exh.: York, 1911(85).
Similar in composition to the lower sketch in (*a*).

(*c*) [pl. 25*a*] Millboard, 11 × 8½.
Coll.: as for (*a*).
Exh.: York, 1911(85).
Similar in composition to the lower sketch in (*a*), but the figure of Holofernes is in a twisted pose, showing the back of his head and shoulders. His left arm and hand sag over the edge of the bed. This, and the lower sketch (*a*) include a shield immediately behind the bed.
Royal Scottish Academy, Edinburgh.

(*d*) [pl. 25*b*] Panel, 13½ × 17½.
Coll.: G. P. Dudley Wallis, sold Sotheby's, 21.5.1952(118), bt. Arcade Gallery £70 Mrs. Robert Frank (from June to August 1957).
Exh.: A. C. Etty, 1955(14).
Repr.: Illustrated London News, 20.8.1955, p.321.
Sold as a Géricault in 1952, it also appears on the easel in John Minton's *Portrait of Nevile Wallis* (exh. R.A., 1953).
Mr. George E. Dix, junr., New York.

(*e*) Millboard, 12 × 16.
Coll.: Louis D. Shirlaw, Edinburgh, from whom purchased by York 1911(No. 72/1911).
Exh.: York, 1911(165); York, 1948(13); York 1949(75).
City Art Gallery, York.

(*f*) Millboard aid on canvas, 27 × 21.
Coll.: (?)D. Shirlaw; Miss M. K. Cartwright (until June, 1956); Mrs. E. M. Bean.
Exh.: (?)York, 1911(166) Sketch for *Judith and Holofernes*; York, 1948(8); York, 1949(94). On long loan to York 1936–56.
Mrs. E. M. Bean, Sudbury, Suffolk.

(*g*) [pl. 24*b*] Pencil, 6 × 3⅜.
Coll.: Robert E. Smithson; E. W. Smithson, sold 12.3.1928(140), bt. York, *Sketchbook IV*, pp. 12–13.
Differs only slightly from the final oil painting: Judith holds her arm at a less acute angle than in the later work.

(*h*)–(*k*) Four pencil studies on card, each 4⅜ × 3.
Coll.: as for (*g*).
No. 51(*a*) head of Judith.
Nos. 51(*b*, *d*), (*e*) recto and verso: miscellaneous details.
City Art Gallery, York.

(*l*) Pencil, 3 × 4½.
Coll.: Presented Rev. G. Mountford to British Museum, 1948–11–26–4(verso).
Shows figure of Judith in top third of sheet: Holofernes on his couch is in the lower part.
British Museum, London.

(*m*) Three pencil studies (two recto and one verso), 2 9/10 × 6.
Coll.: J. P. Knight, 1870; P.D. 180 C., Portf. 252F/1/7650/50.
Victoria and Albert Museum, London.

(*n*) Millboard laid on canvas, 27 × 21.
Coll.: On loan to York Art Gallery.
Exh.: York, 1948(8); York, 1949(94).
Study for the head and shoulders of Judith. The model has her head thrown back, and is seen frontally.

25 JUDITH GOING FORTH
Canvas (painted arched top), 118½ × 108.
Coll.: Commissioned by the Royal Scottish Academy 1829, and presented to the National Gallery of Scotland 1910 (No. 187).
Exh.: R.A., 1830(124); R.S.A., 1831(264) and (II); S.A., 1849(III); *International Exhibition*, 1862(354); York, 1911(180). On long loan to York, 1922–50.
Lit.: Autobiography, pp. 39–40; Waagen, *op. cit.*; Gilchrist, i, pp. 278, 285, 329–30, 333–5, 353, ii, pp. 177–8, 337.
The second and right hand wing of the *Judith* series: 'And anon after she went forth; and she gave Holofernes' head to her maid, and she put it in her bag of meat.'
National Gallery of Scotland, Edinburgh.

26 JUDITH: THE MAID OF JUDITH WAITING OUTSIDE THE TENT OF HOLOFERNES TILL HER MISTRESS HAD CONSUMMATED THE DEED THAT DELIVERED HER COUNTRY FROM ITS INVADERS
Canvas (painted arched top), 118½ × 108.
Coll.: Commissioned by the Royal Scottish Academy 1829, and presented to the National Gallery of Scotland 1910 (No. 185).
Exh.: R.A., 1831(79); R.S.A., 1831(III); S.A., 1849(II); *International Exhibition*, 1862(352) York, 1911(178). On long loan to York, 1922–500.
Lit.: Autobiography, pp. 39–40; Waagen, *loc. cit.*;

Gilchrist, i, pp. 323–6, 329–30, 333–5, 353, ii, pp. 177–8, 337.

This is the third and last of the *Judith* series, but depicts the first scene of the narrative and forms the left-hand wing of the triptych.

In the Wethered Sale 27.2.1858 were two studies for the *Judith*: *The Maid of Judah* (54) 'a sketch of figures on the back', bt. Humphrey 20 gns.; and *Head of Judith* (58) 'in a crimson robe and cap', bt. Rippe 12½ gns. Messrs. Rainy & Cameron lent 'studies' for the *Judith* series to York, 1911(28, 29, 30).

National Gallery of Scotland, Edinburgh.

27 THE MAGDALEN

Inscr.: 'Nº 4. Wᵐ Etty R.A.' (on verso).
Millboard laid on panel (painted oval top), 19⅜ × 15⅜.
Coll.: Robert Vernon Gift to the National Gallery 1847 (No. 365). Transferred to the Tate Gallery, 1929.
Exh.: (?)R.A., 1842(6) *A Magdalen*.
Engr.: F. Bacon, *The Art Journal*, XI, August, 1849, p. 258, and *The Vernon Gallery*, 1st Series, 1850, No. 9, as *The Penitent*.
Lit.: Gilchrist, ii, pp. 129–30, 132, 339.

Another version, said to have been painted for the Rev. Issac Spencer and exhibited at the R.A., 1842, was sold Sharpin Sale, 21.3.1863 (158), bt. Rought 380 gns. At the R.S.A., 1851 (115), *The Magdalen* was exhibited as the property of Spencer. Several *Magdalen* subjects were shown at the Society of Arts in 1849, but none of these can safely be identified with surviving pictures.

Tate Gallery, London.

28 MOSES

Panel, 52¾ × 23½.
Lit.: as for *Aaron* (*v. supra*).
St. Edmund the King and Martyr, London.

29 NUDE FEMALE CONTEMPLATING A CRUCIFIX (?A MAGDALEN)

Canvas, 21¼ × 37⅛.
Coll.: (?)William Wethered, sold 27.2.1858 (105) *The Magdalene Reclining*, 'a skull and crucifix before her', bt. Hoskins 11 gns.; acquired for £15 by the Victoria & Albert Museum 1873 (No. 811).
Victoria and Albert Museum, London.

30 THE PENITENT MAGDALEN

Millboard, 23¼ × 18¼.
Signed and dated on the back 1835.
Coll.: (?)C. W. Wass; William Wethered, sold 27.2.1858(100) *The Magdalene reading*, 'before a crucifix', bt. Rought 17½ gns., Ernest I. Nathan,

sold 20.4.1928(113) *The Magdalen*, panel, 23 × 17½, bt. Mrs. Bolton 42 gns.; Mrs. W. F. R. Weldon Gift, 1933.
Exh.: (?)S.A., 1849(XXXVIII) lent Charles Wentworth Wass.
Lit.: Gilchrist, ii, p. 338; *Catalogue of Paintings*, Ashmolean Museum, 1951, No. 146, pp. 34–5, where it is identified with the H. A. J. Munro of Novar painting (No. 538 in the Frost and Reeve catalogue). But the size and description of neither of the two Magdalen subjects in the Munro collection fit the Ashmolean picture. Lot 146 in the Munro Sale, 1867, is described as the painting which once belonged to the Rev. Isaac Spencer.
Ashmolean Museum, Oxford.

31 [pl. 61*b*] THE PRODIGAL SON

Millboard (traces of arched top), 26⅞ × 21⅛.
Coll.: James Stewart, sold 20.4.1839(59) *The Prodigal Son*, 'seated in a posture of sorrow; . . .', bt. Hume 86 gns.;—Child, Esq.; The Duke of Hamilton, K.T., sold 8.6.1882(1070; 10th Day), bt. Agnew 95 gns.; Councillor E. C. R. Litler-Jones, Liverpool (by 1933).
Exh.: B.I., 1836(225); *59th Autumn Exhibition*, Walker Art Gallery, Liverpool, 1933(63); York, 1949(9).
Lit.: *Autobiography*, p. 40; Gilchrist, ii, p. 338.

Another, still unlocated version of this subject was exhibited at the R.A., 1838(46), where it was purchased by William Beckford (Gilchrist, ii, pp. 80, 82). In *Fraser's Magazine*, June, 1838, p. 763, William M. Thackeray describes the prodigal son as kneeling with his hands clasped in prayer. It was about the same size as the 1836 picture, and a 'finished study' for it was bought in at the Benjamin Godfrey Windus Sale, 26.3.1859(39). At York, 1911, there were two versions, both lent by Josiah Rhodes: *The Prodigal* (137), and *The Prodigal in the Far Country* (168).

Numerous studies exist for heads and limbs of boars and goats scattered among the pages of *Sketchbook VI* (*q.v.*).

The Lord Fairhaven.

32 [pl. 72] THE REPENTANT PRODIGAL'S RETURN TO HIS FATHER

Panel, 34 × 46.
Coll.: Purchased from the Artist for 250 gns. by the Marquis of Lansdowne; James Price, sold 15.6.1895(36), illus., bt. Ramus 460 gns.; sold 23.2.1901(117), bt. Lansdowne 120 gns., sold 7.3.1930(15), bt. Leggatt 10 gns.; W. F. R. Weldon Bequest 1937 (No. 147).

Exh.: R.A., 1841(136); S.A., 1849(L); A.C. *Etty*, 1955(32).

Lit.: Autobiography, p. 40; Waagen, *Treasures of Art*, 1854, iii, p. 165; Gilchrist, ii, pp. 118–19, 273, 339.

The R.A. catalogue contained a quotation from *St. Luke*, xv, v. 21. The centre group of father and son compares closely with Murillo's *The Return of the Prodigal* which had recently been acquired by the Duke of Sutherland from Marshal Soult in 1835, and which was exhibited at the British Institution, 1836(22) and again at the R.A. *Seventeenth Century Exhibition*, 1938 (217).

Ashmolean Museum, Oxford.

33 ST. JOHN THE BAPTIST

Paper mounted on plywood, $19\frac{3}{4} \times 16$.

Coll.: (?)Richard Nicholson, sold 13.7.1849 (83), bt. Andrews 38 gns.; G. T. Andrews, sold 31.5.1851(67), bt. Wilkin 52 gns. Bequeathed by Sir Claude Phillips, 1924 (No. 83/1924).

Exh.: York, 1911(114); York, 1948(5).

A pencil study for this figure appears on p. 114 of *Sketchbook II* (*q.v.*), and this suggests that the painting may be dated *c.* 1824–5. Another *St. John the Baptist* was exhibited at the R.A., 1848(404) without a title, but with the quotation: 'Him that crieth from the wilderness, Repent ye.' It was bought at the exhibition by the Rev. Isaac Spencer, sold 23.2.1861 (48), bt. Munro. This is perhaps the same painting as that shown at York, 1911(153), lent by Mr. T. Laughton.

City Art Gallery, York.

34 SKETCH FOR A LARGE PICTURE OF CHRIST BLESSING LITTLE CHILDREN

Canvas, $18 \times 31\frac{1}{2}$ (30 × 45 in B.I. catalogue).

Coll.: Etty Sale, 10.5.1850(651), bt. Owen [?Rev. E. P. Owen] 20 gns., as 'unfinished'; H. A. J. Munro of Novar, sold 11.5.1867(140), bt. Graves 180 gns.; Henry Smith (by 1868); Frederick Nettlefold, sold 5.6.1913(108), bt. Sampson 21 gns.; Anon., sold 14.2.1936(137), bt. Marks 9 gns. Present location unknown.

Exh.: B.I., 1843(40); *National Exhibition of Works of Art*, Leeds, 1868(1139).

Lit.: Gilchrist, ii, p. 339; noted in the Munro of Novar catalogue by W. E. Frost, A. R. A. & Henry Reeve, but not numbered.

A study for a large painting originally intended for St. Margaret's Church, Brighton.

35 [pl. 34a] THE STORM

Canvas, $35\frac{1}{2} \times 41\frac{1}{2}$.

Coll.: Purchased from the Artist by the Royal Manchester Institution, 1832. The price was 85 gns., 15 gns. less than that asked in 1830.

Exh.: R.A., 1830(37); B.I., 1831(82); *Modern Artists*, Royal Manchester Institution, 1832 (325); R.S.A., 1831(V); S.A., 1849(XXV); *Art Treasures*, Manchester, 1857(273); *National Exhibition of Works of Art*, Leeds, 1868(1166); R.A. *Old Masters*, 1876(261); *Art Treasures*, Manchester, May–July, 1878(244); *British Art*, Manchester, 1934(82); B.C. *La Peinture Anglaise XVIIIᵉ et XIXᵉ Siècles*, Louvre, Paris, 1938(42) and repr. in supplement; A.C. *English Romantic Art*, 1947(57); York, 1949(47); R.A. *First Hundred Years*, 1951–2(238), and repr. in illus. souvenir, p. 25.

Lit.: Autobiography, p. 40; Gilchrist, i, pp. 278, 286, 355, ii, pp. 273, 337.

Repr.: Reproductions from the Collection of the Manchester City Art Gallery, 1925, p. 18; Gaunt & Roe, pl. 13.

Version: Anon., sold 7.2.1919(93), bt. Smith £65, described as a 'drawing' $36 \times 41\frac{1}{2}$; Anon., sold 15.2.1929(40), bt. Lacey 21 gns., $35\frac{1}{2} \times 41$; (?)S. Goldman, Houston, Texas. This painting would seem to be of doubtful pedigree.

In the R.A. catalogue for 1830 the following quotation is given: 'They cried unto Thee, and were delivered; they trusted in Thee, and were not confounded', *Psalm* xxii, v. 5; and in the S.A. catalogue further quotations from *Psalm* cvii, vv. 6 and 25, were included.

City Art Gallery, Manchester.

(*a*) Pen and sepia wash, $4\frac{7}{10} \times 4\frac{1}{10}$.

Shows central figures as they are in the final composition.

Miss E. Newmarsh, Windsor.

(*b*) Pencil on oiled tracing paper, $7\frac{4}{5} \times 6\frac{2}{5}$.

Coll.: J. P. Knight, 1870; P.D. 180 C, Portf. 252F/6/7653/32.

A preliminary study for the female figure, seen in reverse and in a slightly different pose from that used in the final painting.

Victoria and Albert Museum, London.

36 THE WISE AND FOOLISH VIRGINS

Canvas (arched top), $83\frac{1}{2} \times 66$.

Coll.: Mr. Sergeant Thompson, sold 5.3.1859 (60), bt. Flatou 160 gns.; C. F. Huth, Tunbridge Wells, sold 19.3.1904(50), bt. Hubbard 20 gns.;—Blyth, sold 15.2.1924(148), bt. Nicoll 20 gns. Present location unknown.

Exh.: R.A., 1840(230) *A subject from the parable of the Ten Virgins;* B.I., 1841(40); S.A., 1849 (XXIV), lent by Sergeant Thompson.

Lit.: Autobiography, p. 40; Gilchrist, ii, pp. 110, 117, 273, 338.

The R.A. catalogue for 1840 had the quotation: 'Five of them were wise, and five foolish: . . . Verily I know you not', *St. Matthew*, xxv.

HISTORICAL, MYTHOLOGICAL AND ALLEGORICAL

37 [pl. 36a] ANDROMEDA

Millboard, 26⅜ × 20.

Coll.: (?)Charles Reade, sold 18.5.1885(243), bt. Bolton 10 gns.; Alexander Huth, sold 14.7.1916(128), bt. Gooden & Fox 10 gns. for 1st Viscount Leverhulme.

Lit.: R. R. Tatlock, *Catalogue of the Lady Lever Art Gallery*, I, 1928, p. 95, No. 2854, repr. pl. 56.

Repr.: Gaunt & Roe, pl. 44.

Although entitled *Andromeda*, this painting might also be a preliminary study for the *Britomart redeemes faire Amoret* in the Lady Lever Art Gallery. A picture *Andromeda*, panel, 25½ × 19½, belonged to Charles Edward Lees, Oldham, sold 24.4.1936(129), bt. Field 31 gns.; Adams Bros., sold anon., 8.6.1951(121), bt. Gough 16 gns. It was exhibited at York, 1949(19).

The Lady Lever Art Gallery, Port Sunlight.

38 [pl. 82b] ANDROMEDA—PERSEUS COMING TO HER RESCUE

Panel, 32 × 25.

Coll.: (?)George Knott, sold 26.4.1845(52), bt. Rought 210 gns.; J. Harris; (?)Charles Macdonald, sold 29.5.1855(76), bt. in 300 gns.; again bought in 23.5.1857(365); sold 5.6.1858 (50), bt. Gregory 400 gns.; Daniel Thwaites; John and Oscar Yerburgh, sold 27.10.1950(73), bt. Agnew 34 gns.

Exh.: R.A., 1840(26); S.A., 1849(CIII); *Royal Jubilee*, Manchester, 1887(584); A.C. *Etty*, 1955(31).

Lit.: The Times, 6th May, 1840: Gilchrist, ii, pp. 110, 205, 338.

Michael Jaffé, Esq., Cambridge.

39 ANDROMEDA AND PERSEUS

Canvas, 30 × 24.

Coll.: (?)James Broughton; George Walthew, who presented it to Manchester, 1894.

Exh.: (?)*Yorks. Exhibition of Science and Manufactures*, Leeds, 1875(767).

This appears to be a later version of the 1840

painting. Louis Huth lent a *Perseus and Andromeda* to the British Institution, 1862(198).

City Art Gallery, Manchester.

40 AURORA AND ZEPHYR

Panel (painted circle), 36 × 36½.

Coll.: Joseph Gillott (*Account Book*, 20th March, 1849, p. 12); William Wethered, sold 7.3.1856 (148), bt. Rought 710 gns.; C. T. Maud; H. A. J. Munro of Novar, sold 6.4.1878(27), bt. Vokins 460 gns.; Anon., sold 8.6.1901(88), bt. Agnew 200 gns.; William Lockett Agnew (1923), sold 15.6.1923(28), bt. Gooden & Fox 240 gns. for 1st Viscount Leverhulme.

Exh.: R.A., 1845(12); *National Exhibition of Works of Art*, Leeds, 1868(1149), lent Charles T. Maud; R.A. *British Art*, 1934(675) and repr. illus. souvenir p. 61, and Commemorative Cat., CXXI.; A.C. *Yorkshire Artists 1600–1900*, Leeds, 1946(10).

Lit.: Autobiography, p. 40; Gilchrist, ii, pp. 204, 340; Gaunt & Roe, pp. 73, 104 (and repr. pl. 54); R. R. Tatlock *Catalogue of the Lady Lever Art Gallery*, I, 1928, p. 95, No. 4690, repr. pl. 57.

The Royal Academy catalogue contained the quotation from Milton's *L'Allegro*:

The frolic wind that breathes the spring—

> Zephyr with Aurora playing,
> As he met her once a Maying.

Gaunt and Roe compare this composition with Titian's *Venus and Adonis* (National Gallery, Angerstein Collection, No. 34); it is almost identical but seen in reverse. Etty's copy after Titian's painting was in the Munro of Novar Sale, 6.4.1878(23; 27½ × 35½), bought by Agnew 220 gns. A smaller version of this subject by Etty, 12½ dia., was in Sir William Eden's collection, sold 15.7.1899(130), bought Maple 34 gns.

The Lady Lever Art Gallery, Port Sunlight.

41 BACCHANALIAN REVEL

Canvas, 13½ × 21¼.

Coll.: Earl of Wemyss, Gosford.

Exh.: R.A. *Old Masters*, 1886(50).

Similar in style to the sketch for *The World Before the Flood*, and probably painted *c.* 1828–30. Possibly based upon a Poussin prototype.

The Earl of Wemyss.

42 [pl. 69] A BIVOUAC OF CUPID AND HIS COMPANY

Canvas, 26 × 36.

Coll.: Richard Colls; Joseph Gillott from Colls for £438 (Gillott *Account Book*, 8th June, 1845); James Fallows, Manchester, sold 23.5.1868 (122), bt. Gambart 220 gns.; David Price,

sold 2.4.1892(53), bt. McLean 260 gns.; R. B. Angus, who presented it to Montreal 1908.
Exh.: R.A., 1838(16); Birmingham Society of Artists, 1846(44), lent by Joseph Gillott; S.A., 1849(XLIX); *Art Treasures*, Manchester, 1857 (226); *Royal Jubilee*, Manchester, 1887(561).
Lit.: Gilchrist, ii, pp. 82, 228.
Museum of Fine Arts, Montreal.

43 [pl. 60a] THE BRIDGE OF SIGHS
Canvas, 31½ × 20.
Coll.: Purchased from the Artist for £100 by Digby Murray (until 1840); W. C. Macready, sold 8.7.1873(382), bt. E. D. Wilmot £75; R. Hanmer, purchased with the aid of the N.A.C.F. by York, 1948 (65/1948).
Exh.: R.A., 1835(235); B.I., 1836(207); S.A., 1849(XL); York, 1948(2); York, 1949(69) and repr.; *Pictures from Yorkshire Galleries*, Sheffield, 1952(63); A.C. *British Subject and Narrative Pictures: 1800–1848*, 1955(18); *Peintures anglaises des collections d'York et du Yorkshire*, Musée des Beaux-Arts, Dijon, 1957(26).
Lit.: *Autobiography*, p. 40; Gilchrist, ii, pp. 31, 114, 338; *Macready's Reminiscences*, ed. Sir Frederick Pollock, London, 1875, ii, pp. 161-2, entries for June 24/25th, 1840.
Repr.: *York Preview* 3, July, 1940 (cover).

Painted between 1833–5 from sketches Etty made in Italy in 1823. Two drawings, one of the Bridge and canal, the other a detailed study of the Bridge, are in Etty's 'Cash Book', c. 1823 (York Art Gallery). The 'Cash Book' also contains an account of Etty's visit to the State Prisons of Venice from which is taken this description printed in the Royal Academy catalogue, 1835: 'Just by the Bridge of Sighs, at the remote extremity of the narrow passage . . . is a strong iron bar, upon and across this, the condemned was thrown and his head severed from his body, unheard, unseen, save by the executioners and the dread eye of Heaven! . . . the body was conveyed to a distant part of the Lagune and there thrown in. Near that spot the fishermen of Venice were forbidden under the severest penalties, to fish.'
City Art Gallery, York.

44 [pl. 46] BRITOMART REDEEMES FAIRE AMORET
Canvas, 35½ × 25⅞.
Coll.: Purchased from the Artist for £157 by 'Mr. L., Manchester', 1833 ('Cash Book', entry for August, 1833); G. T. Andrews, sold 23.6.1849(96), bt. Lord Charles Townshend 520 gns.; Anon., sold 24.5.1851(40), bt. in 510 gns.; sold 13.5.1854(38), bt. E. Gambart

420 gns.; Sir G. A. Drummond, sold 27.6.1919 (141), bt. Gooden & Fox 410 gns. for 1st Viscount Leverhulme.
Exh.: R.A., 1833(7); *Modern Artists*, Royal Manchester Institution, 1833 (193); S.A., 1849 (CXXVIII); A.C. *Etty*, 1955(22) repr. pl. IV.
Lit.: *Autobiography*, p. 40; Gilchrist, i, p. 359, ii, pp. 250, 273, 283, 337; R. R. Tatlock, *Catalogue of the Lady Lever Art Gallery*, I, 1928, p. 96, No. 4031.
Repr.: Gaunt & Roe, pl. 20.

Inspired by lines from Edmund Spenser's *Faery Queene*, Book iii, Canto 12.
The Lady Lever Art Gallery, Port Sunlight.

(*a*) Two drawings, 51 (*c*) and 51 (*d*) verso (both on card, 4⅖ × 3) show that Etty first planned his composition with Britomart on the extreme left, the enchanter being between her and Amoret, all of them standing.
City Art Gallery, York.

(*b*) Pencil sketch on irregular shaped tracing paper, approx. 9⁷⁄₁₀ × 9½, shows Amoret kneeling on right of the composition, with the sorcerer on the left attempting to stab either her or Britomart who is standing between them. Suggestion of arched top, but no architectural details drawn in.
Coll.: J. P. Knight, 1870; P.D. 180 C. Portf. 252F/4/7651/18.
Victoria and Albert Museum, London.

45 CANDAULES, KING OF LYDIA, SHOWING HIS WIFE BY STEALTH TO GYGES, ONE OF HIS MINISTERS: AS SHE GOES TO BED
Canvas, 17¾ × 20.
Col.: Robert Vernon, who purchased it from the Artist and presented it to the National Gallery 1847 (No. 358). Transferred to the Tate Gallery 1929.
Exh.: R.A., 1830(331); York, 1911(149); York, 1949(55).
Lit.: Gilchrist, i, pp. 285–6, ii, p. 337.

The subject (sometimes called the *Imprudence of Candaules, King of Lydia*) is taken from *Herodotus* I, chap. 8. The Queen of Lydia, Nyssia, outraged at the indignity she had suffered gave Gyges the choice either to be executed or to slay the King. The Minister chose the second alternative, married Nyssia, and reigned over Lydia 38 years.
Tate Gallery, London.

(*a*) Pencil study, 9⅘ × 7⁹⁄₁₀, of *Candaules* and other fragments on a letter [*n.d.*] from John Bulmer, with black seal, initials 'J.B.', and Bull's head crest.

Coll.: J. P. Knight, 1870; P.D. 180 C, Portf. 252F/4/7651/38.

Victoria and Albert Museum, London.

46 [pl. 80] CIRCE AND THE SIRENS THREE
Canvas, 46½ × 71½.

Coll.: Purchased from the Artist for 350 gns. by Joseph Gillott (*Account Book*, 7th November, 1845), sold 27.4.1872(261), bt. Agnew 600 gns.; Thomas Walker, Berkswell Hall, Warws., sold 2.6.1888(52), bt. Evans 285 gns.; Mrs. Lewis-Hill, London, sold 20.4.1907(28), bt. Gooden & Fox 140 gns. for F. A. Denny; purchased by Sir James Linton for Perth.

Exh.: R.A., 1846(166); Birmingham Society of Artists, 1848(37), lent by Joseph Gillott.

Lit.: Gilchrist, ii, pp. 150–2, 163–8, 211, 340.

The first of the designs for the fresco in the Garden Pavilion, Buckingham Palace, 1844, inspired by Milton's *Comus*: 'Circe, with the Syrens three / Amidst the flowery-kirtled Naïades.' The actual fresco, which Wethered obtained from Colls, was sold 27.2.1858(111), bt. Woodgate 20 gns., who also bought the following lot, a chalk study for *Circe*, for 8½ gns.

Art Gallery of Western Australia, Perth.

(a) [pl. 83a] Panel (painted circle), 11½ dia.
Coll.: (?)Etty Sale, 10.5.1850(660), *Circe*, bt. Andrews 18½ gns.

A half-length study for the central figure of Circe.

Mrs. Robert Frank, London.

(b) (?)Canvas, presumably quite small, for the reclining naïad on the extreme left of the composition. Known only from a photograph —said to have belonged to P. M. Turner, but not in Turner Sale, December, 1950.

(c) Pen and ink, 1⁷⁄₁₀ × 7⅔. Two studies for naïad (as in (b)), but seen in reverse.
Coll.: J. P. Knight, 1870; P.D. 180 C, Portf. 252F/1/7650/26.

Victoria and Albert Museum, London.

47 [pl. 13] CLEOPATRA'S ARRIVAL IN CILICIA
Canvas, 42¼ × 52¼.

Coll.: Commissioned from the Artist by Sir Francis Freeling for 200 gns., although Gilchrist hints that a much lower sum was paid. Sold 15.4.1837(92), bt. Henry Farrer 210 gns.; Right Hon. Henry Labouchere (Lord Taunton) until 1872; R. K. Hodgson, sold 26.6.1880 (120), bt. in 500 gns., and again sold 2.4.1881 (279), bt. Marsden 430 gns.; J. Pearson, sold 9.6.1883(275), bt. Mrs. Fielden 300 gns.; sold 28.4.1888(57), bt. McLean 240 gns.; A.

Sanderson, sold Knight, Frank & Rutley, 16.6.1911(631) illustrated in catalogue, bt. Gooden & Fox 240 gns. for 1st Viscount Leverhulme.

Exh.: R.A., 1821(261); B.I., 1825(99); R.S.A., 1846(342); *Modern Artists*, Royal Manchester Institution, 1846(266); S.A., 1849(CV); *Art Treasures*, Manchester, 1857(249); *International Exhibition*, 1862 (374); R.A. *Old Masters*, 1872 (23); *British Art 1830–50*, Whitechapel, 1920 (27).

Lit.: *Autobiography*, p. 37; Waagen, *Treasures of Art*, 1854, ii, p. 423; Gilchrist, i, pp. 92–5, ii, p. 336; Malcolm C. Salaman, *The Studio*, LXXXV, no. 385, January, 1923, pp. 3–12; R. R. Tatlock, *Catalogue of the Lady Lever Art Gallery*, I, 1928, p. 94, No. 169; Gaunt & Roe, pp. 23, 78, 85 (repr. pl. 6).

Repr.: *The Magazine of Fine Arts*, I, November, 1905—April, 1906, p. 121.

This painting is also known as *The Triumph of Cleopatra*.

The Lady Lever Art Gallery, Port Sunlight.

An oval study for *Cleopatra* was in the B. G. Windus Sale, 15.2.1868(304), bt. Vokins 22 gns.

(a) Sepia ink, on tracing paper, 10 × 16⅛, study for central group of Cleopatra and her attendants.
Inscr.: 'Raffaelle Michel Angelo Antique.' Agrees in all details with the finished painting.
Coll.: J. P. Knight, 1870; P.D. 180 C, Portf. 252F/6/7653/36.

(b) Three pencil studies on single folded sheet, 12¾ × 10½, for central figure of Cleopatra only.
Coll.: as for (a) Portf. 252F/5/7652/35.

(c) Six pencil outline studies on single sheet, 12⅝ × 7⁹⁄₁₀, for figure of Cleopatra only.
Coll.: as for (a) Portf. 252F/5/7652/47.

(a), (b) and (c) *Victoria and Albert Museum, London.*

48 [pl. 17] THE COMBAT: WOMAN PLEADING FOR THE VANQUISHED. AN IDEAL GROUP
Canvas, 100 × 135.

Coll.: Purchased from the Artist for 300 gns. by John Martin, the painter. Martin then sold it to the Royal Scottish Academy in 1831, and they presented it to the National Gallery of Scotland in 1910 (No. 189).

Exh.: R.A., 1825(1); B.I., 1826(343); R.S.A., 1831(IV), lent John Martin, H.R.S.A.; R.S.A., 1844(341); S.A., 1849(IV); Birmingham Society of Artists, 1849(76); *Art Treasures,*

Manchester, 1857(360); B.I., *Ancient Masters*, 1859(116); *International Exhibition*, 1862(373).
Engr.: G. T. Doo, 1848; J. and G. P. Nicholls, *The Art Journal*, August, 1858, p. 235.
Lit.: *Autobiography*, pp. 39, 40; Waagen, *Art Treasures*, iii, 1854, p. 271; Gilchrist, i, pp. 227–9, 233, 333–4, ii, pp. 178, 202, 273, 336; Gaunt & Roe, p. 71 (repr. pl. 8).
Repr.: *The Art Journal*, 1903, p. 375.

The subject and much of the composition of *The Combat* should be compared with Flaxman's pen drawing *Heracles killing a man, to whom a woman clings* (British Museum, 1862–3–8–11 . . . 7, f. 25a, Binyon Catalogue).
National Gallery of Scotland, Edinburgh.

(*a*) Canvas, 35 × 46½.
Coll.: Possibly the copy made by an unknown Edinburgh artist and almost completely reworked by Etty in January, 1845, for the engraver Doo to work from. Anon., sold 13.6.1851(98) *The Combat* (engraved G. Doo), bt. Grundy 570 gns. [*sic*]; Joshua H. S. Mann, sold 7.5.1886(142), bt. Permain £2; J. M. Naylor, Welshpool, sold 19.1.1923(31), bt. Sampson 5 gns.; Wolf Harris, London, sold 16.7.1926(120), bt. Sampson 15 gns.; Anon., sold 9.4.1934(54), bt. Stern 16 gns.; John and Mable Ringling.
Lit.: Samuel and Richard Redgrave, *A Century of British Painters*, Phaidon ed., 1947, p. 8.
The John and Mable Ringling Museum, Sarasota, U.S.A. (No. 416).

(*b*) [pl. 21*b*] Canvas, 17 × 21.
Coll.: (?)C. W. Wass (1849); (?)G. R. Burnett, sold 18.3.1882(99), bt. Long 10 gns.; again Burnett, sold 23.3.1908(274) *The Combat*, 25½ × 30 (possibly inc. frame), bt. Schroeder 14 gns.; Briton Rivière, R.A., sold 6.12.1920(35), bt. Bunny 14 gns.; L. G. Duke (until 1952); Appleby Bros. (until May, 1953); Julius H. Weitzner.
Exh.: (?)S.A., 1849(XIX); Rhode Island School of Design, 28th November, 1956–2nd January, 1957.
A crayon drawing, buff paper, 8⅗ × 11³⁄₁₀, *Sketchbook I*, p. 88 (York Art Gallery) shows a similar composition to this oil study. Other preliminary pen and pencil studies are on p. 89 (*loc. cit.*), and on pp. 79, 99, and 172, *Sketchbook II*, 11⅝ × 8 (York Art Gallery).
Mr. Julius H. Weitzner, New York, U.S.A.

(*c*) Pencil, 12⅖ × 7⁹⁄₁₀, on notepaper postmarked 'May 7, 1824'.

Coll.: J. P. Knight, 1870; P.D. 180 C, Portf. 252F/5/7652/6.

(*d*) Pencil, 5³⁄₁₀ × 3⁷⁄₁₀, study for vanquished man on right.
Coll.: as for (*b*), Portf. 252F/1/7650/13.

(*e*) Pen and ink on notepaper, 7⅞ × 8⅞, study for whole composition excluding the landscape.
Coll.: E. 4041–1919 (misc. 505).
(*c*), (*d*) and (*e*) *Victoria and Albert Museum, London.*

(*f*) Panel, 36½ × 48½.
Coll.: Described in the 1883 R.S.A. Catalogue as 'Life Study'.
This appears to be an unfinished preliminary study for *The Combat*, although the composition differs greatly from the finished work. The fleeing figure on the right with arms flung up, occurs again in the *Pluto carrying off Proserpine* of 1839.
Royal Scottish Academy, Edinburgh.

(*g*) Canvas, 41½ × 54½.
Coll.: H. E. Leetham, J.P., to his daughter Mrs. E. M. Robinson of Dringhouses, York; bequeathed by her to York, 1957.
Lit.: *York Preview* 38, X, April, 1957, p. 376.
Appears to be a faithful copy after the Edinburgh picture, and not by Etty.
City Art Gallery, York.

Between 1855–91 works entitled *A study for 'Mercy Interceding for the Vanquished'* have appeared on five occasions in the sale room, all being sold for very small prices.

49 THE CORAL FINDER: VENUS AND HER YOUTHFUL SATELLITES ARRIVING AT THE ISLE OF PAPHOS
Two versions:
(i) [pl. 12] Canvas, 29 × 38½.
Coll.: Purchased from the Artist for £30 by Thomas Tomkison, pianoforte maker to the Prince Regent, 77 Dean Street, Soho; T. Charles Appleby, Barrow (by 1841); Charles Birch (by 1844); Joseph Gillott (*Account Book*, 1845, after entry dated 7th November); passed to C. W. Wass (1848), who is said to have owned it whilst executing the engraving (*Art Union, loc. cit.*, 1848); Richard Nicholson, sold 13.7.1849(211) as *The Coral Fishers* [*sic*], bt. Agnew 370 gns.; T. Horrocks Miller (by 1889); Thomas Pitt Miller, sold 26.4.1946(35), bt. Mitchell Gallery 110 gns.; Benjamin Welch, sold 27.11.1953(14), bt. in 52 gns.; with Mitchell Gallery, November, 1955, purchased A. Denvil.

Exh.: R.A., 1820(13); Birmingham Society of Artists, 1844(41), lent by Charles Birch; R.A. *Old Masters*, 1889(29); *Guild Merchant Loan Exhibition*, Preston 1902(96); A.C. *Etty*, 1955 (7).

Engr.: C. W. Wass, published *Art Union*, X, April 1848, facing p. 116; W. Cosmo Monkhouse, *Pictures of William Etty*, London, 1874, pl. II.

Lit.: *Autobiography*, pp. 37, 40; Gilchrist, i, pp. 90–94, ii, p 335.

There is an autograph letter on the back of this picture from Etty addressed to C. Appleby, dated 19th May, 1841, in which he undertakes to retouch the shadows, at the request of the owner. A note in Appleby's handwriting, dated 4th August, 1841, confirms the circumstances of the letter.

A. Denvil, Esq., London.

(ii) Canvas, 29½ × 38½.

Coll.: Charles P. Matthews, sold 6.6.1891(27), bt. Schuster 230 gns.; William Somers Schuster; Mrs. Orr-Ewing.

No documentary evidence exists that Etty painted a second version of this painting. It is possible that another version was painted for Wass in 1848, from which he could do his engraving. Although it agrees in every detail with (i) and seems to be of almost the same quality, it is unlikely to be the painting exhibited at the Royal Academy in 1820. In his letter to Appleby, Etty implies that it was Appleby's picture which brought him the friendship of Sir Francis Freeling. Gilchrist states that the picture often changed hands between 1820–49, but does not mention a second painting.

A copy in miniature of *The Coral Finder*, belonging to Thomas Agnew & Sons, was sold 28.10.1861(1210), bt. Jones 5½ gns.

Mrs. Mary Orr-Ewing, Storrington, Dorset.

50 CUPID AND PSYCHE

Canvas (oval), 14½ × 16¼.

Coll.: G. Webster (by 1825); W. H. Lever (1st Viscount Leverhulme) by 1901.

Exh.: B.I., 1821(100); B.I., 1825(79); *International Exhibition*, Glasgow 1901(565); York, 1911(82); A.C. *Etty*. 1955(9).

Lit.: Gilchrist, i. p. 95, ii, p. 336; R. R. Tatlock, *Catalogue of the Lady Lever Art Gallery*, I, 1928, p. 94, No. 161; Gaunt & Roe, p. 86 (repr. pl. 12).

Illustrates lines spoken by the Attendant Spirit in the Epilogue to Milton's *Comus*:

'Where far above, in spangled sheen,
Celestial Cupid, Venus' fam'd son, advanced.
Held his dear Psyche—
After her wand'ring labours long.'
The Lady Lever Art Gallery, Port Sunlight.

51 CUPID IN A SHELL

Two versions:

(i) Millboard, 9 × 13.

Coll.: (?)Alderman R. J. Spiers, Oxford, sold 14.2.1873(155), bt. Copeland 87 gns.; Richard Newsham Bequest, 1883.

Exh.: (?)S.A., 1849(XII); *Art Treasures*, Manchester, 1857(255); *British Art 1830–50*, Whitechapel, 1920(13).

Engr.: W. J. Linton, 1857; J. and G. P. Nicholls, *The Art Journal*, August, 1858, p. 233.

Lit.: Gilchrist, ii, p. 340.

Repr.: Gaunt & Roe, pl. 53.

Painted 1844. A pen and wash drawing, 3½ × 6, inscribed 'Etty' (top left), is in the Witt Collection (No. 3859), Courtauld Institute of Art. Exhibited: A.C. *Drawings from the Witt Collection*, 1953(7a).

The Harris Museum and Art Gallery, Preston.

(ii) Panel, 9½ × 13½.

Coll.: (?)John Bibby, St. Asaph, sold 3.6.1899 (77) as *A Sea Nymph in a Shell*, 7½ × 10½, bt. Jeffries 18 gns.; J. R. Severn, Gerrards Cross; Anon., sold 14.7.1950(79), bt. Wolmark 5 gns.; Montage Gallery, James St., W.1 (until 1951).

Contemporary and identical with (i). Is inscribed on verso as follows: 'This Sketch of Cupid in a Shell was given to me by William Etty, R.A. when I visited him at Adam St. Adelphi on the introduction of his nephew John Clarke [*sic*].'

Mrs. David Williamson, London.

52 CUPID SHELTERING HIS DARLING FROM THE APPROACHING STORM

Panel, 17 × 13½.

Coll.: John Sheepshanks Gift 1857 (No. 73).

Exh.: R.A., 1822(7); B.I., 1823(120); S.A., 1849(LIV).

Engr.: Simmons, published S. C. Halls, *Book of Gems*, 1836, p. 71 as illustration to Sir Philip Sidney's 'From Astrophel and Stella'; Rolls, published Alaric A. Watts, *Lyrics of the Heart*, 1851, p. 207; F. Joubert, *The Art Journal*, June, 1863, facing p. 92.

Lit.: Gilchrist, i, p. 100, ii, p. 336; Gaunt & Roe, pp. 86–7.

Repr.: *The Magazine of Fine Arts*, I, November, 1905–April, 1906, p. 114.

Victoria and Albert Museum, London.

53 THE DANCE

Canvas, 48 × 77.

Coll.: Bought at the Birmingham Society of Artists' exhibition in 1842 by Mr. Bacon of Nottingham, for the greatly reduced price of 360 gns.; Richard Colls (by 1845); John Clow, Liverpool (by 1849), sold Winstanley's, 21.4.1852(81), bt. (?)Tennant 1,100 gns.; Sir Charles Tennant, Bart.; Lord Glenconner.

Exh.: R.A., 1842(33); Birmingham Society of Artists, 1842(46); R.S.A., 1847(153); S.A., 1849(LXXXII); *Art Treasures*, Manchester, 1857(281); *International Exhibition*, 1862(419); *Royal Jubilee*, Manchester, 1887(691); Guildhall, 1894(82); R.A. *Old Masters*, 1906(147).

Lit.: Autobiography, p. 40; Gilchrist, ii, pp. 127–8, 339.

Repr.: Catalogue of the Pictures forming the Collection of Sir Charles Tennant, Bart., 1896.

Illustrates lines from Pope's translation of Homer's *Iliad* describing the Shield of Achilles:

'A figured dance succeeds, a comely band
Of youths and maidens, bounding hand in hand.
The maids in soft simars of linen drest,
The youths all graceful in the glossy vest:
. . . the sprightly revel ends.'

Etty also had in mind Flaxman's Shield of Achilles bas-relief of 1818.

The Lord Glenconner.

(*a*) Pen and wash, 4⅖ × 4⅖, composition study.

Coll.: J. P. Knight, 1870; P.D. 180 C, Portf. 252F/3/7650/49.

(*b*) Pen and ink, 3½ × 5³⁄₁₀, rapid outline composition study.

Coll.: as for (*a*), Portf. 252F/3/7650/21.

Victoria and Albert Museum, London.

54 DESIGN FOR A CEILING

Paper laid on millboard (circular), 17½ dia. (sight).

Coll.: Henry Burton; T. Gabriel; T. B. Gabriel.

Probably in the Etty Sale, 1850, but cannot be related with certainty (? lot 361: 'Design for a ceiling, from P. Veronese—small circle', bt. Birch £3 5s.), nor does the design itself suggest any particular work. It shows a variety of elements including a figure of Zeus and his eagle, Hebe and the infant Bacchus, Apollo driving his chariot across the sky, Venus and Cupid, and Hercules. The circular balustrade occurs in the work of Le Brun and his contemporaries, but the isolated groups are typical of Etty, and the design is thus most likely to be an invention by him rather than a copy after a known prototype. Painted *c.* 1820–5.

Mrs. E. M. Gabriel, Worplesdon, Surrey.

55 DIANA AND ENDYMION

Canvas, 31 × 27.

Coll.: Purchased from the Artist for £100 by George Knott in 1839; Knott Sale, 26.4.1845 (51), bt. Colls 210 gns.; H. A. J. Munro of Novar, sold 6.4.1878(24), bt. Agnew 300 gns.; Edward Crompton Potter, sold 22.3.1884(21), bt. Agnew 295 gns.; Ralph Brockleback, Haughton Hall, Ches., 7.7.1922(55), bt. Agnew 330 gns.; Lord Lawrence of Kingsgate, sold 15.3.1935(103), bt. Smith 52 gns.; present location unknown.

Exh.: R.A., 1839(195); S.A., 1849(XIV); *Art Treasures*, Manchester, May–July, 1878(231); Guildhall, 1899(185); B.F.A.C., Winter, 1908 (27); Manchester, 1909(104); York, 1911(170).

Lit.: Autobiography, p. 40; Gilchrist, ii, pp. 98, 205, 338; W. E. Frost, A.R.A. and Henry Reeve, *Catalogue of the . . . Collection of the late H. A. J. Munro of Novar* [n.d.], No. 128; Gaunt & Roe, p. 99.

Repr.: The Magazine of Fine Arts, I, November, 1905–April, 1906, colour pl. facing p. 110.

Begun in 1838, Etty originally asked £90 for this painting when it was in his studio.

56 [pl. 87] THE FAIRY OF THE FOUNTAIN

Millboard laid on panel, 27⅞ × 20.

Coll.: Commissioned from the Artist for £300 by Joseph Gillott (*Account Book*, November 1845), sold 27.4.1872(258), bt. A. J. Wigram 470 gns. It may have belonged briefly to G. T. Andrews since he lent a similarly entitled work to the S.A., 1849(CXXXII), but it was not in either of his sales of 1849 and 1851. H. A. J. Munro of Novar, sold 6.4.1878(21), bt. Baker 42 gns.; Anon., sold 11.3.1899(72), bt. Vokins 95 gns.; W. Marchant & Co., 21.12.1917(78), bt. Gooden & Fox 32 gns. for 1st Visc. Leverhulme; presented to the Tate Gallery by his Executors through the N.A.C.F. 1925 (No. 4108).

Exh.: S.A., 1849(CXXXII).

Lit.: Gilchrist, ii, p. 341; W. E. Frost, A. R. A. and Henry Reeve, *Catalogue of the . . . Collection of the late H. A. J. Munro of Novar* [n.d.], No. 544 as *Nymph in Water*.

In two letters to Joseph Gillott, Etty explains his ideas about this painting; the second (dated 15th February, 1847), contains twelve lines of verse: *The Little Song of the Fairy of the Fountain* expressing the moral 'If thou would'st wise and

happy be / See keep thy mind and conscience pure / And thou wilt prove both fair and free / From pangs which others oft endure! / The little Dove gave sweet assent / And joyous flapp'd his snowy wings! . . .' A label on the verso in Etty's handwriting reads: 'Woman with Dove and Cupid / Etty.'
Tate Gallery, London.

57 [pl. 68] A FAMILY OF THE FORESTS
Canvas, 22½ × 31.
Coll.: Purchased from the Artist for £50 by either John or his brother Edward Harper in the summer of 1836. After John Harper's death in 1842 it was owned by Edward. Not in Harper Sale, April 1853. (?)William Wethered, sold 7.3.1856(122) *The Forest Family*, bt. Rought 192 gns.; H. A. J. Munro, sold 11.5.1867(20) *A Family of the Forests*, 16 × 26, bt. Bicknell 40 gns.; Henry Sanford Bicknell, sold 7.4.1881 (403), bt. Smith 39 gns. Alexander T. Hollingsworth, from whom purchased by subscription for York 1911 (No. 90/1911).
Exh.: R.A., 1836(82); York, 1836; S.A., 1849 (CI); York, 1911(164); *Jubilee Exh.*, Bradford, 1930(53); *59th Autumn Exh.*, Walker Art Gallery, Liverpool, Oct.–Dec., 1933(68); R.A. *British Art*, 1934(651); York, 1948(7); York, 1949(72).
Lit.: Gilchrist, ii, pp. 46, 338; W. E. Frost, A.R.A. & Henry Reeve, *Catalogue of the . . . Collection of the late H. A. J. Munro of Novar*, [n.d.], No. 541.

In the R.A. catalogue was this quotation from Hesiod: 'They lived with calm untroubled mind.' Gilchrist says the painting was sold between 1850–5 for £350, but gives no further details. Joseph Gillott owned a painting *The Flowers of the Forest*, 25 × 31, sold 27.4.1872 (257), bt. H. Edwards, M.P. 215 gns., sold 13.6.1874(87c), bt. Agnew 195 gns. This may be the picture once in Wethered's collection. Gillott lent his picture to the Birmingham Society of Artists, 1852(120) *The Forest Family*. In the James Coles Sale, 18.6.1870(37) *The Forester's Family*, was bought by G. C[oles?] 61 gns.
City Art Gallery, York.

58 THE GRACES: PSYCHE AND CUPID AS THE PERSONIFICATION OF LOVE, BURNING THE ARROWS OF DESTRUCTION AND TRAMPLING ON THE INSIGNIA OF WAR
Canvas, 31 × 27.
Coll.: Richard Nicholson, sold 13.7.1849(216), bt. Rennard for John Singleton 370 gns.; Anon., sold 19.12.1919(106), bt. Lacey 320

gns. (bt. in); Mrs. A. B. Lamb, sold 26.7.1929 (140), bt. in (Hathenden) 65 gns. On long loan to York Art Gallery since 1929.
Exh.: R.A., 1843(30); *Yorks. Fine Art & Industrial*, York, 1866(174); *National Exhibition of Works of Art*, Leeds, 1868(1204); *Yorks. Fine Art*, York, 1879; York, 1911(94); York, 1948(1).
Lit.: Gilchrist, ii, pp. 145, 339.
Miss Maude Lamb, Worthing, Sussex.

59 HERO AWAITING LEANDER
Panel, 24 × 19½.
Coll.: P. A. Williamson Gift 1916.

This and the Boston painting (*v. sub.*) are almost identical compositions, and may be dated *c.* 1835–40. Both paintings show a semi-nude female figure seated at an opening overlooking a stormy seascape. She is in profile, seen from the right and her head is turned away from the spectator.
Williamson Art Gallery and Museum, Birkenhead.

60 HERO AWAITING LEANDER
Millboard laid on panel, 24 × 20.
Coll.: Acquired before the museum became corporation property, source not recorded.
Public Library, Boston, Lincs.

61 HERO AWAITING LEANDER
Canvas, 22⅞ × 18¾.
Coll.: (?)R. Colls; Joshua Dixon Bequest 1886 (No. 997–'86).
Exh.: (?)S.A., 1849(CX) as *The Signal* (or according to Gilchrist: *Hero and Leander*—nude reclining figure).
Lit.: Gilchrist, ii, p. 340.

Never shown at the Royal Academy, 1844, as was stated in the Society of Arts catalogue. Entitled *The Ring* in the V. & A. catalogue (1907), but almost certainly a Hero and Leander subject. The figure enclosed within a ring in the sky above the sea may be an attempt at symbolizing the death of Leander. The painting dates from about 1835. A picture entitled *The Signal* was sold anon., 2.6.1888 (126), bt. Permain 15 gns.
Victoria and Albert Museum, London.

62 [pl. 31] HERO, HAVING THROWN HERSELF FROM THE TOWER AT THE SIGHT OF LEANDER DROWNED, DIES ON HIS BODY
Canvas, 30½ × 37¼.
Coll.: Thomas Thorpe, senr.; Thomas Thorpe, junr.; Rev. William Tudor Thorpe; Thomas Alder Thorpe. On permanent loan to York Art Gallery since 1954.
Exh.: R.A., 1829(31); S.A., 1849(XXVI); A.C. *Etty*, 1955(18).

Lit.: Autobiography, p. 40; Gilchrist, i, pp. 266, 273, 275, 286, ii, p. 336; *York Preview 24*, October, 1953, pp. 256–7 (and repr.).

This painting is a sequel to *The Parting of Hero and Leander*, 1827.

Mrs. E. J. Britten, Haslemere, Surrey.

(*a*) Pencil, 4½ × 7³⁄₁₆.
Coll.: J. P. Knight, 1870; P.D. 180 C, Portf. 252F/4/7651/27.

This shows Etty's original idea for the composition with Leander stretched parallel to the bottom edge of the painting, head and arms outspread to the right. Hero is seen full face, foreshortened, hanging over Leander's body.

A *Sketch for Hero—for the 'Hero and Leander'* was sold anon., 12.5.1860(160), by Wallis 11 gns. Another(?) sketch 'in chalk' for *Hero and Leander* appeared in the James Coles Sale, 18.6.1870(12).

Victoria and Albert Museum, London.

63 [pl. 81] HESPERUS
Canvas (painted semi-circular arch and spandrels), 35 × 68.
Coll.: Purchased from the Artist by Edwin Bullock, sold 21.5.1870(116), bt. Agnew 1,005 gns.; John Hargreaves, sold 7.6.1873 (310), bt. Agnew 800 gns.; William Agnew; Property of a Lady, sold 27.2.1920(133), as *A Scene from 'Comus'*, bt. Gooden & Fox £580 for 1st Viscount Leverhulme.
Exh.: R.A., 1844(152); Birmingham Society of Artists, 1845(107), lent by Edwin Bullock; R.A. *Old Masters*, 1891(13); *British Art 1830–1850*, Whitechapel, 1920(77); A.C. *Yorkshire Artists 1600–1900*, Leeds, 1946(12).
Lit.: Gilchrist, ii, pp. 166–9, 276, 340; R. R. Tatlock, *Catalogue of the Lady Lever Art Gallery*, I, 1928, p. 95, No. 4111; T. S. R. Boase, 'The Decoration of the New Palace of Westminster, 1841–1863', *Journal of the Warburg and Courtauld Institutes*, XVII, Nos. 3–4, 1954, p. 335.
Repr.: Illustrated London News, IV, 1844, p. 373; Gaunt & Roe, pl. 52.

Given no formal title when first exhibited, this illustrates lines from Milton's *Comus*: 'All amidst the Gardens fair / Of Hesperus and his Daughters Three, / That sing about the golden tree; / . . . Holds his dear Psyche sweet entranc'd.' It was intended as an alternative design to the unsuccessful *Circe* composition (*v. supra*). The actual fresco, which Wethered obtained from Colls, appears to have been lot

146 in the 1856 Sale (bt. in), and lot 110 in 1858, when it was bought by Woodgate 36½ gns. A copy of this composition by W. D. Kennedy was sold 6.3.1899(17), ex-coll. W. Blinkhorn, bt. Banner 2½ gns.

The Lady Lever Art Gallery, Port Sunlight.

(*a*) Oil on panel (corner lunettes) and tempera on canvas (centre), 34 × 68.
Coll.: (?)William Wethered, sold 7.3.1856 (142), bt. Palgrave 100 gns.; Appleby Bros., London, sold 5.11.1954(158), bt. Bryant 12 gns.; Anon., sold Sotheby's, 9.5.1956(153), bt. in £3.
Exh.: Rhode Island School of Design, 28th November 1956–2nd January 1957.
Mr. Anthony M. Clark, Providence, Rhode Island, U.S.A.

(*b*) Millboard laid on panel, 14⅛ × 26 (including lunettes).
Coll.: with Appleby Bros. since January, 1957 from a private collection in Jersey.

Agrees in all details with the final picture.
Messrs. Appleby Bros., London.

(*c*) Pencil, 4⅘ × 4½.
Coll.: J. P. Knight, 1870; P.D. 180 C, Portf. 252F/1/7650/7.
Study for central group of dancing figures. (*Verso:* sketch of general composition for (?) *Thomas à Becket*.)

(*d*) Pencil, 4⁷⁄₁₀ × 4½. Four studies.
Coll.: as for (*c*), Portf. 252F/1/7650/6. (*Verso:* one study for *Thomas à Becket*.)

(*e*) Pen and ink, 3½ × 5¹⁄₁₀.
Coll.: as for (*c*), Portf. 252F/1/7650/33.
Study of full composition of *Hesperus* (including the lunettes).

(*f*) Pencil, 2½ × 5.
Coll.: as for (*c*), Portf. 252F/1/7650/45(*verso*).
Central figure of *Hesperus*, and lunettes with cupids.

(*c*)–(*f*) *Victoria and Albert Museum, London.*

64 [pl. 47a] HYLAS AND THE NYMPHS
Inscr. on verso: 'No. 1 Wm. Etty R.A.'
Canvas, 35½ × 45⅝.
Coll.: Purchased from the Artist for 160 gns. by Mr. [J. Vincent] Sergeant Thompson at the British Institution, 1834 (Etty's '*Cash Book*', entry for 5th May, 1834), sold 5.3.1859(62), bt. H. Farrar 400 gns., sold 15.5.1866(103), bt. Fountain [*sic*] 270 gns.; Sir Andrew Fountaine, sold 7.7.1894(3), bt. Chester 80 gns.; F. E. Sidney, sold 10.12.1937(30), bt. Leggatt 48 gns.; Lord Fairhaven.
Exh.: R.A., 1833(153); *Modern Artists*, Royal

Manchester Institution, 1833(106); B.I., 1834 (52); Birmingham Society of Arts, 1834(25); York, 1836; S.A., 1849(LI); *International Exhibition*, 1852(335); York, 1949(4).

Lit.: *Autobiography*, p. 40; Gilchrist, i, pp. 359, 364, ii, pp. 46, 337.

Repr.: Gaunt & Roe, pl. 22.

The Royal Academy catalogue printed a quotation from Lemprière's translation of Appollonius Rhodius, recounting the story of Hylas, a favourite youth and squire of Hercules and the infant son of Theiodamus (or Theiomenes) King of the Dryopians and Menodice. Hylas, going in search of water for the Argonauts at Mysia, was lured away by Dryope and her nymphs of Pegae.

The Lord Fairhaven.

65 [pl. 22] THE JUDGMENT OF PARIS

Canvas, $70\frac{1}{4} \times 107\frac{1}{2}$.

Coll.: Commissioned by John, 4th Earl Darnley, for £500; Edward, 5th Earl Darnley, sold Rainy's Gallery, 1838(?), bt. in; sold privately to C. W. Wass, who sold it in 1843 to [Sir] Andrew Fountaine; Fountaine Sale, 7.7.1894(2), bt. Chester 500 gns.; acquired 1911 by Mrs. Fountaine, Narford Hall, Swaffham, Norfolk; 1st Viscount Leverhulme.

Exh. R.A., 1826(24), *The choice of Paris*; B.I., 1827(312); S.A., 1849 (CII); York, 1911(118), lent Mrs. Fountaine; R.A. *First Hundred Years*, 1951–2(240); A.C. *Etty*, 1955(13), but withdrawn.

Engr.: C. W. Wass, 1847.

Lit.: *The Art Union*, 9th June, 1847, p. 224 (and engraving); *Autobiography*, p. 40; Gilchrist, i, pp. 233–5, ii, pp. 80, 336; *The Studio*, LXXXV, 1923, p. 12; *The Connoisseur*, LXV, 1923, p. 70; R. R. Tatlock, *Catalogue of the Lady Lever Art Gallery*, I, 1928, p. 93, No. 642.

The Lady Lever Art Gallery, Port Sunlight.

(*a*) Millboard (painted circle), $12\frac{3}{4}$ dia.

Coll.: (?)C. W. Wass; (?) L.V. Flatou, sold 23.3.1861(115), bt. Dickson £10; (?)Henry Burton, sold 12.7.1890(155) as *A Male Nude Academy Study—circle*, bt. Nathan 8 gns.; T. Gabriel; T. B. Gabriel.

Exh.: (?)S. A., 1849(XXXVII) where dated 1842.

Study for figure of Paris. The pose resembles that in Raphael's *Judgment of Paris* (engraved Marcantonio Raimondi, *see* pl. 23*b*). *Mrs. E. M. Gabriel, Worplesdon, Surrey.*

(*b*) [pl. 24*a*] Pencil, $4\frac{1}{2} \times 7\frac{3}{8}$. Inscribed with colour notes.

Coll.: Rev. G. Mountford; British Museum, 1948–11–26–2.

Full composition of *Judgment of Paris*, but shows *motif* of a flying *putto* about to crown Venus with a wreath.

(*c*) Pencil, $3 \times 4\frac{1}{2}$.

Coll.: as for (*b*), 1948–11–26–3 (*recto*).

Centre group of five figures and *putto*, suggestion of arched bower. Venus holds out her right hand to Paris.

(*d*) Pencil, $3 \times 4\frac{1}{2}$.

Coll.: as for (*b*), 1948–11–26–3 (*verso*).

The Three Graces and a nymph; poses roughly as in (*c*).

(*e*) Pencil, $4\frac{1}{2} \times 3$.

Coll.: as for (*b*), 1948–11–26–4.

Standing figure in profile, turned left (?)Venus. Also faint sketches for the *Judith and Holofernes* composition.

(*b*)–(*e*) *British Museum, London.*

(*f*) Pen and ink, $8 \times 8\frac{4}{5}$. Inscr. 'D'Orville Esqr.'

Coll.: J. P. Knight, 1870; P.D. 180 C, Portf. 252F/3/7650/125.

Two full composition studies, and figures of *putti*.

(*g*) Red chalk and pencil on oiled tracing paper, $8\frac{3}{10} \times 10\frac{7}{10}$.

Coll.: as for (*f*), Portf. 252F/6/7653/35.

Full composition study, but with variations from the finished oil painting:

(i) Pose of Paris is closer to Rubens's *Judgment* (National Gallery) except that Paris' pose is here reversed, and Venus' pose nearer to that in Rubens's Prado *Judgment*. The relationship of Paris and Venus is that used by Etty in the 1846 *Judgment* (*v. sub.*).

(ii) Juno stands on Venus' left, $\frac{3}{4}$ back view looking to right, with her right arm raised above her head. Minerva has almost the same pose as in the final painting, but is striding away (again, closer to 1846 *Judgment*).

(iii) Mercury lounges in the right-hand corner of composition, instead of being between Paris and Juno.

(*f*) and (*g*) *Victoria and Albert Museum, London.*

66 THE JUDGMENT OF PARIS

Canvas, 57×78.

Coll.: Commissioned from the Artist for 600 gns. by Joseph Gillott (*Account Book*, 7th November, 1845), sold 27.4.1872(262), bt. George Attenborough 810 gns.; A. Andrews, sold 16.4.1888(147), bt. Permain 480 gns.; Anon., sold 10.2.1894(63), bt. Wallis 410 gns.;

H. Panmure Gordon, sold 17.1.1903(31), bt. F. E. Sidney 300 gns.; Sidney Sale, 10.12.1937 (28), bt. Fasey 27 gns.; Anon., sold 24.6.1949 (149), bt. Marlborough Gallery 45 gns.; with Roland, Browse & Delbanco (until January, 1950).
Exh.: R.A., 1846(200) *The choice of Paris;* S.A., 1849(XVI); Edinburgh, 1886(1440); York, 1949(18).
Lit.: Autobiography, p. 40; Gilchrist, ii, pp. 117, 210–11, 213, 341; T. Laughton, *Catalogue of the Picture Collection at the Royal Hotel, Scarborough* [n.d.], No. 64, where it is wrongly identified with the 1826 *Judgment of Paris.*
Repr.: The Magazine of Fine Arts, I, November 1905–April 1906, p. 119; T. Laughton, *Royal Hotel,* booklet [n.d.]; *The Connoisseur,* CXXXV, No. 546, May, 1955, p. 220, fig. 3.
R. T. Laughton, Esq., Scarborough.

67 JUDGMENT OF PARIS
Canvas, 23½ × 31.
Coll.: (?)G. T. Andrews, York, sold 23.6.1849 (41) as *Sketch for The Judgment of Paris,* bt. Miller 100 gns.; Anon., sold 9.6.1922(116), bt. B. Weller 2½ gns.; Anon., sold 18.7.1938 (170), bt. Bradley 6 gns.; purchased through G. J. Wolstenholme Bequest by York 1948 (No. 99/1948).
Exh.: S.A., 1849(CXXX), where said to have been painted in 1828, although the York painting looks closer to the 1846 version (*v. supra*)—perhaps the date should read 1848; York, 1949(93).
Repr.: York Preview 4, October, 1948.

If not actually later than the 1846 picture, then this is most likely to be a study for it, although much inferior in quality. A sketch, *Judgment of Paris,* oval, 10½ × 15, ex-coll. Thomas Pitt Miller, was sold 26.3.1946(38), bt. Agnew 28 gns. A pastiche (? by Franklin) combining elements of both the 1826 and 1846 versions was sold 22.6.1956(248), canvas, 44 × 55, bt. Dent 30 gns.
City Art Gallery, York.

68 [pl. 38*a*] LEDA
Canvas, 16 × 20.
Coll.: (?)Sir Thomas Lawrence, P.R.A., sold 19.6.1830(341) *Leda, after the design of Michelangelo,* bt. Norton £4 10*s.*; Ralph Fletcher, Gloucester, sold 9.6.1838(29), title as above, canvas, 22 × 34, bt. Artaria 10 gns.; (?)G. T. Andrews, sold 31.5.1851(82), bt. Rogier 7½ gns.; H. A. J. Munro of Novar (No. 539 in

Frost and Reeve, *Catalogue . . . Munro Collection*), but not in Munro Sales of either 1867 or 1878. Percy Moore Turner, from whom acquired by Lord Sandwich, 1926.
Exh.: British Art, Manchester, 1934(78); R.A. *British Art,* 1934(659); *Paintings by William Etty,* Adams Gallery, May–June, 1936(5); *Centenary Memorial Exhibition of John Constable, R.A.,* Wildenstein, 1937(72); York, 1949(1); A.C. *Etty,* 1955(38).
Lit.: Gaunt & Roe, p. 68 (repr. pl. 36).
Repr.: Commemmorative Catalogue of Exhibition of British Art, R.A., 1934, pl. CXXI.
Painted *c.* 1825–30.
The Earl of Sandwich.

69 [pl. 37*b*] LOVE'S ANGLING
Canvas, 22½ × 21½.
Coll.: Bought at the Manchester Exhibition for 45 gns. by Charles Birch, although originally priced at 50 gns.; Birch Sale, 7.7.1853(44) as *Venus angling,* bt. in 310 gns.; C. F. Huth, sold 6.7.1895(80), bt. Vokins 255 gns.; C. G. Huth, sold 19.3.1904(49), bt. Agnew 250 gns.; Lord Lawrence of Kingsgate, sold 15.3.1935 (104), bt. Permain 50 gns.; with Permain 1935–1947, and sold by Gooden & Fox in May, 1947, to Sir David Scott.
Exh.: (?)R.A., 1831(144) *Nymph angling;* (?)R.S.A., 1831(VII) *Nymph Fishing; Modern Artists,* Royal Manchester Institution, 1832 (415); S.A., 1849(LVIII); *Paintings by William Etty,* Adams Gallery, March–April, 1946(31).
Lit.: Gilchrist, i, pp. 323, 355, ii, p. 337.
Sir David Scott, Boughton, Kettering.

70 [pl. 10*a*] MANLIUS HURLED FROM THE ROCK
Canvas, 45 × 33.
Coll.: George Franklin; W. W. Lewis; Sir James Linton, P.R.I.; T. W. Bacon (by 1898).
Exh. B.I., 1819(72); B.I., 1825(77); *A Century of British Art 1737–1837* (Second Series), Grosvenor Gallery, 1889(107); *Victorian,* New Gallery, 1898(171); *Pictures by Early English and Other Masters,* South London Art Gallery, 1898(15); A.C. *Etty,* 1955(6). On long loan to the Union Club, Manchester.
Lit.: Gilchrist, i, pp. 83–4, ii, p. 335.
Painted 1818. The subject is taken from the story of Marcus Manlius, surnamed Capitolinus because of his heroic defence of Rome against the Gauls. He became Consul in 392 B.C., but was accused by the Roman patricians of high treason in 384 B.C., and hurled to his death down the Tarpeian Rock by the tribunes.
A watercolour, *The Tarpeian Rock,* was in the

Orrock and Linton Sale, 25.4.1895(81), bt. Lewis 5 gns.

A. W. Bacon, Esq., Otley, Suffolk.

71 MARS AND VENUS

Millboard (circular), 8.

Coll.: David Macbeth, sold 15.1.1887(344), bt. Huth £5; Louis Huth, sold 20.5.1905(50), bt. Thrift 15 gns.; Sir Bruce M. Seton, Bart., sold 4.3.1912(263), bt. Permain 28 gns.; Percy Moore Turner; Lord Sandwich (by 1930).

Exh.: A Century of British Art, 1737–1837, (Second Series) Grosvenor Gallery, 1889(26); York, 1949(2); A. C. *Etty,* 1955(45).

Painted *c.* 1840–5.

The Earl of Sandwich.

72 [pl. 50*b*] MARS, VENUS AND CUPID

Panel, 40 × 27.

Coll.: Purchased for 120 gns. by Thomas Wright, sold as *The Bivouac of Cupid,* 7.6.1845 (51), bt. Colls 370 gns.; Charles Oddie, sold 18.3.1854(118), bt. Wallis 205 gns.; Ralph Brocklebank, sold 29.4.1893(145), bt. Laurie [*sic*] 201½ gns.; Messrs. Lawrie & Co., sold 28.1.1905(8), bt. F. E. Sidney 180 gns.; Sidney Sale, 10.12.1937(32), bt. Leggatt 60 gns.

Exh.: York, 1836; R.A., 1837(267); B.F.A.C., Winter 1912(1); *York Artists' Exhibition,* York, 1913–14; *British Empire Exhibition,* 1924(38) illus. in souvenir, p. 38; B.F.A.C., Winter 1938–9(10); York, 1949(10).

Lit.: Gilchrist, ii, pp. 51, 205, 338.

Repr: The Magazine of Fine Arts, I, November, 1905-April, 1906, p. 118; Gaunt & Roe, pl. 45.

A label on the verso of the panel reads: 'No. 4 Wm. Etty R.A. Exhibited at the first opening of the New National Gallery in the year 1837.'

The Lord Fairhaven.

73 MARS, VENUS AND ATTENDANT

Panel, 41 × 25¾.

Coll.: (?)Samuel Mendel, sold 23.4.1875(301), bt. Agnew 500 gns.; Charles P. Matthews, sold 6.6.1891(30), bt. Agnew 150 gns.; C. F. Huth, sold 19.3.1904(91), bt. Permain 190 gns.; Barnet Lewis, 3.3.1930(190), bt. Crawley 150 gns.; Rt. Hon. Lord Leverhulme, sold 2.10.1942(88), bt. Leggatt 60 gns.

Exh.: R.A., 1840(30), *Mars, Venus, and attendant derobing her mistress for the bath;* Birmingham Society of Arts, 1840(50), *The Bivouac of Mars,* priced at £136.

Lit.: Gilchrist, ii, p. 338.

Repr.: Gaunt & Roe, pl. 47.

The Lord Fairhaven.

(*a*) Pen and ink, 7 1/16 × 2⅝.

Coll.: J. P. Knight, 1870; P.D. 180 C, Portf. 252F/1/7650/22.

(*b*) Charcoal, 4 × 5 7/16, on back of envelope from the School of Design, Somerset House (red seal).

Col.: as for (*a*), Portf. 252F/3/7650/106.

The figure of Mars has been omitted.

Victoria and Albert Museum, London.

74 MUSIDORA (THE BATHER 'AT THE DOUBTFUL BREEZE ALARMED')

The subject is inspired by eight lines from James Thomson's *The Seasons: Summer,* which describe how Musidora is surprised by Damon whilst bathing in a woodland stream: 'But desperate youth, / How durst thou risk the soul distracting view; / . . . / With fancy blushing, at the doubtful breeze / Alarmed, and starting like the fearful fawn?'

There are at least four versions:

(i) [pl. 85*a*] Panel, 27 × 22½.

Coll.: Purchased from the Artist for 70 gns. by George Knott in 1843, sold 26.4.1845(60), bt. Farrer 225 gns.; W. J. Broderip (by 1849), sold 18.6.1853(88), bt. Egg 345 gns.; T. Horrocks Miller (by 1889); Thomas Pitt Miller, sold 26.3.1946(36), bt. Leggatt 110 gns.; Anon., sold 21.11.1947(93), bt. Agnew 60 gns., from whom purchased by Mrs. Dunne 1948.

Exh.: R.A., 1843(44) *The Bather 'At the doubtful breeze alarmed';* S.A., 1849(XC); R.A. *Old Masters,* 1889(28).

Lit.: Gilchrist, ii, pp. 138–9, 205, 339.

Mrs. M. A. Dunne, Chadshunt, Warws.

(ii) [pl. 88] Canvas, 25⅝ × 19¾.

Coll.: Presumably purchased from the Artist by Jacob Bell, who bequeathed it to the National Gallery, 1859 (No. 614). Transferred to the Tate Gallery 1900, and returned to the National Gallery 1956.

Exh.: (?)B.I., 1846(229), 35 × 29 [frame included]; S.A., 1849(CIX), lent Jacob Bell, described as not previously exhibited; Birmingham Society of Artists, 1854(283), lent Jacob Bell; *Descriptive Catalogue of Pictures* [Jacob Bell Collection], Marylebone Literary & Scientific Institution, 28th March–16th April, 1859(67).

Lit.: Gilchrist, ii, pp. 210, 340.

Repr.: Sir E. J. Poynter, *The National Gallery,* III, 1900, p. 65; Alfred Leroy, *Histoire de la Peinture Anglaise,* Paris, 1939, facing p. 289, pl. XLII; Gaunt & Roe, pl. 3 (in colour).

National Gallery, London.

(iii) Canvas laid on panel, $13\frac{1}{2} \times 10$.
Coll.: James Gresham Bequest 1917.
Exh.: *British Art*, Manchester, 1934(80).

This is almost identical with the Tate Gallery composition, the landscape and foliage are, however, less freely brushed in.
City Art Gallery, Manchester.
(iv) Canvas, $27\frac{1}{4} \times 23\frac{3}{4}$.
Coll.: Emeritus Professor E. G. R. Taylor, D.Sc., F.R.G.S.

This again follows the Tate version, but is somewhat poorer in quality and may be a mid-nineteenth century student's work.
Professor E. G. R. Taylor, London.

75 NYMPH AND YOUNG FAUN DANCING
Two versions:
(i) Panel, $26\frac{7}{8} \times 19\frac{5}{8}$.
Coll.: Purchased from the Artist for £45 by Richard Colls; G. T. Andrews, sold 23.6.1849 (49) *Dancing Nymph and Faun*, bt. Wass 310 gns.; T. Horrocks Miller; Thomas Pitt Miller, sold 26.3.1946(37), bt. Wolmark 22 gns.
Exh.: B.I., 1835(200); S. A., 1849(CXXIV), no owner given, but probably lent by G. T. Andrews; R.A. *Old Masters*, 1889(47).
Lit.: Gilchrist, ii, pp. 29–30, 79, 337.
Alfred A. Wolmark, Esq., London.
(ii) [pl. 50*a*] Canvas, $30\frac{1}{8} \times 25\frac{1}{2}$.
Coll.: (?)John Windass or W. J. Foot; Anon., sold 27.1.1912(29), bt. Howard 28 gns.; with Knoedler & Co. (until August, 1912); Hon. Evan Charteris.
Exh.: R.A., 1838(97); *Modern Artists*, Royal Manchester Institution, 1838(140); (?)York, 1911(42 or 145); York, 1949(6).
Lit.: Gilchrist, ii, pp. 82, 338.

This composition contains a temple and a landscape vista on the right which are absent from the Wolmark version. Some of the minor figures are also additions, and this greater elaboration suggests that this might be the later painting.
The Lord Fairhaven.

76 [pl. 16] PANDORA
Canvas, $34\frac{3}{4} \times 44\frac{1}{8}$.
Coll.: Purchased from the Artist for about 300 gns. by Sir Thomas Lawrence, P.R.A., sold 15.5.1830(118), bt. Henry Bone 105 gns. for Joseph Neeld, M.P.; Sir John Neeld; Colonel Aubrey Neeld; L. W. Neeld, sold 13.7.1945 (123), bt. Nachemsohn; sold Sotheby's, 14.10.1953(114), bt. Marshall Spink; acquired by Leeds March, 1954.
Exh.: R.A., 1824(213); S.A., 1849(XLII);

R.A. *Old Masters*, 1877(258); *A Century of British Art 1737-1837*, Grosvenor Gallery, 1888 (187); A. C. Etty, 1955(10) and repr. pl. II.
Lit.: *Autobiography*, pp. 39, 40; Gilchrist, i, pp. 88–90, 219–20, 238, ii, p. 336.
Repr.: *Treasures from Yorkshire Collections* (2nd Series), Leeds City Art Gallery, No. 9, 1954; *Illustrated London News*, 20th August, 1955, p. 321.

'Pandora, the heathen Eve, having been formed by Vulcan as a statue, and animated by the Gods, is crowned by the Seasons with a garland of flowers.' See also Elton's translation of Hesiod's *Theogony*:
'To deck her brows, the fair tressed seasons bring
A garland breathing all the sweets of Spring.'
City Art Gallery, Leeds.
(*a*) (?)Canvas, 17×22.
Coll.: Sir James Linton, P.R.I. & James Orrock, R.I.; 1st Viscount Leverhulme, sold Anderson Galleries, New York, 17.2.1926 (81).
Exh.: B.I., 1820(7) *Pandora formed by Vulcan, and crowned by the Seasons*; (?)Birmingham Society of Arts, 1830(123) *Pandora, a sketch*.
Lit.: Letter from James Orrock (dated 12.11.1890), *Birmingham Daily Post*, 15th November, 1890.

Described by Gilchrist, i, pp. 88–9, as a highly finished study. Present location unknown.
(*b*) Canvas, $67\frac{1}{2} \times 95$.
Coll.: Presented by Howard Halton to the Birmingham School of Design (later Society of Arts) 1844, which body then presented it to Birmingham 1867.
Exh.: (?)B.I., 1825(125); York, 1911(140).
Lit.: Letter from Whitworth Wallis (dated 18.11.1890), *Birmingham Daily Post*, 19th November, 1890.

An unfinished *modello* for the 1824 picture, and differing from it in the poses used for the main figures.
City Art Gallery, Birmingham.
(*c*) [pl. 19*a*] Oil and pen on paper stuck to canvas, $6\frac{3}{8} \times 7\frac{3}{4}$.
Coll.: (?)A. T. Hollingsworth, Clapham, sold 11.3.1882(86), bt. Roberts 11 gns.; bequeathed by Henry Vaughan to the Tate Gallery 1900 (No. 1795).
Exh.: A. C. Etty, 1955(11).

The composition agrees in detail with the final version.
Tate Gallery, London.

(d) Black crayon, $11\frac{5}{8} \times 8$, study for group of Venus and Cupid on the left of painting; the sheet contains other miscellaneous studies, including some for the figure of Holofernes.

Coll.: E. W. Smithson, 1928; *Sketchbook II,* p. 30.

(e) Pen, $11\frac{5}{8} \times 8$, composition study with figures of Mercury and one of the Seasons omitted on right side.

Coll.: as for (d); *Sketchbook II,* p. 109.

City Art Gallery, York.

77 [pl. 26] THE PARTING OF HERO AND LEANDER

Inscr. on back of stretcher: 'William Etty A Nº 3'.

Canvas (painted circle), $32\frac{1}{2} \times 33$ on stretcher 34×34.

Coll.: Lord Northwick from the Artist in exchange for an old anonymous copy of Titian's *Ariadne in Naxos* (Prado), sold 12.5.1838(65), bt. Joseph Neeld, M.P. 150 gns.; Sir John Neeld; Colonel Aubrey Neeld; L. W. Neeld, sold 13.7.1945(124), bt. National Gallery 130 gns. (Colnaghi Fund), and transferred to the Tate Gallery 1945 (No. 5614).

Exh.: R.A., 1827(438); York, 1836; S.A. 1849 (XLIV); R.A. *Old Masters,* 1877(46); *A Century of British Art, 1737–1837,* Grosvenor Gallery, 1888(237).

Lit.: Autobiography, p. 40; Gilchrist, i, pp. 236, 259, ii, pp. 46, 274, 336.

The Royal Academy catalogue printed this quotation: 'Hero was a beautiful woman of Sestos in Thrace, and priestess of Venus, whom Leander of Abydos loved so tenderly that he swam over the Hellespont every night to see her.'

Tate Gallery, London.

78 [pl. 43a] PHAEDRIA AND CYMOCHLES, ON THE IDLE LAKE

Canvas (arched top), 25×30.

Coll.: Purchased from the Artist for 100 gns. by Wynne Ellis 1832 ('*Cash Book*', entry for 30th August), sold 2.5.1874(124), bt. in 510 gns., resold 6.5.1876(5), bt. McLean 310 gns.; (?)Charles P. Matthews, sold 6.6.1891(28), bt. Agnew 200 gns.; Anon., sold 14.5.1898 (119), bt. Richardson 200 gns.; James Gresham sold 12.7.1917(55) as *Mars and Venus,* bt. Gooden & Fox 80 gns. for 1st Viscount Leverhulme.

Exh.: R.A., 1832(360); S.A., 1849(XLV); *Art Treasures,* Manchester, 1857(205); (?)York, 1911(121) as *Youth and Pleasure; Modern Paintings and Etchings from the Collection of Visc.*

Leverhulme, Lady Lever Art Gallery, November–December, 1933(9).

Lit.: Waagen, *Art Treasures,* ii, 1854, p. 298; Gilchrist, i, p. 345, ii, pp. 28, 337; R. R. Tatlock, *Catalogue of the Lady Lever Art Gallery,* I, 1928, p. 94, No. 3306; Gaunt & Roe, p. 93, and repr. pl. 19.

The subject is taken from Edmund Spenser's *Faery Queene,* Book ii, Canto 6: 'Along the shore as swift as glance of eye, / A little gondelay, bedecked trim, / With boughs and arbours woven cunningly, / . . . / And therein sate a ladye fresh and fayre.' Another picture, described as a study for this work, belonged to Richard Nicholson, sold 13.7. 1849(85), bt. G. T. Andrews 30 gns.; Andrews Sale, 31.5.1851(76), bt. Grundy 32 gns. This may be the second painting exhibited at the Royal Academy, 1835(310) and at the Royal Manchester Institution, 1835(85): although *The Times'* critic's description (23rd May, 1835) mentions a cupid 'at the end of the boat . . . a sort of May-day climbing boy . . .'

The Lady Lever Art Gallery, Port Sunlight.

(a) Pen, ink and watercolour, $3\frac{1}{2} \times 6$.

Coll.: Gresham; Mountford sold to Sir Robert Witt; Witt Collection (No. 3860).

Exh.: A. C. *Drawings from the Witt Collection,* 1953(7b). *University of London. Courtauld Institute of Art.*

(b) Pencil, $6\frac{3}{10} \times 5\frac{1}{10}$.

Coll.: J. P. Knight, 1870; P.D. 180 C, Portf. 252F/4/7651/32.

Three studies for *Phaedria and Cymochles. Victoria and Albert Museum, London.*

79 [pl. 86] A PIRATE CARRYING OFF A CAPTIVE (THE CORSAIR)

Millboard, $27\frac{3}{4} \times 21$.

Coll.: Edwin Bullock, sold 21.5.1870(27), bt. Agnew 65 gns.; Thomas Walker, sold 2.6.1888 (51), bt. McLean 18 gns.; A. T. Hollingsworth; James Orrock; James S. Inglis, sold American Art Galleries, New York, 11.3.1909(72), probably bought John G. Johnson.

Exh.: B.I., 1846(115); S.A., 1849(XCII); *A Century of British Art, 1737–1837* (Second Series), 1889(21).

Lit.: Gilchrist, ii, pp. 210, 340.

A painting, *The Corsair,* was lent by Messrs. Dowdeswell & Dowdeswell to York, 1911(152), and was sold, 30.6.1916(13), bt. Parker 26 gns. ($25 \times 18\frac{1}{4}$).

John G. Johnson Collection, Philadelphia, U.S.A.

80 [pl. 64] PLUTO CARRYING OFF PROSERPINE

Canvas, 51 × 77.

Coll.: Purchased from the Artist for £350 by Lord Northwick, after being priced at 500 gns. at the opening of the Royal Academy exhibition 1839; Joseph Gillott from the dealer Pennell (Gillott *Account Book*, October, 1846), sold 27.4.1872(263), bt. Baron Albert Grant 1,000 gns.; sold 28.4.1877(177), bt. John Rhodes 710 gns.; sold 27.3.1918(116), bt. Coleman 10 gns.; Mrs. J. R. Freeman, Hove (1930); Colonel Fairfax Rhodes, sold Sotheby's, 11.7.1934(44), bt. Cooling £90, illus. in catalogue; Anon., sold 24.7.1936(135), bt. Vicars 36 gns.; Anon., sold 24.6.1949 (150), bt. Jeales 45 gns.; J. Leger & Son (until March, 1955); I. Oscar Herner.

Exh.: R.A., 1839(241); Birmingham Society of Artists, 1847(56), lent by Joseph Gillott; S.A., 1849(XXVII); *Industrial & Fine Art*, Dublin, 1853; R.A. *Old Masters*, 1872(42); *Yorks. Fine Art & Industrial*, York, 1879(114); Guildhall, 1892(101), illustrated in supplement facing p. 54; R.A. *Old Masters*, 1894(14); *Royal Yorkshire Jubilee*, York, 1897.

Lit.: Letter from Etty to Henry Howard, R.A., 9th April, 1839 (Ir. Thomas H. Etty Coll.); *Autobiography*, p. 40; Gilchrist, ii, pp. 28–9, 96–9, 338; Waagen, *Treasures of Art*, 1857, iv, p. 403.

The subject illustrates lines taken from Milton's translation of Ovid's *Metamorphoses:* 'In that fair field of Enna where Proserpine, / Gathering flowers, herself a fairer flower, / By gloomy Dis was gathered.' Until recently (1934), a fourth horse could be seen rearing up on the further end of the line to complete the quadriga, but this feature and that of a Cupid flying overhead holding a blazing torch, have now been overpainted. Although Etty worked on the painting after the exhibition, it seems unlikely that he would have removed these elements.

Señor I. Oscar Herner, Gallerias Iturbidas, S.A., Mexico.

(*a*) Canvas, 17 × 24½.

Coll.: (?)William Wethered, sold 27.2.1858 (96), bt. Rippe 18 gns.; J. A. Chatwin; Adams Gallery, London (1946); Sir Colin Anderson.

Exh.: Constable and his Contemporaries, Hampstead, 1951(52); A. C. *Etty*, 1955(28).

This study shows the horse and cupid included in the final composition.

Sir Colin Anderson, London.

(*b*) [pl. 65*a*] Paper laid on board, 22 × 15¾.

Coll.: Purchased from Sir James Linton, P.R.I., 1908 (No. 591).

Kneeling figure of a nude woman in a pose similar to that occupied by the nymph in the left foreground of the finished picture. In the H. A. J. Munro of Novar Sale, 11.5.1867 (53) a '*Finished Study of Female Kneeling.* Gathering Flowers—for the Picture of Pluto and Proserpine', 17½ × 23½, was bt. Vokins 46 gns.

National Gallery of Ireland, Dublin.

(*c*) Pen and ink on azure envelope, 7³⁄₁₀ × 4½.

Coll.: J. P. Knight, 1870; P.D. 180 C, Portf. 252F/4/7651/45.

Two studies of Pluto and Proserpine (including one on verso) showing different posing of the figures—both seen frontally. Three studies of frightened nymphs are on the same sheet.

Victoria and Albert Museum, London.

81 [pl. 21*a*] PROMETHEUS

Panel, 27¾ × 30½.

Coll.: William Etty, R.A., sold either 7 or 10.5.1850(299 or 582), both oil studies on millboard: 229. *Prometheus*—'finely foreshortened', bt. Weeks 5 gns.; 582. *A man transfixed by an arrow*—'finely foreshortened', bt. Colls 7 gns.; E. M. Ward, R.A. (until 1879); Anon., sold 5.3.1910(37), bt. Wallis 10 gns.; 1st Viscount Leverhulme.

Lit.: R. R. Tatlock, *Catalogue of the Lady Lever Art Gallery*, I, 1928, p. 95, No. 2849.

Repr.: Gaunt & Roe, pl. 37.

Although described in the 1910 sale catalogue as with 'the background by J. Linnell Sen.', there seems little justification for this. The painting probably dates *c.* 1825–30. The arrow may symbolize both the punishment of Prometheus (*i.e.* to have a griffon-vulture daily gnawing his liver), as well as his deliverance by an arrow shot by Hercules which killed the vulture.

The Lady Lever Art Gallery, Port Sunlight.

82 PSYCHE HAVING, AFTER GREAT PERIL, PROCURED THE CASKET OF COSMETICS FROM PROSERPINE IN HADES, LAYS IT AT THE FEET OF VENUS, WHILE CUPID PLEADS IN HER BEHALF

Four versions:

(i) Canvas, 17 × 21.

Coll.: (?) James Stewart, sold 20.4.1839(53),

bt. Smith 55 gns.; Thomas Baring, M.P.; Anon., sold 5.7.1884(81), bt. Permain 78 gns.; Wed. Ella Pijnacker-Hordijk (from *c.* 1926 until January, 1954), a great-grand-daughter of Charles Etty, senr.

Exh.: R.A., 1836(96); S.A., 1849(C); *International Exhibition*, 1862(262).

Lit.: Waagen, *Treasures of Art*, ii, 1854, p. 189; Gilchrist, ii, pp. 37, 338.

Formerly Wed. E. Pijnacker-Hordijk, The Hague.

(ii) Panel, 16½ × 20½.

Coll.: Henry Burton (but not in Burton Sale, July, 1890); T. Gabriel; T. B. Gabriel.

A note in Burton's copy of Gilchrist suggests that this is the 1836 painting, but this does not agree with the information given in the S.A. catalogue, 1849.

Mrs. E. M. Gabriel, Worplesdon, Surrey.

(iii) Canvas, 20½ × 25½.

Coll.: F. E. Sidney (by 1911), sold 10.12.1937 (37), bt. Robersons 27 gns.; Adams Gallery, London (by 1946). Present location unknown.

Exh.: (?)B.I., 1828(19); (?)*Modern Artists*, Manchester Royal Institution, 1833(287); *International Fine Arts Exh.*, Rome, 1911(23); *Paintings by William Etty*, Adams Gallery, March-April, 1946(16).

(iv) Canvas, 11½ × 8½.

Coll.: (?)Joseph Gillott (not in Gillott Sale, 1872); (?)William Wethered, sold 7.3.1856 (124), bt. Colls 33 gns.; James Fenton, sold 16.2,1903(3), bt. Permain 38 gns.; James Orrock, sold 4.6.1904(258), bt. Permain 95 gns.; Barnett Lewis, sold 3.3.1930(191), bt. Leggatt 28 gns. Present location unknown.

Exh.: (?)S.A., 1849(CVII).

83 SABRINA

Two versions:

(i) [pl. 38*b*] Canvas, 24 × 30.

Coll.: Purchased from the Artist for 100 gns. by Sir Francis Freeling, sold 15.4.1837(79), bt. Farrer 53 gns.; Thomas Baring, M.P.; F. E. Sidney, sold 10.12.1937(35), bt. Martin 36 gns.; Anon., sold 20.9.1946 (31), bt. Seton 50 gns. Present location unknown.

Exh.: R.A., 1831(170); B.I., 1832(6); S.A., 1849(CIV); *International Exhibition*, 1862(264).

Lit.: Gilchrist, i, p. 323, ii, p. 337.

(ii) Inscr. on back of stretcher: 'Sabrina, from / Milton's Comus Painted by me, Wm. Etty / Nov. 9 1841'. Canvas, 23¼ × 31¼.

Coll.: C. W. Wass (until 1852); (?)John Miller, Liverpool, sold 21.5.1858(231), bt. Arkle [*sic*] 148 gns.; Mrs. W. D. Pearson,

Melton Mowbray, from whom purchased by Leicester 1936 (No. 22.A.36).

Exh.: S.A., 1849(LXVI); A.C. *English Romantic Art*, 1947(59).

Lit.: Gilchrist, ii, p. 337.

Apparently a later variant of the 1831 composition. There are no figures in the top right-hand corner, and the background appears to be darker. In the left foreground are wreaths of flowers which do not occur in the 1831 painting. Wass also owned another version, painted in 1840 and only exhibited at the Society of Arts, 1849(XLIII). A 'study' for *Sabrina*, canvas, 21 × 25½, was in the North-brook collection until 1929 (ex-H. A. J. Munro of Novar collection. No. 568).

City of Leicester Museums and Art Gallery.

84 [pl. 63] THE SIRENS AND ULYSSES

Canvas, 117 × 174.

Coll.: Purchased from the Artist by Daniel Grant, 1837; William Grant (brother to Daniel), who presented it to the Royal Manchester Institution, 1839.

Exch.: R.A., 1837(122); *Modern Artists*, Royal Manchester Institution, 1838(213); S.A., 1849(V); *Art Treasures*, Manchester, 1857 (263).

Engr.: J. and G. P. Nicholls, *The Art Journal*, August, 1858, p. 234.

Lit.: *Autobiography*, pp. 39, 40; Gilchrist, ii, pp. 52-5, 61-3, 66-9, 273, 338.

Repr.: *The Magazine of Fine Arts*, I, November, 1905-April, 1906, p. 123.

Illustrates 26 lines from the Twelfth Book of Pope's translation of Homer's *Odyssey*, beginning: 'Next, where the Sirens dwell, you plough the seas; / Their song is death. . . . / . . . O stay, and learn new wisdom from the wise.' A sketch, *The Syrens*, was lent by John Miller of Liverpool to the Royal Scottish Academy, 1851(423).

City Art Gallery, Manchester.

(*a*) Pencil, 5 × 4.

Coll.: J. P. Knight, 1870; P.D. 180 C, Portf. 252F/1/7650/19A.

Composition study for *Ulysses.*

(*b*) Pencil, 4⅖ × 7⅛.

Coll.: as for (*a*), Portf. 252F/1/7650/43.

Studies for *Ulysses* and *Thomas à Becket.*

(*c*) Pencil, 8 9/10 × 7⅛. Folded envelope, 'W.E.' seal.

Coll.: as for (*a*), Portf. 252F/2/7652/25.

Small sketches for *Ulysses* and *The World before the Flood* (*q.v.*) among many unidentified subjects.

(d) Pencil, $7\frac{3}{10} \times 8\frac{9}{10}$.

  Coll.: as for (a), Portf. 252F/5/7652/21.

  Three *Ulysses* sketches on verso of letter from Emma Taylor [n.d.].

(e) Pencil, $9\frac{3}{10} \times 6\frac{4}{5}$.

  Coll.: as for (a), Portf. 252F/5/7652/28.

  The *Ulysses* composition almost as in the final version.

(f) Pencil, $7\frac{3}{10} \times 8\frac{9}{10}$.

  Coll.: as for (a), Portf. 252F/5/7652/32.

  One full composition study for *Ulysses;* two sketches of Sirens, and one of figure of Ulysses. All on verso of a letter from Walter to William Etty (dated 20.3.1835).

  (a)–(f) *Victoria and Albert Museum, London.*

(g) Pencil on card, $3 \times 4\frac{2}{5}$.

  Coll.: E. W. Smithson, sold 12.3.1928(140), bt. York (No. 5l(f)).

  Early composition study showing Sirens on the *right*-hand side of picture.

  City Art Gallery, York.

85 [pl. 30] SLEEPING NYMPH AND SATYRS

Canvas, $51 \times 70\frac{1}{2}$.

Coll.: Presented to the Royal Academy as the Artist's Diploma Work, October, 1828.

Exh.: Art Treasures, Manchester, 1857(240); *International Exhibition*, 1862(263); *National Exhibition*, Leeds, 1868(1246); R.A. *Old Masters*, 1872(30), 1894(100), and 1903(114); R.A. *British Art*, 1934(697); R.A. *First Hundred Years*, 1951–52(417); R.A. *Diploma Works 1768–1868*, May–June, 1955 (no catalogue).

Lit.: Gilchrist, i, pp. 252–3; *Catalogue of the Diploma and Gibson Galleries*, Royal Academy, 1939, No. 61.

Repr.: The Art Journal, 1903, p. 376; C. H. Collins Baker and M. R. James, *British Painting*, 1933, pl. 120 facing p. 183.

  In the 1934 and 1951–2 exhibition catalogues this was incorrectly identified with the similarly entitled picture exhibited at the Royal Academy 1835(325), *Wood Nymphs Sleeping; . . . Morning* (q.v.).

  The Royal Academy of Arts, London.

86 THE THREE GRACES

Panel, $35\frac{1}{2} \times 26\frac{3}{4}$.

Coll.: (?)G. T. Andrews, sold 23.6.1849(45), bt. in 280 gns., resold 31.5.1851(80), bt. Hatch 200 gns.; Anon., sold 28.6.1907(51), bt. Wright 34 gns.; 1st Viscount Leverhulme.

Exh.: A.C. *Yorkshire Artists 1600–1900*, Leeds, March, 1946(11) and repr. pl. 5.

Lit.: R. R. Tatlock, *Catalogue of the Lady Lever Art Gallery*, I, 1928, p. 94, No. 1381;

Gaunt & Roe, p. 105, and repr. pl. 60. In both books this painting is incorrectly identified as ex-collection John Singleton and as exhibited Royal Academy, 1847(339). The 1847 picture belonged to Joseph Gillott, and was lot 259 in the Gillott Sale, 1872.

The Lady Lever Art Gallery, Port Sunlight.

THE THREE GRACES (Metropolitan Museum, New York). *See* VENUS AND HER SATELLITES (No. 100).

87 [pl. 73] TO ARMS, TO ARMS, YE BRAVE!

Canvas, $31 \times 43\frac{1}{2}$.

Coll.: Purchased from the Artist for £200 by Thomas Wright in 1842, sold 7.6.1845(55), bt. Hawker 390 gns.; Richard Nicholson, sold 13.7.1849(214), bt. Agnew 450 gns.; George Pennell, sold 19.5.1866(98), bt. in 660 gns.; Sir William Eden, sold 30.5.1874(77), bt. M. Colnaghi 180 gns.; C.B.O. Clarke, Steyning, Sussex, sold 8.5.1936(13), bt. Clarke 60 gns.; S. H. Baker's Art Gallery, Hove, sold to C. G. Doward, New York, 1952.

Exh.: R.A., 1841(206); (?)Birmingham Society of Artists, 1845(46) *Mars taking leave of Venus;* Rhode Island School of Design, 28th November, 1956–2nd January, 1957.

  Another small version, or study seems to have existed; sold Anon., 30.1.1886(161), bt. Permain $16\frac{1}{2}$ gns. It was exhibited *Yorks, Fine Art & Industrial*, York, Summer 1882(296), lent H. Smith and priced at £8 (from annotated catalogue in York Art Gallery).

  Mr. C. G. Doward, New York, U.S.A.

(a) Pencil, $2\frac{9}{10} \times 5$.

  Coll.: J. P. Knight, 1870; P.D. 180 C, Portf. 252F/1/7650/8.

  Study of central female figure of Venus(?).

  Victoria and Albert Museum, London.

88 TOILET OF VENUS

Canvas, $24 \times 17\frac{1}{2}$.

Coll.: James King, from whom purchased 1924.

Exh.: York, 1949(29).

  Williamson Art Gallery and Museum, Birkenhead.

89 TOILET OF VENUS

Canvas (painted oval), $26 \times 28\frac{1}{2}$.

Coll.: (?)George R. Burnett, sold 24.3.1860 (50) *The Bath of Venus*, bt. Connolly 135 gns.; F. E. Sidney, sold 10.12.1937(34), bt. Leggatt 98 gns.; Lord Fairhaven.

Exh.: B.F.A.C., Winter, 1938–9(2).

Repr.: Gaunt & Roe, pl. 11.

  Painted *c.* 1825–30.

  The Lord Fairhaven.

90 VENUS AND CUPID
Canvas, 12 × 15.
Coll.: Messrs. Agnew, from whom purchased by Lord Sandwich.
The Earl of Sandwich.

91 [pl. 35*a*] VENUS AND CUPID
Canvas, 12½ × 17½.
Coll.: (?)C. W. Wass (until 1852); (?)John Burton (by 1882); Rev. James S. Holden, Derby, from whom purchased by York, 1911 (No. 77/1911).
Exh.: (?)B.I., 1830(240) as *Venus and Cupid*; S.A., 1849(XXXV); York, 1911(23); *Paintings by Famous British Artists*, Sunderland, February–April, 1924(16); *British Empire Exhibition*, 1925(W.46) and illus. in souvenir, p. 42; *Commemorative Exh. of Opening of the New Gallery*, Harrogate, January–April, 1930 (30); *Inaugural & 59th Autumn Exh.*, Walker Art Gallery, Liverpool, Oct.–Dec., 1933(46); R.A. *British Art*, 1934(657); York, 1948(9); York, 1949(73) and repr.; *Peintures anglaises des collections d'York et du Yorkshire*, Musée des Beaux-Arts, Dijon, 1957(24).
Lit.: Gilchrist, i, p. 285, ii, p. 337.
Repr.: *York Preview* 8, II, October, 1949; *The Burlington Magazine*, CXXV, January, 1950, p. 25, fig. 25.
    Although Gilchrist identifies the 1830 painting as a *Venus and Cupid Descending*, the measurements given in the catalogue of 22 × 28, allowing for the frame, fit this painting. Stylistically it belongs to the early 1830s.
City Art Gallery, York.

92 VENUS AND CUPID
Canvas, 17 × 12.
Coll.: Charles Pemberton, sold Foster's, 17.6.1863(71), bt. (?)Levy; Albert Levy, sold 31.3.1876(108), bt. Graves 69 gns.; A. T. Hollingsworth, sold 11.3.1882(91), bt. Agnew 84 gns.; Sir Charles Tennant; Lord Glenconner.
Exh.: (?)B.I., 1825(99) as *Nymph and Cupid: a finished Sketch.*
Lit.: Gilchrist, i, p. 227, ii, p. 336; *Catalogue of the Pictures forming the Collection of Sir Charles Tennant, Bart.*, 1896, as *Cupid and Psyche.*
The Lord Glenconner.

93 VENUS AND CUPID
Canvas, 46 × 35½.
Coll.: Miss Helen Gilbert, who presented it to the Gallery.
Public Library, Museum and Art Gallery, Bilston, Staffs.

94 VENUS AND CUPID
Millboard, 30 × 14.
Coll.: Purchased 1946.
Lit.: *Bulletin and Annual Report of the Russell-Cotes Art Gallery and Museum*, September, 1946, p. 3.
Repr.: Gaunt & Roe, pl. 7.
Russell-Cotes Art Gallery and Museum, Bournemouth.

95 VENUS AND CUPID
Canvas, 9½ × 13½.
Coll.: Lord Lawrence of Kingsgate, sold 15.3.1935(106), bt. Cooling 12½ gns.; Lord Fairhaven.
Exh.: B.F.A.C., Winter 1938–9(13).
Repr.: Gaunt & Roe, pl. 2 (in colour).
    The title should be *Venus and Cupid*, although it was sold as *Venus, Cupid and Nymph.*
The Lord Fairhaven.

96 VENUS AND CUPID
Panel, 11 × 6¾.
Coll.: Purchased from the Artist for £30 by Welbore Ellis, 2nd Earl of Normanton; by descent to the present Earl.
Exh.: R.A. *Old Masters*, 1885(37).
Lit.: *Catalogue of Pictures at Somerley* (MS.), 1884, No. 86 (1948 revised catalogue, No. 85).
    Painted *c.* 1830–35. The Somerley catalogue gives no date of purchase.
The Earl of Normanton.

97 VENUS AND CUPIDS
Inscr. (? by Etty): 'W. Etty 1831' (bottom left).
Canvas, 14 × 18.
Coll.: Purchased from Thomas McLean, 7 Haymarket, London 1912 (No. 12:1).
Exh.: York, 1949(25).
Victoria Art Gallery, Bath.

98 [pl. 18] VENUS AND CUPID DESCENDING
Panel, 27 × 20.
Coll.: George Young, Ryde, sold 19.5.1866(20), bt. Colnaghi 490 gns.; (?)McConnel, Liverpool; P. & D. Colnaghi, sold 16.3.1867(983), bt. Agnew 400 gns.; (?)James Price, sold 15.6.1895(35) described as panel, 20 × 20½, bt. Agnew 200 gns.; Sir William Agnew; Miss E. M. Agnew (by 1933).
Exh.: B.I., 1822(164); S.A., 1849(XXXII); *International Exhibition*, 1862 (314); R.A. *Old Masters*, 1896(2); *Paintings by William Etty, R.A.*, R. E. A. Wilson, 24 Ryder St., November, 1933(23); *Art Treasures in the West Country*, April–May, 1947(10); B.C. *Cien Años*

de Pintura Británica, 1730–1830, Madrid and Lisbon, 1949(17).

Engr.: R. W. Sievier, pub. J. Sweet, November, 1824.

Lit.: Gilchrist, i, pp. 98–9, ii, p. 336.

Private Collection.

A companion piece to No. 98 was *Cupid and Psyche Descending*, commissioned by Sir Francis Freeling and exhibited British Institution, 1822(186). Freeling Sale, 15.4.1837(85), bt. Smith, Lisle Street, 59 gns. Engraved by C. W. Wass, *Art Union*, X, July, 1848, p. 227. Later passed to W. J. Broderip, sold 18.6.1853 (83), bt. Agnew 220 gns.; John Graham, sold 30.3.1887(37), bt. Agnew 175 gns.; (?)James N. Graham, sold 11.5.1923(46), bt. Alexander Reid 50 gns.; Anon., sold 23.4.1926(57), bt. Sampson 14 gns. Present location unknown.

99 [pl. 57*a*] VENUS AND HER DOVES

Canvas, $25\frac{1}{2} \times 24$.

Coll.: Painted for Daniel Grant, Manchester; J. Grant Lawson, sold 18.7.1891(39), bt. Agnew 38 gns.; Dr. Lloyd Roberts (by 1901), who bequeathed it to Manchester, 1920.

Exh.: R.A., 1836(167); *Modern Artists*, Royal Manchester Institution, 1836 (110); *International Exhibition*, Glasgow, 1901(179); *Works of Art in the Cartwright Memorial Hall*, Bradford, 1904(14); Whitechapel, Spring, 1905(37); York, 1911(91); *British Art*, Manchester, 1934(91); York, 1949(51).

Lit.: Gilchrist, ii, pp. 37, 338.

City Art Gallery, Manchester.

100 VENUS AND HER SATELLITES (THE TOILET OF VENUS)

Two versions:

(i) [pl. 56] Panel, 32×43.

Coll.: Purchased from the Artist for just under 300 gns. by the Rev. E. P. Owen, 1835; H. D. Owen; Anthony Gibbs, J.P. (by 1888); Lord Wraxall; with Frost & Reed, Ltd., February, 1955, bt. Devas.

Exh.: R.A., 1835(94); *National Exhibition*, Leeds, 1868(1191); R.A. *Old Masters*, 1878 (275); *International Exhibition*, Glasgow, 1888 (203); *A Century of British Art, 1737–1837*, Grosvenor Gallery, 1888(247); Guildhall, 1892(91) and repr. in supplement, facing p. 52; A.C. Etty, 1955(42).

Lit.: Autobiography, p. 40; Gilchrist, ii, pp. 31–2, 337.

Repr.: The Connoisseur, CXXXV, February, 1955, p. xix.

Anthony Devas, Esq., A.R.A., London.

(ii) Panel, $31 \times 43\frac{1}{2}$.

Coll.: Marquis de Chateauneuf, sold Oesterreichischer Kunstverein, Vienna, 20.10.1910 (26) repr. pl. 17, bt. P. S. Larsen; purchased from Larsen by York, 1926 (No. 67/1926).

Exh.: Commemorative Exhibition of Opening of New Gallery, Harrogate, January-April, 1930 (87); York, 1948(24); York, 1949(79); A.C. Etty, 1955(25).

Although agreeing closely in composition with (i), it is much more thinly painted and may be a studio copy. A watercolour sketch, 15×10, initialled 'W.E.' on base of urn on the left, repeats the composition faithfully in every detail. It was purchased in England by the Montreal artist John Hammond on behalf of the School of Fine and Applied Arts, Mount Allison University, Sackville, New Brunswick, Canada, where it now is. It is possibly the same work as that in the Orrock and Linton Sale, 25.4.1895(113), *Venus at the Bath* [watercolour], bt. Heaps 3 gns. An oil *Toilet of Venus*, ex-coll. John Hargreaves, was sold 5.6.1873 (285), bt. Agnew 420 gns.

City Art Gallery, York.

(a) [pl. 57*b*] Millboard, $22\frac{1}{2} \times 18\frac{3}{4}$, study for the group of THE THREE GRACES.

Coll.: G. T. Andrews, sold 23.6.1849(76), bt. in 84 gns.; Thomas MacKenzie, J.P., sold 10.5.1902(110), bt. T. Smith 38 gns.; Henry E. Heyman, London, from whom purchased by New York in December 1905.

Exh.: Rhode Island School of Design, 28th November, 1956–2nd January, 1957.

Repr.: The Burlington Magazine, VIII, February, 1906, facing p. 351, pl. II; *The Connoisseur*, LXXVIII, May, 1927, p. 53.

The Metropolitan Museum of Art, New York.

(b) Pencil, $8 \times 9\frac{1}{10}$.

Coll.: J. P. Knight, 1870; P.D. 180 C, Portf. 252F/5/7652/7.

An elaborate study for a *Toilet of Venus*, but not closely related to the Devas painting.

Victoria and Albert Museum, London.

101 VENUS, CUPID AND PSYCHE

Canvas, $21\frac{3}{4} \times 14\frac{3}{4}$.

Coll.: W. F. R. Weldon Bequest, 1937(No. 150).

Ashmolean Museum, Oxford.

102 VENUS, CUPID WITH A DOVE

Panel, 26 × 19.

Coll.: Jonathan Peel, sold 11.3.1848(75) as *Bacchante, and Cupid with a Dove*, bt. Roake 72 gns.; George Roake, sold 13.4.1850(65), bt. Gambart 110 gns.; Sir Charles Tennant, Bart.

Lit.: Catalogue of the Pictures forming the Collection of Sir Charles Tennant, Bart., 1896.

Painted *c.* 1840.

The Lord Glenconner.

103 [pl. 27*b*] 'VENUS NOW WAKES, AND WAKENS LOVE'

Canvas, 20 × 24.

Coll.: Joseph Strutt (No. 595, Strutt Collection Catalogue, Derby, 1835), but not in Strutt Sale, 22.6.1889; Sir Merton Russell-Cotes.

Exh.: B.I., 1828(5); Birmingham Society of Arts, 1829(45); A. C. Etty, 1955(15).

Lit.: Gilchrist, ii, p. 336.

Repr.: Bulletin and Annual Report of the Russell-Cotes Art Gallery and Museum, XIV, No. 2, June 1935, p. 21; Gaunt & Roe, pl. 46.

The original title is a quotation from Milton's *Comus*, but the picture is also now called *The Dawn of Love*.

Russell-Cotes Art Gallery and Museum, Bournemouth.

(*a*) [pl. 27*a*] *Nude Female Study*

Panel (circular), 18.

Coll.: James Holland; Dr. Henry Barton; Sir James Linton, P.R.I.; T. W. Bacon (by 1898).

Exh.: (?)Earls Court, 1897(19); *Victorian*, New Gallery, 1898(168); *Pictures by Early English & Other Masters*, South London Art Gallery, 1898(17); A. C. Etty, 1955(16) and repr. pl. III*b*. On long loan to Birmingham City Art Gallery.

Probably a study for the figure of Venus in '*Venus now Wakes, and Wakens Love*'.

A. W. Bacon, Esq., Otley, Suffolk.

(*b*) Pencil, 2 × 3.

Coll.: J. P. Knight, 1870; P.D. 180 C, Portf. 252F/1/17650/12.

Detailed composition study for '*Venus now Wakes*'.

Victoria and Albert Museum, London.

104 VENUS RISING FROM THE SEA

Canvas, 27¼ × 22.

Coll.: Presented by Sir Charles E. Swain, 1917.

City Art Gallery, Manchester.

105 VENUS, THE EVENING STAR

Millboard, 27½ × 21.

Coll.: Purchased from the Artist by Digby Murray (until 1840); A. Andrews, sold 16.4.

1888(146), bt. Lawrie 24 gns.; (?)J. S. Inglis, New York, sold 27.3.1914(153), bt. Wallis 5 gns.; Anon., sold 4.2.1921(131), bt. Kent £7; Anon., sold Sotheby's, 15.12.1950(141), bt. Colnaghi 40 gns., and passed to Lord Methuen.

Exh.: R.A., 1828(357); *A Century of British Art, 1737–1837*, Grosvenor Gallery, 1888(250).

Lit.: Gilchrist, i, p. 249, ii, p. 336.

The Lord Methuen.

106 [pl. 53] THE WARRIOR ARMING (GODFREY DE BOUILLON)

Canvas, 34 × 28.

Coll.: Purchased from the Artist for 100 gns. by Robert Vernon, sold 16.5.1842(106), bt. in 93 gns.; Charles W. Wass (by 1849); Sir Joseph Whitworth, Bt., who presented it to Manchester, 1882.

Exh.: R.A., 1835(287); *Modern Artists*, Royal Manchester Institution, 1842(207); R.S.A., 1843(10); S.A., 1849(LXVIII); R.A. *First Hundred Years*, 1951–2(239) and repr. in supplement.

Lit.: Gilchrist, ii, pp. 5, 30–1, 338.

Begun in September, 1833, and reworked during the latter part of 1834.

City Art Gallery, Manchester.

107 [pl. 55] WOOD NYMPHS SLEEPING; SATYR BRINGING FLOWERS—MORNING

Canvas, 18 × 27½.

Coll.: Purchased from the Artist for £50 by Richard Colls ('*Cash Book*', entry for 1st April, 1835); said by Gilchrist to have been sold in 1851 for £500; H. A. J. Munro of Novar, sold 11.5.1867(15), bt. Colls 81 gns.; Edward Bright, sold 22.11.1890(138) as *Nymphs and Satyrs* [*sic*], bt. Innes 42 gns.; Henry Smith, Josiah Bradlee & Others Sale, American Art Galleries, New York, 20–21.2.1924.

Buyer and present location unknown.

Exh.: R.A., 1835(325); R.A. *Old Masters*, 1880(9).

Lit.: Gilchrist, ii, pp. 29, 338; W. E. Frost, A.R.A. & Henry Reeve, *Catalogue of the . . . Collection of the late H. A. J. Munro of Novar* [n.d.], No. 140.

108 [pl. 29] THE WORLD BEFORE THE FLOOD

Canvas, 59 × 80.

Coll.: Purchased from the Artist for 500 gns. by the Marquis of Stafford (later Duke of Sutherland, K.G.), 1828, sold 8.2.1908(11), bt. F. E. Sidney 230 gns.; Sidney Sale, 10.12. 1937(29), bt. Rees for Southampton 195 gns. (Chipperfield Bequest funds).

Exh.: R.A., 1828(193); R.S.A., 1841(90);

S.A., 1849(XLVI); B.I., *Ancient Masters*, 1854(160); Birmingham Society of Artists, 1856(48); *International Exhibition*, 1862(336); *West Ham Free Pictures*, Easter, 1898; *Pictures from the Permanent Collection*, Southampton, 1939(117); included in the York, 1949, exhibition catalogue (No. 64), but not shown; A.C. *Etty*, 1955(41).

Lit.: M. Passavant, *Tour of a German Artist*, 1836, i, p. 146; Mrs. Anna Jameson, *Private Galleries of Art in London*, 1844, p. 214; *Autobiography*, pp. 39–40; Waagen, *Treasures of Art*, 1854, ii, p. 73; Gilchrist, i, pp. 248–50, ii, p. 336; *Catalogue of Pictures, Stafford House*, 1862, No. 104; W. T. Whitley, *Art in England, 1821–1837*, 1930, pp. 145–6; R. B. Beckett, *John Constable and the Fishers*, 1952, pp. 527–8.

The subject is taken from the eleventh book of *Paradise Lost*: 'He look'd, and saw a spacious plain, . . . With feast and music all the tents resound.' Etty later referred to it both as *The Origin of Marriage* and as *The Bevy of Fair Women*.

Southampton Art Gallery.

(a) Millboard, 8 × 12.
Coll.: (?)Sir Thomas Lawrence, P.R.A., sold 15.5.1830(26) as *A Bacchanalian Scene—a sketch*, bt. Martin 27 gns.; (?)Anon., sold 27.7.1932(272) as *Landscape with figures*, millboard, 9 × 13, bt. Arthurton £8 10s.; Arthur Coulter, York, from whom purchased by York, 1953 (No. 689/1953).
City Art Gallery, York.

(b) Pencil, $8\frac{9}{10} \times 7\frac{1}{5}$, on folded envelope.
Coll.: J. P. Knight, 1870; P.D. 180 C, Portf. 252F/2/7652/25.
Small sketches for this composition and *The Sirens and Ulysses* (q.v.).

(c) Four pen and three pencil studies, $12\frac{7}{10} \times 8\frac{9}{10}$, on folded London Institution paper (dated 21st November, 1831).
Coll.: as for (b), Portf. 252F/2/7652/46.
The seven studies must be revised ideas for another composition similar to *The World Before The Flood;* perhaps intended for *The Dance* (q.v.).
(b) and (c) *Victoria and Albert Museum, London.*

109 [pl. 39] YOUTH ON THE PROW AND PLEASURE AT THE HELM
Inscr. on back of stretcher: 'No 1 W^m. Etty, R.A.'
Canvas, $62\frac{1}{2} \times 46\frac{1}{4}$. Enlarged along top edge by $2\frac{1}{4}$ wide strip.

Coll.: Purchased from the Artist by Robert Vernon ('*Cash Book*', 7th August, 1832: £250 from Vernon 'in part payment for Pleasure at the Helm'); Vernon Gift to the National Gallery, 1847 (No. 356). Transferred to Tate Gallery, 1949.
Exh.: R.A., 1832(196); B.I., 1833(358); York, 1911(96); *Two Hundred Years of British Painting*, Huddersfield, May–July, 1946(235); York, 1949(45).
Engr.: C. W. Sharpe, *The Vernon Gallery*, 1st Series, 1850, No. 19, as *Youth and Pleasure*, and *The Art Journal*, XII, April, 1850, p. 128.
Lit.: *Autobiography*, p. 40; Gilchrist, i, pp. 98–9, 345, ii, p. 337; Gaunt & Roe, pp. 78–9, and repr. pl. 14; Martin Davies, *The British School*, National Gallery, 1946, p. 52.
Repr.: Sir E. J. Poynter, *The National Gallery*, III, 1900, p. 65.

Exhibited at the Royal Academy without a title, but with the following quotation from Gray's *The Bard*: 'Fair laughs the Morn, and soft the Zephyr blows, . . . Youth on the prow, and Pleasure at the helm; . . . That, hush'd in grim repose, expects his evening prey.' Gray's lines refer to the magnificence of Richard II's reign, and although the critic of *The Times*, 24th May, 1832, could see no particular meaning, Etty later explained to C. W. Wass (*The Vernon Gallery, loc. cit.*, quotes an undated letter from Etty to Wass) that 'the view I took of it as a general allegory of Human Life, *morally*, where what we see here portrayed in its fabulous sense, is often real'. Youth in its carefree pursuit of pleasure is heedless of impending doom, symbolized here by a dark shadowy, cloud-like figure, the 'Being of the Whirlwind'. The subject had been in his mind since 1818–19.

Tate Gallery, London.

(a) Millboard, $16\frac{1}{2} \times 12\frac{1}{2}$.
Coll.: Acquired when the museum was privately administered, no records appear to survive.
Exh.: (?)B.I., 1822(128) as *Sketch from one of Gray's Odes*, 21 × 18 (in its frame).
Shows several variations from the 1832 painting; there are no figures swimming around the boat and the group of figures at the prow is reversed.
Public Library, Boston, Lincs.

(b) [pl. 41a] Canvas, 19 × 13.
Coll.: (?)G. T. Andrews, sold 23.6.1849(99) bt. in by Colls 80 gns.; sold again 31.5.1851

(98), bt. Lefray 130 gns.; (?)Henry Burton; T. Gabriel; T. B. Gabriel.
Exh.: (?)S. A., 1849(CXXXI) as painted in 1848.

This agrees more closely with the 1832 painting, but again the figures at the prow have been reversed in pose. It is possible that '1848' in the Society of Arts catalogue may be a misprint for 1828, if so, this would fall into place as a preliminary study.

Mrs. E. M. Gabriel, Worplesdon, Surrey.

(*c*) Panel, $18\frac{1}{4} \times 14\frac{1}{8}$.
Coll.: (?)Sir William Richard Drake, F.S.A., sold 27.6.1891(27), bt. Shepherd $6\frac{1}{2}$ gns.; Right Hon. Lord Derwent, sold Sotheby's, 29.3.1950(90), bt. Countess of Listowel £36, who presented it to York through the N.A.C.F., 1952 (No. 651/1952).

A group of the three central figures aboard the boat. It is just possible that this is a good student's copy of this central feature.

City Art Gallery, York.

(*d*) Pencil, $4\frac{1}{2} \times 9\frac{3}{8}$, on envelope postmarked '30 Jan 1830'.
Coll.: J. P. Knight, 1870; P.D. 180C, Portf. 252F/4/7651/23.

Preliminary composition study.

(*e*) Pencil, $15 \times 11\frac{3}{8}$, oiled tracing paper.
Coll.: As for (*d*), Portf. 252F/6/7653/33. Composition study which agrees most closely with oil study (*b*).

(*d*) and (*e*) *Victoria and Albert Museum, London.*

GENRE

110 BATHERS SURPRISED BY A SWAN

Inscr. on label on verso: 'No. 1 Wm Etty RA'.

Panel enlarged by 1 inch strip all round and at four points of the painted circle by another, shorter, $\frac{1}{2}$ inch strip. Overall, $38\frac{7}{8} \times 38\frac{1}{2}$.

Coll.: Purchased from the Artist for 200 gns. by Robert Vernon (letter from Etty to Thomas Bodley, 3rd May, 1841); Vernon Gift to the National Gallery, 1847 (No. 366). Transferred to the Tate Gallery, 1929.

Exh.: R.A., 1841(379) *Female Bathers surprised by a Swan;* B.I., 1842(34); York, 1911(117).

Engr.: E. J. Portbury, *The Art Journal*, XI, July, 1849, p. 223; *The Vernon Gallery*, 1st Series, 1850, No. 31.

Lit.: Gilchrist, ii, pp. 118, 339.

On the verso of the painting is an outline composition in oils of a central female figure, (?)Terpsichore, surrounded by three dancing *putti* with a female lyre player on the right. On the left, in the background, one male and one female *putti* recline on a bank. A *Bathers Surprised*, ex-coll. Mrs. Gibbons, was sold 5.5.1883 (34), bt. Polak 48 gns.

Tate Gallery, London.

(*a*) Pen and ink, $3\frac{3}{8} \times 2\frac{1}{8}$. Composition study.
Coll.: J. P. Knight, 1870; P.D. 180 C, Portf. 252F/2/7650/97.
Victoria and Albert Museum, London.

THE CROTCHET WORKER. *See* PORTRAITS: MISS MARY ANN PURDON (No. 194).

111 THE DANGEROUS PLAYMATE

Inscr. on verso: 'Wm Etty RA N° 4'.

Panel (painted circle), $10\frac{3}{4} \times 11$; overall, $14\frac{1}{8} \times 11\frac{3}{8}$.

Coll.: Probably purchased from the Artist by Robert Vernon in 1833 ('*Cash Book*' records payment of £20 for unspecified work 30th July, 1833); Vernon Gift to the National Gallery 1847 (No. 360). Transferred to the Tate Gallery, 1919.

Exh.: B.I., 1833(19); York, 1911(174); Sheffield, 1934(280).

Engr.: Edward Norton, lithograph published by Ackermann 1836; E. J. Portbury, *The Art Journal*, January, 1852, facing p. 16, and *The Vernon Gallery*, 3rd Series, 1853, No. 1.

Lit.: Gilchrist, ii, p. 337.

Tate Gallery, London.

112 A DOMESTIC SCENE

Canvas, $25\frac{1}{4} \times 30$.

Coll.: Charles Etty (1793–1856); Charles Etty (1812–91, son of Thomas Etty, senr., b. 1779) m. Ann Maria (daughter of Charles Etty, senr.) and their eldest daughter, Jane Elizabeth, m. Thomas (1832–1904), grandson of John Etty, 1775–1865). Thomas and Jane Elizabeth adopted a nephew, Tom (1884–1932), whose son Thomas Hendrik Etty thus inherited the collection.

Exh.: (?)R.A., 1812(21) *A domestic scene.*

The painting shows the interior of a drawing room with seven members of Walter Etty's family seated around the fire, and at the piano on the right of the picture. The picture has been clumsily overpainted, and it is not possible to identify all the figures.

Ir. Thomas H. Etty, Leidschendam.

(*a*) Pencil, $16\frac{1}{5} \times 12,\frac{3}{10}$ two sheets stuck together, paper watermarked '1812'.
Coll.: J. P. Knight, 1870; P.D. 180 C, Portf. 252F/8/7655/5.

A detailed sketch of front (keyboard) side of a piano; covered with colour notes. Probably related to *A domestic scene.*
Victoria and Albert Museum, London.

113 [pl. 10*b*] DRUNKEN BARNABY
Canvas, 29½ × 25 (heavily overpainted in foreground).
Coll.: as for above.
Exh.: R.A., 1820(196); A.C. *Etty*, 1955(8).
Lit.: Gilchrist, i, p. 92, ii, p. 335.

Illustrates the following quotation from Richard Brathwait's *Barnabae Itinerarium, or Barnabee's Journal*, first published in 1638: 'Mihi mirus affuit status, / A duobus sum portatus.' The *Journal* is an amusing record of English travel, in Latin and English doggerel verse with a fictitious hero, Barnaby Harrington. Etty has used Joseph Haslewood's 1818 edition, and taken the six lines from the second part, p. 55, beginning 'Thence to Cock at Budworth, . . .' for his theme.
Ir. Thomas H. Etty, Leidschendam.

114 IL DUETTO (THE DUET)
Inscr. on verso: 'No. 2 Wᵐ Etty RA'.
Panel, 15 × 19⅝, including a narrow wooden strip added along bottom edge by the Artist.
Coll.: Purchased from the Artist by Robert Vernon; Vernon Gift to the National Gallery 1847 (No. 363). Transferred to the National Gallery of Ireland 1883 (No. 188) and returned 1926. Transferred to the Tate Gallery, 1949.
Exh.: R.A., 1838(112), although begun in 1834.
Engr.: R. Bell, *The Art Journal*, XII, April, 1850, p. 224; *The Vernon Gallery*, 2nd Series, 1851, No. 2 as *The Duett.*
Lit.: Gilchrist, ii, pp. 83, 338; Martin Davies, *The British School*, National Gallery, 1946, p. 52.
Version(?)*:* Guildhall Exhibition, 1899(187) *The Duet*, 8½ × 10, lent Sidney N. Castle.

There are faint traces of another composition painted on the verso of the Tate picture.
Tate Gallery, London.

115 [pl. 94*a*] 'GATHER THE ROSE OF LOVE WHILE YET 'TIS TIME'
Millboard (circular), 19⅝.
Coll.: James Coles, sold 18.6.1870(43) as *Venetian Lovers*, bt. G. C[oles?] 57 gns.; (?)Edward Fox White, sold 7.3.1891(283) as *Venetian Courtship*, bt. Smith 10½ gns.; Alfred Coles, who presented it to Birmingham, 1931.
Exh.: R.A., 1849(178).
Lit.: Gilchrist, ii, pp. 265, 341.

The title recalls Robert Herrick's 'Gather ye rose-buds while ye may'. A label on the back is inscribed 'Painted by William Etty, R.A. for his friend James Coles, Esq., Aug. 1848.'
City Art Gallery, Birmingham.

116 A GIRL READING
Millboard, 12¾ × 11¾.
Coll.: Presented to York by George Benson 1919 (No. 91/1919).
Exh.: York, 1948(20).
Painted *c.* 1845–49.
City Art Gallery, York.

117 THE GLEANER (attributed to Etty)
Canvas, 32½ × 27¼.
Coll.: William Carpenter, who presented it to the Gallery 1899.

This painting has also been ascribed to John Constable, R.A. If by Etty, it may date from *c.* 1815.
South London Art Gallery, Camberwell.

118 HEAD OF A JEW
Canvas, 30⅛ × 25¼.
Coll.: Richard Godson-Millns Bequest 1904 (No. '04–30).
Exh.: (?)B.I., 1827(365); York, 1911(84); York, 1949(52).
City Museum and Art Gallery, Nottingham.

119 HEAD OF A MAHOMEDAN
Millboard, 14 × 10.
Coll.: (?)John Miller, Liverpool, sold 21.5. 1858(146) *Head of a man, in a turban*, bt. in 7 gns.; Henry Burton (in the Burton Sale, 1890, lots 165, 166 and 171 were all called *Head of a Man*); T. Gabriel; T. B. Gabriel.
Exh.: Birmingham Society of Arts, 1840(300) *Head of a Mahomedan*, priced at 15 gns.; B.I., 1841(290).
Lit.: Gilchrist, ii, p. 338.
Mrs. E. M. Gabriel, Worplesdon, Surrey.

120 HEAD OF A WOMAN
Millboard laid on panel, 20 × 15¾.
Coll.: Purchased from the Adams Gallery, London.
Exh.: *Paintings by William Etty, R.A.*, Adams Gallery, 20th May–13th June, 1936(24 or 35).
Painted *c.* 1830–5. The model and composition of this painting are similar to *Lucy Ashton*, which was engraved by H. Robinson for the first Waverley edition of Sir Walter Scott's novels 1833.
Arnold Haskell, Esq., London.

121 [pl. 94*b*] 'LET BROTHERLY LOVE CONTINUE'
Millboard, 20¼ × 20⅛.
Coll.: as for *A Domestic Scene*. Given by William

Etty to his brother Charles to commemorate the meeting of the five brothers at York, 8th September, 1844.

Ir. Thomas H. Etty, Leidschendam.

122 THE LUTE PLAYER

Three versions:

(i) [pl. 43*b*] Panel, 17 × 19 (¼ added on four sides).

Inscr. on verso: 'No. 3 Wm Etty R.A.'

Coll.: Painted for Thomas Bodley for £100 ('*Cash Book*', 29th May, 1833, and letter from Etty to Bodley 15th April, 1833); Miss J. A. Bodley, sold Sotheby's, 14.5.1930(16), bt. Savile Gallery £50 and acquired by Gerald Reitlinger; Reitlinger Sale, Sotheby's, 13.10. 1954(100), bt. Fine Art Society, Ltd., from whom acquired by J. Woolf.

Exh.: R.A., 1833(168).

Lit.: Gilchrist, i, p. 359, ii, p. 337; *The Burlington Magazine*, XCVI, December, 1954, *Notable Works of Art now on the Market*, pl. XXIX.

For a discussion of the painting *v. sub.* (ii). Illustrates the couplet (printed in the R.A. catalogue): 'When with sweet notes I the sweet lute inspired, / The fair ones listen'd and my skill admired.' These lines also appear on a label stuck to back of this painting. But the writing is not Etty's and '*soft* notes' instead of 'sweet notes' has been transcribed.

John Woolf, Esq., London.

(ii) [pl. 48] Panel, 24¾ × 21.

Inscr. on verso: 'WM ETTY R.A. No 1'.

Coll.: Purchased from the Artist by Robert Vernon; Vernon Gift to the National Gallery, 1847 (No. 359). Transferred to the Tate Gallery, 1900.

Exh.: B.I., 1835(59); Dublin, 1861(164); York, 1911(99); Longford Hall, Stretford, 1927(20); *Works of British Artists 1750–1850*, Plymouth, 1939(14); A.C. *Etty*, 1955(24).

Engr.: J. C. Armytage, *The Vernon Gallery*, 4th Series, 185[3?], No. 18, as *The Balcony*, and *The Art Journal*, June, 1854, facing p. 176.

Lit.: as for (i).

Repr.: Sir E. J. Poynter, *The National Gallery*, III, 1900, p. 65; Gaunt & Roe, pl. 16.

This is a larger and more elaborate version of (i). Although (i) was described in *The Burlington Magazine* (*loc. cit.*) as the 1835 painting, it is now clear that the provenance of this picture establishes it as the earlier version. In the British Institution catalogue this version of the couplet appears: 'When with soft notes

the sweet lute I inspired, / The fair ones listen'd and my skill admired.' The sizes recorded in Gilchrist and the B.I. catalogue for both paintings do not fit either panel (even allowing for the frame) and cannot be used as reliable evidence. Furthermore, both pictures derive from an earlier prototype *Window in Venice, during a Festa*, 1831 (*q.v.*).

Tate Gallery, London.

(iii) Canvas, 24¼ × 20.

Coll.: Emeritus Professor E. G. R. Taylor, D.Sc., F.R.G.S.

Differs from (ii) in that a hanging red curtain has replaced the archway, the balcony is bowed out and no drapery falls across the ledge. This may be an unfinished trial study, or a contemporary student's copy.

Professor E. G. R. Taylor, London.

123 MAN IN ARMOUR ('CAPTAIN MARIO')

Millboard, 13½ × 10.

Coll.: Henry Burton, sold 12.7.1890(148) *Head of a Soldier*, bt. Bayliss 13 gns.; James Bayliss, sold 22.3.1897(43) *Captain of the Guard: A Portrait of Signor Mario*, bt. Cook 6 gns.; T. Gabriel; T. B. Gabriel.

Exh.: S.A., 1849(XX), described as painted in 1845.

Mrs. E. M. Gabriel, Worplesdon, Surrey.

124 MATERNAL AFFECTION

Millboard (painted arched top), 15 × 12.

Coll.: Anon, sold 24.5.1856(39), bt. Nunnerly 25 gns.; Thomas Nunnerly, F.R.C.S., sold 22.3.1872(97), bt. in 14½ gns.; Mr. Hogarth of Leeds; George Carnes.

Exh.: York, 1911(162).

A painting of this title was exhibited at the R.A., 1822(121) and again at the B.I., 1824 (341), *see also* Gilchrist, i, p. 99, ii, p. 336; but neither the style nor the size of the Carnes picture agrees with the recorded facts. It looks more like a work of *c.* 1811.

John Carnes, Esq., Kingswood, Surrey.

125 MEMORIAL TO HENRY BURTON

Millboard (depressed arch top), 12¼ × 8.

Coll.: Henry Burton; T. Gabriel; T. B. Gabriel.

The stone (rather like a milestone) in the centre of the composition is inscribed 'Presented in grateful remembrance to H. BURTON, Esq., for kindnesses received by Wm Etty.' Henry Burton (1814–89) was an amateur artist and friend of both Etty and Constable. He was supposed to have painted a view of Arundel Park from a point identical to that chosen by

Constable. He was a relation of Mrs. Gabriel's mother.

Mrs. E. M. Gabriel, Worplesdon, Surrey.

126 THE MOURNER

Canvas, 25 × 19.

Coll.: C. W. Wass (until 1852); W. Cox; Richard Godson-Millns Bequest, 1904 (No. '04.29).

Exh.: (?)S.A., 1849(LXXXVIII), described as painted in 1842; *Deceased Masters of the British School*, Suffolk Street Galleries, 1878 (156); York, 1949(53).

Lit.: Gilchrist, ii, p. 339.

City Museum and Art Gallery, Nottingham.

127 A NOBLEMAN

Panel, 10 × 8½.

Coll.: (?)John Miller, Liverpool, sold 21.5.1858 (96) *Head of a Venetian Nobleman*, bt. Gambart 21 gns., Henry Wallis, sold 17.11.1860(199), bt. Wilmer, £8 10s.; John Elliot Bequest, 1917.

Exh.: York, 1949(27).

Williamson Art Gallery and Museum, Birkenhead.

128 [pl. 52] THE PERSIAN

Inscr. on verso: 'No 3 Wm Etty R.A.'

Canvas, 16 × 12.

Coll.: Robert Vernon, presumably purchased direct from the Artist; Vernon Gift to the National Gallery, 1847 (No. 357). Transferred to the Tate Gallery, 1949.

Exh.: B.I., 1834(82) *The Persian*; York, 1911 (125); *Autumn Loan Exhibition, Some Victorian Painters*, Hanley Museum and Art Gallery, Stoke-on-Trent, December, 1936–January, 1937(10).

Engr.: C. Cousen, *The Art Journal*, August, 1852, facing p. 252, and *The Vernon Gallery*, 3rd Series, 1853, No. 18 as *A Persian Warrior*.

Lit.: Gilchrist, ii, p. 337; Martin Davies, *The British School*, National Gallery, 1946, p. 52, *Study of a Man in Persian Costume*.

Tate Gallery, London.

PREPARING FOR A FANCY DRESS BALL *See* PORTRAITS: THE MISSES WILLIAMS WYNN (No. 183).

129 SOMNOLENCY

Canvas, 29½ × 24½ (sight).

Coll.: G. T. Andrews, sold 23.6.1849(51), bt. in 210 gns., resold 31.5.1851(10), bt. Thomas Todd of Maryculter, Aberdeenshire, 205 gns.; Alexander Macdonald, Kepplestone, Aberdeen, by bequest to the Gallery (Macdonald Collection).

Exh.: R.A., 1838(490); S.A., 1849(CXXVI); York, 1949(24).

Lit.: *Autobiography*, p. 40; Gilchrist, ii, pp. 82, 338.

Art Gallery and Industrial Museum, Aberdeen.

130 THE STANDARD BEARER

Panel, 16¾ × 13¼.

Coll.: (?)Charles Hawker; (?)John Miller, Liverpool, sold 21.5.1858(123), bt. J. H. Mann 5 gns.; James Orrock; F. E. Sidney (by 1907), sold 10.12.1937(41), bt. Leggatt 16 gns.; Lord Fairhaven.

Exh.: S.A., 1849(XVII), described as exhibited at B.I., 1843, but no painting of this title appears in that year's catalogue: Edinburgh, 1886(1420); B.F.A.C., Winter, 1907 (24); B.F.A.C., Winter, 1938–9 (9).

Repr.: Gaunt & Roe, pl. 49.

The Lord Fairhaven.

131 THE STANDARD BEARER

Canvas, 11½ × 10.

Coll.: H. A. J. Munro of Novar, sold 6.4.1878 (16), bt. Colls 49 gns.; Anon., sold 22.4.1927 (111), bt. Cornish 1 gn.; C. D. Rotch, who presented it to York through the N.A.C.F. 1955(No. 857/1955).

Lit.: W. E. Frost, A.R.A. and H. Reeve, *A Catalogue of the . . . Collection of the late H. A. J. Munro of Novar* [n.d.], No. 141; *York Preview* 33, IX, January, 1956, p. 336.

The figure is almost a direct copy of the standard bearer who appears in Titian's *Madonna of the Pesaro Family*, S. Maria dei Frari, Venice. Etty had noted the Titian painting in his list in *Sketchbook II*.

City Art Gallery, York.

132 STUDY OF A MAN'S HEAD

Panel (circular), 10½ dia.

Coll.: Rev. Chauncy Hare Townshend Bequest 1869 (No. 1390–'69).

Exh.: *British Art, 1830–50*, Whitechapel, 1920 (112).

Painted *c.* 1841–2.

Victoria and Albert Museum, London.

133 THE WATER CARRIER

Millboard, 17½ × 12⅛.

Coll.: Presented Alfred A. de Pass, 1936.

Painted *c.* 1840–45. Inscribed on back: 'W. Etty, R.A. Isaac E[rest illegible].' The face appears to have undergone some retouching.

City Art Gallery, Bristol.

134 WINDOW IN VENICE, DURING A FESTA

Two versions:

(i) [pl. 37a] Inscr. 'W + E' (bottom centre)

and on verso: 'No. 3 Wm Etty R.A.', '2', and 'No. 2 Wm Etty R A'.

Canvas laid on panel, 24 × 19¾.

Coll.: Purchased from the Artist for £100 by Robert Vernon in 1831 ('*Cash Book*', 13th August, 1831). Vernon Gift to the National Gallery, 1847 (No. 364). Transferred to the Tate Gallery, 1919.

Exh.: R.A., 1831(163); R.S.A., 1831(VI); York, 1836.

Engr.: A. Linley, *The Art Journal*, May, 1853, facing p. 141, and *The Vernon Gallery*, 4th Series, 185[3?], No. 4 as *The Brides of Venice*.

Lit.: Gilchrist, i, p. 323, ii, pp. 46, 337.

On the back of this picture is a composition study of two seated nude female figures.

Tate Gallery, London.

(ii) Canvas, 24 × 91½.

Coll.: (?)Anon., sold 11.1.1896(54) *The Bride of Venice*, bt. Cappel 7 gns.; on permanent loan to York Art Gallery since 1948 (No. 97/1948) from the Yorkshire Philosophical Society.

Exh.: York, 1911(32) lent E. L. Cappel.

Probably a copy by another artist of the Tate painting.

City Art Gallery, York.

135 WOMAN WITH DOVES (THE DOVES)

Two versions:

(i) Panel (painted oval), 11¼ × 8⅜.

Coll.: James Orrock, R.I., who presented the painting to Nottingham, 1909 (No. '09–50).

Exh.: A.C. *Paintings by English Masters*, Nottingham, 1946(17); York, 1949(54).

Repr.: Illustrated Catalogue of the Permanent Collection, 1913, pl. 23.

A *Venus with Doves* was sold from the H. A. J. Munro of Novar collection, 11.5.1867(23), bt. E. White 19 gns. It was not listed in the Frost and Reeve catalogue. Another, similarly entitled work was sold anon., 26.1.1889(53), bt. Bower 15 gns. The motif is closely related to classical bas-reliefs: e.g. *Grave Stele of a Little Girl*, mid. fifth century B.C., ex-coll. 1st Earl of Yarborough, now Metropolitan Museum of Art, New York (*see* Gisela Richter, *Catalogue of Greek Sculptures in the Metropolitan Museum*, Oxford, 1954, No. 73, p. 49, illus. pl. LXa). Painted *c.* 1835.

City Museum and Art Gallery, Nottingham.

(ii) Canvas (painted oval), 30 × 25.

Coll.: N. G. Terry, York, from his father-in-law.

Exh.: Yorks. Loan Exhibition of Pictures, Judges'

Lodgings, Lendal, York, July–August, 1934 (24).

Noel G. Terry, Esq., York.

136 THE WRESTLERS

Millboard, 20 × 15¾.

Coll.: Nicholson Gallery, where it was exhibited 1942.

Lit.: Gaunt & Roe, p. 117, No. CXXVI note in parentheses.

Male nude study on verso: painted *c.* 1840, the work has been retouched.

John Woodward, Esq., Birmingham.

137 THE WRESTLERS

Linen laid on panel, 19⅝ × 20½.

Coll.: Purchased from the Carroll Gallery, London 1919 (No. 1919.313).

Pictures of this title were sold 21.1.1855(52), bt. Palser £4 17s., and in the Viscount Oxenbridge Sale, 9.12.1899(49), bt. Hardy £2 5s. Painted *c.* 1840.

The Worcester Art Museum, Worcester, Massachusetts.

138 THE WRESTLERS

Millboard, 27 × 21.

Coll.: Anon., sold 31.10.1947(70), bt. Roland 30 gns.; presented by the York Civic Trust, 1947 (No. 89/1947).

Exh.: (?)S.A., 1849(CXVI) described as painted 1840, lent C. W. Wass, although this may be the Worcester painting (*v. supra*); York, 1948(27); A. C. *Twelve Yorkshire Artists of the Past*, 1951(7).

Painted *c.* 1840.

City Art Gallery, York.

PORTRAITS: MALE

139 JOSEPH ARNOULD, J.P., D.L.

Canvas, 30 × 25.

Coll.: By descent to the sitter's great, great-grandson, from his cousin Ernest Arnould.

The owner considers the painting to date from about 1820, and the sitter is almost certainly the same man who is mentioned in Etty's letter to his brother Walter, *c.* 1817–20, here published in Appendix I, Letter 4, British Museum, Add. MS.38794 E, ff. 100–101. Joseph Arnould lived at White Cross, Berkshire.

See also: Mrs. Arnould.

Lieut.-Col. W. H. Olivier, Ashford Hall, Bakewell, Derbyshire.

140 [pl. 42] JAMES ATKINSON

Canvas, $29\frac{1}{2} \times 24$.

Coll.: Miss Atkinson, presented to the Yorkshire Philosophical Society by her sister and executrix Lady Chatterton, 1857.

Exh.: (?)York, 1836; *Yorkshire Fine Art & Industrial*, York, 1866(8); *National Exhibition of Works of Art*, Leeds, 1886(3226); *Old York Views & Worthies*, York, 1905(278); York, 1911(98); A. C. *Etty*, 1955 (21); R.A. *British Portraits*, Winter, 1956–7(419), and repr. in souvenir, p. 35.

Lit.: Gilchrist, i, pp. 350–1; *York Preview* 37, X, January, 1957, p. 371.

Painted September-October, 1832. For further biographical details about James Atkinson (1759–1839) *see* G. F. Willmot, 'The Yorkshire Philosophical Society', *Museums Journal*, LIII, No. 6, September, 1953, p. 143.
Yorkshire Philosophical Society, York.

141 JAMES BAILEY

Canvas, 30×25.

Coll.: By descent to the present owner from his cousin Ernest Arnould.

James Bailey was the father of Joseph Arnould's first wife. Probably painted 1820.
Lieut.-Col. W. H. Olivier, Ashford Hall, Bakewell, Derbyshire.

142 SAMUEL ADLAM BAYNTUN

Canvas, 23×17.

Coll.: N. G. Terry, York, from his father-in-law. Samuel Adlam Bayntun was the eldest son of the Rev. H. Bayntun, of Browfort House, Devizes. At one time a Lieutenant in the Guards, he was returned as M.P. for York from 1830–2. He died in London, September, 1833, his age at death being given variously as 28 and 30 years old. The portrait probably dates from between 1830–2.
Noel G. Terry, Esq., York.

143 THOMAS BODLEY

Canvas, 30×25.

Coll.: T. Bodley. Present location unknown.

Exh.: *National Portraits*, Part III, April, 1868 (407).

Thomas Bodley, cousin to the artist and husband of Martha, 'Uncle' William Etty's daughter, died 1858.

144 [pl. 6] THE REV. ROBERT BOLTON

Canvas, $50\frac{3}{4} \times 41\frac{1}{4}$.

Coll.: Reginald Pelham Bolton (grandson of the sitter), who bequeathed it to the Society 1942.

Lit.: Robert Bolton, *The Genealogical and Bio-*

graphical Account of the Family of Bolton in England and America, New York, 1862, p. 155.

Exh.: Rhode Island School of Design, 28th November, 1956–2nd January, 1957.

Painted 1818.

See also: Mrs. Robert Bolton and her Children.
The New-York Historical Society, New York.

145 JOHN BROOK

Two versions:

(i) [pl. 59] Canvas, $29\frac{1}{2} \times 24$.

Coll.: Presented to the Yorkshire Philosophical Society by the York Musical Society, 1872.

Exh.: *Old York Views & Worthies*, York, 1905 (21); York, 1911(95); York, 1949(43).

Lit.: Gilchrist, ii, pp. 85–6; James M. Biggins, *Etty and York*, York, 1949, p. 6.

Painted 1838. The *Gentleman's Magazine*, March 1851, contains an informative obituary notice about John Brook (1770–1851).
Yorkshire Philosophical Society, York.

(ii) Canvas, $30 \times 24\frac{3}{4}$.

Coll.: C. Harker(in 1866); Percy Moore Turner, sold Sotheby's, 12.12.1951(1), bt. Johnson £11; Anon., sold Sotheby's, 11.6.1952(94), bt. Godfrey £10. Present location unknown.

Exh.: *Yorkshire Fine Art & Industrial*, York, 1866(269); York, 1949(21).

Engr.: James Scott, 1849.

Lit.: Gilchrist, ii, p. 86.

146 JOHN CAMIDGE, MUS. DOC.

Millboard, $12\frac{1}{8} \times 9\frac{5}{8}$.

Coll.: Bequeathed by Dr. Camidge's only daughter, Mrs. Hustwick 1907.

Exh.: York, 1911(128); York, 1949(36).

Lit.: J. W. Goodison, *Catalogue of Cambridge Portraits*, I The University Collection, Cambridge, 1955, p. 112, No. 186.

Repr.: *The Principal Pictures in the Fitzwilliam Museum*, Cambridge, 1929, p. 61.

John Camidge (1790–1859), was assistant organist to his father at York Minster, then organist 1842–58. He took his Mus. Doc. in 1819, and this portrait probably dates from *c.* 1825.
Fitzwilliam Museum, Cambridge.

147 CHARLES ETTY

(*a*) Millboard laid on panel, $16\frac{7}{8} \times 14\frac{5}{8}$.

Coll.: Charles Etty (1793–1856); Charles Etty (1812–91), son of Thomas Etty, senr., born 1779, m. Ann Maria (daughter of Charles Etty, senr.) and their eldest daughter, Jane Elizabeth, m. Thomas (1832–1904, grandson of John Etty, 1775–1865). Thomas and Jane Elizabeth adopted a nephew, Tom (1884–1932), whose son Thomas Hendrik Etty thus inherited the collection.

William's youngest brother, the seventh of Matthew's sons, two of whom died young. Charles Etty became a captain in the merchant service and in 1831 set up as a sugar planter in Wonolangan, Java, where he died in December, 1856. This portrait probably dates from *c.* 1811.

Ir. Thomas H. Etty, Leidschendam.

(*b*) [pl. 84] Panel, 36 × 28.

Coll.: Charles Etty (the sitter) to his son Matthew, who m. Johanna Christina Pereira. After Matthew's death Johanna m. Van Vloten and their daughter Elizabeth Adriano m. Sleyster.

Exh.: Oude Engelsche schilderijen, miniaturen en teekeningen in Nederlansche verzamelingen, Museum Boymans, Rotterdam, November–December, 1934(11), lent Mevr. E. A. Sleyster-Etty.

Repr.: In reverse and showing some distortions, on cover of *Indië,* 'Cultuur-Maatschappij Wonolangan, 1895–1925', 9de Jaargang, Afl. 19, 9 December, 1925.

Painted 1844–5 during Charles's visit to England. The painting was destroyed by bombs when in store at Arnhem, 1944.

148 JOHN ETTY

(*a*) [pl. 3*b*] Canvas, 30 × 25.

Coll.: Presumably in the sitter's possession until his death in 1865, after which it passed to the Company of Merchant Adventurers. No Company records survive prior to 1929.

Exh.: York, 1949(34); A.C. *Etty,* 1955(4), and repr. pl. I.

Painted *c.* 1811–12. John Etty was the third of the five surviving brothers, and William's senior by twelve years. He carried on the family concern as baker and confectioner, moving from 20 Feasegate to Huntington Mill 1830.

Company of Merchant Adventurers of the City of York.

(*b*) Millboard, laid on panel, 25¼ × 19½.

Coll.: as for *Charles Etty* (*a*).

Lit.: Gilchrist, ii, p. 49.

Painted in 1836 for the artist's niece Elizabeth whose father is the subject of the portrait.

Ir. Thomas H. Etty, Leidschendam.

149 MATTHEW ETTY

(*a*) [pl. 3*a*] Canvas, 25½ × 19¼.

Coll.: as for *Charles Etty* (*a*).

The artist's father (1746–1818), painted at York in 1811 and begun soon after Catherine Etty's portrait (MS. letter, Etty to Walter, 19th June).

(*b*) Cardboard, 12 × 9.

Coll.: as for *Charles Etty* (*a*).

Like the small portrait of Esther, his wife, this is a detail of the head taken from the 1811 painting (*v. supra*). It may be either a preliminary study or a copy made specially for Charles Etty.

(*a*) and (*b*) *Ir. Thomas H. Etty, Leidschendam.*

150 THOMAS ETTY, JUNR.

Millboard, 18 × 13⅝.

Coll.: as for *Charles Etty* (*a*).

Born 1832, the grandson of John Etty, Senr., he appears to be aged about ten years in this portrait which was probably painted at York *c.* 1842.

Ir. Thomas H. Etty, Leidschendam.

151 THOMAS ETTY, SENR.

Canvas, 25 × 18½.

Coll.: as for *Charles Etty* (*a*).

Inscribed on the back of the canvas: 'Tho:ˢ Etty Painted by Will:ᵐ Etty. Anno 1811'; Thomas (born 1779) was the fourth of the surviving brothers.

Ir. Thomas H. Etty, Leidschendam.

152 WILLIAM ETTY, R.A.

(*a*) [pl. 20] Panel (painted oval), 16½ × 12½.

Coll.: W. Etty, R.A.; Sir Joseph Whitworth, Bt., who presented it to Manchester, 1882.

Exh.: S.A., 1849(LXXVII); Birmingham Society of Artists, 1853(324), lent by Joseph Whitworth; *Royal Jubilee,* Manchester, 1887(672); York, 1911(81); *British Art,* Manchester, 1934(79*a*); R.A. *British Art,* 1934 (658); York, 1949(50), A.C. *Etty,* 1955(12).

Engr.: C. W. Wass 1849.

Lit: The Art Journal, 1849, p. 68.

Repr.: Gaunt & Roe, pl. 5.

City Art Gallery, Manchester.

(*b*) Canvas, 17¼ × 14¼.

Coll.: as for *Charles Etty* (*a*).

Ir. Thomas H. Etty, Leidschendam.

(*c*) Millboard, 17⅜ × 13⅞.

Coll.: Mrs. Margaret Marr, Pudsey, nr. Leeds.

A free copy after the Manchester painting. *J. Lunn, Esq., Bradford.*

(*d*) Millboard (painted oval), 17 × 12¾.

Inscr.: 'Etty' (bottom left).

Coll.: E. W. Smithson, sold 12.3.1928(149),

Martin 7 gns.; Grenville L. Winthrop Bequest 1943 (1943.191).

Perhaps a preliminary study, or more likely, a studio copy.

Fogg Art Museum, Harvard University, Massachusetts.

(*e*) Millboard, 16½ × 10¾.

Coll.: Purchased York Art Gallery 1913 (No. 85).

Exh.: York, 1948(15); York, 1949(76).

Repr.: York Preview 8, II, October, 1949(cover).

This, and the National Portrait Gallery version were done from a photograph taken by D. O. Hill and Robert Adamson *c.* 1843–5, which is reproduced in H. Gernsheim, *Masterpieces of Victorian Photography,* London, 1951, pp. 11, 105. The photograph was in the Arts Council exhibition of the same title held at the Victoria and Albert Museum 1951(61). It is not clear whether the poor quality of both versions is due to their being copies by Etty from a photograph, or whether they are, in fact, by another hand. It should be noted that the paintings are not an exact copy of the photograph, but such differences as exist are of negligible importance.

City Art Gallery, York.

(*f*) Millboard, 15¼ × 12.

Coll.: John Billington, who bought it *c.* 1875 from an unnamed source; sold Sotheby's, 28.3.1903(305), bt. E. Parsons £10; with Leggatts, from whom purchased by the Gallery 1904 (No. 1368).

Lit.: Catalogue of the National Portrait Gallery 1856–1947, London, 1949.

National Portrait Gallery, London.

(*g*) Pen and brown ink, 9½ × 6.

Coll.: Presented by the Artist to Mr. Hepple, Newcastle; Mr. Halfnight, senr., of Sunderland, Mr. Halfnight, junr. (until June, 1877); Anon., sold 21.1.1949(75), bt. P. & D. Colnaghi (with another lot) 7 gns., and acquired by the Ashmolean.

Exh.: R.A. *British Portraits,* Winter, 1956–7 (707).

Engr.: Published in *Arnold's Magazine of the Fine Arts,* 1834.

On the back is a long inscription giving details of the history of the portrait up to 1877; unfortunately, there is no clue to the writer's identity. A drawing by J. H. Mole (repr. *York Preview* 3, July, 1948, and discussed *ibid.,* 37, X, January, 1957, p. 371) which is now at York, was either drawn

from the engraving, or, less likely, a preparatory study for it.

Ashmolean Museum, Oxford.

153 [pl. 75*a*] JOHN HARPER

Millboard, 19½ × 15½.

Coll.: Purchased for 10 gns. in 1918 at a sale of Mrs. Harper's effects by Arthur Laws of Brighton from whom York acquired it 1919 (No. 71/1919).

Exh.: Paintings by William Etty, R.A., Adams Gallery, May–June, 1936(30); *British Art,* Stedelijk Museum, Amsterdam, 1936(35); B.C. *La Peinture Anglaise: XVIIIᵉ et XIXᵉ Siècles,* Louvre, Paris 1938(43) and repr. in supplement; York, 1948(6); York, 1949(71); A.C. *Twelve Yorkshire Artists of the Past,* 1951(5); *Peintures anglaises des collections d'York et du Yorkshire,* Musée des Beaux-Arts, Dijon 1957(25).

Lit.: The Connoisseur, XCVIII, September, 1936, pp. 147 & 150 (repr.), and CXXIV December, 1949, p. 131; *York Preview* 8, II, October, 1949; *The Burlington Magazine,* XC; January, 1950, p. 25 (and repr. fig. 23).

Probably painted *c.* 1841.

City Art Gallery, York.

154 WILLIAM HESSLEGRAVE

Panel, 8 × 6.

Coll.: By descent to the sitter's great, great-nephew Geoffrey Hedley.

Painted *c.* 1840–5. William Hesslegrave was a silversmith in York. *See also: Mrs. William Hesslegrave.*

Geoffrey Hedley, Esq. (on loan to York Art Gallery).

155 JOHN HOPPS

Canvas, 33¼ × 25½.

Coll.: By descent to the sitter's great granddaughter Miss Lucy B. Kitchin, who presented it to York, 1952 (No. 651/1952).

Presentation portrait to John Hopps (born 1794) a York surgeon, and lecturer at the York School of Medicine. The painting is badly damaged by bitumen.

City Art Gallery, York.

156 JOSIAS INGHAM

Canvas, 30 × 24.

Coll.: By descent to the sitter's great granddaughter Mrs. Littler.

Josias Ingham, a York linen draper, married Maria Moiser 1820. Painted *c.* 1825 (?). The picture has suffered from overcleaning.

See also: Mrs. Josias Ingham.

Mrs. Marion Littler, Warwick.

157 JOHN THORNTON

Canvas, 30 × 25.

Coll.: No records survive of its entry into the Company of Merchant Adventurers' possession.

Exh.: (?)R.A., 1819(420) *Portrait of a gentleman.*

Lit.: Gilchrist, i, p. 78, ii, p. 335.

Company of Merchant Adventurers of the City of York.

158 PORTRAIT OF A GENTLEMAN (Attributed to Etty)

Canvas, 30 × 26½.

Coll.: On loan to the Gallery since 1932; owner unknown.

The painting is of exceptionally fine quality, and if by Etty, probably dates from about 1818–20. The sitter bears some resemblance to the Rev. Robert Bolton, and may be another member of that family.

City Art Gallery, York.

PORTRAITS: FEMALE

159 MRS. ARNOULD

Canvas, 30 × 25.

Coll.: By descent to the sitter's great, great-grandson, from his cousin Ernest Arnould.

Mrs. Arnould was the mother of Joseph Arnould, J.P., D.L. (*q.v.*). Probably painted 1820.

Lieut.Col. W. H. Olivier, Ashford Hall, Bakewell, Derbyshire.

160 [pl. 7] MRS. ROBERT BOLTON AND HER CHILDREN

Canvas, 50¾ × 41¼.

Coll. & Lit.: As for *Rev. Robert Bolton.*

Exh.: Rhode Island School of Design, 28th November, 1956–2nd January, 1957.

Anne Jay (1793–1859) married Robert Bolton (1788–1857) in 1811; by 1818 they had five children, of whom Robert (born 1814) and Anne (born 1815) seem to be of the right age to correspond with the children in this portrait.

The New-York Historical Society, New York.

161 MRS. GEORGE BULMER

Millboard (irregular shape), 7⅗ × 4½.

Coll.: Painted for Mr. and Mrs. George Bulmer *c.* 1845, possibly as a study for a larger portrait; J. B. Willows (by 1885); J. W. Watson, Bradford (until 1907); H. S. Cropper.

Sketch of nude head and bust. A MS. note on verso of painting describes how J. B. Willows called on Mrs. [Margaret] Lotherington, a niece of the artist, to verify the identity of the sitter.

H. S. Cropper, Esq., Newton, West Kirby.

162 MISS MARGARET CAMIDGE

Canvas, 54 × 42 (sight).

Coll.: By descent to the sitter's grand nephew, Dr. Thomas Kirsopp.

Miss Camidge was the daughter of John Camidge (*q.v.*), and judging from the age of the sitter, this portrait must date *c.* 1840.

Dr. Thomas Kirsopp, Fareham, Hants.

163 MRS. SARAH CLAYTON

Oil on paper, 9⅘ × 7½.

Coll.: Sarah and Alfred Clayton to their son, George Smith Clayton; Edward Clayton.

Exh.: *Spring Exhibition,* Whitechapel, March–May, 1905(66) as *Head.*

Sarah (*née* Howey) Clayton was married in 1824 and died in September, 1829, aged 22 years. The portrait is unfinished.

C. E. Ansell Clayton, Esq., London.

164 [pl. 67] MISS ELIZA COOK

Canvas, 15 × 12½.

Coll.: Miss Maude Wethered; V. D. Wethered, sold Sotheby's, 4.1.1947(145), bt. Sir David Scott.

Exh.: *Paintings by William Etty, R.A.,* R. E. A. Wilson, 24 Ryder St., November, 1933(1); B.F.A.C., Winter, 1938–9(11); A. C. *Etty,* 1955(43).

Probably painted *c.* 1837–40, this portrait is of the popular poetess and editor of *Eliza Cook's Journal.* She was born in December 1818, and although almost entirely self-educated, her first poems were published as early as 1835. Her work is characterized by a sincere domestic sentiment and often contains some moral lesson. She died in September, 1889.

Sir David Scott, Boughton, Kettering.

165 [pl. 45*b*] MISS EMMA DAVENPORT

Canvas (painted oval), 30 × 25.

Coll.: Painted as a present for the sitter's mother Hannah, wife of Burrage Davenport (died 1863) *c.* 1827–9; Miss Sophia Frances (died 1887) and Caroline Burns Davenport (died 1897); Mrs. Anna (*née* Carew) Powell.

Emma Davenport (1807–30) married Frederick Joseph Keene 1829. She died in childbirth.

Richard C. Powell, Esq., East Grinstead, Sussex.

166 [pl. 2*b*] MISS CATHARINE ETTY ('KITTY')

Canvas, 23¾ × 19.

Coll.: Catharine m. Robert Purdon (*c.* 1829), and their daughter Mary Ann m. Admiraal (1854). Upon her removal from Java to South Africa the painting passed to her cousin Charles Etty (1845–1937), brother-in-law to

Thomas Etty (1832–1904, grandson of John Etty, 1775–1865); Charles's daughter Jane Elizabeth m. Verloop, their son Thomas inheriting the portrait.

Exh.: A. C. *Etty*, 1955(2).

Painted 1811. In a MS. letter to his brother Walter (19th June, 1811; *see* Appendix I, Letter 1), Etty mentions that he has painted John Etty's eldest [surviving] daughter Kitty, 'who by the bye, is grown a tall genteel girl, . . .'.

Thomas Verloop, Esq., Bradford.

167 MISS ELIZABETH ETTY ('BETSY')
Millboard, 18¼ × 14.
Coll.: as for *Charles Etty* (*a*).

Very much overpainted and thus difficult to date, perhaps *c.* 1840. This was the niece who became the painter's devoted housekeeper for nearly thirty years. She married Stephen Binnington, a chemist, in May, 1850.

Ir. Thomas H. Etty, Leidschendam.

168 MRS. ESTHER ETTY
Millboard, 12 × 9¼.
Coll.: as for *Charles Etty* (*a*).

The large original painting of 1811, from which this is a detail of the head only, belonged to Mevr. Elizabeth Adriano Sleyster-Etty but was destroyed whilst in store at Arnhem in 1944. This may be either a preliminary study or a copy specially made for Charles Etty.

See also: Matthew Etty.

Ir. Thomas H. Etty, Leidschendam.

169 MRS. WILLIAM HESSLEGRAVE
Panel, 8 × 6.
Coll.: as for *William Hesslegrave* (*q.v.*).

170 MRS. MARIA INGHAM
Canvas, 30 × 24.
Coll.: as for *Josias Ingham* (*q.v.*).

171 [pl. 91*b*] MISS JENNY LIND
Canvas, 36 × 28.
Coll.: Mme Lind-Goldschmidt; Dr. Bailey (by 1887); sold at a South Kensington auctioneer's 1951, bt. Knox.
Exh.: A.C. *Etty*, 1955(36).

Probably painted summer 1847, during Mlle Lind's first visit to England. A note in Jenny Lind's handwriting on the back of the picture states that 'This painting by W. Etty, R.A., a portrait of myself. Becomes the property of Dr. Baily [*sic*] at my death. 1858 Aug. signed E. Bailey Jenny Lind.' Another portrait attributed to Etty of Jenny Lind, which was bought in, anon. coll., 13.11.1953 (142), is of very doubtful authenticity.

George Knox, Esq., Newcastle.

172 MRS. ARABELLA MORRIS
Canvas, 30 × 25.
Coll.: Bequeathed by the sitter's granddaughter Miss Christina B. Ashworth Macdonald, Nov. 1947; Miss Macdonald's twin sister Mrs. Claude Magniac retained life interest until her death in December, 1956.

Arabella, daughter of the Rev. William Montague Higginson, Rector of St. Peter's, Alvescot, Oxon., married William Morris, 1817. The portrait dates from about 1816–18.

Thomas Stanford Museum, Preston Manor, Brighton.

173 MRS. MARY NEWMAN
Two versions:
(i) Canvas, 34¼ × 30.
Coll.: By descent to the present owner.

An inscription on the back of the canvas reads: 'Mary Newman (*née* Clarke) / Painted by *Etty* 1822 / Copied in November 1909 / Copy in the possession of / Miss Newman / 1 Pittville Lawn, Cheltenham.' The copy was disposed of during the early 1930s. The portrait is close in style to *The Coral Finder*.
(ii) Canvas, 22 × 18.
Coll.: as for (i).

On the frame is chalked 'Mr. Etty 16 Stangate Walk'. This and the style of the painting date it to the early part of 1824, when Etty had not then moved to Buckingham Street. The pose is similar to (i), but the dress is different.

Mrs. Margaret E. Orr, Aberdeen.

174 [pl. 90] THE HON. MRS. CAROLINE NORTON
Millboard (painted oval), 17½ × 13¼.
Coll.: By descent to the present owner.
Exh.: *Victorian*, New Gallery, 1891–2(283); *International*, Glasgow, 1901(564); York, 1911 (157).

The Hon. Mrs. Caroline Norton (1808–77) was the famous social beauty and authoress of her day. A grand-daughter of R. B. Sheridan, she was unhappily married to the Hon. George Chapple Norton, and late in life married again to Sir William Stirling Maxwell, Bt., M.P. An unfinished life-size portrait head of Mrs. Norton also belongs to Sir John Stirling Maxwell, Glasgow.

Lieut.-Colonel William F. Stirling, Keir, Perthshire.

175 [pl. 93] THE HON. MRS. NORTON AND HER SISTERS
Canvas (painted oval), 13¼ × 16⅞.
Coll.: Anon., sold 22.4.1912(103), bt. Jackson 13 gns.; G. Beatson Blair Bequest, 1941.

Probably painted *c.* 1847. Caroline Norton's sisters were Georgiana, the youngest, and Helen, the eldest. The identification has never been doubted, but both sisters look considerably younger than Mrs. Norton herself. Etty either painted them from earlier portraits by other artists, or they must be other members of the Sheridan or Norton families. All Mrs. Norton's children were boys.
City Art Gallery, Manchester.

176 [pl. 91*a*] PORTRAIT OF AN UNKNOWN LADY
Canvas, 23½ × 19½.
Coll.: Galerie G. H. Sedelmeyer Sale, Paris, May–June, 1907, 1ᵉʳ vente; C. D. Rotch, who presented it through the N.A.C.F. to York 1954 (No. 696/1954).
Repr.: York Preview 28, VII, October, 1954 (cover); *The Burlington Magazine*, XCVI, November, 1954, p. 358, fig. 27.

The portrait dates from 1846–8. A dealer's label on the back reads: 'portrait d'une femme par R. Bonington', and on the centre stretcher is inscribed '(?)Mr. Simmons(?), 35 Rue des Couteau [*sic*]'.
City Art Gallery, York.

177 PORTRAIT GROUP OF THREE SISTERS (?)
Millboard laid on panel (painted circle), 13 dia.; enlarged on three sides.
Coll.: (?)William Wethered, sold 7.3.1856(128) as *The Three Sisters*, bt. Pennell 60 gns., and again 27.2.1858(74) bt. Rippe 126 gns.; (?) Henry Burton; T. Gabriel; T. B. Gabriel.

The composition is similar to the *Fleur de Lys*, illustrated in the Charles Birch Sale catalogue, Foster's, 15.2.1855(XVII); sold for 700 gns. Painted *c.* 1845–9.
Mrs. E. M. Gabriel, Worplesdon, Surrey.

178 [pl. 45*a*] MISS ELIZABETH POTTS
Canvas, 33½ × 28¼.
Coll.: Thomas Potts; Mrs. Elizabeth Bolton (*née* Potts); Mrs. John McDonald (*née* Potts-Chatto) to her daughter Mrs. Margaret Mary Fisher.
Exh.: R.A., 1834(37); A. C. *Etty*, 1955(23). On loan to York 1954–6.
Lit.: Gilchrist, ii, pp. 2, 337.

Painted during the latter part of 1833. At the request of Mrs. Potts, her daughter's identity was not disclosed when the portrait was shown at the Royal Academy (MS. letter from Mrs. Elizabeth Potts to Etty, 10th March, 1834). Etty received 65 gns. for the portrait ('Cash Book', 17th January, 1834).
Mrs. M. M. Fisher, Winchelsea, Sussex.

179 [pl. 75*b*] MLLE RACHEL, THE FRENCH TRAGEDIENNE
Inscr.: 'Rachel the French Tragedian' (bottom left).
Pastel on deep pink paper, 22 × 15½.
Coll.: Sir Robert Witt; Courtauld Institute, 1952 (Witt Collection No. 3067).

Mlle Rachel, whose real name was Eliza Félix (1821–58), made her *début* at the Théâtre Français, Paris, in June, 1838, as Camille in Corneille's *Les Horaces*. She visited London first in May, 1841, then again in 1842, 1846 and 1847.
University of London, Courtauld Institute of Art.

180 MISS MARY SPURR
Millboard, 14½ × 12½ (sight).
Coll.: John Spurr; Mrs. Edwin Brightwell, by descent to her grand-daughter Miss Mary C. Brightwell.
Exh.: (?)R.A., 1835(154) *Study from a young lady* [a 'York Beauty' according to Gilchrist].
Lit.: Gilchrist, ii, pp. 34, 338.

A label on the back of this painting records the following: 'Portrait of the second daughter [Mary] of Mr. John Spurr by William Etty in 1834. Entitled "The Beauty of the North".'
Miss Mary C. Brightwell, Scarborough.

181 [pl. 66] MRS. J. F. VAUGHAN
Canvas, 30 × 25.
Coll.: By descent to the present owner; Lord Llangattock; The Hon. Lady Shelley-Rolls.
Exh.: There is a label of the 1908 R.A. Old Masters Exhibition on the back, but the painting does not appear in the printed catalogue; A.C. *Pictures from Welsh Private Collections*, Cardiff, 1951(19); R.A. *British Portraits*, Winter, 1956–7(375).

Louisa Elizabeth, the sister of J. E. W. Rolls of The Hendre, and wife of J. F. Vaughan of Courtfield. One of her sons was Cardinal Herbert Vaughan. Probably painted *c.* 1835–40. There is a *pentimento* on the right shoulder.
The Hon. Lady Shelley-Rolls, The Hendre, Monmouth.

182 [pl. 95] MRS. WILLIAM WETHERED
Canvas (arched top), 23½ × 28.
Coll.: H. A. J. Munro of Novar, sold 6.4.1878 (26), bt. Baker 65 gns.; John Baker, Wisbech, sold 16.5.1885(109), bt. Vaughan 35 gns.; Anon., sold 12.2.1887(121), bt. Bishop 22 gns.; Anon., sold 18.4.1894(69), bt. Smith 5½ gns.; E. W. Smithson, sold 12.3.1928(143), bt. 'Nottnge' 7 gns.; Anon., sold 27.11.1931(116), bt. Mann 11 gns.; Sir Alec Martin; Anon., sold

15.6.1951(107), bt. Dance 60 gns. for Dunedin.
Exh.: R.A., 1849(270) *Three versions of one subject*; *Paintings by William Etty, R.A.*, R. E. A. Wilson, 24 Ryder St., November, 1933(13).
Lit.: Gilchrist, ii, p. 341; W. E. Frost, A.R.A. & Henry Reeve, *Catalogue of the Collection . . . of the late H. A. J. Munro of Novar* [n.d.], No. 127.
Dunedin Public Art Gallery Society, Inc., Dunedin, New Zealand.

183 [pl. 58] THE MISSES WILLIAMS WYNN (PREPARING FOR A FANCY DRESS BALL)
Canvas, 60 × 51½.
Coll.: Painted in 1833 for the Rt. Hon. Charles Watkin Williams Wynn, M.P.; by descent to Mrs. Lewis Motley, great grand-daughter of Mary Williams Wynn.
Exh.: R.A., 1835(14); S.A., 1849(LXXXI).
Lit.: Gilchrist, i, pp. 360–1, ii, p. 337.

The standing figure on the left is a portrait of Charlotte, and the seated figure on the right is Mary, both daughters of Charles Williams Wynn of Llangedwyn, Denbighshire. Mary was married in 1832 to James Milne Gaskell. Charlotte's headdress is similar to Russian costume of the period, although Gilchrist speaks of it as Italian.
Mrs. Lewis Motley, Wenlock Abbey, Shropshire.

PORTRAITS: CHILDREN

184 [pl. 32] THE LADY MARY AGAR AND THE HON. CHARLES AGAR ('GUARDIAN CHERUBS')
Canvas, 49 × 35.
Coll.: Commissioned from the Artist for 150 gns. by Welbore Ellis Agar, 2nd Earl of Normanton, 1828; by descent to the present Earl.
Exh.: R.A., 1828(6) *Guardian Cherubs, in which are introduced resemblances of the Lady Mary Agar and Hon. Charles Welbore Herbert Agar, infant children of the Earl of Normanton*; *Works of Living Artists*, Birmingham Institution, 1829(51) *Guardian Angels*.
Lit.: *Gentleman's Magazine*, XCVIII, June, 1928, p. 538; Gilchrist, i, p. 248, ii, p. 336; Waagen, *Treasures of Art*, iv, 1857, p. 369; MS. *Catalogue of Pictures at Somerley*, 1884, No. 35 (1948 revised list, p. 35, No. 34), where described as 'Three Heads of Mary Countess Nelson and sleeping figure of Captain the Honble. Charles Agar 44th Regiment when a child'; Gaunt & Roe, p. 89, identify the boy incorrectly as James Charles Herbert Welbore Ellis Agar, later 3rd Earl Normanton.

Mary Countess Nelson was the only daughter of the 2nd Earl, and was born in 1822. She married Lord Nelson in 1845. Captain the Honble. Charles Agar was born in 1824 and died on 18th June, 1855, whilst leading his men in the attack upon the Cemetery at Sebastopol. According to the 1884 Catalogue, this was painted as a pendant to a Murillo *Boy Angels flying in Clouds*, panel, 50½ × 37½, bought by the 2nd Earl at Christie's 13.6.1827 for 40 gns., ex-coll. 'Convent of St. Augustine at Seville'. The other parallel is with that of Reynolds's *Heads of Angels* (Tate Gallery, No. 182), of which there is a copy by Mary Carpenter also at Somerley.
The Earl of Normanton.

185 MISS MATILDA BICKNELL
Panel, 19 × 15¾.
Coll.: Commissioned from the Artist by the sitter's father Elhanan Bicknell, 1845; exhibited, but not sold, in Bicknell Sale, 25.4.1863 (29); Henry Sanford Bicknell; Miss Maude Berry (by 1931), who seems to have allowed Sir James Berry (died 1947–8) a life interest in the picture; Grosvenor Berry (by 1948), who bequeathed it to Captain Lindsay-Smith, January, 1953.
Exh.: S.A., 1849(LV).
Lit.: Waagen, *Art Treasures*, ii, 1854, p. 350; Gilchrist, ii, p. 340.

The portrait shows the head and shoulders of a young girl in profile, looking right, aged about six.
Captain L. Lindsay-Smith, East Donyland Hall, Essex.

186 MISS ELIZABETH ETTY ('BETSY')
Inscr.: 'Etty pinxit' (bottom right).
Canvas, 25 × 19⅞.
Coll.: Elizabeth Ince-Binnington (step-daughter to Elizabeth, the sitter); John Etty; Sarah (*née* Etty) Bosch (great grand-daughter of John Etty, senr.); Jacobus Johannes Thomas Bosch.

Painted 1811 at the same time as the *Catherine Etty (q.v.)*.
Mr. Jacobus J. T. Bosch, Voorburg.

187 MISS JANE ETTY
Canvas, 14¾ × 12.
Coll.: as for *Miss Elizabeth Etty* (Bosch Collection).
Lit.: Gilchrist, i, p. 309.

Portrait of Jane Elizabeth (born 1814) daughter of Walter Etty. This is almost certainly the daughter to whom Etty refers in his letter to Thomas Bodley (13th July, 1830; City

Reference Library, York) when Jane was then at school in Paris. Painted *c.* 1830–5. A label on the back reads: 'This portrait of Jane Etty by her Uncle belongs to John Charles Etty her grand nephew Sep. 1919.'

Mr. Jacobus J. T. Bosch, Voorburg.

188 MASTER HART AS CUPID

Canvas laid on millboard (painted oval), $7\frac{1}{4} \times 5\frac{1}{2}$.

Painted *c.* 1820. A label on verso in Etty's writing reads 'Master Hart'.

J. M. Morgan, Esq., Bemerton, Salisbury.

189 HEAD OF A GIRL

Two versions:

(i) Canvas laid on millboard, 18 × 12.

Coll.: The Hon. Mrs. Michael Lambert, London.

(ii) Canvas, $13\frac{3}{4} \times 11\frac{1}{2}$.

Coll.: Sir James Linton, P.R.I. (in 1917); Graves Gift, 1937.

Formerly attributed to Sir Thomas Lawrence, this and (i) may be copies based on the *Calmady Children* by Lawrence.

Graves Art Gallery, Sheffield.

190 MISS ELIZA AMELIA HOPPS (attributed to Etty)

Canvas, 30 × 25.

Coll.: By descent to Miss Doris Makins (until 1952); passed to her sister Mrs. William H. Doughty.

Eliza Amelia Hopps (1825–39) was the daughter of John Hopps (*q.v.*).

Mrs. William H. Doughty, Keswick.

191 [pl. 33] MISS MARY ARABELLA JAY

Canvas, $30 \times 24\frac{3}{4}$.

Coll.: Mrs. Mary Arabella Ashton (*née* Jay); by descent to her great great-niece Mrs. Rose Mary Chamberlen (*née* Rooker), who bequeathed it to the National Gallery, December, 1956 (No. 6268).

Exh.: R.A., 1819(225).

Lit.: Gilchrist, i, p. 83, ii, p. 335.

Painted in 1818. A label on the back reads: 'Mrs. Ashton. *née* Jay—second daughter of Rev. W. Jay—of Bath. painted by "Etty". This picture belongs to Rose Mary Rooker, her Great great niece.' According to *The Autobiography of the Rev. William Jay*, ed. George Redford, D.D., LL.D. and John Angell Thomas, London, 1954, p. 95, Mary Arabella was Jay's third child and second daughter. When still quite young she married Garfit Ashton, a Cambridge solicitor and 'Clerk of the Peace'. She died childless shortly after her father's death in 1853, and her husband died in

November, 1855 (*see also: Gentlemen's Magazine*, 1854, i, p. 443, and 1856; Ralph Thomas, *Notes & Queries*, 4 December, 1909, pp. 445, 485).

National Gallery, London.

192 [pl. 2a] THE MISSIONARY BOY

Inscr.: 'W. Etty' (bottom left). Millboard, $25\frac{1}{4} \times 19\frac{7}{8}$.

Coll.: Mixed properties of Capt. Copplestone, Munro, and Walker, sold 13.6.1859(159), bt. Bewick 2 gns.; James Leathart, sold 9.6.1897 (31) *The Negro Boy*, bt. Corns 13 gns.; Thomas Prosser; Dr. Hoyland Smith, Harrogate, from whom purchased for 20 gns. by York 1952 (No. 641/1952).

Exh.: A Pre-Raphaelite Collection, Goupil Gallery, June–July, 1896 (64) *Negro Boy*, lent Leathart; *Jarrow Industrial and Art Exhibition* (date unknown), lent Thomas Prosser; A.C. *Etty*, 1955(1).

Lit.: York Preview 20, V, October, 1952, p. 227 (and repr.).

Painted *c.* 1805–6. Fragments of two inscriptions on the verso read: 'I well remember . . . missionary boy at Hull painted [at ?] York by W. Etty R.A.' A more accurate title might be *The Mission Boy*.

City Art Gallery, York.

193 MISS MARY ANN PURDON

(*a*) Millboard, $10\frac{3}{4} \times 9\frac{3}{4}$.

Coll.: as for *Charles Etty* (*a*).

Lit.: Gilchrist, ii, p. 49.

Daughter of Catherine (*née* Etty) and Robert Purdon, this painting shows her at the age of about four, *i.e.* 1836. There is a *pentimento* around the left ear.

Ir. Thomas H. Etty, Leidschendam.

(*b*) Cardboard, $14 \times 10\frac{3}{4}$.

Coll.: Mary Ann Admiraal; Mev. J. M. Jonquière-Etty (until November, 1955); Weduwe Edward G. Etty-Hoeyenbos. Painted *c.* 1838.

Wed. E. G. Etty-Hoeyenbos, Utrecht.

(*c*) Panel, $13 \times 10\frac{1}{2}$.

Coll.: John Singleton; Mrs. A. B. Lamb; Miss Maude Lamb. On loan to York since 1929.

Painted *c.* 1840.

Miss Maude Lamb, Worthing, Sussex.

194 MISS MARY ANN PURDON ('THE CROTCHET WORKER')

Two versions:

(i) Millboard laid on plywood, 26 × 20.

Coll.: as for *Charles Etty* (*a*).

Probably a study for the painting exhibited at the Royal Academy 1849(84).

Ir. *Thomas H. Etty, Leidschendam.*
(ii) Panel, 26½ × 20.
Coll.: (?)Etty Sale, 10.5.1850(645) *A Young Lady in a Green Dress Knitting*, bt. Rought 46 gns.; acquired by York through Wolstenholme Bequest 1948 (No. 106/1948).
Exh.: York, 1949(89).
City Art Gallery, York.

At least two other versions may have existed of this subject, including one in the Edward Harper Sale, 16.4.1853(75) *The Crotchet Worker*, 20 × 18, where described as the R.A., 1849 picture. It was bought by Charles Cope for 90 gns. and appeared in the Cope Sale, 8.6.1872(22), bt. White 36 gns. Another version was in the Charles Birch Sale, Foster's, 23–27.2.1857(XVIII), 20 × 15; and possibly a third was in the Etty Sale, 10.5.1850(644), bt. Rought 42½ gns. The Harper picture is mentioned by Gilchrist, ii, pp. 265–6.

195 [pl. 11*b*] MISS WALLACE ('INNOCENCE')
Canvas, 17 × 13.
Coll.: (?)C. W. Wass (until 1852); John Jones Bequest, 1882 (No. 498–'82) as *Innocence, Head of a Young Girl.*
Exh.: (?)S.A., 1849(LXI) as *Portrait of Miss Wallace*, painted 1820.
Lit.: Gilchrist, ii, p. 336.
Repr.: The Magazine of Fine Arts, I, November, 1905–April, 1906, p. 117.

The style of the picture dates it to 1820, although the identification of the sitter is only tentative. A painting *Innocence* was in the Henry Wallis Sale, 17.11.1860(127), bt. Colls £13. The Royal Academy owns a variant, canvas, 15½ × 13½ (pres. by Miss Anna Bridge).
Victoria and Albert Museum, London.

196 [pl. 92] THE WOOD CHILDREN
Canvas, 26¼ × 29½.
Coll.: Henry Wood, who commissioned the portrait 1845; Anon., sold, 4.8.1950(101), bt. Cooling 35 gns.; with the Adams Gallery from whom purchased by the N.A.C.F. and presented to York 1950 (No. 522/1950).
Exh.: S.A., 1849(LVII), where incorrectly dated 1840.
Lit.: Gilchrist, ii, p. 338; *York Preview* 13, IV, January, 1951, pp. 148, 150 (repr. on cover).

The children of Henry and Ann (*née Weller*) Wood of Lewisham are, from left to right: Emily Sarah (1837–75), Frederick William (1840–62), and Mary Ann (1820–1918). Two autograph letters at York Art Gallery, from Etty to Wood, the second dated 13th August,

1845, inform him of the picture's completion.
City Art Gallery, York.

UNIDENTIFIED GROUPS

197 CHILDREN'S HEADS
Panel, 9¼ × 13½.
Coll.: (?)Henry Burton, not in Burton Sale; T. Gabriel; T. B. Gabriel.

The two heads on the left are of the same child but in different positions; the third head and shoulders portrait is of a fair-haired girl. Painted *c.* 1835–40.
Mrs. E. M. Gabriel, Worplesdon, Surrey.

198 GROUP OF THREE CHILDREN
Inscr. on verso in ink: 'Painted by William Etty R.A. Nov. 22. 1839'; and a label: 'No 3 Group of Children. already sold—Painted by William Etty, R.A. 14 Buckingham Street, Strand.'
Coll.: A. C. Mace (by 1903).
Exh.: B.I., 1840(338).
Lit.: Gilchrist, ii, pp. 110, 338.

Six drawings of the head of one of these children appear on a sheet, 4 × 7, belonging to Mrs. Elisabeth Stevens, London.
Mrs. Margaret E. Orr, Aberdeen.

NUDE STUDIES: PUBLIC COLLECTIONS

199 [pl. 65*b*] SEATED NUDE FEMALE BATHER
Panel, 24 × 19½.
Coll.: Presented by P. A. Williamson, 1916.
Painted *c.* 1835–40.
Williamson Art Gallery and Museum, Birkenhead.

200 FEMALE NUDE (BACK VIEW)
Canvas, 11 × 18⅝.
Coll.: W. P. Young; A.C. Wall Gift, 1929.
City Art Gallery, Birmingham.

201 FEMALE NUDE (BACK VIEW)
Millboard, 23½ × 15½.
Boston Public Library, Lincs.

202 STANDING FEMALE NUDE (THE BATHER)
Canvas, 74 × 40.
Coll.: Presented by Mr. & Mrs. F. V. Gill, 1921.
Exh.: York, 1911 (according to label on back).

Painted *c.* 1825–30, probably as a pendant to the Manchester Academy of Fine Arts painting now at Burnley. A *Venus entering the bath*—'life size' was bought in 38 gns., John Davies, of Manchester, Sale, 26.5.1855(104).
City Art Gallery, Bradford.

203 STANDING MALE NUDE (BACK VIEW)
Millboard laid on canvas, 33 × 21.

Coll.: Cecil Rea; Mrs. Constance Rea Bequest 1953.

Painted *c.* 1820; unfinished.

City Art Gallery, Bradford.

204 STANDING MALE NUDE (BACK VIEW)

Canvas, 77½ × 35½ (sight).

Coll.: Manchester Academy of Fine Arts, from whom purchased 1953.

Exh.: York, 1911(112).

Painted *c.* 1825–30 as pendant to the Bradford *Standing Female Nude* (*The Bather*).

Art Gallery and Museum, Burnley.

205 STANDING FEMALE NUDE (BACK VIEW)

Canvas, 25¾ × 17¼.

Coll.: Purchased 1945.

Painted *c.* 1830.

Art Gallery and Museum, Burnley.

206 TWO MALE NUDES

Paper stuck on canvas, 21¼ × 23¾ (1⅝ strip added to top).

Coll.: Charles Ricketts (by 1933) and Charles Shannon Bequest, 1937.

Painted *c.* 1818–20.

Fitzwilliam Museum, Cambridge.

207 RECLINING FEMALE NUDE

Canvas, 14 × 18½.

Coll.: Purchased February, 1953 (No. P. 241).

Art Gallery and Museum, Doncaster.

KNEELING FEMALE NUDE (National Gallery of Ireland). *See* PLUTO CARRYING OFF PROSERPINE (No. 80*b*).

208 [pl. 19*b*] TWO SEATED FEMALE NUDES

Millboard, 27 × 20½.

Coll.: William Brodie, R.S.A., sold Dowell's, Edinburgh, 17.12.1881(338), bt. Royal Scottish Academy.

Lit.: Catalogue of the Permanent Collection, R.S.A., 1883, p. 20, No. 10.

Painted *c.* 1925–30. On the back is a study of a reclining female nude [see pl. 19*b*] which also shows a second study of part of the head and shoulders of the same model on the right of the composition.

Royal Scottish Academy, Edinburgh.

209 RECLINING MALE FIGURE (BACCHANAL)

Millboard (enlarged on three sides), 23 × 28.

Coll.: Etty Sale, 6–9.5.1850 (either 198 or 436), both bt. Sharpin; J. F. Sharpin, sold 21.3.1863(103) *A Bacchanalian Figure reclining on a Leopard's skin,* 'purchased at the Artist's Sale. The background added by C. Baxter'. This, and a 'companion picture' were bt. in 32 gns.

Exh.: York, 1949(67).

Similar in subject and date (*i.e.* 1835–40) to the *Reclining Male Nude* belonging to Mr. A. W. Bacon.

The Watts Gallery, Compton, Guildford.

210 [pl. 28*a*] TWO STANDING MALE NUDES

Canvas, 28 × 23.

Coll.: Cecil Rea; Mrs. Constance Rea; Miss Amy Halford, who presented it to Leeds 1953.

Lit.: Leeds Art Calendar, VII, No. 22, Summer, 1953, p. 5 (repr. p. 4).

Painted *c.* 1820–5.

City Art Gallery, Leeds.

211 STANDING MALE NUDE (THE BOWMAN)

Millboard laid on panel, 33¼ × 27¾.

Coll.: Lord Derwent, Huckness Hall, Scarborough, from whom purchased, 1947 (No. 47.A.47).

Painted *c.* 1825–30.

Museums and Art Gallery, Leicester.

212 STANDING FEMALE NUDE

Canvas, 40 × 25½.

Coll.: L. Lesser, sold anon., 3.1.1880(129) *A Female Figure,* bt. in 3 gns.; J. Leger & Sons from anon. source, bought N.A.C.F. and presented to the Tate Gallery, 1941 (No. 5305).

Exh.: A.C. Etty, 1955(26).

Repr.: Gaunt & Roe, pl. 41.

Painted *c.* 1835–40.

Tate Gallery, London.

213 HALF LENGTH MALE NUDE (BACK VIEW)

Millboard laid on canvas, 12 × 10½.

Coll.: Rev. Chauncy Hare Townshend Bequest 1869 (No. 1421–'69).

Painted *c.* 1820(?).

Victoria and Albert Museum, London.

214 STANDING FEMALE NUDE WITH HELMET

Millboard, 25½ × 18½.

Coll.: Purchased 1868 (No. 872–'68).

Repr.: Gaunt & Roe, pl. 39.

Painted *c.* 1835–40. A copy of this by B. R. Haydon is in the Graves Art Gallery, Sheffield, millboard laid on plywood, 24 × 17½. Appears to be inscribed 'Haydon ——' (bottom right). Another version is at York, millboard, 25¼ × 18½, presented by H. C. Hayes 1947 (No. 93/1947); exhibited York, 1948(26). It also may only be a copy.

Victoria and Albert Museum, London.

215 RECLINING FEMALE NUDE ('THE DELUGE')

Millboard laid on panel (enlarged on all sides: top 2⅜, bottom 4⅛, left 2¼, right 2½), 25 × 27.

Coll.: (?)Charles Oddie, sold 18.3.1854(115) *The Deluge:* 'a female figure, drawn and

coloured with grand effect, and 3 ALs.s of Etty relating to it', bt. in 30 gns.; William Wethered, sold 27.2.1858(60) *The Deluge*: 'female lying on a rock' bt. Colls £24 13*s*.; not in Charles T. Maud Sale 1864, and presented by him to the Victoria and Albert Museum 1871 (No. 225—'71).
Repr.: C. H. Collins Baker & M. R. James, *British Painting*, 1933, p. 183, pl. 120.

Described in the 1907 Catalogue as 'signed and dated on back 1815'. There are two Etty ALs.s (now almost illegible) on the back addressed from Coney Street, York, but the dates are invisible. In one letter Wass, the engraver, is mentioned (he was born 1817), and in the other Etty speaks of the extensions to the painting. The style dates it to *c*. 1835–45.
Victoria and Albert Museum, London.

216 STANDING FEMALE NUDE (BACK VIEW)
Panel, 24⅞ × 18⅞.
Coll.: Purchased 1871 (No. 1607—'71).
Exh.: (?)*Autumn Loan Exh., Some Victorian Painters*, Hanley, Stoke-on-Trent, December, 1936–January, 1937(9).
Repr.: Gaunt & Roe, pl. 40.
Painted *c*. 1835–40.
Victoria and Albert Museum, London.

217 SLEEPING NUDE FEMALE
Canvas, 9½ × 12½.
Coll.: Rev. Alexander Dyce Bequest (No. D. 37).
Painted *c*. 1845–9. Possibly retouched on the hands and feet.
Victoria and Albert Museum, London.

218 WOMAN AT A FOUNTAIN
Millboard, 24¼ × 18¼.
Coll.: Rev. Alexander Dyce Bequest (No. D. 52).
Repr.: Gaunt & Roe, pl. 1 (in colour).
Painted *c*. 1840–5.
Victoria and Albert Museum, London.

CROUCHING FEMALE NUDE 'THE RING' (Victoria and Albert Museum). *See* HERO AWAITING LEANDER (No. 61).

219 SEATED MALE NUDE
Millboard, 36 × 25.
Coll.: F. Hindley Smith Bequest, January 1940.
Two studies for an *Andromeda* are on the back.
City Art Gallery, Manchester.

220 STANDING FEMALE NUDE (TURNING TO RIGHT: BACK VIEW)
Millboard, 21¾ × 14½.

Coll.: J. G. Sampson Bequest 1942 (No. 149).
Painted *c*. 1835–40.
Ashmolean Museum, Oxford.

221 STOOPING FEMALE NUDE (BACK VIEW)
Thick paper laid on panel, 21⅝ × 18½.
Coll.: Presented by Sir J. D. Linton, P.R.I., 1906.
Painted *c*. 1835–40. Appears to be the same model as in the Ashmolean picture No. 149 (*v. supra*).
Art Gallery of Western Australia, Perth.

222 & 223 SEATED FEMALE NUDE LOOKING LEFT (THE BATHER)
SEATED FEMALE NUDE LOOKING RIGHT (THE BATHER)
Both paintings on millboard (circular), 9¾ dia.
Coll.: James Orrock, R.I.
Exh.: Edinburgh, 1886 (1432 & 1435); *A Century of British Art, 1737–1837*, Grosvenor Gallery, 1888(196 & 255); York, 1949(56 & 57).
Lit.: R. R. Tatlock, *Catalogue of the Lady Lever Art Gallery*, I, 1928, p. 95, Nos. 164 & 165, repr. pl. 7.
Repr.: *The Connoisseur*, XCI, April, 1933, pp. 221 and 311.
Painted *c*. 1845–9.
The Lady Lever Art Gallery, Port Sunlight.

STANDING FEMALE NUDE (Musée du Louvre, Paris).
See EVE (No. 12).

224 STANDING MALE NUDE, LEFT ARM UPRAISED
Canvas (enlarged along top by (?)later hand), 27 × 19½.
Coll.: Mrs. Robert Frank, London (1956). Purchased 1956.
Painted *c*. 1816–18.
Rhode Island School of Design, Providence, U.S.A.

225 SEATED MALE NUDE, HEAD BENT OVER KNEES
Paper laid on canvas, 19 × 19¾.
Coll.: Mrs. Robert Frank, London (1956). Purchased 1956.
Painted *c*. 1818–20.
Rhode Island School of Design, Providence, U.S.A.

226 BACK VIEW OF STANDING MALE NUDE IN BOAT
Paper laid on panel, 27 × 20.
Coll.: Anon., sold 18.11.1955(81A), bt. Wells 35 gns.; with Mrs. Robert Frank. Purchased 1956.
Painted *c*. 1818–20. The boat added as an afterthought, perhaps by another hand.
Rhode Island School of Design, Providence, U.S.A.

227 [pl. 28*b*] SEATED FEMALE NUDE

Millboard, 19 × 15.

Coll.: With the Cooling Gallery 1937; purchased 1953 (No. 53.129).

Lit.: Museum Notes, Rhode Island School of Design, XI, No. 2, Winter 1953 (and repr.).

Painted *c.* 1825.

Rhode Island School of Design, Providence, U.S.A.

228 STANDING FEMALE NUDE (FULL FACE)

Millboard laid on panel, 27¼ × 20½.

Coll.: Charles Morgan, sold 20.2.1858(125), bt. Butler 62 gns.; Charles Butler, sold 7.7.1911 (46), bt. Sir Charles Dewar 11 gns.; Marsh F. Oliver; with Savile Gallery; Graves Gift 1937 (No. 161).

Exh.: Sheffield, 1934(297); York, 1949(63).

Painted *c.* 1824–8.

Graves Art Gallery, Sheffield.

229 RECLINING FEMALE NUDE

Millboard, 18 × 23½.

Coll.: Presented to Tel-Aviv by Mr. and Mrs. Claude Hyman, Winnipeg, Canada, 1956.

Exh.: Recent Acquisitions, Fifth Collection, Ben-Uri Art Gallery, June–July, 1956(1).

Painted *c.* 1845–9.

Museum of Art, Tel-Aviv, Israel.

230 [pl. 5*b*] MALE NUDE WITH STAFF

Millboard, 15⅞ × 12.

Coll.: Roberts, sold 18.7.1938(169), bt. in 2½ gns.; purchased G. J. Wolstenholme Bequest Funds 1948 (No. 399/1948).

Exh.: York, 1949(92); A.C. *Etty,* 1955(5).

Painted *c.* 1814–16. Compare with the drawing *Male Nude with Staff* (York).

City Art Gallery, York.

231 STANDING MALE NUDE (THE BOWMAN)

Millboard, 21¾ × 16.

Coll.: Josiah Rhodes, who presented it to York 1911 (No. 68/1911).

Exh.: York, 1911(137); York, 1948(33).

A study for the 1836 *Prodigal Son* is on the back, with a label '140 The Prodigal Son—A Study from the life'.

City Art Gallery, York.

232 STANDING FEMALE NUDE ('THE INDIAN GIRL')

Millboard, 30 × 22.

Coll.: F. R. Meatyard; Sir Kenneth Clark; with Messrs. Ernest, Brown & Phillips, London (1949–50), sold 27.4.1951(78), bt. York 180 gns. (No. 577/1951).

Exh.: British Art, Manchester, 1934(89); R.A.

British Art, 1934(639); *Paintings by William Etty, R.A.,* 132nd Exh., Oxford Arts Club, April–May, 1935(34); B.C. *La Peinture Anglaise: XVIIIᵉ et XIXᵉ Siècles,* Louvre, Paris 1938(44) and repr. in supplement; B.C. *British Painting from Hogarth to Turner,* Hamburg, Oslo, Stockholm and Copenhagen, 1949–50(43); *Pictures from Yorkshire Galleries,* Sheffield, June–July, 1952(62).

Lit.: The Burlington Magazine, LXIV, February, 1934, repr. p. 53; *York Preview* 15, IV, July, 1951, p. 175 and repr.

Repr.: Gaunt & Roe, pl. 25.

Somewhat repainted; lips and drapery are brushed in with colours not found in Etty's palette. The original study probably painted *c.* 1840–5.

City Art Gallery, York.

233 RECLINING MALE NUDE WITH SPEAR

Millboard, 14¾ × 20¼.

Coll.: Presented by T. Grey of York, 1953 (No. 676/1953).

Painted *c.* 1817–18. the pose is reminiscent of *Manlius Hurled from the Rock,* and may be a preliminary study for this painting.

City Art Gallery, York.

234 [pl. 36*b*] MALE NUDE WITH UPSTRETCHED ARMS

Millboard, 23½ × 17.

Coll.: Sir Claude Phillips Bequest 1924 (No. 74/1924).

Exh.: York, 1948(23); A.C. *Etty,* 1955(17) and repr. pl. IIIa.

Painted *c.* 1828–30.

City Art Gallery, York.

235 RECLINING FEMALE NUDE

Canvas, 17 × 21.

Coll.: Presented by Sir W. H. Lever, Bart., 1911 (No. 00/1911).

Exh.: York, 1911(89 or 103); York, 1948(3); A.C. *Twelve Yorkshire Artists of the Past,* 1951(6).

Painted *c.* 1820–5.

City Art Gallery, York.

236 RECLINING FEMALE NUDE IN LANDSCAPE

Panel, 18⅝ × 24¾.

Coll.: May Siward Surtees, Heighington, Co. Durham; Arthur Coulter, York, from whom purchased 1952 (No. 632/1952).

Lit.: York Preview 19, V, July, 1952, p. 216, and repr. p. 217.

Painted *c.* 1830–5. The landscape is unusually detailed for Etty.

City Art Gallery, York.

NUDE STUDIES:
PRIVATE COLLECTIONS

237 SEATED FEMALE NUDE ('CONTEMPLATION')
Millboard laid on panel, 20½ × 16⅞.
Coll.: Augustus Walker; Ralph Edwards, sold
23.12.1943(85), bt. Anderson; sold Sotheby's,
4.6.1947(25), bt. in Gale £24.
Exh.: Constable and his Contemporaries, Hampstead, 1951(51); A.C. *Etty,* 1955(35).
Repr.: Gaunt & Roe, pl. 43.
   Painted *c.* 1840–5.
Sir Colin Anderson, London.

NUDE FEMALE STUDY (A. W. Bacon Collection).
See 'VENUS NOW WAKES, AND WAKENS LOVE'
(No. 103*a*).

238 [pl. 47*b*] RECLINING MALE NUDE (BACCHANAL)
Millboard, 16 × 18.
Coll.: (?)Etty Sale 9.5.1850(436), bt. Sharpin
9½ gns.; Boswell & Son, Norwich, from whom
purchased by T. W. Bacon, 1926; A. W.
Bacon.
Exh.: R.A. *British Art,* 1934(654). On loan to
Birmingham Art Gallery.
Repr.: Gaunt & Roe, pl. 29.
   Painted *c.* 1835–40. Compare with the Watts
Gallery composition of the same subject. *A
Bacchante,* 'lying on a panther's skin' was in the
Wethered sale, 7.3.1856(132), bt. in 104 gns.,
resold 27.2.1858(92), bt. Rippe 15 gns.
A. W. Bacon, Esq., Otley, Suffolk.

239 STANDING FEMALE NUDE WITH NEGRESS GIRL
ATTENDANT
Millboard laid on panel, 26 × 20 (¾ strip
added along top).
Coll.: Adams Gallery, where purchased 1946.
Exh.: Paintings by William Etty, Adams Gallery,
March–April 1946(21) *Nude and Negress.*
   Painted *c.* 1835–40. A *Study of Nude Female
and Negro Attendant* was lent by A. G. B. Russell
to York, 1911(134).
R. A. Bevan, Esq., London.

240 RECLINING FEMALE NUDE (BACK VIEW) IN
LANDSCAPE WITH TWO DOGS
Millboard laid on canvas, 27 × 30½.
   Painted *c.* 1830–5.
M. Pierre Bordeaux-Groult, Paris.

241 [Colour plate, frontispiece.] RECLINING
FEMALE NUDE
Paper laid on canvas, 19 × 25.
Coll.: Mrs. Robert Frank (1956).
   Painted *c.* 1828–30. The same model as that
used for '*Venus now Wakes*'.
Peter Claas, Esq., London.

242 [pl. 39] RECLINING MALE NUDE (FORE-
SHORTENED)
Panel, 17⅜ × 21½.
Coll.: Sir K. Clark (by 1927); on long loan to
Tate Gallery, 1927–9.
Exh.: Paintings by William Etty, R.A., R. E. A.
Wilson, 24 Ryder Street, November, 1933(19);
Paintings by William Etty, R.A., 132nd Exh.,
Oxford Arts Club, April–May, 1935(43); A.C.
Etty, 1955(40).
   Painted *c.* 1825–8.
Sir Kenneth Clark, Saltwood Castle, Kent.

243 STANDING FEMALE NUDE BY A STREAM (BACK
VIEW)
Millboard laid on panel, 31½ × 22½.
   Painted *c.* 1825–6.
G. H. Constantine, Esq., Sheffield.

244 SEATED FEMALE NUDE IN LANDSCAPE
Millboard, 20¾ × 17¾.
Coll.: Chevalier Epifanio Rodriguez, sold
31.1.1913(136) *A Nymph,* bt. Grant 18 gns.;
Emeritus Professor Taylor.
   Painted *c.* 1818–20.
Commander Anthony Dunhill, R.N., London.

245 STANDING FEMALE NUDE FULL FACE, ARMS
UPRAISED
Inscr. (in ink along top): 'Etty Decr. 1842 No.
14'; and in pencil, just below: 'Nature unveiling herself *Etty.*'
Coll.: Knoedler, sold anon., 2.6.1919(59), bt.
Blackwell 10 gns.; Emeritus Professor E. G. R.
Taylor, D.Sc., F.R.G.S.
Commander Anthony Dunhill, R.N., London.

246 FEMALE NUDE HOLDING BASKET UPON HER HEAD
Canvas, 12¾ × 9½.
Inscribed twice on stretcher: 'Painted for
Bishop Luscombe 23 Dec. 1835.'
Miss M. Du Pontet, London.

247 HALF LENGTH MALE NUDE (BACK VIEW)
Panel, 19¼ × 11½.
Coll.: George Acton, York.
Repr.: Gaunt & Roe, pl. 24.
   Painted *c.* 1830–5.
The Lord Fairhaven.

248 DANCING FEMALE NUDE
Panel, 35 × 20¼.
Repr.: Gaunt & Roe, pl. 59.
   Painted *c.* 1835–40.
The Lord Fairhaven.

249 STANDING FEMALE NUDE IN PROFILE, LOOKING
RIGHT
Millboard, 26 × 19¾.
Coll.: Presented to D. L. A. Farr by Miss Helen

W. Henderson, Philadelphia, U.S.A., October, 1953.

Painted *c.* 1845–9, unfinished. This study, and seven more from the same collection which are now at the Courtauld Institute of Art—all on millboard, some painted both sides—form a useful group by which to study the evolution of Etty's technique. They are in varying stages of completion, and cover the years approximately 1815–45. (Courtauld Institute, Nos. 1–7.54, ex-coll. Henderson).

D. L. A. Farr, Esq., London.

250 RECLINING MALE NUDE, LEFT HAND ON KNEE (BACK VIEW)
Millboard, $11\frac{1}{2} \times 17\frac{1}{2}$.

Painted *c.* 1830–5.

Mrs. Robert Frank, London.

251 RECLINING MALE NUDE ('SLEEPING GLADIATOR')
Millboard, $26\frac{1}{2} \times 19\frac{1}{2}$.
Coll.: (?)Henry Burton; T. Gabriel; T. B. Gabriel.

Painted *c.* 1840. Similar in style to A. W. Bacon's *Reclining Male Nude.*

Mrs. E. M. Gabriel, Worplesdon, Surrey.

252 SEATED FEMALE NUDE ('BACCHANTE')
Panel, $23\frac{1}{2} \times 18\frac{1}{2}$.
Coll.: R. E. A. Wilson; Adams Gallery (until 1949); with Roland, Browse & Delbanco, sold to H. E. Bäcker, May, 1949.
Exh.: Paintings by William Etty, R.A., 132nd Exh., Oxford Arts Club, April–May, 1935(41); *Paintings by William Etty, R.A.,* Adams Gallery, May–June, 1936(12); *Paintings by William Etty,* Adams Gallery, March–April, 1946(4); *Aspects of British Romanticism,* Roland, Browse & Delbanco, March, 1949(1).
Repr.: Gaunt & Roe, pl. 42.

Painted *c.* 1835–40. Compare with the *Hero Awaiting Leander* compositions.

L. H. Gilbert, Esq., Lisbon.

253 HALF LENGTH FEMALE NUDE, RIGHT ARM RAISED TO HEAD
Millboard laid on canvas, $34\frac{1}{4} \times 27\frac{1}{2}$.
Coll.: F. W. Hooper, sold 21.2.1880(92), bt. Permain 10 gns.

Painted *c.* 1828–30. The same model as that used for '*Venus now Wakes, and Wakens Love*'.

Sir Eldred Hitchcock, Tanga, Kenya.

254 STANDING FEMALE NUDE (BACK VIEW)
Millboard laid on panel, 24×17.
Coll.: Anon., sold 16.3.1934(173), bt. Jeannerat 15 gns.
Exh.: A.C. *English Romantic Art,* 1947(58); B.C. *Cien Años de Pintura Británica 1730–1830,*

Madrid and Lisbon 1949(16); A.C. *Etty,* 1955 (39).

Painted *c.* 1825–30.

Pierre Jeannerat, Esq., Radlett, Herts.

255 GROUP OF FEMALE NUDES BY A LAKE
Canvas, $17 \times 12\frac{1}{2}$.
Repr.: Sacheverell Sitwell, *Narrative Pictures,* 1937, p. 66, pl. 91, *A Conversation.*

Painted *c.* 1830–5.

Francis F. Madan, Esq., London.

256 RECLINING FEMALE NUDE IN LANDSCAPE
Inscr. (?by Etty): 'Jan. 6 1838' (top centre).
Panel, 17×22.

The style of the painting appears to agree with the date inscribed, and is similar in draughtsmanship to drawings of this period (*e.g.* those at York of 1839–41).

Dr. Donaldo Manuel, Pasadena, California.

257 STANDING MALE PUTTO
Millboard, 13×9 (enlarged on three sides: $1\frac{3}{4}$ left, $1\frac{1}{2}$ top, 1 bottom).
Coll.: Mrs. Patricia (*née* Etty) Dimes, daughter of Walter Etty and niece to the artist; W. Lewis Collins; with the Adams Gallery, 1946; Lord Methuen.

An inscription on the back reads: 'A Study by Etty R.A. Given to me by his niece the wife of Mr. Dimes Squire of Olboton Hall near Blackawton, Devonshire W. Lewis Collins, Ringmore Tower near Teignmouth Devonshire.' Martha, daughter of Walter Etty, married William Piercy Dimes, 'Law Student', at St. James's, Westminster, 6 February, 1847.

The Lord Methuen.

258 TWO MALE NUDES IN LANDSCAPE
Panel (circular), $8\frac{3}{4}$ dia.
Coll.: Purchased *c.* 1934–6 in London saleroom.

Painted *c.* 1818–20. The painting has been attributed to Alfred Elmore, R.A.

E. C. Norris, Esq., Polesden Lacey.

259 SEATED FEMALE NUDE, HANDS CLASPED
Millboard, $12 \times 14\frac{3}{4}$.
Coll.: Gerald Reitlinger, sold Sotheby's, 13.10.-1954(97), bt. E. Speelman £20.
Repr.: Drawing and Design, IV, No. 25, July, 1928, p. 181.

Painted *c.* 1830–5.

E. Speelman, Esq., London.

260 [pl. 85*b*] STANDING MALE NUDE WITH SWORD (BACK VIEW), AND SEATED MALE NUDE (FULL FACE)
Inscr. (top right): 'Etty Nov.ʳ 1842 No. 10'.
Millboard, $24\frac{1}{2} \times 18$.

Coll.: Spink & Son, Ltd. (February, 1956); Mrs. Robert Frank.

Repr.: The Burlington Magazine, XCVIII, February, 1956, p. viii (advertisements).

The same model is shown in two poses. The seated figure is similar to the man holding a ram in the *Repentant Prodigal's Return to His Father* (Ashmolean, Oxford).

John Tillotson, Esq., London.

261 SEATED MALE NUDE, HEAD BENT OVER KNEES
Canvas, $20\frac{3}{4} \times 16\frac{3}{4}$.

Exh.: Montage Gallery, James Street, W.1, 1951.

Painted *c.* 1816–18, is similar in style and composition to the Rhode Island School of Design painting of the same description, except that the pose is seen here in right profile.

Alfred A. Wolmark, Esq., London.

262 HEAD AND SHOULDERS OF MALE NUDE
Millboard laid on panel, $25\frac{1}{4} \times 20$.

Exh.: Montage Gallery, 1951.

Painted *c.* 1830–5, this may be a study for either a Prometheus or a Crucifixion subject. A *Head of Saint Sebastian*, panel, $24 \times 19\frac{1}{2}$, was in the Wallis Sale, 19.3.1910(122), bt. A. N. Smith $2\frac{1}{2}$ gns.

Alfred A. Wolmark, Esq., London.

LANDSCAPES

263 [pl. 78*a*] ACOMB, 'THE PLANTATION'
Inscr. (?by Etty): 'Etty 1842' (bottom centre). Millboard (circular), $8\frac{1}{2}$ dia.

Coll.: Colonel M. H. Grant, sold 5.11.1954 (257), bt. York (No. 714/1954).

Lit.: Gilchrist, ii, p. 133; *York Preview* 29, VIII, January, 1955, p. 295.

Repr.: M. H. Grant, *History of English Landscape Painters*, 1926, pl. 172; *York Preview* 31, VIII, pp. 320–3.

A view of the stream in the grounds of the Rev. Isaac Spencer's house at Acomb, near York. J. J. Leeman, M.P., who afterwards owned 'The Plantation', misnamed it 'Acomb Priory'. The pond is now used as a settling pond by the Poppleton sugar beet factory. A drawing, $9\frac{1}{5} \times 12\frac{7}{10}$, shows what is probably 'The Plantation', with lake, cypress trees and house. (J. P. Knight Coll., 1870; P.D. 180 C, Portf. 252F/8/7655/7; Victoria and Albert Museum, London).

City Art Gallery, York.

264 CHURCH RUINS (?BOLTON ABBEY)
Millboard, $7\frac{7}{8} \times 12$.

Coll.: Elizabeth Ince-Binninington (step-daughter to Elizabeth ('Betsy') Etty); John Etty; Sarah (*née* Etty) Bosch (great grand-daughter of John Etty senr.); Jacobus J. T. Bosch (until 1956).

Possibly painted 1841, at the same time as *The Strid, Bolton Abbey* (*q.v.*).

Wed. E. Etty-Hoeyenbos, Utrecht.

265 CHURCH RUINS (?BOLTON OR FOUNTAINS ABBEY)
Millboard, 12×8.

Coll.: as for *Church Ruins* (*?Bolton Abbey*).

Painted *c.* 1841.

Mr. Jacobus J. T. Bosch, Voorburg.

266 GIVENDALE CHURCH
Millboard, $11\frac{1}{4} \times 8\frac{1}{4}$.

Coll.: John Singleton, Givendale; presented by Mrs. Elizabeth Rose Challoner, 1946 (No. 78/1946).

Exh.: R.A., 1848(161) *A Sketch of Landscape, Givendale, Yorkshire*; York, 1911(20) *Givendale Church, before Restoration*, lent Mrs. Singleton; York, 1948(31); York, 1949(84) and repr.

Repr.: York Preview 8, II, October, 1949; *The Burlington Magazine*, XC, January, 1950, fig. 24, facing p. 25.

City Art Gallery, York.

267 GIVENDALE, THE FISHPOND
Panel, $11 \times 7\frac{3}{4}$.

Coll.: as for *Givendale Church*, presented 1946 (No. 79/1946).

Exh.: York, 1911(22); York, 1948(32); York, 1949(85).

Painted *c.* 1848. The site was built over during the 1930s, and the stream tapped for Pocklington's water supply.

City Art Gallery, York.

268 [pl. 79] LANDSCAPE
Millboard, $18\frac{1}{2} \times 24$.

Coll.: Purchased locally by York, 1949 (No. 29/1949).

Exh.: York, 1949(96); A.C. *Etty*, 1955(33).

Lit.: York Preview 16, IV, October, 1951, p. 183 (and repr.).

Painted *c.* 1840. Perhaps a view of the grounds at 'The Plantation', Acomb, near York. A standing female nude study (back view) is painted on the back.

City Art Gallery, York.

269 [pl. 78*b*] LANDSCAPE WITH HOUSE
Millboard, $12\frac{1}{2} \times 11\frac{3}{4}$.

Coll.: Elizabeth ('Betsy') Etty, niece and house-keeper to the artist; Elizabeth Binnington; John Charles Mellor (Elizabeth Binnington's adopted son, died 1929) to his sister Sarah Bosch; Jacobus J. T. Bosch (until 1954).

Exh.: A.C. *Etty*, 1955(30).

Painted *c.* 1840. The subject may be either the Rev. Isaac Spencer's house 'The Plantation', Acomb, or the Singleton's home at Givendale.

Ir. Thomas H. Etty, Leidschendam.

270 POCKLINGTON(?) CHURCH

Millboard, 8 × 11⅞.

Coll.: as for *Church Ruins (?Bolton Abbey).*

Painted *c.* 1840. A faint pencil sketch of a standing female nude is on the back, also an inscription: '8ᵈ P. G. Pater(?) 26.'

Mr. Jacobus J. T. Bosch, Voorburg.

271 [pl. 74] THE STRID, BOLTON ABBEY

Millboard, 8¼ × 11½.

Coll.: John Wood; Colonel M. H. Grant, sold 17.12.1954(84), bt. Agnew for York (No. 723/1954).

Exh.: S. A., 1849(XXXVI) lent John Wood; A.C. *Early English Landscapes from Colonel Grant's Collection*, 1952–3(20); A.C. *Etty*, 1955(44); *Peintures anglaises des collections d'York et du Yorkshire*, Musée des Beaux-Arts, Dijon, 1957(27).

Lit.: Gilchrist, ii, pp. 124, 339; *York Preview* 31, VIII, July, 1955, pp. 320–1 (and repr.).

Exhibited at the Society of Arts as *A Landscape View of the Stid [sic] Bolton Abbey, Yorkshire*, and there dated 1843. An inscription on the back reads: 'Mr. Wood purchased at the sale of the late / Mr. W. Etty's pictures a parcel of sketches / of which this is one. Lot. No. 375 at Christies'. On the panel in the back of the frame is another inscription: 'Strid, Bolton Abbey / Wm. Etty R.A. / 1843'. Neither of these is to be trusted: lot 375 was in fact an Etty copy after Titian; Etty visited Bolton Abbey in August, 1841, and probably made this study direct from the subject. The 'Strid' is a famous stepping-stone across the River Wharfe, where the 'Boy of Egremont' (son of Lady Alice de Romilly) was supposed to have been drowned in the twelfth century.

City Art Gallery, York.

272 THREE SEASCAPES

All three are on canvas laid on hardboard, 10¾ × 7⅞.

Coll.: Thomas Bodley; Miss J. A. Bodley, sold Sotheby's, 14.5.1930(23) *Three Studies of the Sea and Sea Coast*, bt. Dr. Tancred Borenius £1. [Lot 22 was also of three similar studies, millboard, 7½ × 15½, bt. Morant £8.]

Exh.: *Paintings by William Etty, R.A.*, R. E. A. Wilson, 24 Ryder Street, November, 1933(20)

A Study of the Sea. Two other studies were lent by Mrs. Vitale Bloch (Nos. 14 & 26), and a third (No. 17) was owned by Wilson.

Possibly among the studies Etty made of the sea at Brighton, 1836, in preparation for his *The Sirens and Ulysses*. They seem to be of one place and date, and show an autumn or winter sea.

Mrs. Anne Marie Borenius, Coombe Bissett, Wilts.

273 [pl. 60b] YORK, MONK BAR

Canvas, 30 × 24.

Coll.: Etty Sale, 10.5.1850(652) *Monk Bar, York*, bt. Rought 11½ gns.; sold Foster's, 3.5.1865(132) *The York Gate*, 30 × 20, from an anonymous Lancashire collection; purchased from Mr. and Mrs. Bolton, Bradford, 1938 (No. 64/1938).

Exh.: York, 1948(11); York, 1949(74); A.C. *Etty*, 1955(27).

Repr.: James M. Biggins, *Etty and York*, York, 1949 (cover).

The painting has a label on back 'The York Gate'. There were two other pictures in the Etty Sale (lots 661 and 662), listed as 'Inner View of Walmgate Bar, York', and 'Outer View of the same', painted in 1838 (Gilchrist, ii, p. 85). It seems likely that *Monk Bar* also dates from 1838. A picture entitled *Micklegate Bar, York*, was lent by Benson Rathbone to an exhibition at the Liverpool Art Club, 1881 (314).

City Art Gallery, York.

STILL-LIFE AND BIRDS

274 GRAPE FRUIT AND GRAPES

Panel, 10 × 10.

Coll.: John Elliot Bequest 1917.

Williamson Art Gallery and Museum, Birkenhead.

275 DEAD PHEASANT

Millboard, 12½ × 17½.

Coll.: (?)Edward Harper, sold 16.4.1853(58) *A pheasant and a snowdrop*, bt. Colls 42 gns.; (?)H. A. J. Munro of Novar, sold 11.5.1867 (116), bt. Ensom [*sic*] 16½ gns.; Mrs. A. B. Lamb (by 1911); H. D. Molesworth, sold Sotheby's, 9.5.1956(130), bt. Mrs. Bohener £4.

Exh.: York, 1911(43).

Lit.: W. E. Frost, A.R.A. & Henry Reeve, *Catalogue of the Collection . . . of the late H. A. J. Munro of Novar (n.d.)*, No. 574, *Study of a Pheasant* 'Vase of Flowers, to right. Snowdrop, Forget-me-not, etc. 12½ × 16½'.

Mrs. V. R. W. Bohener, London.

276 [pl. 70b] STILL-LIFE WITH EWER
Panel, 8 × 12.
Coll.: Edwin Bullock, sold 21.5.1870(68) *Fruit in a Shell and a Silver Ewer*, bt. Holmes 40 gns.; Edward Dinwoody Wilmot (until 1887); J. A. Chatwin.
Lit.: P. B. Chatwin, *Life Story of J. A. Chatwin, F.R.I.B.A., F.S.A.Scot., 1830–1907*, Oxford, 1952, p. 40.
Painted *c.* 1843–5.
Philip B. Chatwin, Esq., Leamington, Warws.

277 [pl. 70a] FLOWER STUDY
Millboard, 17½ × 23½.
Coll.: Mrs. Thomas Collier, sold 11.2.1921(63), bt. Sampson £60. Present location unknown.
Repr.: Drawing and Design, IV, 25, July, 1928, p. 181.
Painted *c.* 1838–40.

278 [pl. 71] STILL-LIFE WITH GLASS
Panel, 12½ × 16¼.
Coll.: Henry Burton; T. Gabriel; T. B. Gabriel.
Exh.: (?)B.I., 1843(318) *Fruit*, 15 × 19; (?) R.S.A., 1843(294) *A Study of Fruit*; A.C. *Etty*, 1955(34).
Mrs. E. M. Gabriel, Worplesdon, Surrey.

279 STILL-LIFE WITH PHEASANT
Millboard, 14¼ × 20¼.
Coll.: as for *Still-life with Glass*.
Painted *c.* 1845–9.
Mrs. E. M. Gabriel, Worplesdon, Surrey.

280 STILL-LIFE WITH STONE JAR
Millboard, 13 × 19¾.
Coll.: as for *Still-life with Glass*.
Painted *c.* 1845–9.
Mrs. E. M. Gabriel, Worplesdon, Surrey.

281 BOWL OF FLOWERS
Panel, 9⅜ × 15¼ (on white gesso ground).
Coll.: Robert Cochorane; with Fine Art Society (May–July, 1956); Lady Hodder Williams.
Painted *c.* 1840–5. The name 'Keir' is inscribed on the back.
Lady Hodder Williams, London.

282 STUDY OF A PEACOCK
Canvas, 22½ × 31½.
Coll.: Presented by Sir Joseph Whitworth, Bt., 1882.
Exh.: Animals in Art, Whitechapel, 1907(48); *British Art*, Manchester, 1934(88); R.A. *British Art*, 1934(645), repr. pl. CXX in commemorative souvenir; B.C. *Cien Años de Pintura Británica 1730–1830*, Madrid and Lisbon, 1949 (15); B.C. *British Painting from Hogarth to Turner*, Hamburg, Oslo, Stockholm, Copenhagen 1949–50(42).
Repr.: Basil Taylor, *Animal Painting in England, from Barlow to Landseer*, Penguin Books, 1955, pl. v (in colour), facing p. 48.
This, and the Tate Gallery *Study of a Peacock*, may be studies for the 1826 *Judgment of Paris* (*q.v.*), although the pose of the Manchester peacock is repeated exactly in the 1846 *Judgment of Paris* (T. Laughton Collection, *q.v.*).
City Art Gallery, Manchester.

283 PHEASANT AND BOWL
Millboard, 20 × 26¼.
Coll.: F. B. Buckland, sold 3.4.1922(67) *Still Life*: 'A pheasant, fruit, and vase of flowers', panel, 20 × 26, bt. Sampson 22 gns.
Exh.: A.C. *Etty*, Museum & Art Gallery, Luton, August, 1955 (*hors catalogue*).
Painted *c.* 1845–9, on grey primed millboard and left unfinished.
F. J. Manning, Esq., Streatley, Beds.

284 STUDY OF A PEACOCK
Millboard, 19¾ × 25¼.
Coll.: Robert E. Smithson; E. W. Smithson (great-nephew of the artist), sold 12.3.1928 (146), bt. Martin 17 gns. for Tate Gallery (Clarke Fund; No. 4384).
Perhaps painted 1826; compare with the Manchester version.
Tate Gallery, London.

285 STILL-LIFE: DEAD PHEASANT
Millboard, 11½ × 9.
Coll.: Mrs. John Singleton; Susan Singleton; presented by Mrs. E. R. Challoner 1946 (No. 92/1946).
Exh.: York, 1948(29), York, 1949(82).
Lit.: Gilchrist, ii, pp. 135–6.
Painted 1842. An ink inscription on the back reads: 'Susan Singleton / by Wm. Etty, R.A. / The Gift of Her Mother / Sepr. 2nd. 1844.' Mrs. Elizabeth Rose Challoner (previously Mrs. Chisnal Hamerton) was a niece of the Misses Singleton of Givendale.
City Art Gallery, York.

286 [pl. 82a] STILL-LIFE: DEAD PHEASANT AND FRUIT
Paper laid on millboard, 17½ × 15.
Coll.: (?)R. Nicholson, sold 13.7.1849(74) *Pheasant and Fruit*, bt. Morgan 14½ gns.; presented by Mrs. E. R. Challoner 1946 (No. 81/1946).
Exh.: York, 1948(28); York, 1949(81); A.C. *Etty*, 1955(29) *Still Life with Pheasant and Peach; Peintures anglaises des collections d'York et du Yorkshire*, Musée des Beaux-Arts, Dijon, 1957(22).

Lit.: Gilchrist, ii, pp. 107–8; *The Burlington Magazine*, XC, January 1950, p. 25.

Perhaps painted c. 1839. A torn label on the back reads: ' "Dead [pheas]ant [an]d [pea]ch" by W. Etty [painted or purchased ?] at G——. W. B. Morgan.'

City Art Gallery, York.

287 STILL-LIFE WITH LEMON, PEACHES AND GRAPES
Millboard, 8 × 12.
Coll.: Presented by Mrs. E. R. Challoner 1946 (No. 80/1946).
Exh.: York, 1948(30); York, 1949(83); A.C. *Twelve Yorkshire Artists of the Past*, 1951(8); *Peintures anglaises des collections d'York et du Yorkshire*, Musée des Beaux-Arts, Dijon, 1957(23).
Repr.: York Preview 8, II, October, 1949.
Painted c. 1840–5.
City Art Gallery, York.

COPIES AFTER OLD MASTERS
ANTHONY VAN DYCK

288 PORTRAIT OF A LADY AND CHILD
Watercolour on thin card, $3\frac{4}{5} \times 2\frac{3}{10}$.
Coll.: Robert E. Smithson; E. W. Smithson, sold 12.3.1928(140), bt. York.
Copy made in July, 1830, after the painting in the Louvre (Glück, 1931, No. 338).
City Art Gallery, York.

289 PORTRAIT OF A STANDING MALE FIGURE AND CHILD
Watercolour on thin card, $3\frac{7}{10} \times 2\frac{1}{5}$.
Coll.: as for the above.
Copy made in July, 1830, after the painting in the Louvre (Glück, 1931, No. 339).
City Art Gallery, York.

290 HALF LENGTH PORTRAIT OF A MAN
Watercolour on thin card, $2\frac{7}{10} \times 2\frac{1}{10}$.
Coll.: as for the above.
Copy made in July, 1830, after the painting in the Louvre (Glück, 1931, No. 347).
City Art Gallery, York.

GIORGIONE

291 FÊTE CHAMPÊTRE
Two versions:
(i) [pl. 35*b*] Canvas, 28 × 36.
Coll.: William Etty, R.A., sold 8.5.1850(379), bt. Hobson 32 gns.; Lady Eastlake, sold 2.6.1894(51), bt. Agnew 220 gns.; Sir Luke Fildes, R.A., sold 24.6.1927(50), bt. Sampson 42 gns.; Sir Alec Martin (by 1933).
Exh.: *Exhibition for the Benefit of the Distressed Peasantry of France*, The French Gallery, then removed to the Society of British Artists, Suffolk Street, c. 1871–2(170); York, 1911(119);

Paintings by William Etty, R.A., R. E. A. Wilson, 24 Ryder Street, November, 1933(18); A.C. *Etty*, 1955(19).
Lit.: Gilchrist, i, p. 292.
W. A. Martin, Esq., London.
(ii) Canvas, 17 × $21\frac{1}{2}$.
Coll.: F. E. Sidney (by 1908), sold 10.12.1937 (39), bt. Howard 12 gns.
Exh.: B.F.A.C., 1908(140); B.F.A.C., Winter, 1912(15); B.F.A.C., Winter, 1924–5(19).

This version lacks the nude female figure on the left. There are no sure grounds for the attribution to Etty of this picture. Another, poor quality copy attributed to Etty was sold anon., 12.3.1954(137), bt. Schreisheimer £7.

SIR THOMAS LAWRENCE

292 STUDY OF A BOY'S HEAD
293 STUDY OF A GIRL'S HEAD
Both paintings on canvas, 14 × 12.
Coll.: Purchased with the G. J. Wolstenholme Bequest Funds, 1948 (Nos. 96 & 107/1948).
Exh.: York, 1949(88 & 87).
Lit.: Kenneth Garlick, *Lawrence*, 1954, p. 18.
The boy's head is a copy of one of the *Pattison Boys*, and the girl is a copy from the *Lady Templetown and Child* (National Gallery, Washington, c. 1802) by Lawrence. Perhaps painted c. 1807–8.
City Art Gallery, York.

REMBRANDT

294 SELF PORTRAIT
Watercolour on thin card (oval), 3 × $2\frac{3}{10}$.
Coll.: Robert E. Smithson; E. W. Smithson, sold 12.3.1928(140), bt. York.
Copy made in July, 1830, after the painting in the Louvre (Bredius, No. 29).
City Art Gallery, York.

295 SELF PORTRAIT
Watercolour on thin card, $3\frac{1}{5} \times 2\frac{1}{5}$.
Coll.: as for the above.
Copy made in July, 1830, after the painting in the Louvre (Bredius, No. 53).
City Art Gallery, York.

SIR JOSHUA REYNOLDS

296 CYMON AND IPHIGENIA
Panel, $16\frac{1}{2} \times 19\frac{1}{2}$.
Coll.: R. Nicholson, sold 13.7.1849(182), bt. White 26 gns.; William John Broderip, sold 18.6.1853(46), bt. Fuller 18 gns.; H. A. J. Munro of Novar, sold 11.5.1867(121), bt. Hodgkin 14 gns.; Anon. (27 × 36), sold 15.2.1904(71), bt. Wood 6 gns.; W. Y. Baker,

sold (11 × 14) 17.11.1916(512), bt. Partridge 17 gns.; Sir Colin Anderson; Anon., sold Sotheby's, 4.6.1947(26), bt. Roland, Browse & Delbanco £19, from whom purchased by Walton.

Lit.: W. E. Frost, A.R.A. and Henry Reeve, *Catalogue of the Collection . . . of the late H. A. J. Munro of Novar*, [n.d.] No. 579 (16¼ × 19¼).

Sir William Walton, London.

297 GEORGIANA, DUCHESS OF DEVONSHIRE AND HER DAUGHTER

Canvas 43½ × 55¾ (*i.e.* the size of the original).

Coll.: Commissioned from Sir Thomas Lawrence by George IV in 1825, but Lawrence gave the task to Etty. The picture appears as No. 687 in an inventory for 'Carlton Palace'. Lawrence received 400 gns. for the work. A MS. inventory of the royal pictures drawn up under Redgrave's supervision contains a note stating that the compiler was told by Etty himself of the real authorship of the copy. In a letter to Walter (n.d., (?)1827, British Museum Add. MS. 38794E, ff. 115–16) Etty mentions a sum of £40 for the 'Sir Joshua copy'.

Lit.: *The Art Journal*, January, 1855, p. 6.

H.M. the Queen (Windsor Castle).

PETER PAUL RUBENS

298 [pl. 41*b*] APOTHEOSIS OF THE DUKE OF BUCKINGHAM

Panel, 12½ × 9¾ (painted circle, 9½ dia.).

Coll.: Charles H. Lewis, sold 23.2.1951(96), bt. Tooth 8 gns. for York (No. 571/1951).

Exh.: A.C. *Etty*, 1955(20).

Copy after the painting in the National Gallery, London (No. 187), formerly in the possession of Sir David Wilkie, R.A. The original is a sketch intended for a ceiling at Osterley Park, and was once thought to be an *Apotheosis of William the Silent*. Another copy of this work, (24½ square), attributed to Eugène Delacroix, was advertised in *The Burlington Magazine*, XCVIII, September, 1956, p. vii, as the property of French & Company, Inc., New York.

City Art Gallery, York.

299 DIANA RETURNING FROM THE CHASE (Copy attributed to Etty)

Inscr. (?by Etty): 'William Etty 1824' (bottom left).

Canvas, 25 × 29.

Coll.: Mrs. A. Anderson (from her father) Gift 1948.

Exh.: York, 1949(61).

Copy after the picture at Dresden. The copy is clumsy and appears to be heavily overpainted. A *Diana and nymphs* 'after Rubens' was in the Etty Sale, 1850(112), bt. with lot 113 by Hulton £9 5s.

Museum and Art Gallery, Rotherham.

300 IXION AND THE FALSE JUNO

Canvas, 14 × 18¼.

Coll.: Etty Sale, 6.5.1850(108) *Jupiter and Juno*, 'after Rubens', bt. Birch 14½ gns.; Metchley Abbey Sale, Foster's, 23.2.1857(LVI), measuring 15½ × 11; 1st Earl of Northbrook; disposed of after death of the 2nd Earl 1929, present location unknown.

Exh.: York, 1911(8).

Major L. C. Floyd McKeon, Worcester, possesses a work attributed to Etty entitled *Ixion Embracing the False Juno*, measuring 36 × 26.

301 THE RAPE OF THE SABINE WOMEN

Canvas, 25½ × 30.

Coll.: Benson Rathbone; purchased with the G. J. Wolstenholme Bequest Funds 1948 (No. 105/1948).

Exh.: York, 1911(54); York, 1949(91).

This is a free adaptation of a series of details from the foreground group in the painting in the National Gallery, London (No. 38). The soldier who is bending down and seizing a woman's dress has been moved across the composition to the right, and the horse on the right of the original painting has been put next to the central group of the two men and two women. A watercolour study (6$\frac{9}{10}$ × 5) for the soldier seen full face on the left of the York painting, belongs to Mr. K. Fraser, Llandudno.

City Art Gallery, York.

TINTORETTO

302 ECCE HOMO

Paper laid on thin card, 4 × 5⅞.

Coll.: Edward Harper, not in the Harper Sale 1853; Robert E. Smithson; E. W. Smithson, sold 12.3.1928(140), bt. York.

Inscribed on the back: 'Painted by W. Etty, R.A. at Venice [*i.e.* 1822–23] from a painting by Paul Veronese [*sic*] and given by him to E. Harper of 8 Brunswick Terrace Hove.' The sketch is of the panel over a doorway opposite the great *Crucifixion* in the Sala dell' Albergo, Scuola di San Rocco. The door pediment has been omitted, and the two side figures are on a level with the seated Christ.

City Art Gallery, York.

TITIAN

303 CHRIST AND THE MAGDALEN ('NOLI ME TANGERE')

Canvas, $42\frac{1}{4} \times 35\frac{1}{4}$ (*i.e.* the size of the original).

Coll.: Robert E. Smithson, sold 28.11.1891(66) *Noli Me Tangere*, bt. Moore £13; H. G. Simpson, Bristol (until 1951/52); Appleby Bros., London.

Exh.: *Yorks. Fine Art & Industrial*, York, July, 1866(514) *Copy of 'Rogers' Titian', in the National Gallery*, lent R. E. Smithson.

A copy after the painting in the National Gallery, London (No. 270), bequeathed by Samuel Rogers in 1855.

Messrs. Appleby Bros., London.

304 THE EDUCATION OF CUPID

Canvas, $15\frac{3}{4} \times 24\frac{1}{2}$.

Coll.: Etty Sale, 8.5.1850(378) *Venus binding Cupid* 'after Titian', bt. Birch 35 gns.; Metchley Abbey Sale, Foster's, 23.2.1857(LIX); 1st Earl of Northbrook; disposed of after the death of the 2nd Earl 1929.

Exh.: York, 1911(14).

Copy after the painting in the Borghese Gallery, Rome. A watercolour, 4×5, which was purchased by the City Art Gallery, Bradford, 1920, shows the composition in reverse. It was exhibited York, 1949(101).

Miss Walker, Mirfield, Yorks.

305 SUPPER AT EMMAUS

Canvas, $18 \times 26\frac{1}{2}$.

Coll.: J. I. Jefferson; purchased with the G. J. Wolstenholme Bequest Funds 1948 (No. 98/1948).

Exh.: York, 1911(34); York, 1949(90).

Lit.: Gilchrist, i, p. 293.

Painted July, 1830, after the painting in the Louvre, Paris.

City Art Gallery, York.

306 VENUS OF URBINO

Canvas, $47\frac{1}{4} \times 65$ (*i.e.* the size of the original).

Coll.: Etty Sale, 10.5.1850(632), bt. in Francklin [*sic*] 70 gns.; bought from Etty's executors by the Royal Scottish Academy 1853 (No. 6 in the 1883 R.S.A. catalogue).

Lit.: *Sketchbook II*, p. 48; *Autobiography*, pp. 38–9; Gilchrist, i, pp. 174, 181–4.

Painted in the Uffizi, July, 1823.

Royal Scottish Academy, Edinburgh.

VERONESE

307 EMBLEMATICAL FIGURE OF FORTUNE

Canvas, 14×12.

Coll.: (?)Etty Sale, 8.5.1850(376) *A legendary subject*, 'after P. Veronese', bt. Dr. Hamilton $12\frac{1}{2}$ gns.; Lord Leighton, sold 14.7.1896(376) *Fortune* 'after Veronese' ($12\frac{1}{2} \times 14$), bt. Shannon 2 gns.; Charles Shannon, R.A., sold 15.2.1935(18) bt. Heather $1\frac{1}{2}$ gns.; Emily and Gordon Bottomley Bequest 1949.

Exh.: York, 1949(37).

A copy made in 1823 after one of the allegorical figures from the ceiling decorations of the Sala del Collegio, Palazzo Ducale, Venice.

Public Library, Museum and Art Gallery, Carlisle.

308 [pl. 61a] ST. JOHN PREACHING

Canvas, $27\frac{1}{4} \times 21\frac{1}{4}$.

Coll.: Etty Sale, 6.5.1850(113) *St. John in the desert*, 'after P. Veronese' bt. with lot 112 by Hutton £9 5s. [presumably bt. in]; purchased from Etty's executors by the Royal Scottish Academy 1853 (No. 7 in the 1883 R.S.A. catalogue). Presented to the National Gallery of Scotland 1910 (No. 127).

Lit.: *Sketchbook II*, p. 48.

A free copy of the painting in the Borghese Palace, Rome, executed 1822–3.

National Gallery of Scotland, Edinburgh.

NOTE: The copies catalogued above represent a tiny fraction of the total number Etty made after Old Masters. In the Etty Sale (the catalogue of which provides a useful, if summary, check list of copies) there were almost sixty items, eleven of which were bought by Charles Birch of Metchley Abbey, Harborne. The 1st Earl of Northbrook later owned five of the Birch paintings in addition to five from other sources. Some of these were exhibited at Whitechapel in 1908, and again at York 1911. The collection was dispersed in 1929. For details of other copies consult Appendix II.

DRAWINGS

NOTE: A number of drawings and watercolours which relate to particular compositions have been catalogued with their appropriate paintings.

309 STUDY OF A WOMAN'S HEAD

Pastel, 14×10.

Coll.: Purchased from McDonald and Nicholson, 1931.

Williamson Art Gallery and Museum, Birkenhead.

310 SEATED FEMALE NUDE

Black chalk, heightened with white chalk on grey paper, $13\frac{5}{8} \times 9\frac{1}{4}$.

Coll.: Presented by W. A. Grist, 1939 (No. 132 '39).

Towards the upper left corner is a study of a man's head, apparently of Giovanni Battista Belzoni (1778–1823), African traveller. There are other 'action study' diagrammatic figures lower left. The style suggests a date *c.* 1825–30.
City Art Gallery, Birmingham.

311 [pl. 76a] SLEEPING FEMALE NUDE
Inscr.: 'Etty, R.A.' (bottom right).
Pencil heightened with white body colour, $11\frac{3}{4} \times 20\frac{5}{8}$.
Coll.: Presented by Alderman Lloyd, 1930 (No. 326 '30).
Possibly *c.* 1828–30.
City Art Gallery, Birmingham.

312 SAILING BOATS AND MISCELLANEOUS FIGURE STUDIES
Pencil, $4\frac{1}{2} \times 7\frac{3}{8}$ (two $\frac{1}{2}$ sheets of inside of a letter).
Coll.: Presented by Rev. G. Mountford 1948 (No. 1948–11–26–1).

The two sheets are inside an undated letter addressed to [Henry] Bone, from Buckingham Street, *c.* 1824–30.
British Museum, London.

313 STUDIES OF A WOMAN'S HEAD
Pencil, $4\frac{1}{2} \times 3$.
Coll.: as for *Sailing Boats* (No. 1948–11–26–5).

On recto are sketches of a woman's head seen in profile (? for *Judith*), and scribbled around these are names including those of Sir Thomas Lawrence, [Joseph] Strutt, Barker, [Earl of] Northbrook, and Hilton the painter. On the verso is part of a draft of a letter, now almost indecipherable.
British Museum, London.

314 RECLINING FEMALE NUDE
Black, white, blue and red pastel, $12 \times 18\frac{3}{4}$.
Coll.: Acquired 1895 (No. 1895–12–14–2).

Similar in style to the York *Female Nude Study*, and probably *c.* 1825–30. The feet have been left unfinished.
British Museum, London.

315 WOMAN IN PEASANT COSTUME
Inscr.: 'W. Etty/Miss Lisle 18[2?]7'.
Watercolour, $7 \times 4\frac{11}{16}$ (enlarged on three sides).
Coll.: Presented G. W. Duffet 1908 (No. 1908–1–6–1).
British Museum, London.

316 NUDE FIGURE OF A YOUNG GIRL
Black, red and white chalk, on light brown paper, $22\frac{3}{8} \times 16\frac{1}{8}$.

Coll.: Sir Robert Witt; Courtauld Institute (Witt Collection No. 3068).
Lit.: *Hand-list of Drawings in the Witt Collection*, London University, 1956, p. 18.
Executed *c.* 1840.

317 FIGURE STUDIES
Black chalk, on light brown paper, $22 \times 15\frac{3}{8}$.
Coll. & Lit.: as for above (No. 3069).
c. 1840.

318 FEMALE NUDE WITH DRAPERIES
Black and white chalk, on light brown paper, $20\frac{5}{8} \times 16\frac{1}{8}$.
Coll. & Lit.: as for above (No. 3070).
Study for (?)*Circe*, *c.* 1844.

319 STUDY OF A FEMALE NUDE
Black chalk, on light brown paper, $17\frac{1}{2} \times 13$.
Coll. & Lit.: as for above (No. 3071).
c. 1840.

320 A RECUMBENT FEMALE NUDE
Black, red and white chalk, on buff paper, $15\frac{1}{4} \times 22\frac{1}{4}$.
Coll. & Lit.: as for above (No. 3224).
c. 1840.

321 STANDING FEMALE NUDE
Black, red and white chalk, on light brown paper, $22\frac{1}{4} \times 15\frac{1}{4}$.
Coll. & Lit.: as for above (No. 3225).

The female nude stands against a statue of *Venus Pudica*. Daniel Maclise (quoted by Gilchrist, ii, p. 59) recalls that Turner once arranged a female model in the pose of the *Venus de' Medici*, standing her next to a cast of the latter.
c. 1835–40.

322 A FEMALE NUDE AND A SWAN
Black, red and white chalk, on buff paper, $23\frac{3}{8} \times 17\frac{1}{2}$.
Coll. & Lit.: as for above (No. 3226).

The same model appears here as in No. 3068. The artist does not seem to have intended representing a *Leda and the Swan* in the traditional manner.
c. 1840.
University of London, Courtauld Institute of Art.

323 TWO MALE NUDES
Red chalk, $19\frac{1}{4} \times 13\frac{1}{8}$.
Coll.: Purchased 1907 (No. '07–75).
c. 1815–18.
City Museum and Art Gallery, Nottingham.

324 RECLINING FEMALE NUDE (ODALISQUE)
Black chalk and watercolour, $9\frac{1}{2} \times 14\frac{1}{2}$.
Coll.: Alfred Beurdeley, Paris, sold 1920 and acquired by Cabinet des Dessins, Musée du Louvre (R.F. 5193).

A female nude reclines on a couch, looking to right at her image in a mirror. Her left arm is raised to her head. She appears to hold an arrow in her right hand. A curtain hangs behind her head and a landscape background is indicated on the right.

c. 1830.

Le Musée du Louvre, Paris.

325 [pls. 8a & 8b] GROTESQUE HEADS

Pen & ink, $12\frac{1}{2} \times 20$ (recto & verso).

Coll.: Purchased from Mr. G. Vickers, Gillygate, York (No. 103/1949).

Exh.: York, 1949(100).

Repr.: York Preview 9, III, January, 1950.

c. 1810–15.

City Art Gallery, York.

326 [pl. 5a] MALE NUDE WITH A STAFF

Inscr.: 'Etty' (bottom left). Pencil, $14\frac{1}{4} \times 9\frac{3}{4}$.

Coll.: Sir Hugh Walpole; Milligan Grundy; with Roland, Browse & Delbanco and sold to York through the York Civic Trust 1947 (No. 73/1947).

Exh.: Collection of the late Sir Hugh Walpole, Leicester Galleries, April, 1945(17); York, 1948(37), York, 1949(97); A.C. *Twelve Yorkshire Artists of the Past,* 1951(9).

Repr.: York Preview 1, January, 1948 (cover).

Executed *c.* 1816–18; compare with the oil painting of the same subject.

City Art Gallery, York.

327 [pl. 15a] FEMALE NUDE STUDY

Inscr.: 'W. Etty' (bottom left).

Red chalk, $10\frac{1}{2} \times 13$.

Coll.: Presented by John Moult, Esq., York, 1915 (No. 101/1915).

Exh.: York, 1949(99).

c. 1825–30.

City Art Gallery, York.

328 STANDING FEMALE NUDE

Pencil, heightened with white, on buff paper, $21\frac{1}{2} \times 14$.

Coll.: Gould (November, 1947); with Roland, Browse & Delbanco, sold to York, January, 1948 (No. 102/1948).

Exh.: York, 1948(38); York, 1949(98); A.C. *Twelve Yorkshire Artists of the Past,* 1951(10).

City Art Gallery, York.

329 THE RIALTO BRIDGE, VENICE

Pencil, $9\frac{1}{10} \times 13\frac{3}{10}$.

Coll.: Robert E. Smithson; E. W. Smithson, sold 12.3.1928(140), bt. York.

c. 1823.

City Art Gallery, York.

330 TWO VIEWS OF LAKES AND MOUNTAINS

Watercolour, on thin card, $4 \times 5\frac{7}{10}$ (painted on both sides).

Coll.: as for No. 329.

The subjects are either of the Lake District or, less likely, of Scottish scenery. They probably date from Etty's visit to Scotland and Cumberland which he made in 1831.

City Art Gallery, York.

331 STUDIES FROM MICHELANGELO'S 'LAST JUDGMENT'

Pencil, $7\frac{3}{10} \times 9\frac{2}{5}$ (on recto & verso).

Coll.: as for No. 329.

Studies made in Rome, August–October, 1822, of souls in torment and of Satan falling to his doom.

City Art Gallery, York.

THE SKETCHBOOKS

(City Art Gallery, York):

Nos. I to IV come from the collection of Robert E. Smithson; E. W. Smithson, sold 12.3.1928(140), bt. York.

332 [pls. 9a & 9b] SKETCHBOOK I

Some pen & ink, but mostly pencil, black and white chalk, on coarse-grained paper, $8\frac{3}{5} \times 11\frac{3}{10}$, 118 pp. (pp. 1–2 blue paper; pp. 3–62 white; pp. 63–74 dark buff; pp. 75–84 pale green; pp. 85–102 pale buff; and pp. 102–18 blue). Board covers.

Probably *c.* 1816–24. Contains studies from the Elgin Marbles and other antique statues and bas-reliefs, *e.g.* Borghese Vase (Louvre) p. 15; as well as outline sketches after compositions by Poussin, *e.g. Bacchanal,* pp. 20–1, *The Nurture of Jupiter,* p. 77 [pl. 9b]; Le Brun, *Entry of Alexander the Great,* pp. 29, 85; and Titian, *Bacchus and Ariadne,* p. 9. There are also numerous studies of children; a few landscapes, *e.g. Genoa Harbour,* pp. 46–7; mountain scenes and life studies.

333 [pl. 14a] SKETCHBOOK II

Mostly pencil, white paper throughout, $11\frac{5}{8} \times 8$, 267 pp., vellum spine, mauve boards. Etty has used part of this as a diary for his Italian visit of 1822–3, some of which consists of a draft of a long letter to Thomas Bodley.

Among the more important sketches should be noted those after Michelangelo's Medici Chapel Tomb figure *Dawn,* p. 196; *The Last Judgment* (Sistine Chapel), pp. 234, 240 and 242; the Sistine Chapel ceiling, pp. 248, 252, 254, 256–60, 262–4, and 266 (mainly of the

'Ignudi'); and a study from the figure of Abraham in Titian's *Sacrifice of Isaac*, p. 173. There are also many landscape sketches scattered throughout, a few studies after the antique and from the life; some oddments of still life (*e.g.* tankards, candlesticks and snuffers), as well as several Venus and Cupid groups and other, unidentifiable miscellaneous head and figure drawings.

It also contains a list of the copies which Etty set himself to do whilst in Italy (p. 48, *see* Appendix II).

334 [pl. 4*a*] SKETCHBOOK III
Mostly pencil, on thin cream paper, $7\frac{1}{2} \times 6$, 24 pp., limp blue cloth covers.

Probably *c.* 1810–16. Miscellaneous diagrammatic 'action studies', heads drawn in varying poses, and some studies of children.

335 [pl. 4*b*] SKETCHBOOK IV
Mostly pencil, on white paper, $8 \times 6\frac{1}{2}$, 48 pp. (76 pp. have been cut out and are missing).

The date '8th July 1818' occurs on p. 49 [pl. 4*b*], and most of the drawings may be dated *c.* 1817–19. The contents are similar to those of *Sketchbook III*, there being in addition several carefully finished studies of feet and hands (*e.g.* pp. 15, 30, 31 and 33).

336 [pl. 14*b*] 'CASH BOOK'
Pencil, with some pen and ink, white paper, $13\frac{3}{8} \times 9\frac{1}{4}$, green spine and grey boards. Pages not numbered, but approximately the same as for *Sketchbook II*.
Coll.: as for *Sketchbooks I–IV*.

Known as the '*Cash Book*' because of the four pages of Etty's private accounts for the period 26th May, 1831 to 1st April, 1835, contained therein.

Also has drawings of the Rialto and Bridge of Sighs, Venice; studies after Michelangelo's *Victory*, and *Day*, *Night* and *Dawn* (Medici Tombs, Florence); Titian's *Votive Picture of the Vendramin Family*; an Egyptian figure statue; and sketches of Titian's and Veronese's tombstones.

337 SKETCHBOOK V
Pencil, white paper, $6\frac{1}{4} \times 3\frac{3}{4}$, 135 pp., calf-bound pocket sketchbook with brass clip.
Coll.: Thomas Bodley, by descent to George H. Scott, sold Sotheby's 9.11.1954(450), bt. York.

Sketches date from *c.* 1809. They are mostly studies of figures of children and women at play and walking; of drapery and costume; and some slight anatomical studies of bones and limbs.

338 SKETCHBOOK VI
Black chalk, white paper (watermarked 'T. Sweet 1829'), $4\frac{1}{2} \times 3\frac{1}{2}$, 100 pp., red leather-bound pocket book with clip.
Coll.: as for *Sketchbook V*.

On the front inside cover is written 'Chiefly Animals', and most of the drawings are of goats and pigs probably intended for the *Prodigal Son* of 1836. Also includes some studies of drapery, figures and heads of eagles.

339 [pls. 76*b* & 77] SEVENTEEN FIGURE DRAWINGS
Pen, white paper, $12 \times 9\frac{1}{2}$.
Coll.: Purchased 1952 (No. 653/1952, I–XVII).
Lit.: *York Preview* 21, VI, January, 1953, p. 231.

From an album formed in 1863. The drawings date from between 1839–June, 1841, according to the inscriptions on several of them in the artist's handwriting.
City Art Gallery, York.

NOTE: An album of some 500 drawings and watercolours, many of them quite small (average size is $7 \times 4\frac{1}{4}$), which have been attributed to Etty, are in a private collection in Stockholm, Sweden. Unfortunately, it has not been possible to examine these before this catalogue went to press.

INDEXES

A. GENERAL

Excluding paintings and drawings by or attributed to Etty, and their present and past owners.
Titles of paintings, drawings and books are in italics.
References to plates are in italics.

B. TITLES OF PAINTINGS AND DRAWINGS
BY OR ATTRIBUTED TO ETTY

Identified works are in ordinary type; recorded but unidentified works in italics.
In all cases, only the name of the last known owner is given.
Works whose owners are marked with an asterisk are definitely not by Etty.
Catalogue numerals are in **bold** type; references to plates are in italics.

PAINTINGS

Aaron
    London, St. Edmund the King and Martyr 66, **1**, *49*
Aaron, the High Priest of Israel
    Sunderland, Museum and Art Gallery **2**
Ablution [sic] of Cupid 99
Acomb, 'The Plantation'
    York, City Art Gallery 93, 94, **263**, *78a*
Adam and Eve at their morning orisons 75, 76
Agar, The Lady Mary, and The Hon. Charles Agar ('Guardian Cherubs')
    The Earl of Normanton 52, **184**, *32*
Andromeda
    Gough (1951) **37**
    Manchester, City Art Gallery **219**
    Port Sunlight, The Lady Lever Art Gallery **37**, *36a*
Andromeda—Perseus coming to her rescue
    Michael Jaffé 88, 89, 91, **38**, *82b*
Andromeda and Perseus
    Manchester, City Art Gallery **39**
Apotheosis of the Duke of Buckingham (after Rubens)
    York, City Art Gallery **298**, *41b*
Arnould, Joseph
    Lieut.-Col. W. H. Olivier **139**
Arnould, Mrs.
    Lieut.-Col. W. H. Olivier **159**
Atkinson, James
    York, Yorkshire Philosophical Society 64, 65, 84, **140**, *42*
Aurora and Zephyr
    Maple (1899) **40**
    Port Sunlight, The Lady Lever Art Gallery **40**

Bacchanal, *see* Reclining Male Figure **209**
Bacchanal, *see* Reclining Male Nude **238**

Bacchanalian Figure reclining on a Leopard's skin, A, *see* Reclining Male Figure (Bacchanal) **209**
Bacchanalian Revel
    The Earl of Wemyss **41**
Bacchanalian Scene,—a sketch, A, *see* The World Before the Flood **108**(a)
Bacchanalians 25
'Bacchante', *see* Seated Female Nude **252**
Back View of Standing Male Nude in Boat
    Providence, Rhode Island School of Design **226**
Bailey, James
    Lieut.-Col. W. H. Olivier **141**
Bath of Venus, The, *see* Toilet of Venus **89**
    Bather, Archdeacon 73 and *n.*
Bather, The, 'At the doubtful breeze alarmed', *see* Musidora **74**
Bather, The, *see* Seated Female Nude Looking Left **222**
Bather, The, *see* Seated Female Nude Looking Right **223**
Bather, The, *see* Standing Female Nude **202**
Bathers Surprised
    Polak (1883) **110**
Bathers surprised by a Swan
    London, Tate Gallery **110**
Bayntun, Samuel Adlam
    Noel G. Terry **142**
Benaiah
    Edinburgh, National Gallery of Scotland 11, 55, **3**, *34b*
    York, City Art Gallery **3**(a)
Bevy of Fair Women, The, *see* The World Before the Flood **108**
Bicknell, Miss Matilda
    Capt. L. Lindsay-Smith **185**

INDEX OF TITLES

DRAWINGS

C. PAST AND PRESENT OWNERS OF PAINTINGS AND DRAWINGS BY OR ATTRIBUTED TO ETTY

Last known owners of a work are in ordinary type; earlier owners in italics.
Identified works are in ordinary type; recorded but unidentified works in italics.
Works marked with an asterisk are definitely not by Etty.
Catalogue numerals are in **bold** type; references to plates are in italics.

Aberdeen, Art Gallery and Industrial Museum
    Somnolency **129**
Adams Gallery
    Psyche having, after great peril, procured the casket of cosmetics from Proserpine in Hades, lays it at the feet of Venus, while Cupid pleads in her behalf **82**(**iii**)
Agnew and Sons
    The Flowers of the Forest **57**
    The Judgment of Paris **67**
    Toilet of Venus **100**
    Venus and Adonis (after Titian) **40**
Anderson, Sir Colin
    Pluto Carrying off Proserpine 85–7, **80**(**a**)
    Seated Female Nude ('Contemplation') **237**
Anderson, R. W. & Sons
    Joan of Arc (drawings) **22**
Appleby Brothers
    Christ and the Magdalen ('Noli Me Tangere': after Titian) **303**
    Hesperus **63**(**b**)

Bacon, A. W.
    Manlius Hurled from the Rock 27, 62, **70**, *10a*
    Nude Female Study 52, **103**(**a**), *27a*
    Reclining Male Nude ('Bacchanal') **238**, *47b*
Barlow, George H.
    'He was despised and rejected of men' **16**
Bath, Victoria Art Gallery
    Venus and Cupids **97**
Bean, Mrs. E. M.
    Judith **24**(**f**)
Beckford, William
    The Prodigal Son 84 and *n.,* **31**

Bevan, R. A.
    Standing Female Nude with Negress Girl Attendant **239**
Bilston, Public Library, Museum and Art Gallery
    Venus and Cupid **93**
Birch, Charles
    Miss Mary Ann Purdon ('The Crotchet Worker') **194**
Birkenhead, Williamson Art Gallery and Museum
    Grape Fruit and Grapes **274**
    Hero Awaiting Leander **59**
    An Israelite **18**
    A Nobleman **127**
    Seated Nude Female Bather **199**, *65b*
    Study of a Woman's Head **309**
    Toilet of Venus **88**
Birmingham, City Art Gallery
    Female Nude (Back View) **200**
    'Gather the Rose of Love While yet 'tis Time' **115**, *91a*
    Pandora 45, **76**(**b**)
    Seated Female Nude **310**
    Sleeping Female Nude **311**, *76a*
Bloch, Mrs. Vitale
    Two Seascapes **272**
Blyth
    The Wise and Foolish Virgins 88, **36**
Bodley, T.
    Thomas Bodley 57, **143**
Bohener, Mrs. V. R. W.
    Dead Pheasant **275**
Bordeaux-Groult, Pierre
    Reclining Female Nude (Back View) in a Landscape with Two Dogs **240**
Borenius, Mrs. Anne Marie
    Three Seascapes **272**

INDEX OF OWNERS

1. WILLIAM ETTY IN THE LIFE SCHOOL

Drawing by C. H. Lear, October 1845

$6\frac{1}{2} \times 5\frac{1}{2}$

2b. MISS CATHERINE ETTY ("KITTY")
23¾ × 19 (166)

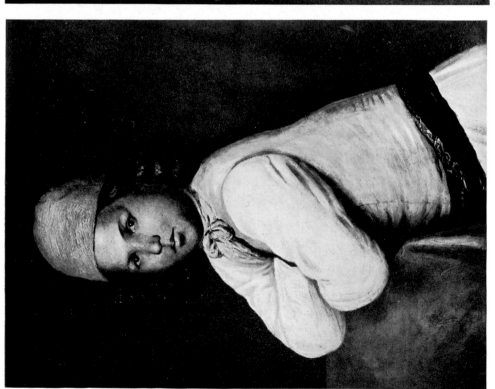

2a. THE MISSIONARY BOY
25¼ × 19⅞ (192)

3b. JOHN ETTY
30 × 25 (148a)

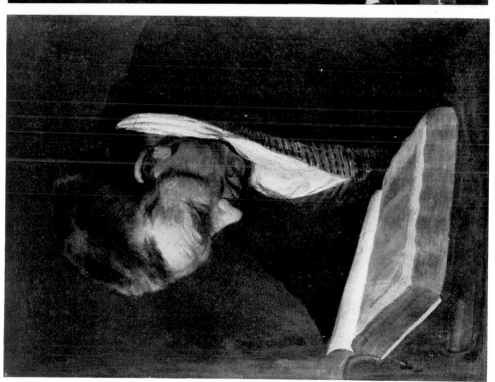

3a. MATTHEW ETTY
25½ × 19¼ (149)

4b. GROUP OF FIGURE STUDIES
Sketchbook IV, p. 49
$8 \times 6\frac{1}{2}$ (335)

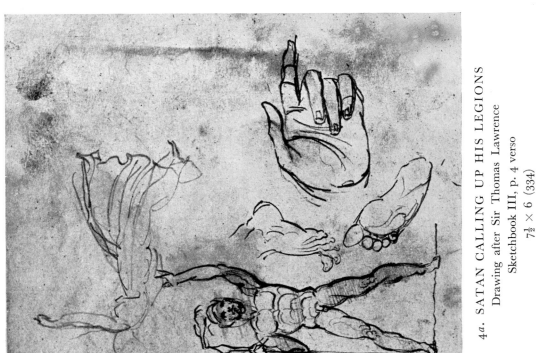

4a. SATAN CALLING UP HIS LEGIONS
Drawing after Sir Thomas Lawrence
Sketchbook III, p. 4 verso
$7\frac{1}{2} \times 6$ (334)

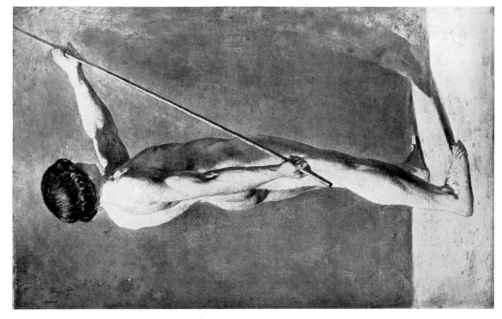

5b. MALE NUDE WITH A STAFF
$18\frac{7}{8} \times 12$ (230)

5a. MALE NUDE WITH A STAFF
$14\frac{1}{4} \times 9\frac{3}{4}$ (326)

6. THE REV. ROBERT BOLTON

$50\frac{3}{4} \times 41\frac{1}{4}$ (144)

7. MRS. ROBERT BOLTON AND HER CHILDREN
$50\frac{3}{4} \times 41\frac{1}{4}$ (160)

8a. GROTESQUE HEADS (recto)
12½ × 20 (325)

8b. GROTESQUE HEADS (verso)
12½ × 20 (325)

9a. STUDIES OF CHILDREN
Sketchbook I, p. 117
$8\frac{3}{5} \times 11\frac{3}{10}$ (332)

9b. THE NURTURE OF JUPITER (Dulwich Art Gallery). Sketch after Poussin
Sketchbook I, p. 77
$8\frac{3}{5} \times 11\frac{3}{10}$ (332)

10b. DRUNKEN BARNABY

29½ × 25 (113)

10a. MANLIUS HURLED FROM THE ROCK

45 × 33 (70)

11b. MISS WALLACE ("INNOCENCE")
17 × 13 (195)

11a. THE REV. WILLIAM JAY
Engraving by J. Thomson, *European Magazine*, January, 1819

12. THE CORAL FINDER: VENUS AND HER YOUTHFUL SATELLITES ARRIVING AT THE ISLE
OF PAPHOS

29 × 38½ (49i)

13. CLEOPATRA'S ARRIVAL IN CILICIA

$42\frac{1}{4} \times 52\frac{1}{4}$ (47)

14a. ITALIAN LANDSCAPE SKETCH
Sketchbook II, p. 25
$11\frac{5}{8} \times 8$ (333)

14b. VIEW OF FLORENCE FROM THE ARNO
"Cash Book"
$13\frac{3}{8} \times 9\frac{1}{4}$ (336)

15*a*. FEMALE NUDE STUDY
Red Chalk
$10\frac{1}{2} \times 13$ (327)

15*b*. ALLÉGORIE À LA GLOIRE DE NAPOLÉON
Engraving by C. Normand, 1809, after J.-B. Regnault

16. PANDORA
$34\frac{3}{4} \times 44\frac{1}{8}$ (76)

17. THE COMBAT: WOMAN PLEADING FOR THE VANQUISHED. AN IDEAL GROUP

100 × 135 (48)

18. VENUS AND CUPID DESCENDING

27 × 20 (98)

19*a*. Study for PANDORA
$6\frac{3}{8} \times 7\frac{3}{4}$ (76*c*)

19*b*. RECLINING FEMALE NUDE STUDY
$20\frac{1}{2} \times 27$ (208)

20. SELF PORTRAIT

$16\frac{1}{2} \times 12\frac{1}{2}$ (152a)

21a. PROMETHEUS
$27\frac{3}{4} \times 30\frac{1}{2}$ (81)

21b. Study for THE COMBAT
17×21 (48b)

22. JUDGMENT OF PARIS

70¼ × 107½ (65)

23a. THE JUDGMENT OF PARIS

Engraving by John Flaxman, *The Iliad*, 1793, pl. 37

23b. THE JUDGMENT OF PARIS

Engraving by Marcantonio Raimondi after Raphael

24*a*. Study for the JUDGMENT OF PARIS
$4\frac{1}{2} \times 7\frac{3}{8}$ (65*b*)

24*b*. Study for JUDITH
Pen, Sketchbook IV, p. 13 (and part of p. 12)
$8 \times 6\frac{1}{2}$ (24*g*)

25a. Oil study for JUDITH
$11 \times 8\frac{1}{2}$ (24c)

25b. Oil study for JUDITH
$13\frac{1}{2} \times 17\frac{1}{2}$ (24d)

26. THE PARTING OF HERO AND LEANDER

$32\frac{1}{2} \times 33$ (77)

27a. NUDE FEMALE STUDY
18 × 18 (103a)

27b. "VENUS NOW WAKES, AND WAKENS LOVE"
20 × 24 (103)

28b. SEATED FEMALE NUDE
19 × 15 (227)

28a. TWO STANDING MALE NUDES
28 × 23 (210)

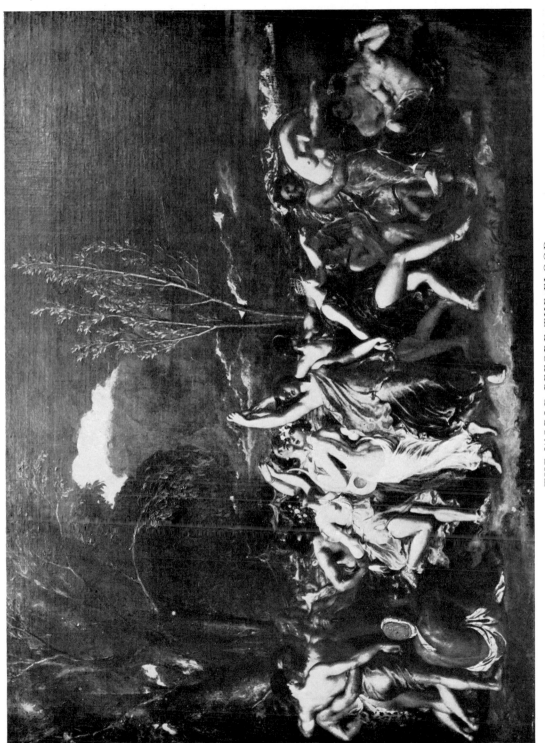

29. THE WORLD BEFORE THE FLOOD

59 × 80 (108)

30. SLEEPING NYMPH AND SATYRS

51 × 70½ (85)

31. HERO, HAVING THROWN HERSELF FROM THE TOWER AT THE SIGHT OF LEANDER DROWNED, DIES ON HIS BODY

$30\frac{1}{2} \times 37\frac{1}{4}$ (62)

32. THE LADY MARY AGAR AND THE HON. CHARLES AGAR
("GUARDIAN CHERUBS")

49 × 35 (184)

33. MISS MARY ARABELLA JAY

30 × 24¾ (191)

34*a*. THE STORM
$35\frac{1}{2} \times 41\frac{1}{2}$ (35)

34*b*. BENAIAH
120 × 157 (3)

35a. VENUS AND CUPID

$12\frac{1}{2} \times 17\frac{1}{2}$ (91)

35b. FÊTE CHAMPÊTRE (after Giorgione)

28×36 (291i)

36b. MALE NUDE WITH UPSTRETCHED ARMS
23½ × 17 (234)

36a. ANDROMEDA
26⅜ × 20 (37)

37b. LOVE'S ANGLING
$22\frac{1}{2} \times 21\frac{1}{2}$ (69)

37a. WINDOW IN VENICE, DURING A FESTA
$24 \times 19\frac{3}{4}$ (1341)

38*a*. LEDA

16 × 20 (68)

38*b*. SABRINA

24 × 30 (83i)

39. YOUTH ON THE PROW AND PLEASURE AT THE HELM
$62\frac{1}{2} \times 46\frac{1}{4}$ (109)

40. RECLINING MALE NUDE
$17\frac{3}{8} \times 21\frac{1}{2}$ (242)

41b. APOTHEOSIS OF THE DUKE OF BUCKINGHAM
(after Rubens)
$9\frac{1}{2} \times 9\frac{1}{2}$ (298)

41a. Study for YOUTH ON THE PROW
19×13 (109b)

42. JAMES ATKINSON
$29\frac{1}{2} \times 24$ (140)

43*a*. PHAEDRIA AND CYMOCHLES, ON THE IDLE LAKE
25 × 30 (78)

43*b*. THE LUTE PLAYER
17 × 19 (122i)

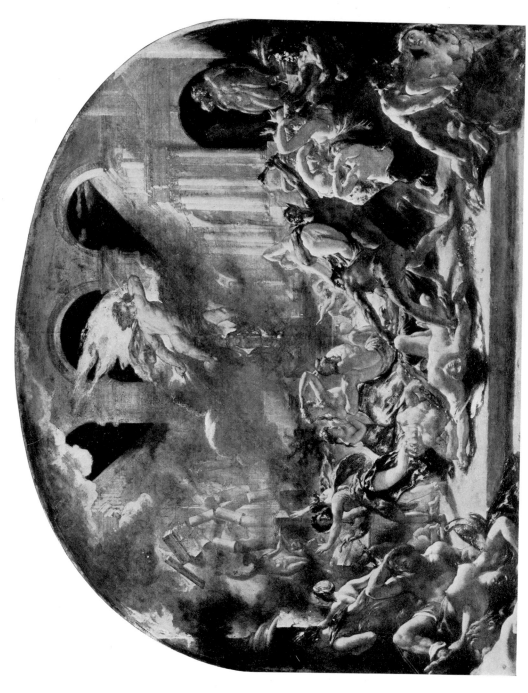

44. THE DESTROYING ANGEL AND DAEMONS OF EVIL, INTERRUPTING THE ORGIES
OF THE VICIOUS AND INTEMPERATE

36 × 46 (10)

45*b*. MISS EMMA DAVENPORT

30 × 25 (165)

45*a*. MISS ELIZABETH POTTS

33½ × 28¼ (178)

46. BRITOMART REDEEMES FAIRE AMORET

$35\frac{1}{2} \times 25\frac{7}{8}$ (44)

47a. HYLAS AND THE NYMPHS
$35\frac{1}{2} \times 45\frac{5}{8}$ (64)

47b. RECLINING MALE NUDE (BACCHANAL)
16×18 (238)

48. THE LUTE PLAYER
$24\frac{3}{4} \times 21$ (122 ii)

49. AARON

$52\frac{3}{4} \times 23\frac{1}{2}$ (I)

50b. MARS, VENUS AND CUPID
40 × 27 (72)

50a. NYMPH AND YOUNG FAUN DANCING
30⅛ × 25¼ (75ii)

51a. SEATED FEMALE NUDE

Pen and wash drawing by W. E. Frost, R.A.

$4\frac{1}{2} \times 3\frac{3}{8}$

51b. FRONTISPIECE TO AN ALBUM OF DRAWINGS

Pen and wash drawing by W. E. Frost, R.A.

$4\frac{1}{2} \times 3\frac{3}{8}$

52. THE PERSIAN
16 × 12 (128)

53. THE WARRIOR ARMING (GODFREY DE BOUILLON)

34 × 28 (106)

54*a*. CHRIST APPEARING TO MARY MAGDALEN
By J. P. Knight, R.A.
$27\frac{3}{4} \times 35\frac{3}{4}$

54*b*. CHRIST APPEARING TO MARY MAGDALEN AFTER THE RESURRECTION
$15\frac{3}{4} \times 26$ (5)

55. WOOD NYMPHS SLEEPING; SATYR BRINGING FLOWERS—MORNING

18 × 27½ (107)

56. VENUS AND HER SATELLITES (THE TOILET OF VENUS)
32 × 43 (1001)

57b. THE THREE GRACES
22½ × 18¾ (100a)

57a. VENUS AND HER DOVES
25½ × 24 (99)

58. THE MISSES WILLIAMS WYNN (PREPARING FOR A FANCY-DRESS BALL)

60 × 51½ (183)

59. JOHN BROOK

$29\frac{1}{2} \times 24$ (145i)

60b. MONK BAR, YORK

30 × 24 (273)

60a. THE BRIDGE OF SIGHS

31½ × 20 (43)

61b. THE PRODIGAL SON

$26\frac{7}{8} \times 21\frac{1}{8}$ (31)

61a. ST. JOHN PREACHING (after Veronese)

$27\frac{1}{4} \times 21\frac{1}{4}$ (308)

62a. THE SIRENS

Engraving by John Flaxman, *The Odyssey*, 1805, pl. 19

62b. THE GOOD SAMARITAN

$21\frac{5}{8} \times 26\frac{1}{4}$ (14)

63. THE SIRENS AND ULYSSES
117 × 174 (84)

64. PLUTO CARRYING OFF PROSERPINE

51 × 77 (80)

65b. SEATED FEMALE NUDE BATHER
24 × 19½ (199)

65a. KNEELING FEMALE NUDE
22 × 15¾ (80b)

66. MRS. J. F. VAUGHAN

30 × 25 (181)

67. MISS ELIZA COOK

15 × 12½ (164)

68. A FAMILY OF THE FORESTS
$22\frac{1}{2} \times 3^{\scriptscriptstyle\mathrm{I}}$ (57)

69. A BIVOUAC OF CUPID AND HIS COMPANY

26 × 36 (42)

70a. FLOWER STUDY
$17\frac{1}{2} \times 23\frac{1}{2}$ (277)

70b. STILL-LIFE WITH EWER
8×12 (276)

71. STILL-LIFE WITH GLASS
$12\frac{1}{2} \times 16\frac{1}{4}$ (278)

72. THE REPENTANT PRODIGAL'S RETURN TO HIS FATHER

34 × 46 (32)

73. TO ARMS, TO ARMS, YE BRAVE!

31 × 43½ (87)

74. THE STRID, BOLTON ABBEY
$8\frac{1}{4} \times 11\frac{1}{2}$ (271)

75b. MLLE. RACHEL, THE FRENCH TRAGEDIENNE
22 × 15½ (179)

75a. JOHN HARPER
19½ × 15½ (153)

76a. SLEEPING FEMALE NUDE
Pencil drawing
$11\frac{3}{4} \times 20\frac{5}{8}$ (311)

76b. SLEEPING FEMALE NUDE
Pen drawing
$9\frac{1}{2} \times 12$ (339)

77. BACK VIEW OF STOOPING FEMALE NUDE

12 × 9½ (339)

78b. LANDSCAPE WITH HOUSE

$12\frac{1}{2} \times 11\frac{3}{4}$ (269)

78a. 'THE PLANTATION', ACOMB

$8\frac{1}{2} \times 8\frac{1}{2}$ (263)

79. LANDSCAPE
$18\frac{1}{2} \times 24$ (268)

80. CIRCE AND THE SIRENS THREE

$46\frac{1}{2} \times 71\frac{1}{2}$ (46)

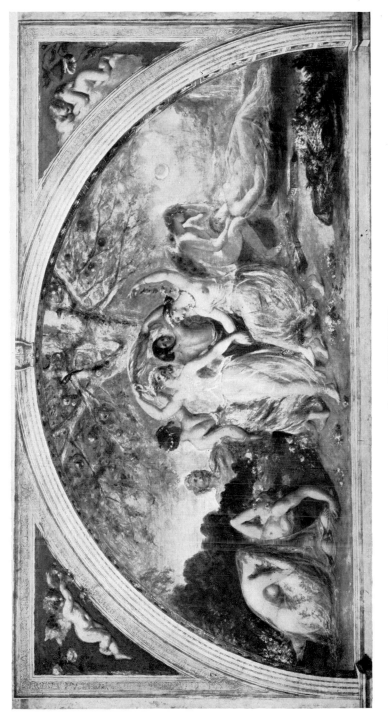

81. HESPERUS
35 × 68 (63)

82b. ANDROMEDA—PERSEUS COMING TO HER
RESCUE
32 × 25 (38)

82a. STILL-LIFE: DEAD PHEASANT AND FRUIT
17½ × 15 (286)

83b. AN ISRAELITE INDEED

$26\frac{1}{4} \times 19\frac{3}{4}$ (19)

83a. CIRCE, study of head and shoulders

$11\frac{1}{2} \times 11\frac{1}{2}$ (46a)

84. CHARLES ETTY
(Destroyed 1944)
36 × 28 (147*b*)

85b. BACK VIEW OF STANDING MALE NUDE.
AND SEATED MALE NUDE
24½ × 18 (260)

85a. MUSIDORA
27 × 22½ (74i)

86. A PIRATE CARRYING OFF A CAPTIVE (THE CORSAIR)
$27\frac{3}{4} \times 21$ (79)

87. THE FAIRY OF THE FOUNTAIN

$27\frac{7}{8} \times 20$ (56)

88. MUSIDORA

$25\frac{5}{8} \times 19\frac{3}{4}$ (74 ii)

89*a*. Studies for the MARTYRDOM OF JOAN OF ARC
Pen drawing
$4\frac{3}{8} \times 7\frac{1}{4}$ (*22 a*)

89*b*. Study for JOAN OF ARC ATTACKING FROM THE GATES OF ORLÉANS
Pen and brush drawing
$3\frac{2}{5} \times 5$ (*21 a*)

90. THE HON. MRS. CAROLINE NORTON

$17\frac{1}{2} \times 13\frac{1}{4}$ (174)

91b. MISS JENNY LIND

36 × 28 (171)

91a. PORTRAIT OF AN UNKNOWN LADY

23½ × 9½ (176)

92. THE WOOD CHILDREN
$26\frac{1}{4} \times 29\frac{1}{2}$ (196)

93. THE HON. MRS. NORTON AND HER SISTERS
$13\frac{1}{4} \times 16\frac{7}{8}$ (175)

94b. "LET BROTHERLY LOVE CONTINUE"

$20\frac{1}{4} \times 20\frac{1}{8}$ (121)

94a. "GATHER THE ROSE OF LOVE WHILE YET 'TIS TIME"

$19\frac{5}{8} \times 19\frac{5}{8}$ (115)

95. MRS. WILLIAM WETHERED
23½ × 28 (182)

96. A GROUP OF CAPTIVES: "BY THE WATERS OF BABYLON"
23 × 26½ (15)